MELANCHTHON
The Quiet Reformer

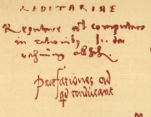

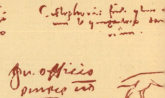

Gott für uns,
r mag wider uns sein

Antichristi.

1526
VIVENTIS·POTVIT·DVRERIVS·ORA·PHILIPPI
MENTEM·NON·POTVIT·PINGERE·DOCTA
MANVS

Clyde Leonard Manschreck

MELANCHTHON
The Quiet Reformer

Ist Gott für uns,
wer mag wider uns sein

New York • Nashville
ABINGDON PRESS

MELANCHTHON: THE QUIET REFORMER

Copyright © MCMLVIII by Abingdon Press

Library of Congress Catalog Card Number: 58-5147

SET UP, PRINTED, AND BOUND BY THE
PARTHENON PRESS, AT NASHVILLE,
TENNESSEE, UNITED STATES OF AMERICA

DEDICATION

To ARDIS, THEO, LEE, and ANN

FOREWORD

I wish to express my gratitude to the directors of the Carnegie Research Fund for making it possible for me to purchase the Melanchthoniana necessary for this biography and to the Fund for the Advancement of Education of the Ford Foundation for a fellowship that enabled me to take the time for the study. I am also indebted to the Sterling Library of Yale University, Folger Shakespeare Library of Washington, D.C., and the Library of Congress for the use of their Reformation materials. I am also grateful for the encouragement, assistance, and kindness of Dr. Roland H. Bainton of Yale University, and for the patience and inspiration of my wife, Ardis, who has endured the ups and downs of the research and writing.

When I found myself hospitalized and unable to meet the indexing deadline, valuable assistance was given by my colleagues at Duke University, Dr. David G. Bradley, Dr. Creighton Lacy, Dr. Thomas A. Langford, Dr. James L. Price, Dr. McMurry S. Richey, and Dr. R. H. Sales.

Clyde Leonard Manschreck

Duke University

[7]

CONTENTS

LIST OF ILLUSTRATIONS

Introduction

PHILIP MELANCHTHON IS ONE OF THE CHIEF FIGURES in the founding of Protestantism; he is also one of the most enigmatic. Because he does not fit neatly into the usual humanistic patterns of the late Renaissance nor into the patterns of the evangelical Reformation as expressed in Calvin and Luther, his role in the turbulent sixteenth century has baffled theologians and historians alike. He has been caricatured and formalized, praised and damned, valued by alien standards and transvalued, and even ignored, but not forgotten. Only now in the travail of modern Protestantism to understand itself and in the perspective of four hundred years is the place of Melanchthon becoming clear. To understand Melanchthon and to assess his significance one must recognize the two historical movements which combined in him and which have never been reconciled in Protestantism—the Renaissance and the Reformation. Like the arms of a cross they join, only to separate, neither forming a complete symbol alone, one vertical, the other horizontal. Attempts to divide them have ended in the extremes of secularism with its sacrifice of Christ and in fundamentalism with its sacrifice of culture. Perhaps Melanchthon's coat-of-arms, the wilderness serpent uplifted, is not without its own prophetic symbolism.

Like the Greek dichotomy of body-spirit, the Renaissance and Reformation divisions in Protestantism have proved fruitful but at the same time disastrous. In Melanchthon these divisions were a living unity. He cannot be explained in terms of either, for he transcended both. This is his greatness. This is his tragedy.

Through the Augsburg Confession Melanchthon influenced all the major denominations of Christendom. He established the first public school system since the days of ancient Rome. Protestant historians recognize him as the first systematic theologian of the Reformation.

[13]

Luther regarded him as the greatest theologian that ever lived and declared that the *Loci* deserved to stand next to the Bible. Yet, his name was in his own day, and still is, beclouded by suspicion. His gentleness was mistaken for weakness, his learnedness was regarded as questionable rationalism, his refusal to accept Luther without discrimination was painted as rebellion, his struggles to unify Christendom were labeled pro-papalism, and his recognition of the worth of Geneva's great leader was slurred as crypto-Calvinism. Today reference books subject him to such diverse interpretations that one wonders if he should be monumentalized as a reformer or condemned as a traitor. For his educational work he has been extolled, and, for the very same endeavors, denounced as a fore-runner of Hitler. He has been exalted for his moral purity and accused of sexual promiscuity.

Those who wished to honor Melanchthon have not been least respon-sible for this ironic fate. The Melanchthon Synod of the Evangelical Lutheran Church held its first annual meeting in 1857 in Middletown, Maryland. It officially subscribed to the Augsburg Confession, but added "we owe it to ourselves and to the cause of evangelical truth to disavow and repudiate with equal clearness and emphasis certain *errors which are said by some to be contained in said Confession.*" After listing four sus-pect statements about the mass, confession, baptism, and the Eucharist, the official report continued, *"With these exceptions, whether found in the Confession or not, we believe and retain the entire Augsburg Con-fession with all the great doctrines of the Reformation."* [1] Here was a synod, professedly honoring Melanchthon, which did not know whether or not he held certain objectionable doctrines, but which fervently re-pudiated such obnoxious errors if he did, as some said!

In 1624 a Roman Catholic book appeared in England bearing the motto: "By theire fruictes you shall knowe them: Doe men gather grapes of thornes or figges of thistles?" In it the author marshaled numerous facts to disparage the "supposed worthe" of Melanchthon. He said that Melanchthon wrote "suspiciouslie" on the Trinity, denied the divine glory of Christ, fostered libertinism, and promoted sexual promiscuity com-parable to that of Solomon "who in likinge of his concubines became an idolater." The writer concluded by saying such was the evangelical leader who in his day was supposed to have been the most singular instrument of the Holy Ghost—better than a hundred Augustines! [2]

Others have hurled accusations and made generalizations without evidence. In 1947 Melanchthon's use of reason was called a "blight," the "source of the abridgment of the essential vitality of Luther's thought" which led to a cultural and political lag in Germany, the Thirty Years' War, and the collapse of Lutheranism under Hitler! [3] This, of course, is preposterous.

Such ignorance, prejudice, and aspersion root basically in the neglect which has been this reformer's historical lot, for he did not fit into either one of the main streams of Protestant culture. He received the titles of "preceptor of Germany" and "theologian of the Reformation" during his own lifetime. He was the official representative of Protestantism at almost every colloquy in Germany from 1529 to 1560. He helped write the Protest which gave Protestantism its name. His works have influenced almost every major development in Protestantism, and historians commonly rank him second only to Luther and Calvin. But for three hundred years after his death he remained in obscurity.

The immediate causes of this neglect centered in the last fifteen years of Melanchthon's life, those years after the death of Martin Luther. This period was racked with bitter controversies concerning the *correct* Lutheran interpretation of such matters as adiaphora (nonessentials), the Lord's Supper, good works, and justification by faith. Melanchthon was branded a traitor to Lutheranism, a weakling, and a compromiser with the papal Antichrist. This was as skillful a piece of character assassination as has ever been perpetrated in history.

After Melanchthon's death in 1560 the controversies continued to rage. The Formula of Concord, as the name implies, attempted to state a reconciliation, but concord was not achieved. From 1574 when the Wittenberg divines published their "Exegesis on the Perpetual Controversies over the Lord's Supper" until the bicentennial of Melanchthon's death, a pall of suspicion, reproach, prejudice, and calumny hung about Melanchthon. His supporters were deposed and imprisoned; his writings were condemned and suppressed. In 1610 the government ordered his *Loci* stricken from the list of approved textbooks, and the author of the new textbook, Hutter, following a public disputation, tore down Melanch-thon's portrait and kicked it into bits.

Beyond a cursory notice or sketch nothing was done to restore Melanch-thon until 1760. In that year his death was commemorated for the first time! In 1777 Strobel's excellent edition of Camerarius' life of Melanch-thon appeared. But this brief period of recognition was like a small shaft of light, for, astonishing as it may seem, until 1840, the only other biographies of Melanchthon worthy of the name were those by the Dutch writer Abraham vande Corput in 1662 and the British author F. A. Cox in 1816. In 1840 and 1841 two German books appeared as a result of the feeling that Melanchthon had been unjustly neglected! [4]

Through the personal efforts of Prof. Nikolaus Müller, of Berlin, on October 20, 1903, the Melanchthon house in Bretten was made a memo-rial. The house, as well as most of the town, had been destroyed in 1689 by the French. Prof. Müller supervised its reconstruction. It now contains many of Melanchthon's first editions and other mementos. When this Melanchthon house was opened, eminent delegates from the Lutheran and Reformed churches, universities, and learned bodies of Germany came to honor him, and the Bretten house is today a center for reformation renaissance. [5]

Since the middle of the nineteenth century many admirable researches have been done on Melanchthon by German scholars, and his writings are being reissued in Europe. Especially noteworthy is the work of Bretschneider and Bindseil who collected and edited the writings of Melanchthon, published as *Melanchthon Opera, Corpus Reformatorum,* twenty-eight volumes. Carl Schmidt published a good biography in 1861, and Karl Hartfelder surveyed Melanchthon's work as a teacher in 1896. But none of these has been translated. In English only a few biographies have appeared; the latest and by far the best, by J. W. Richard, was published more than fifty years ago.

In spite of this neglect, in 1897, William Kelly wrote:

We hesitate not to declare that Melanchthon's influence instead of waning, in some directions at least, is still in the ascendant. By virtue of the fact that the Augsburg Confession, written by him, is not only the doctrinal standard of the Lutheran Church throughout the entire world, but the source from which the Church of England drew the Thirty-Nine Articles of the English confession . . . the influence of Melanchthon will continue to be felt, as long as these great churches continue to endure. But with the churches mentioned that influence does not stop. The twenty-five articles of Methodism, largely based on the Thirty-Nine Articles of Anglicanism, may with justice be claimed indirectly at least as an outgrowth of the Augsburg Confession, so that the Methodist Church also is indebted to Melanchthon. The slightest acquaintance with the Westminster Confession, with the Dort and Heidelberg Catechisms, will show . . . that the Augsburg Confession was consulted by the authors of the later confessions, and that portions were substantially drafted from that Confession into the later productions.[6]

Even though Melanchthon was condemned and rejected, his influence, or infiltration as some would say, continued. The Formula of Concord condemned his rationalism but employed his dialectic through theologians who had been trained by him. In France his books were banned by the Catholic hierarchy, but they were still used. The old French libraries contain many books by Melanchthon, but rarely one from which the author's name has not been carefully effaced and the frontispiece mutilated.[7]

In some circles Melanchthon has been regarded as a replica of Luther. "My own opinion," a professor once remarked, "is that Melanchthon said nothing different from Luther, and if he did, it is false." Knowledge of Melanchthon is often limited to what has been interwoven with the story of Luther. A relatively insignificant book, published in 1813, illustrates this treatment. The book contains a translation of the Augsburg Confession "composed by Luther and Melanchthon," plus a short life of Luther. In spite of the fact that Melanchthon is the acknowledged author of the Augsburg Confession and its Apology (which the writer admits, with qualifications, on page 92), the reader of the book is left with the impression that Luther was the real author.[8]

Melanchthon and Luther worked closely together, and they were lifelong friends. But Melanchthon was not a mouthpiece for Luther. Lutheran scholars who have perpetuated this view, thinking thereby to enhance Luther, have done even Luther a disservice, for Luther will be better understood when Melanchthon enjoys his rightful place. In the bitter controversies after Luther's death, Melanchthon was sharply condemned, whether rightly or wrongly, precisely because some people thought that he was an "untrue" Lutheran.

Skillful propagandists of the sixteenth century also branded Melanchthon as a "crypto" or "secret" Calvinist. In Calvinist circles this was an attempt to make him a rubber stamp of Calvin; in Lutheran circles it was an accusation of the most serious treachery. Uncritical historians have furthered these clever fictions.

The key to the mystery of Melanchthon is his recognition that human beings are finite, that no human being has final truth, that no human action is final, and that the gospel cannot be absolutely translated into human thought and action, that man stands in a faith relationship to God which breaks through all forms of human finiteness so that man does not contain but is contained. This knowledge made him work with "fear and trembling"—not before men, but before God.

Melanchthon negotiated and appeared to be weak; he rejected parts of Luther and appeared to be antievangelical; he used Renaissance culture and appeared to be humanistic; he changed opinions and appeared to be vacillating. But appearances are deceiving. He knew that neither he nor any other man could absolutize his own light. He held on to what he had in faith; he was willing to seek further. His was the ageless problem of reason and revelation—the Renaissance and the Reformation. He was a finite man seeking to serve an infinite God. This is what must be kept in view if one is to understand and evaluate Philip Melanchthon.

Wittenberg's New Professor

HEN PHILIP MELANCHTHON RODE INTO WITTENBERG ON the afternoon of August 25, 1518, he little imagined that he would soon be a heretic, nor that he would for the next twenty-eight years be the closest friend of Martin Luther. He did not know that he would be the official spokesman for the "schism" of Christendom, that he would be the author of its most influential creed; nor did Philip have the remotest notion that he would die in Wittenberg under such a pall of suspicion that for the next two hundred years to call a man a "Philippist" would be to insult him.

The two-hundred-mile journey from Tübingen on horseback was at an end! When Melanchthon first saw Wittenberg with the Elbe River flowing gently on the south side, he was glad. The town's white soil made it look like a giant crescent on the bank of the river and caused Melanchthon to recall the legend that the place had been named "Wittenberg" or "White Mountain" by its ancient Flemish settlers. Around the rest of the city stretched a low wall and moat. On the river front was a market where farmers brought produce several days a week. There, he was to learn, the guilds presented their plays, the state publicly put to death its criminals, and the gala fairs came twice a year. The village skyline was dominated by the twin-pointed towers of the *Stadtkirche,* or Town Church, and the spires of the castle and the *Schlosskirche,* or Castle Church.

A smile crossed his lips as he remembered journeying through Ingolstadt and Leipzig only a few days before. That drunken dolt at Leipzig!

The professors at both these universities tried to persuade him to join their faculties.[1] They were willing to double the one hundred florins he had been offered to go to Wittenberg, and they royally toasted him at banquets. He had heard, too, that Duke Ulrich of Württemberg had sent the well-known Conrad von Sickingen to ask Philip's mother to persuade her son to enter the priesthood where he would be assured a rich benefice.[2]

These reveries faded as he and young Spalatin, his official escort, rode through the Elster gate and got a close-up view of Wittenberg with its little shops and not very tidy clay cottages, its public baths with dishpans hung outside to indicate they were open, and its two cleanly swept paved streets which followed the banks of the two brooks that met at the castle and supplied power for a huge grinding mill.[3] All this fell into the shadows when compared to the eminence of the university and the Augustinian monastery.

The next day, August 26, while still only twenty-one, Melanchthon officially received his position. The rector of the University of Wittenberg was Nicholas Gingelm, Master of Arts. In the Codex Bavari he entered a brief, singularly unimpressive note: "Philip Melanchthon of Bretten, a Tübingen Master of Arts, was registered as the first professor of the

JOHN FREDERICK (*Cranach*)

THE SCHLOSSKIRCHE AT
WITTENBERG, 1499

Greek language." [4] The rector then reminded him that within three days he was expected to give an inaugural speech to the faculty and student body.

As Melanchthon met members of the faculty—Martin Luther in theology; Jerome Schurf, a lawyer from Tübingen, with whom Melanchthon was already acquainted; John Rhagius and Otto Beckman, lecturers on the Latin classics; Caspar Borner, a teacher of mathematics and astronomy; Andrew Bodenstein (Carlstadt), a theologian; Jacob Premsel and John Gunkel, lecturers on Thomistic physics and logic—he became uncomfortably aware of a certain coolness. Many on the faculty had preferred Peter Mosellanus of Leipzig, an established Greek scholar-teacher, rather than this relatively inexperienced young instructor. Philip began to stutter a little more than ordinarily, and he wondered if anyone would notice that one shoulder was lower than the other. He saw some students winking and making circular gestures with their fingers. His first days in Wittenberg were anything but auspicious. [5]

In his tour of the town Melanchthon included the *Stadtkirche,* with its chapel dating back to the time of the thirteenth-century Flemish settlers, its twin Gothic towers, its painting of the Virgin Mary, and its outside inscription showing that the Jews were expelled from the city in 1304. He visited the *Schlosskirche,* with its thousands of special, holy relics displayed in fabulous gold and silver casements—17,443 relics which could help a person reduce his future stay in purgatory by as much as two million years. [6]

There was the thorn that had pressed into the brow of Jesus, a fact which could be authentically documented. King Philip VI of France had presented the thorn to Elector Rudolf, who in 1353 built a chapel to house this precious gift. Rudolf dedicated his chapel to the Virgin Mary and the saints, and provided for masses every Tuesday in honor of St. Anne. Thousands of other relics were gathered, and as the years went by the electors of Saxony collected large sums of money from curious and pious pilgrims who wanted to see the sacred pieces. In 1490 Elector Frederick the Wise used some of this money to build a more elaborate Castle Church. The magnificent new structure was finished in 1509. Two years before this new *Schlosskirche* was completed, Frederick took still more funds from the traffic in relics and endowed the University of Wittenberg, thus providing a financial link between the university and relic veneration.[7]

The thorn that had brought blood to the brow of Jesus was always displayed on a special altar on All Saints' Day, while the other relics were shown from emporiums and balconies built along the sides of the church. Pilgrims came to behold, and they contributed. Melanchthon gazed at a piece of the cloak of John the Baptist, a rock from Mount Calvary, a portion of the rock on which Jesus stood when he wept over Jerusalem, some of the milk of the Virgin Mary's breast, a part of Mary's gown, four strands of Our Lady's hair, four pieces of Our Lady's girdle, a tear that Jesus shed at Lazarus' tomb, thirty-five splinters from the cross of Christ, three pieces of myrrh and one piece of gold brought by the Wise Men to the baby Jesus, a strand of Jesus' beard, one of the nails driven into his hands, a piece of bread served at the Last Supper, a part of the stone on which Jesus stood before ascending into heaven, a twig from Moses' burning bush, an angel feather, and bones and teeth from an array of saints including Chrysostom, Bernard, Augustine, Jerome, Anastasia, Apollonia, and Lucia, along with one complete skeleton and 204 odd bones of the innocent children of Bethlehem slain by the order of Herod.[8]

With many questions half-formed and unexpressed, Melanchthon left the *Schlosskirche* and returned to his quarters. Like Martin Luther who had only ten months before nailed his Ninety-five Theses on the Castle Church door, Melanchthon had begun to question the value of the relics and indulgences. In his Greek New Testament he did not find an emphasis on relic veneration, saints' tales, or indulgent absolution.

On August 29, 1518, four days after arriving in Wittenberg, with many misgivings Melanchthon delivered his inaugural address before the assembled university. He had resolved not to compromise the new learning in which his great-uncle John Reuchlin was a pioneer, nor to bow to mediocrity. He took as his subject, *The Improvement of Studies*.[9]

Melanchthon first congratulated the university on being placed under the auspices of an illustrious prince, and commended to the entire faculty the study of classical literature, although, he said, some uncultured boors will look upon the Greeks as queer and will object to Hebrew. He briefly sketched the historical plight of classical learning. With the fall of the Roman Empire, he declared, study of the classics virtually ceased; only here and there, in England and Ireland, did classical learning flourish, in men like The Venerable Bede. Italy and Gaul, he said, slumbered torpidly, and Germany concerned herself more with the art of war than with the art of letters. Charlemagne tried to revive scholarship in Gaul and succeeded in bringing the renowned Alcuin from England to Paris, which flourished temporarily as a cultural center. Gradually, however, decline and darkness took over. Aristotle and other classical writers, mutilated by inferior translations, became obscure. Men lost facility in Greek. When the scholastics arose, "more numerous than the seed of Cadmus," classical study continued to decline, to the detriment of medicine, law, and theology. Mediocre literature became the vogue. Ceremonies, capitularies, pilgrimages, and glosses consumed more time than sincere study, and genuine scholarship lay dormant. "Who is not affected in our lamentable times by the loss of our ancient writers and the advantages that might have been ours had their writings been preserved?" [10]

Having traced the demise of learning in western Europe, Melanchthon placed his formula for improvement of studies before the university: Learn thoroughly the ancient languages of Hebrew, Greek, and Latin; recover the original wellsprings of the classics and Christianity. He pleaded for a renaissance through a study of original sources. To drink from the sources of theology and to cultivate the liberal arts, he said, we must comprehend the Greek, Latin, and Hebrew languages, for only in this way can we avoid the frigid glosses and jangling comments interposed by men.[11]

If we turn our minds to the sources, said Melanchthon, we will begin to understand Christ, his commands will be beacons leading us, and we will be filled with the holy nectar of divine wisdom. But the one who would be initiated in divine things must first be transformed, the old Adam sloughed off and the new Adam put on, the precepts of men exchanged for genuine piety.[12] He closed by announcing he would begin his work in the university with a study of Homer and the Epistle to Titus.

Melanchthon had hurled a challenge in the face of the obscurantism of his day. He proposed in effect to rejuvenate society and regenerate theology by scrapping several centuries of traditional methods and secondary studies.

The speech impressed the university audience. The applause was

thunderous and exhilarating. Luther's earlier disappointment changed
into unqualified approval. He was happy to have the frail youth with
the high forehead.[13] Jubilantly he wrote to Spalatin:

As regards our Philip Melanchthon, everything shall be done as you suggest. On the fourth day after his arrival he delivered a most learned and
chaste oration and there was so much applause and admiration on every
side that you need not now commend him to us. We quickly retracted the
opinion which we had formed when we first saw him. Be at pains to commend
him most heartily to the Prince. I desire no other Greek teacher so long
as we have him. But I fear that his delicate constitution may not bear the
mode of life in this country. Also, I hear that because of the smallness of
his salary the boastful Leipzig professors hope soon to take him from us.
They solicited him before he came here. I suspect that Dr. Pfeffinger has been
trying to save the Elector's purse a little too much. This man is deserving of
all honor.[14]

It is not too much to imagine that after dinner that night the monks
of the Black Cloister plied Melanchthon with questions about his great-
uncle Reuchlin's conflict with the Dominican monks of Cologne, nor is
it too much to imagine that Melanchthon denounced the Dominicans as
base, flattering parasites and greedy dolts.[15] The Reuchlin fight with
the Dominicans had been raging for over a decade and showed no signs
of diminishing. It had all started when Nicholas V commissioned a
preaching campaign against all "insubordinate Hussites" and "dis-
believing Jews." Burnings were common, ghettos in some towns were
depopulated, and Jewish children were often mercilessly carried away.
A converted Jew, Johann Joseph who at the time of baptism took the
name Pfefferkorn, headed the Dominican preaching crusade. In 1506
he had just been released from prison where he had been serving a
burglary sentence. Aided by the monks at Cologne, particularly Ortuinus
Gratius of the theological faculty, Pfefferkorn issued a series of hate
pamphlets.[16] He declared that all Jews should be compelled to hear
sermons, forsake usury, and destroy their heretical books (the Old Testament excluded). Furthermore, they should be made scavengers. Many
Jews, he said, became doctors to facilitate a systematic murder of Christians. He ridiculed the Jewish Day of Atonement, saying that modern Jews
were using chickens instead of goats in this ritual because the chickens

were cheaper. He described the Jews as fanatics who whirled fowls about their heads and cried, "I am released of my sins! Thou goest to thy death, and I to eternal life." Then, he said, they ate the hapless fowls. Occasionally, however, the Jews would simply wait for a high wind to blow away their sins.

In August, 1509, the Emperor Maximilian gave Pfefferkorn a mandate to destroy any Jewish literature that opposed Christianity. A fanatic, who often resorted to violence and who could not read Hebrew, was thus empowered to sweep away an ancient literature. Reuchlin, a humanist and one of the foremost Hebrew scholars of the time,[17] objected and proposed an alternative which might help Christianity, namely the establishment of chairs of Hebrew in all the leading universities so that Jewish literature could be studied and judiciously pruned if necessary.

He was viciously attacked by Pfefferkorn, the Dominican Inquisitor Jakob van Hoogstraten, and the Cologne monks. In 1511 Reuchlin issued a spirited defense called *Augenspiegel,* Eye-Mirror, which attracted much attention. Realizing that freedom of scholarship was at stake, men like Sir Thomas More, Colet, Hugh Latimer, and others rallied to the side of Reuchlin. The Dominicans enlisted the aid of the universities of Louvain, Cologne, and Erfurt.[18] In the legal battle at the court of the youthful Bishop of Spires, Reuchlin was acquitted of heresy, but the case dragged on in Rome. *Clarorum Virorum Epistolae (Letters of Renowned Men),* a collection of letters supporting Reuchlin, came from the Anshelm press in 1514. For this book Melanchthon wrote a preface in praise of his uncle.[19] Then, late in 1515 the famous *Epistolae Obscurorum Virorum, (Letters of Obscure Men)* appeared.[20] Supposedly they were letters addressed to Ortuinus Gratius from ignorant monks who thought they were asking about profound theological problems. Ortuinus was asked to declare how much guilt was occasioned if on Friday one ate an egg with a chicken in it, or whether worms in cheese should be classified as meat. The letters were cruel and witty, and at first some of the monks did not know they were being ridiculed. Erasmus is said to have laughed so hard that he burst a facial abscess.[21]

The affair attracted so much attention that Pope Leo X ordered the burning of all copies of the book and excommunicated the author or authors, whoever they might be. In 1518 the Dominicans had not yet convinced the pope that he should reverse the decision of the Bishop of Spires, condemn the *Augenspiegel,* and saddle Reuchlin with all the court costs. That came in 1520. Five years later Reuchlin died, broken and discouraged.

In the Wittenberg cloister that night in 1518 there was an atmosphere of expectancy. Many believed that the new Greek teacher, Melanchthon, was one of the authors of the "obscure" letters. Luther thought of himself and was hailed by his friends as a new Reuchlin. But now the nephew of Reuchlin had arrived, bringing humanistic scholarship with him to the seat of the Protestant Reformation. "I most heartily commend Philip," said Luther. "He is an excellent Greek scholar, very learned and highly cultured. He has his auditorium full of hearers. Principally because of his scholarship, all the theological students, high, middle, and low, are studying Greek." [22]

It is now known that while Melanchthon did help edit some of the letters, he was not their author. He also wrote a satire on Hoogstraten for which he was vilified as "dangerous," and he bluntly called Pfefferkorn an impostor who was blackmailing the Jews.[23]

Erasmus was perhaps not too extravagant in his jubilant expectations. Only a few years before he had written:

Eternal God, what promising hopes does not Philip Melanchthon raise, who though only a youth, indeed, scarcely more than a boy, deserves equal esteem for his knowledge of both Latin and Greek! What wisdom in argument, what purity of expression and style, what comprehensive knowledge, what varied reading, what delicacy and mental elegance he displays! [24]

The Devil, Latin, and Philosophy

THE HUMANISTIC SCHOLARSHIP THAT MELANCHTHON brought to Wittenberg had its genesis in his formal education. His early training furnished him with the Renaissance tools of study and set the stage for further development.

Bretten, the place of his birth, was a village of only three hundred people, but the Kraichgau Valley in which Bretten was located could boast the beauty of nature's harvest, for, as the Latin poet Jacob Micyllus remarked, Ceres and Bacchus had both bestowed their gifts upon it.[1] The wine of Bretten, perhaps as much as its location, influenced leaders of sixteenth-century caravans en route from the Rhine

MELANCHTHON'S BIRTHPLACE IN BRETTEN   MELANCHTHON'S HOME IN WITTENBERG

to the Italian peninsula to drive their wagons that way. From this village and its people Melanchthon received a fear of the devil, his early education, and a deep sense of piety.

In 1504 five Bretten citizens were convicted of devil-inspired witch-craft, and, in keeping with the biblical injunction not to let a sorceress live, they were put to death by fire. Philip was seven.

Villagers of the sixteenth century imagined the world filled with demons. These devils could change form and do untold harm to an unwary man. Merchants at the town fairs hawked pamphlets containing lurid tales about wrathful witches and weird warlocks. To ward off evil

WITCH BURNING

spirits, to protect one's hut, to ensure good crops, they sold charms and relics—a tooth, a hair, a strand of cloth, a piece of palm. Books on the art of dying ranked high in popularity, for it was commonly believed that Satan and his minions, unless foiled, would attend the dying and whisk wavering souls away to perdition if they abandoned hope in Christ. Guidebooks for a good death were therefore in demand. Satan might marshal a man's sins before him in the last minutes, as the books said, confronting him with this adultery and that theft. Preparation for such onslaughts might save the dying from eternal torment, especially if at the proper time the victim could quote sacred writings, repeat the *Pater Noster,* praise the Mother of God, and call upon the saints.

Melanchthon absorbed the superstition of his day. John Wesley, two hundred years later, retold one of Melanchthon's stories. When Philip was out walking one evening with some students, the sky was suddenly filled with uncommon singing, after which a strange bird appeared. A student asked, "In the name of the Father, Son, and Holy Ghost, what art thou?" It answered, "I am a damned spirit!" As the horrible apparition disappeared, agonizing words could be heard, "Oh, eternity, eternity! Who can tell the length of eternity!" [2]

In adulthood Melanchthon developed elaborate theories of astrology and demonology. Luther chided Philip about this and once remarked that when Melanchthon talked about astrology he sounded like Luther under the influence of too many beers. But Luther himself moved in a world of imps and demons, for these were as much a part of the sixteenth century as science is a part of the twentieth.

But Bretten gave Melanchthon something else. Camerarius, a close friend of Melanchthon, described the villagers of Bretten as incredibly humanitarian, ingenuous, polite, and good.[3] This was true of Philip's ancestors at least as far back as grandfather Schwartzerd. Schwartzerd, literally meaning "black earth," was Philip's family name. The Greek equivalent, Melanchthon, was given to Philip at the age of twelve by his great-uncle Reuchlin.

Shortly after the death of Melanchthon in 1560, the admiring professors of Wittenberg wrote a brief account of the Schwartzerd family.[4] Melanchthon's grandfather, Claus Schwartzerd, "a worthy, pious man," said the professors' account, lived with his wife Elizabeth in Heidelberg. Their two sons, John and George, were "diligently trained in the fear of God." John took up the trade of a locksmith, but George, who found favor with the Elector, took up armor-making. His skill aroused the professional jealousy of his fellow craftsmen, and George was "accidentally" burned with some hot lead. The Elector then sent George to Nürnberg for special training. His work was so superior that foreign potentates sought his services, among them the king of Poland and the Emperor Maximilian.

When George was thirty, the Elector thought that he might have a firmer hold on his prize armourer if an honorable marriage could be arranged for him. So he negotiated with a distinguished citizen of Bretten, John Reuter, whose daughter Barbara was a virtuous, well-bred maiden. By the providence of Almighty God and the negotiations of the Elector, she was finally promised to George in marriage. They were wedded at Spires in the presence of many knights who assembled to do them honor.

George Schwartzerd was a just, pious, God-fearing man. . . . No one ever heard him curse, and no one ever saw him drunk or heard of his being drunk to the day of his death. He lived in wedlock four years without children; but after the close of the fourth year, which was 1497, on Thursday after Invocavit [February 16], his first son, Philip, our dear master and teacher, was born in Bretten, in the house of the father-in-law and grandfather, John Reuter. Thus God blessed this pious and God-fearing man with the gift of a son, whom not one land, but many, yea, all Christendom, has enjoyed and without doubt will enjoy to the end of the world!

Another son and three daughters were born to the Schwartzerds in Bretten: Anna, in 1499; George, in 1501; five years later, Margaretha; and in 1508, Barbara.[5] George Schwartzerd, however, did not live to see his family grow up. In 1504 in Manheim, Neuburg, he drank some poisoned well water and never recovered from the effects. During the next four years, he was virtually an invalid.

When George realized that death was near, he called his children and tendered them a legacy which Philip never forgot: "These three things I will leave my children when I die. In the bosom of the true Christian Church, they are one in Him, united with each other, and heirs of eternal life." To Philip, aged ten, he said, "I have experienced many changes in the world, but greater ones are coming. My prayer is that God may rule you in these changes. I counsel you, my son, to fear God and to be honest." [6]

Philip scarcely comprehended what was happening. On October 16 his grandfather died; eleven days later, his father.[7]

The pietism of these early years is difficult to assess. George Schwartzerd diligently kept his devotions, never allowing anything to interfere with his religious observances. He often said prayers in the middle of the night, never uttered an improper word, and never joked. Philip's mother was strong on the practice of pietistic charity, even though she herself had very little of this world's goods. "Alms do not impoverish," was a favorite proverb, along with "Whoever wishes to consume more than his plow can support will at last come to ruin and die upon the gallows." [8] She believed that every farmer should divide his produce into three parts, one for planting, one for taxes, tithes and alms, and one for self-support.[9]

Under his grandfather Reuter's direction Melanchthon received his earliest education. Philip with his brother George and another grandson, John Reuter, were enrolled in the town's only school. However, when the teacher came down with a "wicked and contagious disease," sometimes called the "French plague," grandfather Reuter decided to obtain a private tutor. Reuchlin recommended John Unger, a young scholar from Pforzheim.[10] This young theologian later became a court chaplain for the Margrave of Baden. Fifty years afterwards Philip remembered him as an "excellent linguist."

He was an honest man who taught the Gospel and suffered much for the Gospel's sake. . . . He drove me to grammar and made me do twenty or thirty verses from Mantuan each day. He would not allow me to omit anything. Whenever I would make a mistake, he applied the rod to me, and yet with the moderation that was proper. Thus he made me a linguist. He was a good man; he loved me as a son, and I him as a father; and in a short time we shall meet, I hope, in eternal life. I loved him notwithstanding that he used such severity; although it was not severity, but parental correction which prompted me to diligence. At evening I had to hunt the rules in order to recite. You see, discipline was stricter then than now![11]

However, all was not Latin diagraming. Grandfather Reuter was also interested in music. He purchased a missal that his grandsons might also become familiar with the hymns of the church, and he required that they be in the village church on all holy days.[12]

Observing that Philip could hold his own in arguments with adults, grandfather Reuter pitted young Philip against the great Bacchanti who came roving through Bretten. He kept Philip supplied with books and rejoiced inordinately when his grandson dispatched a supposedly learned Bacchanti.[13]

Melanchthon possessed a quick mind, remembered well, and expressed himself forcefully, despite a tendency to stammer.[14] By the time he was twelve, three things had left their imprints upon him—superstition, piety, and Latin.

When both father and grandfather died, the task of finding a suitable higher school for the boys fell upon Elizabeth Reuter, the grandmother. On the advice of her brother John Reuchlin she took the boys to the

Latin school in Pforzheim near Stuttgart, where Reuchlin was president of the Swabian Court of the Confederates.

The Pforzheim Latin school, under the direction of George Simler and John Hiltebrant, both Reuchlinists, had achieved an excellence which was rare in the sixteenth century. This was fortunate, for the early 1500's seemed to have an unusually large quota of malcontents and misfits in the education system. Even though most of the teachers had theological training, some instructors were ignorant of the Ten Commandments, to say nothing about the Hebraic prophets, the New Testament, and philosophy. Although some of the teachers were well trained, many of the Latin school teachers had no university education whatsoever. Immorality among the teachers more than matched their lack of academic achievement. In almost every locality laws were enacted requiring the schoolteachers to be God-fearing, respectful, upright men. And small wonder, since some of them augmented their incomes by manufacturing and selling alcoholic beverages on the school premises.[15]

Such conditions prompted Melanchthon later to say to the citizens of Antwerp, "If you know a good man, one who can teach, speak and act at the same time, get him at any price; for the matter involves the future of your children who receive the impress of good and bad example with the same susceptibility." [16]

George Simler qualified as one of the better teachers in the sixteenth century. The historian Friedlieb, a fellow student with Melanchthon at Pforzheim, described Simler as a born teacher. Melanchthon also praised him: "When I was a boy I had two very learned men for teachers. One was George Simler. He first explained to me the Latin and Greek poets and introduced me to a purer philosophy. In lecturing on Aristotle, he often referred directly to the Greek." [17] Melanchthon was just twelve at the time!

Simler's major field was Latin, but to his best students he offered private lessons in Greek as well. Through him Melanchthon became grounded in ancient Hellenistic language and thought.[18] Simler's friendship with the printer Thomas Anshelm, who put a press in Pforzheim as early as 1502, enabled Melanchthon to get acquainted with many humanistic publications, including two school comedies of Reuchlin which Simler edited in 1508 and used as textbooks for versification.[19] Philip's progress was amazing. Reuchlin spoke of him as his son, bestowed praise, gave him a red doctor's hat, and presented him with a Greek grammar. At a time when books were valuable enough to be chained to their shelves in the libraries, this was no small gift. For composing verses in Latin, Reuchlin rewarded Philip with his personal Greek-Latin Lexicon.

As a surprise for his uncle, Melanchthon once staged one of Reuchlin's light school comedies at a banquet given by the Pforzheim monks to honor "the old phoenix of Germany." Reuchlin, obviously pleased, declared that a young man so clever should no longer have a common name like Schwartzerd, but instead its Greek equivalent, Melanchthon! While he did not immediately use it, inasmuch as he enrolled in Heidelberg as "Philippus Schwartzerd de Brethenn" and at Tübingen as "Philippus Schwartzerd ex Preten," the name came gradually to prevail. Out of a variety of forms—Melas, Melanthonis, Melancton, Melanchton, and Melanthon—Melanchthon, which was used chiefly by his friends, predominated.[20]

This name change symbolized Melanchthon's relation to the humanistic movement,[21] for the humanists commonly considered themselves citizens of both Greece and Rome and entitled therefore to Hellenized and Latinized names. Schwartzerd and Melanchthon both meant the black earth. Those who wished to do so could point to biblical precedent: Abram, Abraham; Saul, Paul.

When Melanchthon left Pforzheim, he could write with facility in either Greek or Latin and had a thorough acquaintance with the subjects usually taught in the Latin schools at the time: grammar, arithmetic, rhetoric, dialectic, history, and geography. He was thirteen when he entered the University of Heidelberg. Jurist John Weisner was rector, and the official entry read, "Philippus Schwartzerd de Brethenn Spir. dyoc. XIIII Octobris."

Unlike Pforzheim the University of Heidelberg in 1509 could not be termed excellent. Looking back upon it Melanchthon said, "Almost nothing was taught me except trivia compounded with more of the same." Nevertheless, two men made a lasting impression: one Dr. Pallas Spangel, a professor of theology, with whom Melanchthon boarded; the other was Agricola, a man who had been dead for twenty-four years.

For three years Philip lived in the home of Spangel and came to know

him intimately. He often reminisced about the time when he served wine
to Spangel's Pomeranian guests on the occasion of the marriage of Duke
George of Pomerania to the daughter of the Palatine Elector.[22] Spangel
had served as vice-chancellor of the university, three times was rector,
and was professor of theology. He had also been the official spokesman
for the university in the dispute with Elector Philip in 1479 about allowing unmarried laymen to teach in the medical faculty, and he had delivered
an official speech before the Emperor Maximilian urging his highness to
annihilate the enemies of Christ or force their conversion. But it was
Spangel's personality which drew the leading students to him.[23]

Spangel was a bridge between medieval scholasticism and renaissance
humanism. Wide interests in the liberal arts enabled him to stimulate
many students at Heidelberg, but his new learning remained a tool for
the promotion of established dogma. He was not a "reformer before the
reformation." As a scholastic he knew the system of St. Thomas; as a
churchman he accepted the orthodox ecclesiastical teachings; as a humanist he interested himself in the better Latin works of the ancients.[24]

Melanchthon appreciated Spangel, but there was no one at Heidelberg
to carry him further in philosophy. To escape the mental atrophy of
"sophistry, phrase-mongering and empty discussion," Melanchthon and
other young scholars—such as John Sorbil, later a humanist poet; Peter
Sturm, brother of the well-known Jacob Sturm of Strassburg; Theobald
Billican, reformer of Nördlingen; John Brentz, fiery reformer of Württemberg; and Martin Bucer, who eventually left the Dominican order to
become one of the foremost reformers in northern Europe—turned to the
library.[25] There he could be seen standing with one of the chained volumes
in his hands, or seated at a small bench with one that was allowed limited
circulation. Through this extracurricular reading, Melanchthon discovered
his most important teacher at Heidelberg—Rudolph Agricola, who was
the guiding spirit behind the humanism which flourished briefly at Heidelberg and with whom his uncle Reuchlin had been acquainted.

Only the last three years of Agricola's life were spent at Heidelberg,
but his lectures on Aristotle and his translations of Lucian were well remembered.[26] Reading his books and hearing others talk about him left
an indelible imprint on Melanchthon. Probably in 1510, but possibly later
when Melanchthon was at Tübingen, he received a three-volume set of

Agricola's *Dialectics* as a present from his friend Oecolampadius. Philip avidly studied these books, memorized large portions, adopted the order of argument, and came to discover new depths in the classics.[27] When Melanchthon's own textbook on rhetoric, obviously influenced by Agricola, was published, it brought an improved dialectic and good Latin once again to the fore in Germany and was widely used in England during the next two centuries. Queen Elizabeth I and Shakespeare thus came into the orbit of Melanchthon's influence.[28]

Agricola represented a break with scholastic logic and dialectic. His vitriolic attacks on scholastic traditions made him a storm center at Heidelberg. Many of the older universities like Prague, Vienna, Heidelberg, Erfurt, and Cologne, all of which were established in the fourteenth century, were militant, proud strongholds of scholasticism. In the fifteenth and sixteenth centuries, many of the new universities like Greifswald, Freiburg, Basel, Ingolstadt, Treves, Mainz, Tübingen, Wittenberg, and Marburg threatened the old bastions of education by promoting the new learning of humanism. Academic warfare resulted. The scholastics at Heidelberg regarded Agricola as an enemy in camp.[29]

That Melanchthon surpassed some of his teachers is indicated by a classroom incident. When one of the professors could not explain a problem due to his deficiency in Greek and cried out, "Where shall I find a Grecian?" the students unanimously answered, "Melanchthon! Melanchthon!"[30]

While at Heidelberg Melanchthon tutored and produced his first printed works. Although he was only fourteen, in 1511 he tutored the two sons of Count Ludwig von Löwenstein. This was probably the first teaching Philip ever did.[31] In 1510 Melanchthon's first published poem appeared in a volume honoring a highly respected preacher of the day, Geiler von Kaiserberg. Jacob Wimpfeling included it in his biographical sketch of Geiler.[32] Wimpfeling also published Philip's second poem, in which he called on the gods and muses to yield to the only true wisdom that can teach us about the universe and lead us to piety.[33] Significantly, Wimpfeling and Geiler were only halfway humanists: loyal to the church, but critical of ecclesiasticism and interested in the researches of the new learning.[34]

After being at Heidelberg only two years Melanchthon passed the required examination for the B.A. degree, and on June 11, 1511, was made a Bachelor of the Liberal Arts. Eager to acquire the M.A. so that he could begin teaching, Melanchthon spent the next year diligently pursuing the necessary scholastic thought. At the end of the year, however, his application was denied, "on account of his youth and his boyish appearance." Deeply hurt, and weakened by persistent attacks of fever, Melanchthon resolved to leave Heidelberg.[35]

Simler and Reuchlin recommended Tübingen for the M.A. degree. This newly founded university on the banks of the Neckar had little tradition of which to boast. Duke Eberhard, the Bearded, set it up in 1477 so that the duchy of Württemberg might also have the prestige of a university. His agents toured Italy for library books, well-trained men were invited to the faculty, and the new center soon had a reputation for energetic learning. By 1512, however, the university was already beginning to entrench.

The entrenchment was not so evident when Melanchthon arrived in Tübingen. Different schools of thought were still vigorously advocated, and disputes often ended in fights with clubs and stones. Students lined up on the side of nominalism or realism, the two prevailing philosophies, and were assigned to their *bursen* or dormitories accordingly.[36] The realists had chosen the eagle as their banner symbol, and the nominalists, the peacock. To these banners the students rallied. Philip liked the peacock! The disputes were often dangerous. Ludvicus Vives reported that he saw fighting not only with fists, but with clubs and swords, so that many were wounded and even killed. Camerarius, Melanchthon's first biographer, reported such disorders at Tübingen.[37]

In 1473 Louis XI, king of France, published an edict against the nominalists. He ordered that all nominalist books be fastened with iron chains in the libraries so that they could not be read and that students take oaths against nominalism. John Heynlin, who helped Louis XI suppress nominalism, became professor of theology and rector of Tübingen in 1478 only to be forced to leave the following year because of the opposition of the nominalists. He sought the peace of a monastery in Basel. His successor, Gabriel Biel, appointed in 1484, was a nominalist and taught the criticial, negative system of William Occam, although he did accept the teachings of the church. But the war of the philosophies was too much for him, too; he finally became a member of the Brethren of the Common Life.

The realists, generally speaking, advocated a Neoplatonic view of this world. The idea "chair," they said, is more real than an actual chair, inasmuch as the idea "chair" transcends time and exists in Divine Mind. The idea "Church," accordingly, they said, is more real than particular churches. This philosophy, of course, helped substantiate many of the universal claims of the Roman Catholic Church.

The nominalists, on the whole, advocated a neo-Aristotelian view of this world. The idea "chair" does not exist apart from a particular chair. And, consequently, an idea like the "Church" has no existence, except as a name. Ideas apart from actual existence are mere names, *nomen,* hence the term *nominalism.* Because the scholastic realists were using Aristotle to support their views, Melanchthon undertook to re-edit Aristotle in the Greek to show that the realists were mistaken. Francis Stadian, professor of philosophy, goaded him to this ambitious task. He proposed that Philip prepare a new edition of Aristotle in the original so that this great philosopher, "who, maimed, mutilated and translated into barbarous Latin, had become more obscure than a sibylline oracle," might again be seen in his pristine greatness. Stadian, Reuchlin, Pirkheimer, Simler, Oecolampadius, and Fabricius promised assistance on this project, but it had to be laid aside on account of Reuchlin's fight with Pfefferkorn and the "monkish bigots of Cologne." This interest in Aristotle was a revolt against scholasticism.

Through an independent study of William Occam, that peerless champion of nominalism in the fourteenth century, Melanchthon came to doubt many church dogmas. Occam pointed out that universals do not exist outside the mind. Universals, or ideas, are subjective; they are intentions of the mind. They do not ever correspond to objective realities which call them forth. Occam concluded from this that reason is almost useless as a foundation for revealed dogma. On faith, without reason, he said he would accept church dogma. This philosophical view tended to limit papal power, which in the system of Aquinas was undergirded by reason. Occam was not a forerunner of the evangelical reformation, but the reformers used his system of thought against Roman Catholicism.

Luther called him "my dear master" and referred to himself as an Occamist. Melanchthon pursued Occam with great interest, but later found the intricacies of his system unsatisfying.[38] Occam, while pointing the way to scriptural authority and undercutting reason, nevertheless remained faithful to the Roman Catholic Church, even adopting transubstantiation simply because the church taught it; it was not taught in Scripture and could not be rationally demonstrated, said Occam.

In the writings of John Wessel, Melanchthon found ideas that accelerated his inclination toward evangelical reform. Philip wrote in one of his Postils: "On many points of evangelical doctrine he taught exactly as we do, now that the church is reformed, and that God has caused the glorious light of the Gospel to shine again in marvellous ways. The writings of Wessel are good!" [39] Luther was so pleased with Wessel, although not with Wessel's figurative view of the Lord's Supper, that he alluded to him as being taught of God and, he added, that papists might have charged Luther with having derived his doctrines from Wessel had he known his writings before.[40]

This pre-Lutheran reformer, John Wessel (1419-89), early in his career embraced nominalism and influenced both Reuchlin and Agricola. Although he did not depart completely from the medieval church, some of his ideals were especially shocking. Wessel rejected the church as an institution for the dispensation of the treasures of the sacraments. He defined the church as a communion of all who are united with Christ in one faith, hope, and love; he made the invisible church paramount. The pope, and the external unity represented by him, he said, was incidental, and therefore not necessary. Ecclesiastical vows, he declared, have no binding power, and indulgences have no efficacy. Wessel pointed to the fallibility of the church with its "pestilential errors" and called submission to such an institution blasphemous and irrational, but he was not for reform, because he considered the visible institution incidental anyway. Since all depends on the relation of the individual to God, sacerdotal priesthood has little value. His goal was to rediscover the primitive church by sloughing off the accumulated additions of the centuries. This likewise became one of Melanchthon's goals. Significantly, Melanchthon studied Wessel before he knew Luther, and this made him ready for conversation with

Luther. It also prepared him for his early rejection of transubstantiation, a step in which Melanchthon anticipated Luther.

While enrolled at Tübingen Melanchthon often visited his uncle Reuchlin in Stuttgart where he spent long hours in the private library and in discussions of current topics. Reuchlin in turn often visited his nephew, actually rooming with him in the burse, eating at the students' tables, and taking sides with the nominalists. A gift from Reuchlin at this time was cherished by Melanchthon the rest of his life—a Latin Bible. During church services when the priest was discoursing, or piously relating a fable about some saint or telling how the wooden soles of the Dominicans' sandals came from the tree of knowledge, Melanchthon would be reading Scripture. More than once he was reprimanded for reading his Bible in church! [41]

Melanchthon's professors at Tübingen varied in academic attainment, a fact which prompted him to read widely. To supplement Bebel's instruction in poetry, he studied both Vergil and Cicero.[42] To offset Jacob Lemp, "the old Doctor of Theology, who pictured transubstantiation on the blackboard," he studied nominalism. But Melanchthon did not read beyond John Stöffler, the mathematician who taught astronomy and astrology. In 1513 Melanchthon wrote a highly complimentary Latin verse for Stöffler's *Elucidatio fabricae ususque astrolabii* and found in Stöffler's lectures confirmation of his own superstitions about the stars and their effects on human life.[43] Melanchthon heard lectures on medicine and virtually memorized Galen. But his outside studies were more significant. With a fellow student, Oecolampadius, he read Hesiod and other Greek works, and later said that no one did more for him in his youth than Oecolampadius.[44]

The degree that was denied at Heidelberg was duly awarded at Tübingen. On January 25, 1514, Melanchthon, the first of eleven candidates, received the M.A. Along with the degree went the right as *Privatdocent* to lecture on the classics. He began to do so, with conspicuous success, in his old dormitory.

But Philip was not content to lecture on Vergil, Terence, Livy, and Cicero. He wanted to go further. "His didactic skill, his extraordinary thoroughness, his enthusiasm for classical literature, awoke a new life in the university." [45]

When Professor Hiltebrant died in 1514, Melanchthon became corrector for the printer Thomas Anshelm who had set up a press in Tübingen. This added to his income and also gave him an opportunity to read many new humanistic writings.[46] While working for Anshelm he edited and largely rewrote the *Chronicon,* or Universal History, by John Nauchler, a ponderous folio of fable, fact, and fiction, which carried a preface by Reuchlin.[47]

The first book to carry Melanchthon's name was probably the *Dialogus Mythologicus* of Bartholomew of Cologne; in 1516 Melanchthon wrote a preface for it.[48] About the same time Melanchthon published a metrical arrangement of the comedies of Terence, which up to that time had appeared only in prose. In the following year translations of Plutarch, Pythagoras, and Lycidas came out, and works on both Aratus and Aristotle were projected.[49]

Melanchthon's oration on the liberal arts before the University of Tübingen in 1517 aroused praise and envy. Dramatically he appealed for devoted pursuit of the classics and sacred studies.[50] In 1518 Anshelm published Melanchthon's *Rudiments of the Greek Language.*[51] The youthful Philip stayed in Anshelm's home while this book was being printed and anxiously scanned each page as it came from the press. He need not have been so worried; the grammar was an immediate success and went through many editions.

Melanchthon's work attracted the attention and praise of men like Erasmus, and he was known even in England.[52] But in Tübingen his success brought the deadly hate of professionals less competent than he. Although the Reuchlin controversy with the Dominicans was still raging, Tübingen did not rally to his support, nor did Reuchlin's nephew receive encouragement. The university had gradually become subservient to conservative ecclesiasticism. Jacob Lemp, for example, combated the new "heresy" of Luther; Simler and Stadian did nothing; and Melanchthon found himself standing alone, suspected, and slandered as a "dangerous man." The relative freedom of teaching once known at Tübingen had slowly faded away. Melanchthon's popularity with the students did not help matters. So, in 1518 Melanchthon prepared to leave "a school where it was a major offence to study good literature." [53] That year he wrote to his friend Bernhard Maurer:

The method of teaching which ought to improve both the understanding and the manners is neglected here. What is called philosophy is a weak and empty speculation, which produces strife and contention! The true wisdom of heaven which should regulate the affections of men is banished.[54]

Melanchthon knew that he must leave Tübingen!

Calls to teach in other universities were not long in coming, for his name was known throughout northern Europe. Erasmus had already prophesied that Melanchthon would excel and eclipse all humanists, even Erasmus, and the humanist Willibald Pirkheimer of Nürnberg had sung his praises.[55] The first position that opened was at the University of Ingolstadt, but Ingolstadt was too much like Tübingen. On the advice of Reuchlin, Philip turned it down. A short while afterwards the Elector Frederick of Saxony asked Reuchlin to recommend suitable professors for two new language chairs in the rapidly expanding University of Wittenberg.

Reuchlin rejoiced, saying that only by studying the languages could scholarship be saved from the "prostitution of fools." For the chair of Hebrew he suggested either Dr. Paul Riccius, a converted Jew and physician to Cardinal von Gurk, or Conrad Pellican, a barefoot prior, a former student of his, who in 1507 had published a Hebrew grammar. For the chair of Greek, Reuchlin nominated his own nephew, Master Philip Schwartzerd of Bretten, with the stipulation that Melanchthon should be returned free of expense if he did not fill the position acceptably. He also mentioned that Melanchthon might journey to Saxony in September with the merchants of Frankfort who could transport his books, "for without books, especially in the university, one can neither rightly teach nor read." [56]

For a while the decision of the Elector hung in the balance. Luther and Spalatin were both supporting Peter Mosellanus, a well-known Greek scholar of Leipzig, but the recommendation of the "old phoenix" prevailed. On July 24, 1518, Reuchlin jubilantly relayed a formal call to Melanchthon. For the occasion—prophetic of the change in Melanchthon's career—Reuchlin drew upon biblical rather than classical metaphors:

Lo! A letter has arrived from our gracious Prince, signed with his own hand, in which he promises you pay and favor. I will not now address you in the language of poetry, but will quote the faithful promise of God to Abraham: "Get thee out of thy country, and from thy kindred, and from the house of thy father, and go unto a land that I will show thee; and I will make thee into a great nation, and I will bless thee, and magnify thy name, and thou shalt be a blessing." So the Spirit tells me, and so I hope the future will be for you, my Philip, my work and my consolation. Go, therefore, for a prophet is not honored in his own country.[57]

To the Elector, who was then attending the diet in Augsburg, Reuchlin wrote:

He will come to Augsburg with his library, to wait on your Electoral Grace with honor, praise and profit. Of this you need have no doubt, for I know among the Germans no one who excells him except Erasmus of Rotterdam, who is a Hollander. Melanchthon also excells us all in Latin.[58]

Philip hurried to Stuttgart to discuss the new position. After a short visit with his family in Bretten and friends in Pforzheim, he said farewell to Reuchlin, and early in August set out on horseback for Augsburg. There he paid his respects to the Elector and met Spalatin who was to be his escort to Wittenberg. When Melanchthon left Tübingen, Simler noted that his "learned" colleagues were unmoved, for "although they were learned men, they were not learned enough to understand how great was the learning of him who had been called from their midst." [59] Camerarius observed, "They did not know that they were losing the one who would become Germany's greatest teacher." [60]

The Idle Spectator

ELANCHTHON'S ARRIVAL IN WITTENBERG SEEMED TO IM-
bue the university with new life. He presented a clarion
challenge to lead forth in education, and within a remarkably short time the outward effects could be seen. "At
the university," said Luther, "they are as industrious as
ants!" Subjects that were devoted almost exclusively to
scholasticism became fewer, studies in languages increased, new lectures
on the classics were offered, and interest in biblical sources awakened.[1]
Philip sought to lead the students to the sources of theology by means of
language, logic, and classical literature, and they responded to his enthusiasm and sincerity. From all over Germany and from foreign countries
young men came to hear him.[2] Melanchthon's teaching and the fame of
Luther drew more and more students to Wittenberg. In the winter
semester of 1518, when Melanchthon first came to the university, only
120 students were enrolled; the following semester the enrollment doubled.
By the summer semester of 1520, 333 were on the official rolls. In the
autumn of 1520 Spalatin reported that 600 were present at one of Philip's
lectures.[3] Another writer observed:

Sometimes he had nearly two thousand hearers, among whom were princes,
counts, barons, and other persons of rank. He taught over a wide range of
subjects, including Hebrew, Latin, and Greek grammar, rhetoric, physics,
and philosophy; thus serving the common weal of Church and State, and in
teaching accomplishing as much in all his subjects as other professors did
in one.[4]

Luther sent students to Philip's lectures at six in the morning.[5] So genuine was the success of the "Grecian" that Luther exclaimed, "No one living is gifted with such talents. He is to be esteemed. God himself will despise anyone who despises this man." [6]

Melanchthon lectured on the classics, drilled students in Greek, and within a year began presenting theology and instruction in Hebrew. Before the end of September he had dedicated to the Elector a translation of one of Lucian's works. In October he published the Epistle to Titus with a small lexicon, and before the year was up had completed two treatises of Plutarch, a dictionary, a Greek hymn, *Athenagoras,* Plato's *Symposium,* and miscellaneous prefaces and discourses. By January his three books on rhetoric appeared.[7] Such energy had not been seen at Wittenberg!

Most important was Melanchthon's interest in theology. Conversations with Luther and wide reading stimulated his study. "Justification by faith" was easy to accept for he brought to it compatible knowledge and experience, and his youthful energy carried him beyond even Luther. By September, 1519, he had completely rejected the fundamental Roman Catholic dogma of transubstantiation. He did not believe that the bread of the Lord's Supper became flesh, and the wine, blood. In this he superseded Luther's *Babylonian Captivity* by a full year.

It was the Leipzig debate, however, which dramatically thrust Philip into the forefront of the evangelical movement. He described himself as an "idle spectator," but this debate and his theses on transubstantiation placed him squarely beside Luther in a dispute little short of open revolt.

Martin Luther's *Ninety-five Theses* had caused an emotional tremor to sweep across Europe, and other tremors followed with rising intensity until both the papacy and the empire felt the shocks. On August 7, 1518, Luther received a summons to appear in Rome for a "trial on suspicion of heresy." But political expediency prevented this. Elector Frederick, Emperor Maximilian, and Pope Leo X had to consider the delicate balance of power and their own interests which might suffer from a disturbance in Germany. Cardinal Cajetan was therefore dispatched to Germany to stop the "infectious spread of doubt." [8] Luther had reason to fear for his life, and as the time approached for the interview with the Cardinal at Augsburg a sense of martyrdom filled Luther and his colleagues. The

Elector's advice that he wait for an imperial promise of safe conduct did not allay the tension.[9] Luther vowed he would rather die than revoke what he had been teaching, and Melanchthon never expected to see Luther again, a feeling which Luther shared. "Play the man, as you do," he said to Philip, "and teach the youth the things that are right. If it please the Lord I am going to be sacrificed for you and for them. I prefer to perish and, what is my greatest sorrow, to lose your sweetest society forever rather than to recant . . . and thus become the occasion for the ruin of the noblest studies." [10]

For three days, October 12-14, Cajetan tried to persuade Luther. Because Luther would not say "Revoco" without being shown the errors of his arguments, and because Cajetan could not argue with a common, suspect priest, the conference came to an impasse. When rumors of imprisonment began circulating, Luther departed from Augsburg in great haste.

Cajetan demanded that the Elector put Luther in chains and send him to Rome. Luther answered with an impassioned call for a general council, even though this was itself heretical. Melanchthon defended Luther in numerous letters and sent a copy of the heretical call for a council to Spalatin asking him to influence the Elector. "I am sending you Martin's statement. Do not fear the raging of the Romanists. That is what such men usually do. Unless they act like tyrants they do not think they rule. But, good God! There is a difference between such ruling and serving as stewards." [11] Just when Luther was preparing to leave Wittenberg for exile, word came that the Elector had written the Curia that he would not surrender Luther for an unfair Roman trial nor banish him for alleged heresy.[12]

Fearing that Frederick might support the emperor in the coming elections, the papacy sent Charles Miltitz to Germany with a Golden Rose relic to make amends, with power to name a new cardinal if necessary. But no one was fooled. Luther promised only that he would not debate nor publish, provided his opponents did likewise.[13]

But his opponents did not keep quiet. John Eck, sensing that the situation was latent with publicity and fame, challenged Luther to a debate. Officially Eck challenged Carlstadt, but actually Luther, although Luther was not sure he would be allowed to debate until he reached Leipzig where Duke George had arranged for the affair.[14]

Eck arrived first in Leipzig and used the time to cover himself with pomp. He was wined and dined and given a coat by the Leipzig professors; he asked for and was given a bodyguard of seventy-six men. This impressive guard marched here and there with fife and drums playing and banners streaming.[15]

The Wittenberg party arrived on June 24 in two open wagons. Carlstadt with his books rode in the first; in the second rode Melanchthon, Luther, John Lange, vicar of the Augustinians, Nicholas Amsdorf, John Agricola, and three doctors of law. Two hundred students armed with spears and battle-axes walked alongside. On entering the city a wheel on Carlstadt's wagon broke hurling him and his books into a mudhole.[16]

Thousands came to hear the debaters. Benches and chairs in the large castle auditorium were appropriately decorated with emblems of St. Martin for the Wittenbergers and St. George for Eck. The debate began on June 27 and lasted eighteen days. First the parties attended six-o'clock mass in St. Thomas Church. Then they assembled in the castle auditorium where Duke George's secretary delivered a "splendid" two-hour speech in which he discussed rules for debate.[17] Duke George marveled that this should be necessary. After this unusual oration, the audience knelt, and the choir accompanied by the town band rendered *Veni, Sancte Spiritus*. Then it was time to eat. To Eck, Duke George sent a deer; to Carlstadt, a roe; and to everyone, wine.

That afternoon the contestants skirmished over rules. Eck opposed having stenographers record the debate, for he feared it might interfere with the spontaneous heat of the arguments. Melanchthon commented that the truth might fare better at a lower temperature. Eck lost.[18] Luther opposed having judges, thinking that a judgment might prejudice his case with the pope. Luther lost. Both sides promised not to publicize the debate until after the theological faculties of Erfurt and Paris made their decisions. Neither side kept this promise.

For a week Eck and Carlstadt disputed the depravity of man. Then Luther and Eck argued papal primacy. Was the papacy divinely or humanly instituted? Duke George did not see that it mattered; whether divine, or human, he said, the pope is still the pope! But Eck knew that the papal

ECK EIN GROSSER FEIND CHRISTI WAR
HAT SEHR VERFOLGT DIE CHRISTLICH SCHAR
MIT SCHREIBEN VND VNNVCZEM GSCHWECZ
BRACHT ER DIE EINFELTIGEN INS NECZ
EIFRIG VND BÖS WAR ALL SEIN SIINN
VERGEBS IM. GOT ZR IST LANG HIINN.

THE PRINCIPALS AT LEIPZIG—LUTHER, ECK, AND MELANCHTHON
(*Note the ditty satirizing Eck.*)

claim of unquestioning obedience rested on divine institution, and he pushed Luther into an agreement not only with the burned heretic Hus but also into an admission that a council might err. The debates on purgatory, indulgence, and penance were anticlimatic, for Eck admitted that he could agree with Luther except when his opponent assailed papal primacy. Eck knew that the great point had been made.[19] Although Eck boasted victory and was privately rewarded by Duke George, it is significant that a large number of students transferred from Leipzig to Wittenberg. Among the number was Caspar Cruciger, who soon became one of Melanchthon's closest friends.

Melanchthon called himself an "idle spectator." He did not debate, but he kept the Wittenbergers supplied with a constant stream of information and arguments to use against Eck and his party. At times he seemed to be one of the disputants, and Eck protested, "Keep silent, Philip. Mind your own business. Don't bother me!" At other times Eck tried to discredit him as the "very arrogant nephew of Reuchlin." [20]

Luther felt quite different. To Spalatin he wrote:

I return to Philip, whom no Eck can make me hate. In my profession I count nothing better than his favorable testimony. This one man's opinion and authority mean more to me than many thousands of miserable Ecks. I would not hesitate to yield my opinion to this ingenuous grammarian, if he should disagree with me, even though I am a master of arts, philosophy and theology and adorned with nearly all of Eck's titles. I have often done this, and I do it daily, on account of the divine gift, bountifully blessed, which God has placed in this frail vessel, so contemptible to Eck. I do not laud Philip, however, for he is a creature of God, and nothing. I revere in him the work of my God! [21]

Four days after the debate Melanchthon wrote to Oecolampadius. Although he refrained from pronouncing judgment, he described the debate as an attempt to distinguish the early theology of Christ from the recent Aristotelian innovations of scholasticism. He praised Eck but noted that the famed debater tried to incite the people against Luther.[22]

Eck read the letter and burned with rage. Although Melanchthon's report was restrained, Eck could not bear being criticized by one who was not even a doctor of theology. Once before he had tried to discredit Philip in the eyes of Erasmus, only to find himself discredited as an "intriguing informer." [23] He now saw an opportunity for revenge.

On July 25 he sent forth from Leipzig a venomous reply to "the Wittenberg grammarian who knows some Greek and Latin." In sixteen terse paragraphs he tried to show that Melanchthon falsely reported or did not understand the fine points of the debate. He sprinkled the reply with derogatory comments and evidences of a spirit of proud contempt. He satirized Melanchthon as "the Wittenberg teacher of languages who fared like the shoemaker who wanted to know more than his last," "the literalist," "the upstart who tried to assume the office of the University of Paris," and "the dusty schoolmaster." Melanchthon might have made a name for himself by keeping silent, but now, said Eck, he has "consigned himself to obscurity." He hesitated to write against a person who was not a theologian, Eck commented, but since Augustine had done so, so would he. [24]

Eck, however, had chosen an opponent who could strike back. Melanchthon wrote in a letter to John Lange that he would answer not as his adversary deserved but as "our own character and cause" justify. [25] The rejoinder appeared in August, "dedicated to the candid reader." [26] He referred to Eck's personal incriminations only to say that he would not return ranting for ranting. With a clear insight into the basic issues he reviewed the Leipzig dispute, sustained the arguments of Luther, and enunciated the principle of scriptural authority in unmistakable terms. The church fathers, he said, on whom Eck relied to defend the primacy of the pope, have no binding authority whatsoever. The canonical Scriptures alone are inspired, true, and pure in all things.

I greatly revere the historic leaders of the Church, those illustrious vindicators of Christian doctrine. However, the holy fathers often have conflicting views, and when they do, they are to be judged by Scripture, not vice versa. Sacred Scripture has a simplicity and unity that can be comprehended by anyone who will carefully follow the text. For this reason, we are told to search the Word. It is an anvil on which to test the doctrines and views of men.

All of us interpret Scripture differently, because we have had different experiences and feelings. As the polyp reflects the color of the stone to which it clings, so we strive to confirm our prejudices, first this and then that interpretation pleasing us. Frequently we get the right meaning and sincerely pursue a proper course, but we are diverted, too, sometimes quite unconsciously. So it was with the Fathers. Their emotions often led them astray, and they abused the Word, interpreting it not necessarily maliciously but inappropriately.

The scholastics, Melanchthon continued, have turned Scripture into a Proteus, a sea god who can change at will; they have metamorphosed the Word of God into a word of man. "But why go on? The divine, canonical Scriptures alone are inspired and true and pure in all things." [27]

In recognizing how much reason can be influenced by experience, Melanchthon called attention once again to the limitations of human rationalism. Over against it he placed the revelation of the Bible. Philip's able reply marked the beginning of his active participation in the overt movement of the Reformation. For him the papacy was a comparatively recent innovation and not *de jure* divine, some of Hus's propositions were right, popes and councils could err, and Scripture alone affords authority! He could no longer be brushed aside as a grammarian, buried in Greek and Latin declensions; he was a lay theologian with penetrating insight. Many now hailed him as a champion of the truth. He was never again an "idle spectator."

Eck made no reply. He was already on his way to Rome with a glowing report of victory over the heretical Wittenbergers.

"Little did Eckius imagine," wrote a historian of the Reformation, "that the public disputation in which he had foreseen nothing but victory and exultation, and the downfall of Lutheranism would give rise to another theological champion, who could contend for Christian truth and Christian liberty, with the spirit of an apostle." [28]

Following the Leipzig debate Melanchthon produced a series of critical writings which struck at the foundation of the church's pretension. He desired not to institute a rebellion but to restore his church to its pristine purity.

Melanchthon pursued his course with youthful vigor, beginning his day's work at 2:00 A.M. "The faithfulness and diligence of the man are so great," said Luther, "that he scarcely takes any leisure." [29]

For his Baccalaureate of Theology, Melanchthon posted on the university bulletin board twenty-four brief statements on justification by faith which he stood ready to defend publicly regardless of consequences. The most radical statement was the assertion that it is not a heresy to disbelieve such dogmas as transubstantiation. It was a conclusion drawn from two of the theses: "That the Roman Catholic Christian needs no articles of faith except those furnished by the Scripture, and that the authority of councils is inferior to the authority of the Bible." [30] Melanchthon could find no clear evidence in Scripture for the dogma of transubstantiation, nor for the indelible character of the priest, and so he boldly concluded it could not be heresy to reject a dogma which had only the inferior authority of human councils. Thus he struck at papal power.

Melanchthon directed a blow at the Pelagian heart of the sacerdotal system by showing the necessity of justification by faith. We naturally love ourselves, he said. We do not naturally love God. Inasmuch as both divine and natural laws command us to love God above all else, when we do not do this, fear comes into our hearts, and out of fear is born an active hatred of God. Thus, we cannot even begin to make ourselves righteous, for all our righteousness is stained with fear and self-concern. If we are righteous at all, it is not on account of what we have done but on account of what God has done through Christ. Our righteousness is the gratuitous imputation of God. The self-centered good works with which we imagine we can coerce God are no more than sins. The love of self is so powerful that we cannot even *will* to love God alone, much less actually do it. If we offend in one thing, we offend in all: Can anyone say that he has kept the plain commandments to love his enemies, to share with them, to seek no vengeance? [31]

When Eck saw these theses, he knew immediately that the very foundation of the priestly system of Catholicism had been challenged. On November 8, 1519, he hurriedly dispatched a letter to the Elector Frederick in which he warned of the errors and heresies that would spring from a rejection of transubstantiation and all that it implied.[32]

"You have seen, or will see, Philip's theses," Luther wrote to Staupitz. "They are bold, but they certainly are true. He defended them in such a way that he seemed to us all a veritable wonder, and such he is. Christ willing, he will surpass many Martins and will be a mighty foe of the devil and of the scholastic theology. He knows their tricks, and also the Rock Christ." [33]

For these theses Melanchthon received a Bachelor of Theology, formally bestowed upon him on September 9, 1519.[34] It was the only theological degree that he accepted, although Luther said many times that he considered Philip a doctor above doctors.

Back of Melanchthon's vehement criticism of papal doctrines lay a thorough study of Scripture and a feeling that the church in high places had become corrupt. He had already lectured on Romans and Matthew and was about to finish a commentary on Matthew. Luther was saying that Philip had surpassed him in theology.[35] The extent to which Melanchthon had carried his objections to the "human" doctrines of the papacy and the depth with which he held his convictions were disclosed in two letters, written early in 1520, one to John Hess and the other to his uncle Reuchlin.

With John Hess of Nürnberg, Melanchthon wanted to share his views on transubstantiation to get the opinion of a learned man. Sometime in February, he wrote saying that he thought transubstantiation should not be numbered among the articles of belief. It has never been proved, said Melanchthon; it has remained in doubt in the schools; it was not taught by the ancient fathers; it came only recently from the scholasticism of Scotus and Thomas. It came not from the Holy Spirit, he said, but from the spirit of men who often placed the Scripture itself in doubt. Our greatest duty is to abandon the theology of human traditions and return to the words of God. Scripture is above human traditions, and a Christian need believe only what is substantiated in the Bible. "Good God! What a maze of ecclesiasticism has been manufactured—one man following an opinion on the authority of the papacy; another following a council; but no one consulting Holy Scripture. In the citadels of scholasticism one learns theology not according to the Bible but according to the pronouncements of men." Melanchthon questioned whether the pope should have secular power, asserted that rejection of Peter Lombard's arguments on the number of sacraments would not be heresy, and said that it would not be heresy to resist papal bulls of indulgence.[36]

Philip's new convictions faced a much more severe test late in 1519. For some unexplained reason his uncle Reuchlin accepted a professorship at Ingolstadt. He wrote a letter to Melanchthon begging him to join the Ingolstadt faculty, and promising him the forgiveness of Eck for the Leipzig aftermath. Reuchlin was actually living in Eck's home at the time. One can feel the poignancy with which Melanchthon wrote the letter which was to mark his separation from the uncle he had loved so dearly:

Many things call me to you—the desire to be near you, love of home, the prospect of association with many learned men, a wonderful library to use, and my health. However, I cannot break my pledged word to the Elector, and I do not want to do anything to cause him to doubt my veracity. I love my native land certainly, but I must consider what Christ has called me to do more than my own inclinations. Trusting in the Holy Spirit, I shall do my work here until the same Spirit calls me away. I ask not to live happily but righteously and Christlike.[37]

The letter alienated Reuchlin, and he requested Philip never to write him again lest he be suspected of sympathy for a heretic![38] Reuchlin willed his library to the monks of Pforzheim even though he had promised before witnesses to leave it to his nephew.[39] The break was final. Melanchthon never saw his uncle Reuchlin again. Nothing could more forcefully have indicated the commitment of Melanchthon to the evangelical reform movement, nor have demonstrated so effectively that humanism was not his final standard.

In July, 1520, Melanchthon made another startling attack on papal traditions when he posted eighteen theses for academic discussion.[40] "Justification takes place through faith," he stated. And then that love might not be misunderstood as a good work deserving righteousness, he declared that love flows from faith and is not a natural action of man. "Faith and love are works of God, not of nature, and love necessarily follows faith. Inasmuch as the sum of our justification is faith, no work can be called meritorious. All human works are only sins." Melanchthon scored still other doctrines that had issued in the malpractices of indulgences and sacerdotal imperialism: "The Mass is not a work the benefit of which avails for another. Baptism benefits only him who is baptized, and the Mass only him who partakes. The keys are given to all Christians alike, nor can the primacy be allowed to Peter by divine right." The final thesis asserted scriptural authority: "It is better to derive our notion of blessedness and like things from the Holy Scripture than from the nonsense of the vain sophists."

In these theses Melanchthon had again expressed the basic principles of the Reformation. He was irrevocably committed! Or was he?

Questions inevitably arise. Was Melanchthon a humanist, so that there was a basic conflict between him and Luther? Was he simply a mouthpiece of Luther? Both of these questions have been answered in the affirmative. But the questions obviously contradict each other and the same answer could not be right for both. Those who saw a difference between Luther and Melanchthon said that Philip was a humanist. Those who saw little or no difference said he was a mouthpiece of Luther. Both were wrong.

Immediately after coming to Wittenberg and during the next few years Melanchthon fell under the spell of Luther. "There was a spirit in the man which drew me to him," he said. But if Melanchthon was reiterating the views of Luther, he could hardly be considered an enemy inside the evangelical camp. Was Melanchthon, then, a humanist? Was his humanism incompatible with the developing evangelical reform? Why did Melanchthon and Luther immediately become and remain friends?

There is little doubt that the two thought highly of each other. Luther exclaimed, "Anyone who does not recognize Melanchthon as his instructor is a stupid, stolid ass . . . for, although he has only the title of Master, he excels all the doctors in the arts and true philosophy." [41] On his side Philip thought as highly of Luther. He ranked him along with Isaiah, John the Baptist, Paul, and Augustine.[42] "I would rather die than be separated from this man; nothing worse could happen than to have to do without Martin." [43]

Luther estimated their respective talents.

I am rough, boisterous, stormy, and altogether warlike. I am born to fight against innumerable monsters and devils. I must remove stumps and stones, cut away thistles, and thorns, and clear the wild forests; but Master Philip comes along softly and gently sowing and watering with joy, according to the gifts which God has abundantly bestowed upon him.[44]

Writers with a strong belief in divine providence have frequently said that God brought Luther and Melanchthon together to accomplish an otherwise impossible reformation.

Whoever is accustomed to observe the movements and to admire the wisdom of superintending Providence will mark this occurrence. He will not be disposed to attribute it to a happy casualty, but consider it as the result of a superior and wise arrangement. He will connect it with all its circumstances, and trace it to all its consequences. . . . Melanchthon was selected by Providence for great purposes, and qualified by a suitable process for the part he was destined to act. . . . Shortsighted indeed, or criminally blind must he be who does not perceive the same superintendence here as in the guidance of Joseph to Egypt, or David to the camp of Saul.[45]

Others thought differently. "Being called to Wittenberg in the twenty-second year of his age, Melanchthon fell into the hands of Luther, who abused his easy disposition, and availed himself of all those fine talents which ought to have been devoted to the service of the Catholic Church!"[46]

When he came to Wittenberg, Melanchthon was not yet an evangelical, but his thought had already taken a path that would lead him inevitably into community of thought and action with Luther. It was natural that Luther would impress Melanchthon, for Martin was almost fifteen years older and was rapidly becoming the most controversial figure in the empire. But Melanchthon did not become a puppet. Differences emerged later because Melanchthon had already developed a point of reference—the Bible. He could not condone Luther's "stoic" predestination because he believed it was incompatible with Scripture, nor could he bring himself to emphasize the word *alone* which Luther added to "justification by faith." Adherence to Scripture rather than humanism was the basis.

The fundamental emphases of evangelical religion were already a part of Melanchthon before he came to Wittenberg. His ingrained piety and acquired biblical lore revealed to him the inadequacies of a scholastic religion whose dogmas were both offensive and unreasonable to him.[47] His evangelical insights had sharpened as he read Occam, Wessel, and the Scriptures. From Occam he learned to question the boundless claims of rationality, and to look to revelation and faith as the fountains of religious belief; he learned to question the authority of the papacy, and to turn to the Bible for a firmer foundation. In Wessel he found a rejection of the system of indulgences, an emphasis on the individual's relation to God, and an exaltation of the primitive church as the deposit of pure Christianity. In Wessel he also found an understanding of the church not as a sacerdotal institution but as a communion of those united with Christ in faith, hope, and love. The Dominican controversy opened Melanchthon's eyes to entrenched self-seeking, pushed him into open criticism of the church, and prepared him for the reformation break at the side of Luther.

This is the key to the immediate friendship which developed between Luther and Melanchthon; they complemented each other. This also explains the major evangelical treatises which Melanchthon published within a remarkably short time after going to Wittenberg, treatises such as the one on transubstantiation in which he anticipated Luther in rejecting the sacerdotal system of Roman Catholicism. These nascent works were the result of his studies of Wessel, Occam, and the Bible, and association with Luther called them forth. Melanchthon's first speech at Wittenberg notified Luther that here was a kindred spirit.

Was Melanchthon really a humanist when he came to Wittenberg? If he was, then it is strange that Luther failed to recognize this alien spirit, for Luther dramatically and without hesitation broke with Erasmus in the mid 1520's. Luther found no "humanistic" fault in Melanchthon during their twenty-eight years of common residence in Wittenberg. This is both significant and mysterious, for in the years following Luther's death, after Melanchthon himself was dead, there were bitter charges that "Philippist" humanism had been allowed to corrupt the evangelical message. This raises another question: What aspect of humanism was considered incompatible with the evangelical movement? And still another: Was Melanchthon a bearer of this kind of humanism?

Not all aspects of humanism were eyed suspiciously by the evangelicals. The reformers openly fostered the Renaissance attempt to recover antiquity. Luther himself accepted a classic name, Eleutherius, and thought of himself as a second Reuchlin. At Wittenberg Melanchthon continued to translate and interpret ancient Greek and Roman writers throughout his lifetime. This aspect of humanism which was considered an aid in the recovery of the purity of early Christianity was generally lauded. There was, however, another element in humanism which eventually led to conflict with the Reformation. This was the humanistic ideal of the Renaissance, the ideal that men should embrace all knowledge and bend every domain of life to their rational control. The individual man was to grasp all the skills of which he was capable; he was to be scholar, politician, explorer, artist, lawyer, and author all in one. Man was placed at the center of the universe. In rejecting the Roman Catholic doctrine of salvation through meritorious works Luther set himself against this humanistic tendency in religion which exalted man's part in salvation. Luther rejected Aristotle because he saw in him only a prop for papal doctrines which he could not accept.

In his early years Melanchthon was a grammarian. As Anshelm's corrector he read the grammars of Manutius, Henrichmann, Brassican, Simler, Wimpfeling, and others, besides publishing his own. Involved as he was in the absorbing task of making easier the appropriation of the learning of the ancients, he was a humanist. This brought Melanchthon into the company of those who were criticizing an ecclesiastical system which was based in part on a faulty translation of ancient culture. In 1440 Lorenzo Valla discovered the forgery of an important document. This paper had been widely used in the church to show that Constantine gave the papacy control of western Europe. This forgery was revealed through a study of language. Quite early Melanchthon became disgusted with ecclesiastical sophistry based on corrupt translations. In this sense he was a critical humanist. But Melanchthon's ingrained piety and his early study of the Bible prevented him from displacing God in an acceptance of the humanistic ideal of man's universal domination. In humanism he found the educational tools by which he promoted evangelical principles. He did not deify man, nor did he believe man could merit his own salvation. He said in his inaugural speech at Wittenberg that everything must be brought into the service of the kingdom of God. In doing this he became the real author of the German evangelical theology and its most influential academic instructor.[48]

This is why Luther, who did not hesitate to break with even a humanist as powerful as Erasmus, did not break with Melanchthon but continued to admire him, in Christian love, and to recommend that his books be read second only to the Bible itself.[49] Far from accepting the lordship of man's rational faculty, Melanchthon recognized the fallibility of all human reason—in the papacy, in Luther, and in himself. At Wittenberg the thoughts of Melanchthon took shape, and Luther had much to do with the mold, but Philip had learned to study and think for himself.

In the Wake of Leipzig

ELANCHTHON PURSUED HIS WORK SO UNREMITTINGLY IN 1520 that his friends began to fear a physical breakdown. The Elector Frederick was moved to write Philip a letter asking him to be careful of his health. Luther, however, had more than mere words of advice. He believed two things would help Melanchthon—a raise in salary and a good wife. Through Spalatin he approached the Elector and begged for an increase in Melanchthon's salary, and at the same time he schemed to find a suitable young lady. On June 25 Luther wrote to Spalatin:

Dear Spalatin, I and many others think Melanchthon should not be burdened with lecturing on Pliny on account of his lectures on the Apostle Paul, which are so fruitful. The hearers ought not to be deprived of this good, since what they would get from Pliny would not be enough to compensate them. . . . I know not what Melanchthon will do about marrying, especially the girl you suggest. I want him to take a wife, but wish neither to dictate nor to advise whom he shall marry, nor do I see that he is particularly anxious to marry.

Although I hope Melanchthon will not go to Bavaria, yet I have always wished that he might have a larger salary, so that they might lose the hope they have conceived of getting him, since they see that he is paid less here than he would be there. If there is any chance, be vigilant.[1]

Both the salary and the romance negotiations moved slowly. By August 5, Luther had decided all was lost. He wrote again to Spalatin:

If you are not successful, I will write nothing to the elector about Melanchthon's salary. What I wrote formerly I did so that the man might have no reason for leaving us; but if nothing can come of it, the Lord's will be done. Finally I tried to get him to marry for the profit of the gospel, for I thought he would live longer in this state; but if nothing comes of this, let it pass. I fear he will not long survive his present manner of life. I try to do what I can for the Word; perhaps I am unworthy to accomplish anything.[2]

Melanchthon wanted to resist the matchmaking of his friends, "for the sake of the Gospel," and declared that he was robbing himself of study and pleasure in order to follow the counsel and desires of others.[3] Nevertheless, he found himself becoming interested in Katherine, the attractive daughter of Hieronimus Krapp, mayor of Wittenberg, and Scripture had little to do with it.[4] Luther lost hope on August 5, but on August 15, Melanchthon announced his engagement to Katherine! "She has the qualities I could expect only from the immortal gods," he exclaimed.[5] Camerarius described her as "a most pious woman, ardently devoted to her husband, liberal and kind to all." [6] Philip feared that he would not be worthy of her.

The engagement was short, in order that "the gossips would not wag their tongues too much." [7] On the day of his marriage, November 25, 1520, Melanchthon posted a Latin verse on the university bulletin board saying he would not lecture that day on St. Paul's doctrines. Thus he followed his usual procedure in announcing a holiday or a special event.[8]

Present at the nuptials were Luther's father, mother, and two sisters. The Elector sent a personal representative with best wishes, news of a raise in salary, advice, and presents of wine, wild game, and fish for the wedding celebration.

Only three weeks after Melanchthon's marriage, on the morning of December 10, 1520, he posted a significant announcement on the university bulletin board:

All friends of evangelical truth are invited to assemble, about nine o'clock, at the church of the Holy Cross, beyond the city wall. There, according to ancient, apostolic usage, the godless books of the papal constitutions and the scholastic theology will be burned inasmuch as the presumption of the enemies of the Gospel has advanced to such a degree that they have cast the godly, evangelical books of Luther into the fire. Let all earnest students, therefore, appear at the spectacle; for it is now the time when Antichrist must be exposed.[9]

This announcement was the result of a series of actions on the part of the papacy to squelch the "monkish squabble" in Germany. John Eck, late in 1519 and early in 1520, had been in Rome arousing Pope Leo X to the gravity of the situation, and the Roman Curia officially reopened the "suspicion of heresy" case against the German "hydra." Eck assisted the committee that drew up the famous bull of June 15, *Exsurge, Domine* ("Arise, O God, and judge thy cause . . ."). Forty-one of Luther's statements were denounced as erroneous and excommunication was threatened if recantation did not come within sixty days after the bull was served. Any who dared to stand with Luther were threatened with the same treatment.

Eck was picked to carry the bull to Germany, and rumors that Luther would be burned at the stake preceded him.[10] When Eck reached Germany, he did not receive any ovation. In Mainz he was stoned and threatened with death if he attempted to burn Luther's books. In Leipzig students insulted him with satirical verses, and he fled by night. Many towns refused to publish the bull; others hedged. Eck's instructions allowed him to name cohorts of Luther if he so desired, and he lost no time in doing so. Luther doubted the authenticity of Eck's papers, but declared that he would not obey the Antichrist.[11]

On December 10, the sixty days of grace were up. Melanchthon's announcement summoned the doctors, masters, and students of the university to congregate at the Holy Cross just outside the city gates at a spot where cattle were sometimes butchered and infected clothing burned. When the bonfire was lighted, Melanchthon watched his colleague throw volumes of the Canon Law and various theological writings along with the *Exsurge, Domine* into the flames.[12] After singing *Te Deum* and *De profundis,* the faculty returned to the university and the students riotously celebrated—parading, burning the pope in effigy, and conducting a funeral for a six-foot copy of the bull.

Adding to the ferment with which all Germany now seethed were the three essays published by Luther in 1520. Melanchthon took no credit for these essays, but he was "Hercules'" silent assistant. The first essay was a bold *Address to the Christian Nobility of Germany* to reform the church. The theme of the essay was that Christians have a duty to correct one another. Because we are all Christians through the same Spirit, we are equal; no one part of Christendom is superior to another. If one part is corrupt, then the other part must admonish. Every Christian is a priest with the responsibility of upholding Christianity. If the papacy has become corrupt, then Christian princes must rectify this situation for the glory of God's kingdom.

While some thought Luther's action precipitous and likely to cause rioting, Melanchthon fully approved. In a letter to John Lange he said:

> The purpose of writing the letter to the German nobility I approved from the beginning. Luther was encouraged in it by those on whom we both rely. Besides, it is of a nature to glorify God. I was not willing to have it delayed. I did not want to curb the spirit of Martin in a matter to which he seems to have been divinely appointed. The book is now published and circulated and cannot be recalled.[13]

Melanchthon spoke with a note of finality and well he might for he assisted in the writing. Luther referred to the essay as "our treatise" and to himself in the writing of it as the "court fool." [14]

The second essay, *The Babylonian Captivity,* appeared on October 6 and assailed the sacramental system of the church. "Martin seems to be driven by a spirit. He accomplishes more by prayer than we do by considered deliberation," said Melanchthon. "Nothing worse could happen than for us to be deprived of him." [15]

The third tract, *Freedom of the Christian Man,* came out late in the year. It asserted that a Christian does not have to keep certain rules in order to be saved, for his salvation comes not from good works but from justification through Christ. Nevertheless, in love a Christian will keep all rules and completely serve his fellow man.

Despite guilt of association with a heretic, and in spite of warnings from Luther that he was next on the list, Melanchthon would not stand idly by. Not only did he assist in the writing of these essays, he also risked property and life in protesting the highhanded judgments of the evangelical cause made by Thomas Rhadinus and the University of Paris.

The *Oration of Thomas Rhadinus Against the Heretic Martin Luther* appeared in Leipzig in October. This oration by Thomas Rhadinus Todiscus of Placentia had been published in Rome in August, but both Melanchthon and Luther believed the real author was Hieronymus Emser, nicknamed "the goat" on account of his coat of arms.[16] The oration attempted to flatter the Elector and to condemn Luther as a heretic by calling him a Herostratus, a Pontius Pilate, a Wyclif, and a Hus bent on destroying all Germany. His ideas on idulgence, penance, and the priesthood of all believers were called "dangerous."

Melanchthon answered this new attack with an *Oration* of his own, even though he himself would thus be classified and condemned with Luther. He wrote as Didymus Faventius, "the twin but credulous brother of Thomas who knows how to speak the graces of Luther," [17] and garnished his learned work with frequent, sarcastic references to the he-goat. Within a month the reply was being read throughout the country.

Melanchthon called on his readers to render judgment according to Holy Scripture and to test the purity of evangelical doctrines and practices by biblical writings rather than by the bleating of a goat hiding behind an Italian-German mask. The goat's oration against Luther has no scripture to back it up; it merely scatters papal sophistry, Philip wrote. Luther did not seek tumult; he sought only to protect religious truth and the liberty of Germans from the tyranny of the Roman Antichrist.

Luther is most iniquitously condemned for having delivered his country from the papal impositions, for daring to eradicate the errors of so many centuries, and restoring to the light pure Christianity, which had been nearly extinguished by the impious decrees of the Popes, and the vain sophistries of the schoolmen. The present commotions ought to be imputed to those who have done nothing else during the past three years than plot the destruction of Luther. Do not suppose their object is the peace of the community—no—it is solely that they might be able to tyrannize completely over it.

In answer to Rhadinus' claim that Luther opposed philosophy because he knew so little about it, Melanchthon said that Luther is opposed only to that philosophy which leads to adulteration and disturbance of the consciences of men, such as the Aristotelian philosophy of scholasticism which takes a partial image of the Creator in this world and tries to grasp the divine majesty itself. This not only departs from Scripture but also tends toward idolatry. When Christian ethics is based on philosophy and entrenched in human traditions, the Christian suffers a double Babylonian captivity. Philosophy adulterates law, sin, and grace; law becomes expediency, sin becomes simple deviation, and grace becomes human merit, for philosophy knowing nothing of the unfathomable sinfulness of man's heart supposes that man can become virtuous without the assistance of God. This has expressed itself in work righteousness, human traditions, and innovations, until the words of Christ have become unintelligible. Christian authority is not philosophy but Holy Scripture.

Philosophers imagine that men may obtain the highest pitch of virtue by exercise and habit; on the contrary the sacred writings teach that all human performances are polluted by sin, and can be cleansed only by the Spirit which Christ procured for men. Philosophers attribute everything to human power; but the sacred writings represent all moral power as lost by the fall. . . . Who does not perceive that this utter rejection of the Scriptural representations of the Spirit as the author of sanctification and of everything good in man and this shameless, arrogant assumption of human merit obscure and lose the truth of Christ? Hence have originated those endless disputes respecting offerings, rewards, and cardinal virtues in which everything is attributed to human nature and nothing to Christ. . . . What is their authority for teaching that Christian minds must hope for salvation from human merits?

Melanchthon charged that scholastic philosophy had been used to set up the Kingdom of Antichrist with the papacy on the throne. Historically and scripturally, Melanchthon pointed out, there is no ground for the papal claim to primacy. The Petrine passage in Matthew does not mean that Christ's church is founded on Peter, the man, but on the rock of revealed truth whereby Peter recognized Christ as the Son of God. The revelation of God is Christ; the Rock is Christ. On this the Church is founded, not on Peter the man. The keys belong to all bishops as shepherds, not as tyrannical lords.

History tells us that primacy belonged first to Jerusalem, but this makes no difference, for the apostles were to be servants like Christ; in no event were they to be tyrannical lords. The Roman claim to primacy is more than an unrighteous usurpation; it is the march of Satan in history. The spiritual and secular tyranny of the papacy has extended over most of Europe and has entrenched itself in orders of monks, scholasticism, and canon law.

Melanchthon called upon the princes as Christians and as rulers of Christian peoples to throw off the yoke of Antichrist and to rescue the church from a new Babylonian captivity. He proposed that the reform begin in the university citadels of scholastic philosophy.

The quick reply of Rhadinus was full of emotional venom, "Furnishing ample proof that Melanchthon had trod upon a snake." Testifying to the widespread effect of the essay, Cochlaeus even as late as 1534 felt called upon to answer.[18]

In the meantime the papacy continued to urge Emperor Charles V to move against Luther. For political reasons Charles hesitated, but on March 6 he summoned Luther to appear on April 16 before the imperial diet at Worms. Unable to guess the outcome of the journey, on April 2 when he left the university, Luther bade Melanchthon good-by, saying:

> If I should not return, and my enemies should kill me at Worms, as may very easily come to pass, I adjure you, dear brother, not to neglect teaching, nor to fail to stand by the truth. In the meantime also do my work, because I cannot be here. You can do it better than I can. Therefore it will not be a great loss, provided you remain. The Lord still finds a learned champion in you.[19]

Melanchthon did not see Luther again for eleven months. After a triumphal journey to Worms, Luther made his famous stand against the papacy and the empire, saying that he would not recant unless proved by right reason and Scripture that his writings were heretical. Fearing the kind of treachery that had befallen Hus at Constance, Luther requested permission to leave the city. True to his promise of safe conduct, Charles had Luther escorted from the city by an imperial herald. The date was April 26. Knowing that Luther was by no means safe, the Elector secretly contrived to have him kidnapped. On May 3, near nightfall, while Luther was passing through a deep forest, he was suddenly taken prisoner by a robber band and whisked away to the old Wartburg Castle, where he lived disguised as a knight. Melanchthon, as well as many others, believed that Luther had been murdered.

The scheme occurred none too soon, for on April 30 Charles made known his intention of putting Luther under the ban, but political affairs made official proclamation of an edict inopportune until May 25 when the Diet of Worms adjourned. That evening a rump session was called together and the Emperor presented his edict. The Elector Frederick had already departed for home; so had Albert of Mainz, and others, leaving only the conservative Catholic rulers to approve the edict which had actually been drawn by Aleander, the papal delegate to Worms.

The Edict of Worms slandered Luther as a devil, detrimental to the state, religion, and morality. It described the Emperor as duty-bound to place Luther under the imperial ban in order to protect the faith of the fathers. Subjects of the empire were strictly forbidden to deal with Luther and were ordered to deliver him to the authorities dead or alive. His supporters were to be treated in like manner, and their property confiscated. Future writings against the Roman faith were prohibited, upon penalty of death and loss of property, which would be given to whoever executed the edict!

Despite this edict Melanchthon was not deterred from publicly defending his colleague and the principles for which he stood. The University of Paris had been chosen as one of the judges of the Leipzig debate between Eck and Luther, but the Sorbonne did not hand down its judgment until April 15, 1521, about the time Luther was entering Worms. On that day it issued a *Determination of the Paris Theologians on the Lutheran Doctrine.*[20] It simply restated and condemned 104 statements of Luther. It called his views false, schismatic, impious, and heretical, without offering a vestige of scriptural proof. The University of Paris classed Luther as the archheretic who had revived the fanaticisms of the Manichaeans, the Hussites, the Wycliffites, the Begars, Pepuzians, Arians, Lamperians, Waldensians, and Bohemians! The Paris assumption of pompous authority was evident:

Luther: God always freely pardons sins without requiring anything except that afterwards we live a good life.
Paris: This article is foreign to the opinions of the sacred Doctors and leads the faithful foolishly and vainly to trust that they have done enough for their sins, and it is heretical.

The august document said nothing about the main point of the debate, papal primacy, nor did it name a victor.

Melanchthon called the Paris document a report of their spiritual poverty. Luther said such blindness was an omen of their end. Eck, disappointed because he had not been proclaimed winner, hastily gathered fifty-four items from the debate and declared that since they were condemned as heretical by Paris, he had won the debate. When Eck published the Paris decree in Germany, Melanchthon took up his pen.[21]

Disregarding the ban against those who supported Luther, in October Melanchthon published his essay, *Against the Furious Decree of the Parisian Theologasters, an Apology by Philip Melanchthon for Luther.*[22] Combining subtle, scathing satire with polished scholarship, Melanchthon placed the principle of scriptural authority over against the principle of tradition, and the early church over against the scholastics' Aristotle. He said that he was sorry that the mighty Sorbonne had bungled an opportunity to render a real service. Is the University of Paris, noted for its scholarship, so unfamiliar with the original Scriptures, the councils, and the writings of the church fathers that not a single line from any of them could be directly cited to support their lofty pronouncements? "Do the Paris doctors think they are the living oracle of the Church of Christ?" If failure to agree with Paris makes one a heretic, then Luther is, for he upholds Scripture, which alone is the true source of Christian truth.

I can scarcely bring myself to believe that such a thing could have happened by the general consent of all the theologians at the University. In the first place, they have perversely distorted Luther's writings by adding atrocious notes to single sentences lifted from his books. From this one may infer what kind of a spirit, what kind of rage, has possessed the authors of this decree, for the Spirit of God does only what is honest. . . .

Evidently a profane scholasticism has hatched at Paris. The Gospel is obscured; faith is extinguished; and a doctrine of works based on Aristotle prevails. Should we hold Aristotle higher than Christ?

You want it to appear that the ancient councils have condemned Luther's doctrines, so you call him a Montanist, a Manichaean, an Ebionite, and the like. Either this is indulgence in rhetoric or nothing is so malignant, so impudent, as the Paris Sorbonne. Are the Parisian theologians so blind that they earnestly think the views of Luther and those of the Manichaeans are the same? The Manichaeans denied freedom of the human will and they denied there is any substance which can be renewed, hence they concluded the human will is incapable of liberty. Luther, too, denies freedom but maintains there is a substance which when renewed by the Spirit is freed from bondage. . . .

Luther has opposed several of the councils which were convened during the reign of the Roman antichrists. And why should he not oppose them since so many things were done in them contrary to the Gospel? The Council of Vienne denied that the keys of the Church are common to all. The Synod of Constance denied that the Church consists of all the predestinated, and, contrary to the Gospel, it also decreed that there are some good works apart from grace. Luther opposed these councils, yes, and in doing so was following the lead of Christ. Whoever opposes Christ is not of the Church of Christ but of the church of the antichrist. . . .

The Sorbonnists say, if an offender refuses to hear the Church, let him be as a heathen and a publican. Yes, but what do you Sorbonnists call the Church? The French Sorbonne? But can that be the Church which is foreign to the Word of Christ, who testifies that his sheep hear his voice? We call that the Church which is based on the Word of God, which is fed, nourished, sustained, ruled by the Word of God; in other words, the Church derives and judges everything from the Gospel. Whoever is of God hears the Word of God; and they who hear it not are not of God.

When Luther, still at the Wartburg, read Melanchthon's *Apology* he joyfully translated it into German and added a preface and epilogue, saying he would hit them with his farmer's axe, lest they think they have not been hurt.[23]

But they were hurt! When Melanchthon's clever defense was circulated in Paris, an immediate stir resulted. Officials of the church and state ordered all copies gathered up and burned; the publishers received penal threats; even the king issued a mandate forbidding circulation of this as well as other books that had not passed the Sorbonne censors.

Melanchthon's reply was too effective to go unanswered, but the response did not appear until 1523.[24] The faculty of Paris, led by Beda, issued a tirade against the "boy" who had offended them in at least twenty points. "How could a Greek teacher possibly know so much!" They considered it preposterous and presumptuous for a boy of twenty-four, a "married man," a "layman," to challenge the entire Sorbonne. "Those devoted to God's services do not marry, yet this husband pretends to teach priests, monks, and popes." How could the Elector permit this? Women might soon be permitted to get an M.A. and teach. If this is allowed to go on, the Church will become a Tower of Babel.

The Sorbonne set forth its principle of biblical interpretation: "Because Scriptures are obscure, they must be interpreted by Masters, especially the Masters of Paris. Because the Fathers are obscure, they must be interpreted by the same Masters of Paris. Its decrees against Luther and Melanchthon are clear and can be comprehended by anyone."

Many readers could not believe the Sorbonne was so blind; others smiled at the pomposity of their document. Friends of Melanchthon wondered at his courage.

Without Elijah

HEN THE REPORTS CAME TO WITTENBERG ABOUT LUTHER'S capture, Melanchthon believed, as did many others, that the Romanists had in some foul manner put him to death. With the exception of rumor and counterrumor, Philip remained without word about Luther until May 12. On that day he received a letter from Luther and jubilantly wrote to Wencel Link, "Our most beloved father lives!" [1] The message in Luther's letter was another matter, for it warned that Melanchthon was next on the list.

Stand, Philip, as a servant of the Word and guard the walls and gates of Jerusalem until they come upon you also. You know your calling and your gifts. I pray for you before all other things, and I do not doubt that my prayer is heard. Do you likewise. Let us bear our burden together. We stand alone in the battle. After me, they will fall upon you.[2]

Melanchthon's joy on hearing Luther still lived was unbounded, even though he knew that correspondence with Luther was forbidden. As the days passed, Melanchthon longed for his return. "Our Elijah is not yet with us, but we wait and hope for him," he wrote. "My longing for him tortures me grievously." [3]

Luther did not feel that his own absence should cause any anxiety. "Even though I should be lost, the Gospel will lose nothing by that; for in Scripture you now excel me, and you are Elisha who succeeds Elijah with a double portion of the Spirit, which may the Lord Jesus bestow upon you in his mercy." [4]

There was more cause for worry than Luther imagined. The people

[70]

felt a general sense of freedom, their thoughts had been fired by the recent events, and they were no longer willing to wait patiently for reform. Fanatics were saying, "Away with the leaven of Rome!" A papist was reported as saying, "We have lost Luther, as we wished; but the people are so stirred up that I hardly think we shall save our own lives unless we light our candles and seek him everywhere and bring him back." [5]

The trouble centers were Carlstadt, Luther's somewhat frustrated senior colleague at Wittenberg; Zwilling, a fanatic; and the Zwickau prophets with their heaven-sent visions. All of them wanted immediately to institute the practical reforms implicit in evangelical teachings.

Carlstadt grasped the occasion of Luther's absence to assume popular control. He was motivated, at least in part, by professional jealousy, for Melanchthon openly reproved him for his envy and pride.[6] On June 20, 1521, he proposed an academic disputation on celibacy. He argued that all priests should be married and that those living with concubines should be forced into wedlock. He contended that according to I Tim. 5:9 people who had reached the age of sixty should not be allowed to enter a monastery, and that those not yet sixty should be allowed to marry and remain in their monasteries or nunneries. The following month he published still more theses on celibacy.[7]

Luther agreed in general but believed Carlstadt's solution was too simple and likely to lead to fleshly excess. Others joined in the debate, and actions soon replaced words.

One of the first to act was Jacob Seidler, pastor at Glasshütte, in Meissen. He believed that his vow required chastity only to the extent of his ability, and inasmuch as he feared that he could not be chaste, he held it to be more honorable to marry than to fornicate.[8] The second was probably Bartholomew Bernhard of Feldkirch who argued that he had vowed to follow the traditions of the fathers, and that they had not bound themselves to the law of celibacy. The third was a minister in Mansfeld. All three men were, of course, imprisoned![9]

The fate of the Mansfeld pastor cannot be exactly determined, but Seidler fought a lost cause, for his pastorate was within the domains of Duke George, an implacable foe of the Reformation. His dislike for Luther, Carlstadt, and Melanchthon was excessive and personal. To him Luther was a heretic, Carlstadt a "loose, frivolous man," and Melanch-

thon an upstart. The intercession of Carlstadt, Agricola, and Melanchthon, therefore, was in vain; Seidler was executed in prison, one of the
earliest if not the first evangelical martyr in Germany.[10]

In Bernhard's behalf Melanchthon wrote an Apology which was sanctioned by the Wittenberg faculty of law. He pointed out that neither the
Old nor New Testament forbade marriage for priests or laymen. Paul
said it was no sin to marry and I Timothy recommended that bishops be
once married. The apostles and early church fathers did not require celibacy, nor did the Greek church. One should not be bound, contrary to
nature and the Word of God, to keep a vow for the sake of human traditions. In taking a wife, said Melanchthon, Bernhard did not perjure
himself; he asserted his Christian liberty.[11]

This defense, along with a letter of transmittal signed by Melanchthon,
Agricola, and Carlstadt, saved Bernhard from execution.[12]

Melanchthon's *Apology for Bernhard* was translated into German and
widely circulated under the title *Priests May Take Wives.*[13] While it
was not solely responsible for the abolition of celibacy, it awakened
thought. Undoubtedly the wretchedness of the celibate priesthood contributed to the widespread defection. On the one hand the church forbade
marriage for the clergy, and on the other levied a tax on bishops' children.
The church officially advocated celibacy for the religious, and prohibited
marriage, but allowed fornication and concubinage. Melanchthon's vindication of marriage, even for one who had already taken a vow to chastity,
was therefore an important theological step leading toward actual reform.
Melanchthon supplied the scriptural justification; Bernhard set the example; and others followed—perhaps not all in the interest of Christian
liberty.

On September 19 Luther begged Spalatin to influence the city council
officially to urge Melanchthon to yield to popular demand to take up active
preaching. "The people need the Word," he wrote, "and no one is richer
or better qualified than Melanchthon to teach and preach the word. . . .
I beg you to use every effort to accomplish this one thing and get your
friends to help you." [14] On September 29 Melanchthon gave communion
in both kinds to some students at the Town Church, but he would not be
ordained.[15] It is possible that Luther sensed tumult and wanted to have
Melanchthon in a position to speak with power.

The Augustinian monks of Wittenberg during the month of October took a bold step. Led by their intrepid Gabriel Zwilling, they met in solemn convocation and formally resolved to abolish private masses, restore the cup to the laity, abandon their costumes, give up begging, and transform all ceremonies inimical to Christ.[16] When the Elector, sojourning at Lochau, learned of the monks' resolve, he immediately ordered his Chancellor Brück to conduct an inquiry. The Chancellor reported that the theologians, including Melanchthon, were in sympathy with the practical reforms. Realizing that to abolish the mass would have serious legal consequences, inasmuch as endowments had been set up for the masses, Elector Frederick decided to have a committee study the entire matter. He could not risk papal or imperial censure on account of irresponsible or hasty radicalism.[17]

On October 20 this committee, consisting of Jonas, Carlstadt, Melanchthon, Pletner, Amsdorf, Doltsk, and Schurf, made its report. It stated that the Augustinians no longer wished to retain the mass because it had come to be a good work whereby we win forgiveness. It has become perfunctory and commercialized, so that every cloister, chapel, and church rings with masses as if the very number would make a difference. This abuse is contrary to the clear word of God; it is one of the greatest sins on earth. Therefore, the committee recommended that the Elector abolish the abuses of the mass even at the risk of being branded a heretic, for it is better to bear reproach from men on account of God's Word than to be condemned by Christ on the day of judgment. The committee also asked that the cup in the Lord's Supper be given to the laity, just as in the days of Christ, since Christ commanded, "Drink ye all of it." These changes, however, should be made only after due instruction in the Scripture, and private masses should not be considered sinful if conducted without abuse.[18]

Elector Frederick well knew the legal implications of the reforms proposed and prudently sought to move cautiously. He could be accused of not protecting property. Abolition of the masses would also abolish the income from the legacies given for this purpose. He asked the committee to reconsider, since no minority should decide so grave a matter; more people should be consulted.[19]

On December 12, the new report was ready.[20] One thing had been added: a sense of crusade to institute the reforms, come what would. The practice of Christ and the Apostles must be restored, the committee urged; there are things worse than the loss of legacies. Such action might indeed bring offense and trouble, but Christ said, "I have not come to bring peace to the world, but discord between father and son, mother and daughter . . ."

Whoever will not forsake honor, life, and goods for Christ is not a genuine Christian. Let no one be offended because this matter will cause great and widespread offense. For Christ, as it is written, came into the world, and was given to those who believe in him and his word, that they might improve themselves in him, to obtain eternal life. But to those who do not receive him and his word, he has been given and set as a stumblingblock, that they may eternally die.[21]

The document clearly indicated that nearly all the professors were in sympathy with the reforms. However, the canons at Wittenberg, with the exception of Provost Jonas, resented the proposed changes and requested the Elector not to initiate changes in the churches and cloisters. Elector Frederick decided the matter should be discussed until some unanimity was reached.[22]

Melanchthon made his own stand still more clear in a series of sixty-five propositions on the mass which he posted in October. He wanted the mass changed, so that it would not give the impression of being a meritorious work reconciling us to God, for as such he believed the mass was destroying thousands of souls.[23] Justification is by faith, he asserted; works do not merit justification; they are the fruits of justification. In the New Testament there are two sacraments, baptism and the Lord's Supper, signs of the gracious gift of God through Christ, but mere participation in either one or both is not a meritorious work. The mass is not a sacrifice of Christ; Christ's sacrifice on the cross was once and for all. "May Thomas and Scotus and any others who have introduced abuses into the Lord's Supper be damned to hell. May the bishops who are not opposed to the ungodliness in the practice of the Lord's Supper also be damned to hell!" Melanchthon was objecting to work righteousness, for he admitted that private masses might be held if they were not regarded as means of coercing God or buying one's way into heaven.

While these official exchanges were taking place, the reform movement was rapidly catching the popular imagination. Zwilling made impassioned pleas to the people to cease participating in the mass, in order to curb the calamitous abuse, and by October 23 most of the Augustinian monks had resolved not to celebrate mass. On that day masses in the cloister ceased. On All Saints' Day in the Castle Church, which still had its thousands of relics, Justus Jonas delivered a dramatic sermon calling for the abolition of vigils and masses and the nonsense of indulgences.

Luther at the Wartburg became disturbed, chiefly because he did not know exactly what was going on, and decided to make a quick visit, incognito, to see his friends.[24] On December 4, masked by a heavy beard, he appeared in Wittenberg. He was immensely pleased with the progress that had been made at that time, and he warned Spalatin to release his tracts on monasticism for publication or expect worse ones.[25] He even threatened to blast the Elector himself if the gold and silver casements in which the Castle Church relics were displayed were not sold for the benefit of the poor. Subsequently, two of Luther's tracts appeared, adding to the unrest. Luther did not condone disorder, but his words helped breed riots. The day before he arrived in Wittenberg some students and townsmen, armed with knives, invaded the parish church, intimidated the priests, stoned some of those saying masses, and hacked the mass books. This kind of action caused Luther to issue an exhortation to shun riot and rebellion, the weapons of Antichrist! Preach and pray, but do not use force; prepare the heart with the Word; be mindful of the weaker Christians who may be offended; let the constituted authorities take the necessary steps.[26]

The Elector, for reasons of his own, especially with regard to relics, agreed that the reformers should just preach and pray. Melanchthon condoned Luther's words, for he felt the matter should be discussed until some unanimity was reached, as Frederick advised. But the excitement of revolution had spread too far.

Carlstadt, perhaps to attract greater attention to himself, not only demanded a return to the simplicity of the mass as in the days of Christ, but asked the abolition of all education. Christ and the apostles were not educated, he argued, and the gospel was not promised to the wise but to the simple. He discredited all higher learning and urged the students at the university to leave their books and learn practical trades. A contemporary tells us that

these three men [Carlstadt, Zwilling, and a schoolmaster named George Mohr] give out that no one should study or keep school, for Christ has forbidden all this in Matthew xxiii with these words, "Be not ye called Rabbi" or masters. In consequence of this many men of talent about this time left this place and forsook their studies. . . . Dr. Carlstadt went round to the houses of the townsmen, and asked them how they understood this or that passage in this or that prophet. And when the simple townsmen wondered at his question and said to him, "Sir Doctor, how comes it that you learned men and doctors in Holy Scripture thus ask us poor, illiterate unlearned folk such questions? Ye should rather tell us the meaning," then Carlstadt answered them that God had hidden it from them, as the Lord Jesus himself says in Matt. xi and Luke x. . . . Besides, these three persons cast images out of the churches. And they gave out that no learned man should be allowed as preacher or priest in the churches, but laymen and handicraftsmen, who were only able to read.[27]

Carlstadt was not content to wait for matters to take their course. He asked that begging be forbidden, that the poor be maintained from a community chest, that prostitutes be banned from the city, and that images of saints be removed from places of worship.[28] He gave public notice that on January 1 he would omit the canon and would offer to everyone communion in both kinds: "When you partake only of the bread, you sin!" The Elector warned that he would permit no such celebration of the mass, so Carlstadt acted ahead of time on Christmas Eve. He wore no vestments and allowed the people to help themselves to bread and wine directly from the altar. That Christmas Eve there was rioting in the streets. A mob threatened the parish priests, smashed lamps in the church, and riotously sang "My Maid Has Lost Her Shoe." At the Castle Church when the priest was pronouncing the benedictions, the rioters wished him pestilence and hell-fire.[29]

Melanchthon wanted the mass changed, but he desired no part in stirring up violence, nor did he wish to sanction the obscurantism implicit in Carlstadt's plea for an exodus from the schools. Melanchthon and Schurf, a lawyer, united to stem the movement toward dissolution of the university. They could hold the university, but not the stream of popular violence. Philip exclaimed, "The dam is broken; I cannot hold back the waters." [30]

During the Christmas season of 1521 three prophets arrived in Wittenberg, fresh from Zwickau which had been a hotbed of religious strife since 1462 when twenty-seven Waldensians were tried there. With them came Thomas Münzer, a radical, eloquent preacher. These newcomers were even more outspoken than Carlstadt and Zwilling. Calling on their special revelations and conversations with God and Gabriel, they predicted the overthrow of the existing government. Two of the radicals, Nicholas Storch and Thomas Marx, were illiterate weavers; the other, Marcus Stübner, had been a student at Wittenberg. In the new regime, which they predicted, Storch confidently expected to be God's vicegerent, for an angel had said to him in a dream, "Thou shalt sit on his throne." [31]

The Zwickau prophets made a powerful impression and quickly won followers. Melanchthon was puzzled. Storch and Stübner declared that they preached only what God inspired them to utter, and Melanchthon noted their accurate knowledge of Scripture and their many acceptable beliefs. But, were they preaching doctrines of their own or of God? [32] The prophets' abolition of infant baptism upset many people. Melanchthon knew that Augustine and other ancients could not resolve the question and, falling back on original sin, retained infant baptism on account of custom. Augustine, however, rejected the doctrine of infant faith. Melanchthon did not believe that baptism would benefit without faith; hence, he found himself in a dilemma. The Zwickau prophets boldly declared that God had told them there should be no infant baptism, and they said Luther would agree.[33]

Because of their disturbances, their claims of inspiration, and their appeals to Luther, Melanchthon thought Luther should be consulted. In a letter to the Elector he gave an explanation of the situation and urgently asked that Luther be informed. "They have spirits, but I believe only Martin could easily judge which kind." [34]

About the same time Felix Ulscenius reported how "exceedingly well versed in Holy Scripture" Stübner was and how disturbed all Wittenberg had become.[35] He also reported that "Melanchthon continually clings to his side, listens to him, wonders at him and venerates him," but Ulscenius was misinterpreting Melanchthon's action. Philip had invited Stübner into his house in order to observe him more closely; he disapproved of the violent fruits of the Zwickau prophets, but he had no clear ground for condemning them. His problem was the Reformation problem in miniature.

When the Elector received disturbing reports from several quarters, he called Melanchthon and Amsdorf to Bretten for a personal conference. If the prophets are from God, said Melanchthon, then their work should not be impeded; if they are from Satan, then their work of violence should be stopped immediately. He thought only Luther had enough insight to judge.[36]

Since Luther was still under the ban, the Elector was unwilling to ask him to return; the theologians would have to decide, he said, and without any public discussion on account of the general unrest. Melanchthon's decision was soon made. One day Stübner fell asleep near Melanchthon, and upon awakening excitedly asked what Philip thought of John Chrysostom. Melanchthon replied that he esteemed the man but did not like his verbosity. Stübner then declared that he had just seen Chrysostom suffering in purgatory. Melanchthon laughed, for the remark revealed Stübner's inconsistency; he had formerly insisted that there was no such place as purgatory.[37]

Melanchthon was not a preacher, however, and believed that he could do nothing as long as the Elector was not disposed to act. The excesses steadily increased.

On January 6, 1522, the Augustinian monks held a provincial convention in Wittenberg, where they resolved to abolish private masses, cloistral confinement, and other unchristian customs; and they decreed that all who wished might leave the monastery.[38] Five days later Carlstadt and Zwilling led a mob that destroyed the side altars in the old convent church and burned the oil used in extreme unction.

The university faculty and town council hurriedly met and passed a resolution reforming the mass, hoping thereby to quiet the most flagrant rioters.

The mass shall be held as follows: In the first part of the service, a hymn will be sung with the Introit and Gloria in Excelsis, then will come the Epistle, Gospel and Sanctus, and preaching. The Mass shall begin as God our Lord Jesus instituted it. The priest shall speak publicly the words of consecration in German, and admonish the people saying all who feel oppressed by sin, all who hunger and thirst after the grace of God, may receive the body and blood of the Lord. When all have communed, then shall be sung the Agnus Dei, a hymn, and the Benedicamus Domino.[39]

Carlstadt and Zwilling could not wait for slow reform. They led a mob to the Town Church, despoiled the gravestones, and vandalized images both inside and out. They justified their iconoclasm with two scriptures: "Thou shalt not make unto thee any graven image"; and "God is a Spirit: and they that worship him must worship him in spirit and in truth." Duke George officially protested these excesses at Wittenberg, and on February 13, 1522, Elector Frederick laid down a solemn request: that images be unmolested, begging reconsidered, the mass kept in all its essentials, and Carlstadt forbidden to preach. Things had gone too far. He asked for deliberation and less fanatical zeal.[40]

With an obvious note of alarm Melanchthon wrote to Spalatin:

Oh, that with pious hearts we might recognize the divine goodness and show our gratitude by better manners! If I mistake not, Christ is about to avenge the contempt of the Gospel by new darkness. He is blinding the minds of those who, under cover of the name of Christ, are now confounding things divine and human, sacred and profane. In a word, I fear that this light, which a little while ago appeared in the world, will be taken from us.[41]

On the basis of a letter written by Luther, January 13, 1522, many have said Melanchthon was timid and fearful. Unfortunately the letter was not received until the third of March, and by that time Melanchthon had done as the letter suggested.[42] Inability to find a clear basis in either reason or revelation upon which to act was Philip's problem. Reason he did not trust; revelation he did not have. Melanchthon was not willing to absolutize his own partial views. To imply that the situation might have been altered if Melanchthon had not been "afraid" is to make the affair too simple and unjustly to brand Philip. Luther wrote:

Coming now to the prophets, let me first say that I do not approve your irresolution, especially since you are more richly endowed with the Spirit and with learning than I am. In the first place they bear witness of themselves and are not to be listened to at once, but according to John's advice (I John 4:1), the spirits must be proved. If you are not able to prove them, you have the advice of Gamaliel to postpone judgment (Acts 5:38). Hitherto I have heard of nothing said or done by them which Satan could not emulate. Do you, in my place, search out whether they can prove their calling. For God never sent anyone who was not either called by men or attested by miracles, not even His own Son. . . .

But now to discover their private spirit, inquire whether they have experienced those spiritual straitenings, that divine birth and death and infernal torture. If you find that their experiences have been smooth, bland, devout (as they say) and ceremonious, do not approve them even though they say they have been caught up to the third heaven, because they have not the sign of the Son of Man.[43]

Luther saw no reason why he should come home.

Rumors continued, however, to reach Luther, and he became more anxious about affairs in Wittenberg. When a call from the town council implored him to return, he considered it a message from God.[44] On March 1, 1522, he left the Wartburg and journeyed straight across the territory of his implacable foe Duke George. Five days later he arrived in Wittenberg, disguised as a knight, wearing a sword.[45] He spent two days studying the situation and on the following Sunday at the parish church he preached the first of his eight consecutive Wittenberg sermons.[46] Luther probably never preached more effectively. In the name of Christian freedom and love, he assailed on the one hand the threat of papal tyranny and on the other the threat of radicalism. If a thing does not violate the Word of God, it may be tolerated; men may do as they choose. This applies to the practice of marriage, burial, cloisters, private confession, images, liturgical forms, monastic vows, and so forth. In instituting both forms in the Lord's Supper, let restraint be used, for love should follow the Eucharist, not violent disturbances. Force must not be used, only the Word.[47]

Elijah had returned and the storm at Wittenberg subsided. Carlstadt was silenced, but he did not repent. In disgust he left Wittenberg, affected the life of a peasant, engaged in a dispute with Luther over the Eucharist, was ordered out of Saxony, and eventually became an outcast in most of northern Europe. Ironically, he later found refuge in Luther's own house. Zwilling confessed his errors and seemed like a changed man; Luther later recommended him for a pulpit at Altenburg. Stübner and Cellarius, after trading harsh words with Luther and Melanchthon, left in a rage, and from Kemberg sent back a letter filled with deprecatory remarks.[48]

Some of the changes introduced during the ferment were retained, for it was the disorderliness and lack of consideration for others to which objection was raised. The canon, that part of the mass in which the priest offers Christ as a sacrifice, was never restored, nor were private masses said in the parish church. In the Castle Church with its thousands of relics the old forms were preserved and defended by the loyal papal priests. Luther, increasingly vexed at having this infection in Wittenberg, appealed to the Elector to use his authority, but the Elector reminded Luther that the gospel alone should win the opposition, even as Luther had said. Despite Luther's stern insistence, mass was not abolished in the Castle Church until December 2, 1524, and a few of the old papal rites were retained until 1543.[49]

After the Wittenberg disturbances, Luther donned the habit of his Augustinian fraternity and lived in the cloister. But all was not tranquil. The revolutionary spirit had spread. At Erfurt trouble flared up over "intercession of saints." Luther, Melanchthon, and Agricola journeyed to the city, despite threats, and were unable to effect a satisfactory reconciliation.[50]

At home Melanchthon had new cares and hopes. On September 20, Anna was born; she was described by Luther as "Melanchthon's elegant daughter." For many years to come, while his children were small, Philip was often seen holding a book with one hand and rocking the cradle with the other.

6

The Loci and the Passional

HE EARLY EVANGELICAL PERIOD OF MELANCHTHON'S AC-
tivity came to a climax in 1521 with the publication of two
books, one a scholarly work, the first systematic statement
of Protestant theology, and the other a popular, illustrated
booklet depicting the papacy as the Antichrist. After 1521
the evangelical and Renaissance aspects of Melanchthon's
thought gradually merged, the latter coming more and more to be a highly
important "tool" for promoting the former. This is clearly indicated by
the changing attitudes expressed toward Aristotle in the various editions
of the *Loci;* in the early editions Aristotle is regarded as a hindrance to
religion, not so in the later.

In 1521 Melanchthon was not quite ready to publish the *Loci Communes,* but he had little choice. Some students, whom Melanchthon believed
were "blessed with more zeal than judgment," printed and widely distributed his lecture notes on Romans. Unable to recall these notes, Melanchthon resolved to print the material in a more acceptable form. The book
came out in April, 1521, and before the year was out two editions appeared
in Wittenberg and one in Basel.[1] By the end of 1525 eighteen Latin
editions had been published in addition to various printings of Spalatin's
German translation of it. Throughout Germany and in foreign lands the
book won acclaim, for it was something radically new in theological
science—a system of doctrine drawn from the Scriptures!

The *Loci* represented the culmination of Melanchthon's study of Paul's
Letter to the Romans, a study which began at Tübingen and continued
at Wittenberg. In the summer of 1519, at the insistence of Luther, Me-

lanchthon began lecturing on Romans. A few months later he called Paul's letter the "acme of holy writ." [2] In a Latin oration commemorating the experience of Paul on the Damascus road, Melanchthon said that Paul should not be taken for granted in order to hurry on to the truths of scholasticism, for in Paul's letters is the truth about God and his grace, beautifully and fully expressed.[3] By the spring of 1520 Melanchthon told John Hess of Breslau that he was dissatisfied with the current, largely erroneous commentaries on Paul and that he was contemplating a systematic arrangement of Paul's thought under such topics as sin, law, grace, etc.[4] In the summer of 1520 Melanchthon exhorted his students to study Paul's writings because in them one learns how sins are forgiven and how one can participate in that forgiveness.[5] That his students might become more familiar with the original Paul, Melanchthon prepared a Greek text of Romans.[6]

Alongside this developing interest in Paul was an increasing disparagement of philosophy. Melanchthon began to think of Aristotle as the "chief of hypocrites." In the foreword to Luther's commentary on Galatians, September, 1519, Melanchthon rejected rationalism as an "egotistic principle of ancient morality" and said philosophy does not open the way to Christ but on the contrary bars it.[7] In Melanchthon's foreword to the satirical comedy of Aristophanes, *The Clouds,* he said philosophy could not be trusted to guide one to the beginning nor to the end of things. One philosopher says the atom was the beginning, another that an idea was the beginning, and still another that there was no beginning. One says pleasure is the goal of everything, another virtue, another nothing, another rest. Philosophy has discovered doubt and criticism rather than truth, said Melanchthon.[8]

This interest in Paul and disparagement of philosophy came together in the *Loci.*[9] In it he systematized much of the basic thought of the Reformation up to that time, and even enemies of Melanchthon referred to it as a plumb line of belief.[10] At the University of Cambridge, England, it was made required reading, and Queen Elizabeth I virtually memorized it in order to acquire the "foundations of religion, together with elegant language and sound doctrine." [11] For a hundred years it was a textbook of dogmatics in the schools of Germany.

Throughout the *Loci* Melanchthon was concerned with three principal topics—sin, law, and grace; and under these he subsumed free will, vows, love, hope, confession, and so forth. But the real subject was why Christ took upon himself human flesh and was crucified.[12] Melanchthon proposed to draw his principal ideas from the Word of God rather than from the "silly, insipid, and impious arguments" of the philosophers. This reliance on Scripture was both strength and weakness. On the one hand it enabled Melanchthon to cut through the subtleties of scholastic disputations and draw upon invigorating source materials, thus giving his works freshness. On the other hand it prevented him from using the tools of philosophy to develop his thoughts. As the book went through scores of revisions, Melanchthon recognized this handicap and deliberately toned down the malicious invectives which he had hurled, particularly at Aristotle.

In the dedicatory letter to Tileman Plettner, who became vice-rector of Wittenberg in 1521 and then went on to take a Doctor of Theology degree, Melanchthon told how he came to write the *Loci*.[13] His main purpose was to systematize the Scriptures under certain headings in the hope of leading students away from "the subtle pratings of Aristotle" back "to the doctrine of Christ," because "he is mistaken who seeks the form of Christianity in any other source." [14] To avoid the pitfalls of commentaries, Melanchthon said he would treat everything sparingly, for he did not want his book to take the place of a study of Divine Scriptures. "I have nothing in view but to assist in one way or another, the studies of those who wish to be conversant with the Scriptures. If this little work will not seem to fulfill this task, may it certainly perish." [15]

As a prelude to his first main topic, *sin,* Melanchthon discoursed on freedom of the will. Using data from Scripture and psychology, he concluded that man of his own free will cannot perform a single genuinely virtuous act. The Bible teaches, Melanchthon contended, that all things happen by necessity. Furthermore, the Bible also teaches that all men are sinners, and since an evil tree brings forth evil fruit, all human acts are sinful, no matter how virtuous they may appear. Melanchthon admitted a certain kind of liberty in external matters—such as wearing a blue or red shirt, but not in the internal matters of righteousness of the heart.[16]

Melanchthon drew his psychological evidence from an observation of man's reason and will. The reasoning faculty, he observed, is controlled by the will or the emotions. One cannot choose to love or not to love, to hate or not to hate; one emotion can be changed or overcome only by a stronger emotion.[17] Reason may advise some good, but emotions are more powerful. Hence it does not follow that to know is to do. Since sin pertains to man's inner being—his heart, his emotions—and not simply to external acts, it is foolish to say that one is free to do good works and thereby merit the grace of God. The greatest and most tyrannical emotion is self-love which keeps one from loving God and man, and causes him continually to break the commandments.[18]

This inordinate self-concern, reasoned Melanchthon, is original sin. Original sin is a native propensity, an inborn impulse, an energy, a depraved desire, a motion of the heart against the law of God. Without divine guidance, man wanders in darkness, seeking and wishing carnal things and despising God. "The first and chief affection of human nature is self-love, by which it is drawn away to wish for and desire only what seems to its nature good, sweet, pleasant and glorious." [19] Original sin is not a simple defect as the scholastics often teach.

Since this is the condition of man, Melanchthon concluded, so-called human or philosophical virtues are really only shadows of virtues for they proceed out of the cesspool of self-love. "All men according to their natural powers are truly sinners and do always sin." Man cannot truly love God, for to love God for the sake of argument, virtue, or utility, is not really to love God but to love self in an oblique manner. To speak of doing "moral" works in order to merit righteousness is but to fabricate blasphemies and plunge men into spiritual darkness.[20]

Law, natural and divine, was given to reveal to man his constant sinfulness. The natural laws of self-preservation and reproduction man shares with the animals. But in addition there are three natural laws, inscribed on the soul of each man. These are laws of conscience, telling men that God ought to be revered, that other men ought not to be injured, and that all things should be used in common. Melanchthon derived individual ownership from the last, for the best way to serve society and insure public peace, he observed, is for each man to manage a portion of the common property for the benefit of society, and the best way to share is through buying, selling, leasing, etc.[21]

Neither the natural nor the divine laws of Scripture, however, can be kept by man because of the self-interest in his heart. He uses property for self rather than for others. He assumes a love of God and expects a reward so that God is not loved. Self-love perverts every attempt to keep divine and natural laws.

Before God man stands lost in sin, helpless, knowing that he must but that he cannot keep the law. The gospel shows man the *grace* of God, whereby his sins are forgiven and his heart turned from himself to God. He remains a sinner, for his human nature is not transcended, but the sin is not imputed to him, and so he is consoled, and knows himself in his true place before God. This grace, or faith, proceeds from God to man continuously. The law terrifies man with the demands which he cannot keep; and the gospel of grace consoles man in the love of God. Grace is the benevolence of God toward us; it is the forgiveness or remission of sins; it is the gift of the Holy Spirit regenerating and sanctifying the heart.[22]

Man cannot earn the benevolence of God, and without this he cannot be righteous, for righteousness comes through faith, and "faith is the constant assent to every word of God; a thing that cannot be done except the Holy Spirit of God renews and illuminates our hearts. . . . Faith is nothing other than reliance upon the divine mercy promised in Christ." [23]

Melanchthon proceeded to base the Christian ethic on gratitude rather than self-concern. "This reliance on the benevolence or mercy of God first pacifies the heart, and then incites us to give thanks to God for his mercy, so that we of our own accord joyfully do the law." Even though our works are not perfect, they are centered not in self, but in gratitude.

When by faith we have tasted of the mercy of God, and have known the divine goodness through the word of the gospel which pardons our sins and promises grace, the soul cannot but love God in return and be joyful, and express its gratitude by some mutual kindness as it were for such great mercy. . . . Therefore, it imparts itself to all its neighbors and serves them, placing itself at their disposal, considering their wants as its own, doing all things with everyone candidly, sincerely, without self-seeking and with no malice.[24]

Mindful of the different emphases of the epistles of James and Romans, Melanchthon said, "That is indeed a living faith which spends itself in works. A living faith justifies." [25]

Recalling the Wittenberg disturbances, Melanchthon added a section on "faith acting through love." In the name of faith and love one must not do what is contrary to the Word of God. But in love one may keep old practices until education works its leaven; "Love is offended if anyone does not assist a needy brother, or disturbs the public peace." If anyone tries to force a Christian to keep traditions as a condition of salvation, then the Christian should refuse. However, "in the presence of the weak and those who have not yet heard the gospel, the obligation of love must be performed, and human traditions regarded, provided of course we admit of nothing contrary to divine law." [26]

Melanchthon ended his book by urging the reader to seek a more exact and edifying account of these matters from the Scriptures, for only from the Word of God can the Spirit be purely drawn.[27]

Melanchthon obviously depended heavily on Paul's Romans, particularly for views on sin, law, and grace. Much of the thought on Christian liberty he drew from Corinthians. In everything he tried to be biblically rather than metaphysically oriented. He brushed aside discussions of the trinity, incarnation, etc., as "things to be adored rather than investigated," and in doing so he was asserting the truth of revelation over against reason. But Melanchthon's dependence on Scripture also led him into a proof-text method and a reliance on allegory which he despised in scholastic commentaries. Melanchthon could say that God's word about Eve, "Her seed shall bruise the serpent's head," was a promise of mercy to Adam, and that the donning of clothes by Adam and Eve signified "without doubt the incarnation of Christ." This same dependence on biblical forms led Melanchthon to say that because death comes from sin, and because children die, therefore, children have original sin.[28] But most unfortunate of all it led him to make statements about free will which can easily be misunderstood. Melanchthon was not a determinist, not in the philosophical sense of that word. When he said, "The Spirit teaches that all things happen necessarily according to predestination," he was thinking of the salvation that can come only from God. Man cannot determine this with his indulgences, relics, mechanical penances, and pilgrimages; sinful man is not free to be perfect.[29]

When Melanchthon wrote the *Loci,* Luther was still in the Wartburg,

condemned to death by the emperor, excommunicated by the pope. Those
who aided him were subject to the same sentence, and some had already
suffered death. Nevertheless, Melanchthon not only defended the evangelical movement in his *Loci,* he also openly called for disobedience of the
Exsurge Domine.[30]

In the sixteenth century the *Loci* was immediately recognized as a
major theological work. Luther said that it was "worthy not only of
immortality but of being placed in the Canon." [31] Erasmus praised it even
though he could not agree with all the ideas.[32] Nicholas Gerbel lauded it
as a work which "no one studying theology can miss without the greatest
loss. It has so laid hold on me that day and night I cannot think of anything
except Wittenberg." [33] In Venice, Italy, it was published under an Italian
title, *I principii della Theologia di Ippofilo da Terra negra. Terra negra*
meant the same thing as Melanchthon and Schwartzerd, black earth. Large
numbers were sold in Rome and read "with the greatest applause" until
some Franciscan monk realized it was "Lutheran and Melanchthonian,"
whereupon the copies were feverishly seized and burned. Only ignorance
of its true authorship saved it for even a while from the index of forbidden books.[34]

Eck was probably the first Roman Catholic to attack the *Loci.* In 1525,
in *Enchiridion locorum communium adversus Lutheranos,* Eck attacked
its unorthodoxy. Eck again chose the *Loci* as his target in his 404 articles
for the Diet of Augsburg in 1530. The Catholic theologian John Cochlaeus
called it a "new Koran, a pest, more dangerous than Luther's Babylon."
He said it was as if a monster of darkness had been loosened in Germany
by the devil. To him the *Loci* was "heretical, abominable, and putrid—
produced by a Saxon beast in league with Satan." [35] Johann Campanus
in 1532 assailed it as a work of historical inaccuracies, gathered by an
imperious, vanishing lightweight who had written putridly about many
things.[36] In the twentieth century Roman Catholic writers still find it
necessary to berate this "unimportant" work.[37] And well they might for
Philip Schaff has described the book as an "epoch in the history of
theology." [38]

Throughout the sixteenth century it was regarded, with Luther's 1520
essays and the Augsburg Confession, as one of the three foundation pillars

of the Reformation. For fifty years after the author's death it was still widely circulated and used as a textbook. In 1524 Sigismund Grim of Augsburg published the *Loci* with a picture of Hercules destroying Cerberus and a legend saying, "Hercules the Destroyer of Monsters." [39]

The *Loci* was printed and reprinted. Strobel traced the history of the numerous Latin editions and the German parallels through three basic periods: 1521-25, 1525-35, and 1535 on. The first German translation appeared in 1522, almost certainly done by Spalatin. In the second period Justus Jonas was the chief German translator; in the third, Melanchthon himself. The second period was characterized by much editing and amending; and the third period, especially about 1540, was characterized by numerous changes and additions. [40] Victor Strigel and Martin Chemnitz, pupils of Melanchthon, both wrote commentaries on the *Loci*.

The changes that Melanchthon introduced into the various editions of the *Loci* do not indicate that he was departing from Luther but rather that he was continuously questing for truth. If these changes have a tone of humanism, it was because Melanchthon increasingly realized that the tools of humanism were useful for promoting the basic doctrine of the Reformation—justification by faith. Significantly, Luther did not think that Melanchthon had departed from him.

Melanchthon's scathing criticism of the papacy reached its popular climax in *Passional Christi und Antichristi*. It was a booklet of woodcut drawings, on one page showing the way of Christ and on the opposite page the way of Antichrist, the pope. Hans Cranach did the pictures and Melanchthon supplied the texts. [41] It was a forecast of schism, for how could the reformers be unequally yoked with an earthly embodiment of evil?

One picture showed Christ being mocked, beaten, and spit upon by soldiers and monks, and a crown of thorns being pressed on his head. To one side lies a dog (or lion) suggesting evil. The opposite picture portrayed the pope sitting on a throne in royal splendor, a jeweled crown being placed gently on his head, while all about dignitaries of every degree kneel in reverent worship. Outside cannon boom and buglers blow to add to the pompous pageantry.

In another pair of drawings Christ is seen washing and kissing the feet of his disciples; and in contrast the pope is shown regaling in splendor while people line up to kiss his toe. In another set of contrasting pictures Christ is driving the money-changers from the temple, but the pope is in the temple acting as the head of a collection agency. The two final pictures show Christ ascending into heaven while joyful devils rejoice to see the pope being hurled into hell-fire.

Passional Christi vnd   **Antichristi.**

CHRIST: JESUS WASHING THE   ANTICHRIST: SUBJECTS KISSING
         DISCIPLES' FEET   THE POPE'S TOE

Antichrist traditionally stood for the embodiment of evil which would reach its highest pinnacle of power just before the return of Christ. The idea rooted in the Old Testament in the books of Ezekiel and Daniel but found its most effective presentation in the book of Revelation. Antichrist literature expressed the hope that the forces of evil which were weighing heavily on the people of God would eventually be overthrown and God's chosen people vindicated. Social-economic-religious conditions in the sixteenth century were such that it was not difficult to transfer this feeling about Antichrist to the pope.

A century earlier John Wyclif contrasted Christ and Antichrist (the papacy) in a series of twelve descriptive sentences which were widely circulated among the common people of Engalnd. Melanchthon may or may not have known about this work, but he undoubtedly did know about the Christ-and-Antichrist writings of Huss and the Hussites.[42] Many early historians believed that Luther was the author of the *Passional,* so vigorous and bold was its presentation, but in a letter dated May 26, 1521, he makes it clear that he had no part in the execution of the work.[43] The *Passional* was like a brand of fire hurled in the face of the enemy.

7

The Great "Defection"

URING THE SPRING OF 1521 MELANCHTHON'S LECTURES ON
Corinthians greatly stirred the heart of Luther. Such
lectures, he said, should be published for everyone to read.
When Melanchthon insisted that the word of man should
not impede the Word of God, that his commentary might
mislead people, Luther simply stole a copy of the lectures
and published them with a preface addressed to Melanchthon:

It is I who publish these annotations of yours, and send you to yourself.
If you do not please yourself, very good; it is enough that you please me. The
sin is on your side, if there be any sin here. Why did not you yourself publish?
Why did you suffer me to ask, command, and urge you so often to publish?
This is my defense against you: I am willing to be, and to be called, a thief,
fearing neither your complaints nor accusation. But to those, who, you think,
will turn up their noses, or will not be satisfied, I shall say: Publish something better. What the impious Thomists falsely claim for their Thomas, viz,
that no one has written better on St. Paul, that I truthfully assign to you. . . .
I say further that the commentaries of Jerome and Origen are mere trifles
and absurdities as compared with your annotations. . . . I threaten you, that
I will steal and publish what you have written on Genesis, Matthew, and
John, unless you shall anticipate me.

The Scripture, you say, must be read without commentaries. You say this
correctly about Jerome, Origen, Thomas, and the like. They wrote commentaries in which they give their own teaching. . . . Nobody should call your
annotations a commentary, but a guide to reading the Scripture and learning
Christ—something which no commentary has hitherto presented.

When you plead that your notes are not in all respects satisfactory to you,
I am forced to believe you; but behold, I believe you will not satisfy yourself.

This is neither asked nor sought from you without regard for the honor of Paul; nor will anyone boast that Philip is superior or equal to Paul. It is enough that he is next to Paul. . . . I do not beg your pardon, if I offend you in doing this. Cease to be offended, that you may not rather offend us, and have need of our pardon.[1]

The book was published by John Stuchs and carried numerous errors. When Melanchthon saw the disfigurations, he laughed, and said that he hoped Luther, made wiser by experience, would not commit any more thefts! Other editions of the work came out at Strassburg and Basel, and a German translation was printed in Augsburg. This and the *Loci* made Melanchthon famed as an expositor of the Bible.

But Luther was not made wiser. True to his threat, in 1523, almost as before, he appropriated Melanchthon's lecture notes on the Gospel of John and sent them to the printer at Basel.[2]

In view of Melanchthon's marked success in theology, his desire to give up theological lecturing shortly after Luther's return from the Wartburg has caused widespread speculation. Was this prompted by an underlying wish to forsake the theology of the Reformation and return to the peace of humanistic studies in literature and languages? Hartfelder concluded just this: "Despite all his enthusiasm for the Gospel, the old humanistic spirit still lived in him in unbroken strength."[3] Melanchthon did want to return to the classics, despite the fact that his theological lectures were very popular, but this hardly proves he was forsaking the Lutheran evangel. Very late in life Melanchthon wanted to return to the "good old days," and some said this showed a longing to return to humanism when all it indicated was that an old man was tired of many years of strife.[4]

Life is complex, but it is not necessarily shrouded in dark mysteries. Melanchthon wanted to give up lecturing in theology for several very practical, mundane reasons. First, and probably not least, was the simple fact that he was not getting paid for it. His theological lectures virtually doubled his teaching load but not his salary.[5] While Luther was in the Wartburg, Melanchthon felt he must explain scripture; as soon as Luther returned, he was ready to relinquish this additional labor. Luther's letter to Spalatin in the summer of 1522 indicated that money played an important part in the situation. "How I wish you would see that Philip be relieved from Grammar, that he may dovote himself to Theology! It is utterly shameful, as I wrote some time ago, that he should receive one hundred gulden for teaching Grammar, when his theological lectures are beyond price." [6] When Luther continued to try to persuade Philip to teach theology, Philip replied that he was being paid to teach Greek, and that he could no longer do both.

In March, 1524, Luther wrote a revealing letter to Elector Frederick:

Your Grace doubtless knows that by the favor of God there are fine youths here, hungry for the wholesome Word, coming from abroad and enduring poverty to study, so that some of them have nothing but bread to eat and water to drink. Now I have proposed to Melanchthon to lecture on the Bible, as he is richly endowed by God's special grace, even better than I myself. I propose that he lecture on the Scriptures instead of on Greek, which is what the whole university earnestly desires. He avoids it with this excuse only, that he is commanded and paid by your Grace to teach Greek, which he must do accordingly. Therefore, I humbly beg for the good of the youth and the furtherance of the Gospel, that your Grace may see fit to pay him his salary for lecturing on the Bible, as there are young folk here who can very well teach Greek. The day will come again, as it did before, that we shall have to close the university for lack of men, which would be a pity. We must look about us for men while we can. I pray you strictly to command Melanchthon to lecture diligently on the Bible, and give him even a larger salary to persuade him to do so.[7]

Melanchthon still held back, even though he admitted it might be easier to do theological lectures than drill sleepy youths in the necessities of linguistics.[8] But Melanchthon needed a raise in salary and would not consent to anything until this was assured. Since Luther had specifically requested a raise, this may well have been what he meant when he said that Luther was his only friend.[9]

Nothing was done to increase Melanchthon's salary until 1526. At that time the Elector offered him one hundred gulden more on the condition that he lecture daily on theology as well as Greek. Melanchthon considered such a teaching load impossible and would not accept. Luther, too, saw the injustice of the request, and on February 9, 1526, wrote the new Elector John (Frederick had died in 1525):

When your Grace reformed the university you commanded two hundred florins a year to be given to Melanchthon; now the man scruples to take them because he is not able to lecture on the Scriptures every day without exception, and says he cannot take them in good conscience, as he thinks your Grace requires such assiduous lecturing from him, and my words and proofs do not persuade him. So it is my humble petition that your Grace would explain your mind to him and show him that you are content if he helps the theological faculty with lectures and disputations as before, even if only once a week or whenever he can. For if your Grace gave him his pay for nothing for a year or two he would well deserve it, for he formerly lectured on the Scriptures two years without pay but with great diligence and effect, and, perhaps, injured his health by it.[10]

The Elector agreed, and so a compromise was set. Melanchthon would teach in two faculties—in languages regularly and in theology whenever he could. The salary raise relieved a pressing situation at home. Anna was born September 4, 1522. Less than two and a half years later, early in 1525, Philip was born prematurely and with great danger to his mother. Philip, Jr., required special care during his entire life, even though he lived to be eighty. Melanchthon's financial pressure was such that he could not afford even a new dress for his wife.

The second reason for wanting to drop theological teaching was that Melanchthon felt he must give time to languages and the classics if the Wittenberg students were to be adequately prepared as ministers. Without Latin, Greek, and Hebrew, without a study of the source materials, how, Melanchthon asked, could one expect to progress in knowledge? It would be like trying to "fly without feathers." [11]

Melanchthon could not forget the Zwickau prophets and Carlstadt. There seemed to be an element of obscurantism lurking in the reform movement and Melanchthon looked to classical studies as an antidote to this tendency. He had encountered obscurantism in the Reuchlin controversy with the Dominicans. He had seen a disparagement of learning in the fantastic claims of the fanatics from Zwickau who averred direct divine inspiration, and in the activities of Carlstadt who wanted to close the university on the ground that God revealed himself to the ignorant but not to the wise. Believing a study of classical literature in the original languages would be a good prerequisite for theology and peaceful moderation, Melanchthon wanted to work in this direction.

At first Melanchthon joined Luther in heaping invectives on Aristotle and philosophy in general, for both recognized that certain modes and principles of reasoning were injurious to the evangelical religious insights, but Philip soon came to feel that philosophy might be a valuable auxiliary in the propagation of truth. Melanchthon's changed view toward Aristotle, especially after 1525, did not represent a desire to give up the fruits of the Reformation but a more mature understanding of philosophy and its usefulness in education and the Christian community. Luther went along.

I will add something concerning philosophy, and the reasons for believing that of Aristotle to be the most useful for the church. It is agreed, I think, by all, that logic is of prime importance, because it teaches method and order, it defines fitly, divides justly, connects aptly, judges and separates monstrous associations. Those who are ignorant of this art, tear and mangle the subjects of discourse as puppies do rags. I admire the simile of Plato, who highly extols it as resembling the fire which Prometheus brought from heaven, to kindle a light in the minds of men by which they might be able to form correct ideas. But he does not furnish us with the precepts of the art, so that we cannot dispense with the logic of Aristotle. That of the Stoics is not extant.[12]

He noted that if we use piety as an excuse for neglecting this area of knowledge, then what we have is not piety but a high grade of stupidity.[13]

As early as July, 1522, Melanchthon told Spalatin that he would rather give up theology than discontinue Greek:

I hear that Dr. Martin wants me to commit the Greek teaching to another. This I do not wish to do. I would rather discontinue theology. Hitherto, my work was only a substitute for that of Martin, when he was absent, or otherwise engaged. I see the need of many earnest teachers of the classics, which at present not less than in the age of sophistry are neglected.[14]

If we attempt to understand the Scriptures without understanding the classical milieu through which the Scriptures were transmitted, we will be severely handicapped.

Melanchthon feared the obscurantism that would abolish education or chain the intellect. Luther, he knew, like Carlstadt, also thought God revealed his message to the lowly rather than the proud, but Luther had no intention of undercutting education; he intended only to undercut the pride of those who relied on sophisticated speculation to grasp God. Melanchthon regarded the obscurantism of Carlstadt as "a new sophistry more foolish and impious than the old." [15]

A third factor in his desire to relinquish theological teaching was ill health. In 1524 Melanchthon wrote to Camerarius, "I sit at home like a lame shoemaker. In my state of health, this worries me." [16] He grew thinner and frequently complained of insomnia. In 1524 he felt compelled to take a short rest, which, of course, aroused rumors that the two reformers had parted company. It was not, however, that Melanchthon had cooled toward Luther, but rather that he needed money, was in bad health, and foresaw trouble in the "barbarous" element that had become mingled with the reform movement.

After 1526, after he had received a raise in salary, had had a short vacation, and was no longer burdened with a double teaching load, Philip did not complain about teaching theology. His publications, which were largely his lectures, showed that he was working on Cicero, Hesiod, Homer, and Pindar along with Paul, Matthew, and John. By being in the two faculties Melanchthon was able to actualize his ideal of using the classics to serve and promote theology. This became a distinctive stamp of the German evangelical schools which Melanchthon established.[17]

Continued ill health during 1524 prompted Melanchthon to apply for a leave of absence. Learning that some of his friends were riding south, Melanchthon wrote Spalatin on April 4, asking that he be granted a five-week leave. He felt reluctant to do this, but Luther urged him: "Go, brother Philip, go in God's name. Our Lord did not always preach and teach; sometimes he went aside to visit friends and relatives. I demand only one thing of you: that you come back again. I will include you in my prayers day and night. And now, go!"

On April 11 Melanchthon thanked Spalatin for securing the leave, and five days later, he mounted his horse and headed south. For safety and companionship he rode in the company of his trusted friend Joachim Camerarius of Bamberg, who wanted to visit Erasmus in Basel, William Nesen of Frankfort-on-the-Main, Francis Burkhard of Weimar, who was later vice-chancellor of Saxony, and John Silverborn of Worms. They were "wretched cavaliers" but the spring air was invigorating and the scenery beautiful.[18]

Two days later the party arrived in Leipzig and stopped to see Peter Mosellanus who that very day died.[19] At Fulda the party was royally entertained by Crotus Rubianus and Adam Kraft, but saddened by news of the death of Ulrich von Hutten, humanist knight, early champion of the evangelical movement. A few days later Nesen stopped at Frankfort, and the others proceeded to Bretten. When Melanchthon saw his native land, he jumped from his horse, knelt on the earth, kissed the soil, and exclaimed: *"O Vaterlandserde!* I thank you, Lord, for letting me see my homeland again!"

After tarrying briefly, Melanchthon's companions pushed on to Basel to see Erasmus. Melanchthon might have gone with them, but since dissension was rising between Erasmus and Luther, he did not know whether he would be welcome.

Philip reminisced with his brother George and got acquainted with his mother's new husband whom she had married in 1520, a burger of Bretten, Christopher Kolbe. In 1526 she married a third time, Melchoir Höchel. There is no evidence that Melanchthon tried to persuade his mother to forsake Catholicism, nor indeed was there any reason to do so, for Melanchthon considered himself a reformer within the church.[20]

At Bretten Melanchthon received two important visits, one from the University of Heidelberg and the other from the secretary of Cardinal Campeggio.

The university that had refused to give Melanchthon the M.A. now sent a delegation to present him with a valuable silver goblet in recognition of his achievements. Hermann Busch, professor of Latin; Simon Grynaeus, professor of Greek; and the dean, Martin Frecht, made the presentation. Melanchthon recalled that year of study at the end of which the rector told him he was too young to receive the M.A. Nevertheless, he was pleased and wrote a formal letter of thanks.[21]

There may have been some connection between this and the fact that Papal Legate Cardinal Campeggio was then in Heidelberg. Campeggio, to weaken the evangelical fold, had decided to woo Melanchthon. He dispatched his private secretary Frederick Nausea to Bretten. After berating Luther as a disturber of the peace, Nausea assured Melanchthon of a position of brilliance in the church if he would but forsake the insurrectionists.

When I have ascertained that a thing is true, I embrace and defend i, without the fear or favor of any mortal and without regard for profit or honor; neither will I separate myself from those who first taught and now defend these things. As hitherto I have defended the pure doctrine without strife and abuse, so shall I continue to exhort all who in this matter of common interest wish for peace and safety, to heal the wounds which can no longer be concealed, and to restrain the rage of those who with hostile hands do not cease to tear open the wounds. If they will not do this, let them look out lest they themselves be the first to fall.[22]

Before the secretary departed, Philip gave him a letter for the Cardinal:

People are mistaken when they think that Luther simply wants to abolish public traditions. . . . Luther does not fight for external things, he knows something greater, namely, the difference between human righteousness and the righteousness of God. He goes back to the Scriptures in order to know with certainty just how the conscience can be fortified against the gates of hell and to know the real nature of penance. Keeping human rites and traditions do not make one righteous before God, but for the sake of love and peace they may be kept if piety is not shamed. . . . I, too, wish ceremonies to be kept so long as they do not lead any astray. However, in the mass and in celibacy there is too much corruption. . . . It is abominable to think that the essence of religion consists either in despising or in observing ceremonies! [23]

Melanchthon added that Luther was certainly not responsible for the actions of all the people who were using his name.

This was one of the first attempts to entice Melanchthon from Luther's side. As these were renewed from time to time, Melanchthon's enemies said he was an untrue Lutheran, a snake in the bosom of the evangelicals; otherwise, the Romanists would not attempt to woo him.

On the return trip to Wittenberg, as the "cavaliers" were passing through the territory of Philip of Hesse, they were suddenly challenged by a group of armed riders. The leader asked for Philip. When he identified himself and began to dismount as a respectful gesture, the Landgrave Philip told him to stay on his horse and to have no fear. "I am an unimportant person," replied Melanchthon, "but I do not fear you." The Landgrave smiled. "But what if I turned you over to Campeggio? He would be immensely pleased!" It was a threat not to be taken lightly, for the Landgrave was known as a vigorous enemy of the Lutheran movement. He had already exiled and imprisoned several ministers.[24] Under the Edict of Worms Melanchthon could easily have been detained legally. However, the Landgrave, who was on his way to Heidelberg to attend a meeting of the princes, desired only to converse. As they rode along, he questioned Melanchthon about religion and requested that Melanchthon explain in writing the innovations at Wittenberg. When they parted, the Landgrave gave them assurances of safe conduct through his territory.[25]

In October Melanchthon sent the Landgrave *A Summary of the Renovated Christian Doctrine:*

Many bishops and princes follow the pope, Philip said, because it is to their worldly advantage to do so, but people follow Luther because he promotes the freedom of the Christian—a freedom from the tyranny of required works, for man is saved by faith in Christ. Christian righteousness cannot be earned by doing so many good works. Righteousness begins when the human conscience recognizes sin and is frightened. Faith works this fear in our hearts, and faith works repentance and trust. We are justified by faith when we truly believe the promises of Christ. For Christ's sake we are forgiven, not for our supposed good works. From trust and belief in the promises of Christ flow the fruits of faith—chastity, humility, and love. Faith does not flow from the good works. Works required as means for getting justification should not be kept by Christians, for the Word says we are justified by faith through Christ. But celibacy when it is cruelly and godlessly imposed by the pope is just such a work. Lying spirits forbid marriage, says Paul, and those who support papal celibacy are the executors of such spirits. Princes should let the gospel be preached, and restrain the violence of those who use the gospel as a pretext for their own aggrandizement.

Melanchthon ended his letter with a prayer that Christ would enter the Landgrave's heart so that he would no longer impede the gospel nor persecute those whom necessity and conscience compelled to renounce papal authority.

After that the Landgrave Philip of Hesse was called Melanchthon's convert, for on February 25, 1525, he openly declared for the Reformation. He became a vigorous champion of the evangelical cause, but he was not always the most honorable example.

8

Stars, Dreams, and Omens

HILE CROSSING THE DOMAIN OF THE LANDGRAVE, CAM-
erarius, Melanchthon, and Nesen, who had rejoined the
party, stopped to water their horses. The others rode on.
Nesen noticed three crows on a nearby hill cawing and
"doing a victory dance." He wondered what this might
mean. "What else," exclaimed Melanchthon, "than that
one of us three is near death." The augury was recalled a few weeks later
when on July 5 William Nesen was drowned in the Elbe River. He was
peacefully boating when a sudden swell upset his craft.[1]

Melanchthon was deeply disturbed. "The unfortunate fate of Nesen
sometimes troubles me so much that I tremble all over." He saw Nesen's
death not only as a fulfillment of the crows' weird dance but also as a
portent of the catastrophe which astrologers freely predicted for 1524.[2]

Melanchthon's belief in astrology was still another factor in his desire
to re-emphasize the classic graces of humanism and the Renaissance. He
became more and more aware of a current of violence rising with the
evangelical reform. That Luther was not responsible for the disorders
which accompanied the religious changes Melanchthon made abundantly
clear. Nevertheless, in the minds of many people Wittenberg innovations
and general disturbances were definitely linked. The astrological configurations of 1524 alarmed Melanchthon for he felt they presaged an increase
in the general tumult. One practical way which he believed might modify
matters was to teach the best of the culture achieved in the past. In con-
centrating on the classics, he was not deserting evangelical truth; he was
trying to meet a practical situation, the outcome of which was the estab-

lishing of the public schools of Germany. The death of Nesen was to him a dire warning of things to come.

John Stöffler, under whom Melanchthon studied astrology and astronomy at Tübingen, had aroused heated controversies with his predictions about the expected conjunctions of the stars in 1524. In his almanac of 1499 Stöffler predicted that great changes would come in twenty-five years, at which time a double sin offering would be necessary to avert catastrophic evil. Many believed that the sixteen conjunctions, all showing watery signs, portended a second universal deluge. Fifty-six authors published 133 known editions of books about the expected events of 1524.[3]

The paradoxical sixteenth century was an age of criticism. It questioned history, theology, ecclesiasticism, and culture. It was an age of learning, with many strains of culture mingling to produce the foundations of modern life; but it was also an age of superstition, with its books of fantasy, sorcery, astrology, and demonology. Humanism was the great tool of this critical age, but humanism was also used to preserve the past. Some of the most educated men were the most morbidly scrupulous. None of the great leaders of the age escaped this aspect of the dark past. A large circle of astrologers surrounded Pope Paul III. Kepler included astrological predictions in his calendar of 1594 and became court astrologer under Kaiser Rudolf II. The founding of the Wittenberg University was delayed until a favorable astrological moment presented itself, and the first rector, Martin Polich of Mellerstadt, was the author of many annual star predictions.[4] Those who did not accept astrology nevertheless had their dreams, and devils, and angelologies.

Records show that a large circle of the best scholars of the time were directly associated with Melanchthon in pursuing astrology.[5] The belief that the heavenly bodies prophesied fate, and that one's destiny could be known through a study of celestial movements, was probably the most widely accepted form of *aberglaube*. Systematized astrology, which Melanchthon considered a science, fascinated him as well as many humanists of the time.[6] He delved into the theoretical question of astrology and defended this pseudoscience in several solemn Latin speeches at the university. In notes to the king of Denmark he called attention to the position of heavenly bodies and what this might mean for approaching events. In numerous letters he spoke of the anxiety awakened in him by the observation of various planets and stars.[7] He had his own horoscope and those of his children read, and often regretted that he did not take the same precaution with his unruly son-in-law. "Sabinus is headstrong and will not listen to advice; this is due to the conjunction of Mars and Saturn at his nativity, a fact which I ought to have taken into account, when he asked the hand of my daughter." [8]

Every eclipse of the sun or moon was a sign, usually of tragedy. He gave warning to his colleagues that the darkening of the sun on April 30, 1532, was an admonition of God. Eclipses were so important that Melanchthon dismissed his classes on such days.[9] Foreseeing a conjunction of Saturn and Mars in 1560, Melanchthon prophesied a famine and proposed that the university store up food, and this the university did.[10] In 1556 Melanchthon described the strange comet which appeared on May 5 and lighted up the heavens for thirty-six days. It was seen throughout Europe and Asia Minor, and was similar in movement to the comet which was seen shortly before the death of Charles V and Kaiser Mahomet of Turkey, noted by Regiomontanus. Melanchthon attributed a great drought and tumult to it.[11]

It is difficult to understand this element of a bygone age and to orient ourselves to those who accepted it. In Melanchthon's defense of astrology, there is a strange mixture of religion, common sense, stupidity, and fear. On the occasion of a doctoral promotion of Jacob Milich in medicine, Melanchthon wrote a Latin speech *On the Dignity of Astrology,* in which he defended two propositions: Astrology is a true science, and it has great practical value.[12] He admitted that there were many errors in astrological predictions, but declared that a science could hardly be responsible for the mistakes of its representatives. Many astrological prophecies have come to nothing, but many have been accurate, said Melanchthon, and astrology should not be placed under suspicion on account of inexact observation. We should learn to read the signs more carefully. He alluded to its past value in medicine, agriculture, statesmanship, and character,[13] and ended his oration by saying that the sun, moon, stars, and comets are all God's oracles of fate. If the sun affects the changes of seasons, if the moon affects the humidity of our earth, then why should we assume that other heavenly bodies were created without purpose? Accumulations of experience indicate that unusual positions among the heavenly bodies presage extraordinary events. We should study the orderly movements of the planets and the beautiful heavenly lights to know what God intends to bring about. To disdain such things is to disdain the warnings of God.[14]

From the corpus juris Melanchthon learned that some astrology was illegal, and this might have caused him to question his own belief in it, but he discovered that the illegality concerned a priest who pretended to reveal thefts by means of an astrolabe. So Melanchthon concluded that the law condemned superstition, or augury based on insufficient evidence. True and lawful astrology, he said, rests on accurate observations of the order of God.[15]

Melanchthon was strangely credulous about astrology. He would not abandon it because there was not enough evidence for doing so; however, he was willing to accept it without enough evidence.[16] Actually his belief in astrology was based on the Neoplatonic view that the levels of creation are all interrelated, that nothing was created without a purpose, and on his understanding of biblical providence. He thought the stars were created by God to tell men what God intended. There were biblical stories about the pillar of fire by night, the cloud by day, and the star of Bethlehem.

"The world is under the dominion of the heavens, *but not unalterably*," Melanchthon believed. In 1549 in his book on physics he discussed the effects of the stars on humanity. Human temperaments, he said, are affected by environment but are chiefly shaped by the stars, which incline human beings in certain directions and even cause fortuitous events. God may interfere to moderate or to punish the wicked, but so may the man himself. The stars incline some men to crime, but the diabolical impulses of men are also behind crime. The deaths of men before their astrologically appointed time, suggested Melanchthon, may be attributed to the universal corruption of nature.[17] Melanchthon's belief in astrology did not make him a fatalist or a determinist.

No man escapes the past, and *Aberglaube* was a part of Melanchthon's inheritance. On this account he is not to be condemned, but understood. *Aberglaube* actually throws light on the conviction with which he believed in God's providence. Melanchthon's concern with dreams brought out the hollowness of superstition as well as the ring of spirituality. He classified dreams under four headings.[18] First, he said, there are dreams which have some natural causation; they are occasioned by what a man sees or thinks.

The lawyer dreams about contentions, the hunter about hounds and dark forests, the seaman about wind and waves. Or dreams may be occasioned by temperament. The fiery-tempered man dreams of struggle, disunion, and yellow colors flying in the air; the melancholy man dreams of dark places, black smoke, frightful ghosts, and sad things; the sanguine man dreams of joyous meals and beautiful dances. . . . Second, there are prophetic dreams, so-called because they are effected by the stars which awoke inborn prophetic powers. Third, there are divine dreams, inspired by God, such as those experienced by Joseph, Jacob, and Daniel. . . . Fourth, there are satanic dreams, inspired by the devil, dangerous dreams expressed through oracles, magic, hexes, and so forth.

Melanchthon believed that only the prophetic and divine dreams should be trusted. (This was one of the reasons he found the Zwickau prophets so puzzling.) He found prophetic and divine dreams substantiated in Scripture, as in the cases of Joseph and Daniel, but he found that the Bible condemns dreamers and demands the death of dream interpreters. From this somewhat contradictory evidence, Melanchthon concluded that the Bible condemns the dreams of divination and magic, augury, lot-casting, pythons, crystal-gazing, and incantations, but not the dreams which convey the Word of God. But, asked Melanchthon, how does one know a dream is from God? It is from God, he decided, if it agrees with the Word and is not opposed to law or gospel.[19]

And so, Melanchthon's concern with dreams brought him back to the touchstone of the Reformation—the Word of God. He did not think dreams should be followed thoughtlessly, for many of them originate in imagination or through the devil, and might bring shame, misery, or even death.[20]

The eternal struggle between evil and good was objectified during the sixteenth century in demonology. Devils appeared everywhere in countless disguises to work demonic evil in men's lives. Melanchthon warned his students about bathing in the Elbe on account of the evil spirits that attacked the bathers. He believed that the devil caused nightmares whenever an angel failed to guard one's bedroom, that the devil inspired evil thoughts, brought despair into the heart, used hexes and magic, and might use a man's godlessness to take over completely.[21]

Melanchthon recorded one of the oldest forms of the Faust story—a tale about a man by the name of Faust who lived in a small city near Bretten.[22] As a student at Krakau, Faust learned magic. He could come and go by mysterious means. He explained once that he would fly up to heaven; the devil gave the power to ascend into the air, but the devil then let him fall to earth so hard that he was almost killed. Johann Faust, for the most part, appeared to enjoy his unearthly powers. But toward the end of his life, he became noticeably mournful. While staying in a small village in Württemberg, he explained one day to the innkeeper that he should not be afraid if anything happened during the night. Around twelve o'clock the house was violently shaken. When noon the next day came and Faust had not come out of his room, the innkeeper decided to investigate. He found Faust on the floor, dead, his tormented, twisted face turned downward, as if agonizing death had come from the devil. People realized then that the dog which followed the man everywhere was really the devil, who at last took his life in exchange for the occult powers which Faust exercised. Once Duke John commanded that this Faust be seized, but he escaped from Wittenberg, and again from Nürnberg, said Melanchthon. This Faust boasted that the victories of the kaiser's armies in Italy were secured through his magical art.

Perhaps the strangest vision recorded by Melanchthon was that experienced by some honest men of Brunswick while they were traveling home one night in a wagon. The moon with a halo around it suddenly appeared, and beside it a mock moon which turned around the first moon four times. A fiery lion and an eagle lacerating its breast then appeared, and afterwards a likeness of the Elector John Frederick of Saxony, a shape showing the creation of Eve out of a rib of Adam, and then God the Father holding Adam and Eve on his knees. All this was followed by a spectacle of burning cities surrounded by camels, and Christ hanging on a cross and surrounded by apostles. Into this unusual panorama came a man, wounded and dripping blood, who with drawn sword was threatening a girl kneeling and weeping before him. Such a spectacle meant something, but Melanchthon was not sure just what![23]

Melanchthon wrote about strange happenings experienced by his friends—about the snakes in Hungary that fought in the sky, a female mule that foaled a colt, a fiery ship seen in the sky by a man in Breslau, a glowing rainbow, the sun split into two parts, bleeding ears of corn, and a calf with two heads. He recorded that in the year 1547 a sinister being with an effeminate voice appeared on the ramparts of the castle—an omen of the soon-to-follow imprisonment of Elector John Frederick by Emperor Charles V.[24]

Because such superstitions were common in the sixteenth century, Melanchthon's booklet *Of two Woonderful popish monsters, to wyt, Of a popish Asse found at Rome and a Monkish Calf which was found at Friberge in Misne* received ready acceptance. In 1579 John Brooke of London, England, published a translation of Melanchthon's interpretation of the popish ass and Luther's statement on the monkish calf found at Freiberg. Two garish woodcuts depicted the unusual beasts.[25]

These beasts were supposed to be signs of "God's wrath" soon to fall on the "blinde, obstinate, and monstrous papistes." Brooke vouched for their authenticity, said they represented the "pope and his rablement of Cardinals and abbots," and urged repentance and prayer to keep from falling into the monster's clutches.[26]

Before explaining each part of the beast's anatomy, Melanchthon called attention to the Antichrist passages in Dan. 8 and Matt. 24, which he said were signs for the faithful lest they be trapped by Satan. The ass clearly indicates, Melanchthon wrote, that the pope's kingdom is abominable. God has taken this means to declare his "horrible indignation on account of the tyrannical domination of the pope."

First of all, the head of the ass is a description of the pope. For the church is a spiritual body, assembled in spirit. Therefore, it cannot and ought not have a man as its head, but only the Lord Jesus. . . . Nevertheless, the pope has made himself the visible and outward head of the church, and so the pope is signified by the head of this ass, joined with a man's body. For it is not seemly that a man's body should have an ass's head, even so it is altogether unseemly that the pope of Rome should be the head of the church.

As the ass in Scripture signifies carnal, worldly life, said Melanchthon, so this ass signifies the carnal traditions of the papacy.

Second, the right hand—an elephant's foot—denotes the heavy tyranny of the pope with his multitudinous decrees and intolerable ordinances. Third, the left hand, which is the hand of a man, signifies the civil power of the pope, which is altogether forbidden in Luke 22.

Der Bapſteſel zu Rom

THE POPISH ASS

The right ox foot signifies, said Melanchthon, the oppressive ministers and doctors who make the papal bulls and issue pardons for a price. The griffin foot stands for all the rascals who abet the papacy with their "abominable avarice and ambition." The scales signify worldly power but the uncovered belly represents the "gluttony, whoredom, and unlawful voluptuousness" of the papacy which cannot be hidden. The old man's head issuing from the buttocks implies the coming end of the pope's kingdom which like all other flesh will perish. The dragon with his flaming mouth denotes the horrible bulls and excommunications of the Antichrist. Melanchthon reached a climax in vituperation when he described

the belly and the stomach, which signify the body of the pope, that is to say the cardinals, archbishops, bishops, abbots, monks, priests and other execrable spiritual martyrs, and all the rest of his bawdes and fat hogs, which have no other care all their life time but to feed and pamper their paunches with delicious wines and delicate dishes, to seek their ease and all the allurements and enticements to whoredom, and to keep themselves in all pleasures and idleness, and to give themselves unto all monstrous infamies. . . . As this popish ass shows before all men's eyes openly and without any shame his belly of a woman, naked and bare, even so these without any shame, lead a dissolute and wanton life . . . and they do cover and cloak themselves with the name of Christ!

He did not call for men to overthrow the papacy, for the beast was found dead. This was to him a sign that God himself would wreak his destruction.

Luther added a short statement and a similar interpretation of the monkish calf found at Freiberg. If this seems exaggerated, the modern reader must remember that this was an age of superstition and violent words intermingled with religion and truth. The mule figure had originated in Rome and Melanchthon adapted it to the polemic of the Reformation. The calf had been interpreted as referring to Luther who now reversed the statements.[27]

Astrology, dreams, and omens were a part of Melanchthon's inheritance, a legacy which he did not transcend. He inherited some of his religious nature from his father, who was unusually pious and god-fearing, but also superstitious about such things as astrology, for he had Philip's horoscope read. Melanchthon's tendency toward astrology might be

Das Münnichkalb zu Freiberg

THE MONKISH CALF OF FREIBERG

analyzed as an attachment to his father. Philip was also greatly influenced by his uncle Reuchlin, who, in spite of the fact that he criticized alchemy and astrology as magical arts of the devil, was strongly attached to the cabala. Reuchlin sought to find in Jewish words and numbers the secret depths of religion.[28] Even enlightened, critical humanism was not without its *Aberglaube*. Renaissance popes Julius II and Paul III honored astrology, and chairs of astrology were actually established in many universities. Almost every court had its astrologer.[29]

This *Aberglaube* ran deep in Melanchthon's life. When exitement mounted to the point of tumult, especially when the Peasants' Revolt flared, Melanchthon felt that an emphasis on the virtues of education was again very necessary. Astrology must not be underestimated as a factor in the change which so many scholars have noted in Melanchthon about this time. Melanchthon believed that stars and dreams were portents of the future, *but that man was not helpless before the portent*.[30] He thought education would mitigate the disorders, and significantly his work to establish the public schools of Germany began shortly after the peasants' uprising.

Attack, Tumult, and Gossip

ATE IN 1524 AND IN THE SUCCEEDING YEAR THREE EVENTS
threatened the entire Reformation: the bitter controversy
between Erasmus and Luther, the Peasants' War, and the
marriage of Luther. The first caused the defection of
many humanists, the second affected the popular support
of the evangelical reform, and the third presented the
papalists with ammunition for character assassination. While some positive effects for the development of Lutheranism resulted from these oc-
currences, the ill consequences were much more evident.

A clash between Erasmus and Luther was almost inevitable. Although
they both wanted to reform the church and used the Bible as their arsenal,
their personalities and circumstances were very different, and their interpretations of Holy Writ varied widely. Erasmus tended toward a ration-
alistic-moralistic explanation of the Scriptures, based chiefly on the
Sermon on the Mount, which would make Catholicism more moralistically
earnest, but would leave its foundations untouched. The Wittenbergers
emphasized man's sinfulness and looked to Christ crucified as the redeemer of fallen man. Galatians and Romans served as their point of
departure. Their interpretation of the Word undercut the sacerdotal,
merit-earning system of the Catholic ecclesiastical system.

At first Erasmus welcomed and supported the Lutheran movement. He
keenly felt the shortcomings of the papal system, and like other intelligent
and sensitive humanists of his day sought to bring about reform. When
Luther posted the *Ninety-five Theses,* Erasmus hailed him as a fellow
champion. From 1518 to 1521, without ever taking Luther's side, Erasmus
helped Luther by insisting on a fair hearing for him. As Luther became

[113]

more famous, Erasmus drew back. He openly confessed that he would
rather play safe than face martyrdom, especially since there was no manifest way of knowing that Luther's way was right.[1] He was willing to
battle for clean walls but not for new foundations in the house of his worship. But Erasmus was too famous to remain neutral. He was pressured
by his fellow professors at Louvain, taunted by papal spokesmen such as
Aleander and Hoogstraten, accused of being the brains behind Wittenberg, and even denounced as a Luther sympathizer. Duke George, King
Henry VIII, and Pope Adrian VI all urged him to combat.[2]

Erasmus undoubtedly chafed as Luther became more and more eminent,
since it was evident that Luther did not think much of Erasmus' renowned
gifts as a humanist. As early as 1516 Luther expressed doubt about
Erasmus' ability as a theologian, and in 1517 noted that "human considera-
tions weigh with him more than divine."[3] By June of 1523 Luther
boldly wrote to a mutual friend that Erasmus obviously did not understand Holy Scripture and could not lead Christendom into the promised
land.[4] Erasmus told the same friend that he was teaching about the
same material as Luther but with far less rancor, fewer paradoxes, and
no riddles. Erasmus saw no reason why Luther's interpretation of scripture was theoretically better than that of the church. Abuses followed
the one and tumult the other; judged by their fruits both should be rejected. Nevertheless, as late as 1524 Erasmus was saying publicly in his
Inquisitio de Fide that Luther was not a heretic, even though he alluded
to the doctrine of justification by faith alone, without works, as an
absurdity.[5]

About the middle of April, 1524, Luther wrote directly to Erasmus
asking him to cease his "pricking" in various publications and begging
that if he were unable to join the reformers at least to mind his own
business and leave them alone. He vowed he would write no book against
Erasmus, if Erasmus would write none against him.[6]

When Melanchthon visited Bretten he desired also to visit Basel, but
he felt that current developments would make a meeting with Erasmus
embarrassing, for by that time rumors were circulating that Erasmus
had taken up his pen against Luther. Actually Erasmus would have welcomed Philip, for he wished to retain "this pure soul" among his ad-
mirers.[7]

But Melanchthon was hardly a disciple of Erasmus. In 1522 in a miscellany of minor writings Melanchthon noted the difference between Luther and Erasmus:

In theological matters we especially seek two different things: one, how we shall be consoled in regard to death and the judgment of God, the other, how we shall live chastely. One is the subject of true, evangelical, Christian preaching, to the world and to human reason unknown; that is what Luther teaches, and that is what engenders righteousness of the heart, in which good works then originate. The other is what Erasmus teaches us—good morals, the chaste life. It is also what the heathen philosophers knew about. What, however, has philosophy in common with Christ, blind reason with the revelation of God? Whoever follows this knows only affection; he does not know faith. However, if love does not proceed out of faith, then it is not genuine, only an external Pharisaic hypocrisy. Nevertheless, I do not hesitate to explain that Erasmus is superior to the ancients.[8]

Melanchthon was not wrong in supposing that Erasmus had begun to write against Luther. In August, 1524, his book appeared—*De Libero Arbitrio*. Erasmus sent copies to Henry VIII, Duke George, Pope Clement VII, Cardinal Wolsey, and other patrons. Erasmus' arguments were cogent, and abundantly supplemented with biblical quotations, but he pretended the entire argument about free will was an academic matter with which laymen should not be troubled. After confessing that he could not treat the entire subject and that he may have misunderstood some of Luther's writings, he expressed a willingness to be converted.

Man's will is not entirely bound, Erasmus contended. The fall of Adam dulled man's faculties but left him with enough moral sense to refrain from evil and to choose the things necessary to salvation. A man must have the power to choose between good and evil, for the Scriptures exhort men to do so. He cited examples from the Old and New Testaments, and pointed to the "moral laxity" that results from the contrary view. In effect Erasmus reasserted the medieval system of work-righteousness whereby a man merits his own salvation. Erasmus did not understand, apparently, that when Luther was talking about man's inability to do good, he was speaking about man before justification. After justification, or during the process of sanctification, man could do something; Luther might have agreed in large measure with Erasmus if he had been talking about man sanctified, even though Luther held that the sanctified man cannot be perfect. Luther was not an antinomian. But Erasmus did not draw the distinction between the justified and the sanctified.

Almost simultaneously with the publication of the book Erasmus wrote a long letter to Melanchthon, explaining that he wrote on free will because he had been attacked, accused, and misunderstood by a "triple array of enemies" who left him only the choice of writing against Luther or not writing and thereby alienating the rulers (pope and princes) or of siding with Luther. In the interest of "good letters," religious thought, and peace, he chose to assail Luther's doctrine.[9]

It was not so much disagreement in doctrine as Erasmus' uncomfortable position which motivated the attack. Before ending his letter Erasmus took care to compliment Melanchthon as the happy genius who wrote the *Loci,* which he called an admirable attack on pharisaic tyranny. "But there are some things, which, to speak frankly, I cannot accept. There are some things, which, even though it were safe, I would not teach on account of conscience. There are some things that I might teach, but without profit."

In quite a different vein Erasmus wrote the same day to Duke George, explaining why he reluctantly entered the gladiatorial arena. He declared that he was never in collusion with Luther, and that he disliked the "wordy, shameless, and intractable" people the movement had begotten. He wrote in defense of literature, for, he said, he preferred popes and bishops to the new low tyrants.[10]

Melanchthon replied to Erasmus' letter on September 30:

You are quite right in your complaints of those who profess the Gospel these days, my dear Erasmus. Those who have railed at your dignity seem to me to have forgotten both humanity and religion. Of the republic of letters and of this age you have earned better thanks than this, and those who with seditious speeches are rousing the multitude against the churches are preparing themselves a kingdom; they are not teaching Christ. Luther is altogether different from these men, and he often laments that the name of religion has been made a pretext for private ambitions, even by the men who wish to appear that they are waging war against the Pharisaical kingdom of the Pope. Though he is greatly moved by these evils, nevertheless he says that he ought not to draw back or desert the public cause, since he judges these scandals the work of the devil for the purpose of oppressing the Gospel in every way.

You seem, however, to have taken such offense at the faults of certain bad men that you are angry with the cause and the doctrine. Perhaps you think this reasonable, but I fear that by this way of reasoning the Gospel may be imperiled. . . . Therefore, I ask, my dear Erasmus, first that you do not believe that Luther is acting with those men whose manners you rightly reprehend; and, second, that you be not unjust to doctrine because of anyone's foolishness or rashness. It is impossible to guess at Luther's opinion about anything, for, to say nothing of the matter of the Pope, he now stoutly declares how much he abhors cruelty and flattery, and, at great risk of life and reputation, he is opposing a certain faction of sanguinary teachers. . . .[11]

I cannot condemn Luther's teaching with a clear conscience, though I shall do it boldly if the Holy Scriptures compel me. That other people interpret this as superstition or folly, gives me no concern. Certainly I shall not suffer myself to be recalled from this way of thinking either by human authority or by any offense it gives.

So far as the Diatribe on the Freedom of the Will is concerned, it has been received here very calmly. It would be tyranny to forbid anyone in the Church to speak his mind about religion. Everyone ought to have the right to do that so long as private motives do not enter in. Your moderation has given great pleasure, though here and there you do sprinkle in some pepper, but Luther is not so irritable that he can swallow nothing. Moreover he promises that in his answer he will use equal moderation. Perhaps it will be to the advantage of many people to have the topic of freedom of the will threshed out, and if it helps their consciences, what place have private feelings in such a public matter? Indeed, if hard feeling begins to enter into the differences of opinion, I do not see how anyone can do justice to so great a subject. I observe that Luther is well disposed toward you, and this makes me hopeful that he will only answer you. On the other hand, it is your duty, my dear Erasmus, to beware lest you make the case more difficult by any ill will, since it is clearly supported by Holy Scripture; then lest you condemn yourself as one who seems to act against his own conscience by too vigorous an opposition. Finally, you know that prophecies are to be tested, not despised.

You can safely trust me with whatever you write. I would rather die than betray a confidence. I wish to convince you also that we honor and love you. . . . Luther reverently salutes you. I do not wish to burden you with a longer letter, else I should have written more. Farewell.[12]

Melanchthon had mingled feelings about the situation. He did not agree with Erasmus, but believed that everyone should speak his mind about religion. He accepted Luther's evangelical insight, but said even

Luther should be judged by Scripture. We must not assume that we are right and the other person wrong; every view must be tested, not despised. This is the explanation of what appeared to be weak vacillation on the part of Melanchthon!

Melanchthon was glad, from an academic viewpoint, that the entire topic of free will was being aired, but he feared that bitter contention on both sides might obscure the truth of earnest dialectic. Sometime during September he expressed this anxiety to Spalatin.[13] Melanchthon sought to restrain the opponents. He respected Erasmus, and he loved Luther. To the latter he talked; to the former he wrote that Luther had promised to reply with the same moderation shown by Erasmus.[14]

But Erasmus did not remain moderate. He seemed to be on edge in anticipation of Luther's answer. He issued sharp stabs at the reformers, and, in letters to Duke George and to Melanchthon he bewailed the "disorders" accompanying the "barbaric" movement.[15] Apparently believing that Melanchthon was aiding Luther in the preparation of a reply, Erasmus deplored the fact that Philip was even so much as associated with a movement which had degenerated into barbarism. He had wished, he wrote, that Melanchthon would remain true to letters instead of taking part in the religious controversies. His protest was not against Luther's doctrine but against his violence. This was, of course, a dissimulation, for he had made contradictory statements to his Roman Catholic patrons. Erasmus was not above dissimulation, if it served Erasmus.[16]

Erasmus' book was popular among Roman Catholics. Duke George had it translated into German, and Pope Clement VII, after seeing an advance copy, sent Erasmus two hundred gold florins in appreciation.[17] Misgivings crept into the Lutheran circles, for many thought Erasmus' pen and influence would be too much for Luther, but Luther appeared unperturbed. A year passed. Rumors circulated everywhere. On December 27, 1524, in a letter to Ludwig Vives, Erasmus manifestly concocted a lie saying Melanchthon feared that Luther's cause would be lost if Erasmus continued to write against it.[18]

Finally, in December of 1525 Luther's *De Servo Arbitrio* (*The Bondage of the Will*) appeared.[19] It was an excellent controversial piece. While exasperated by the "pepper" and "pricks" of Erasmus, Luther remained moderately restrained. He bowed willingly to Erasmus' literary skill, but he could not agree that the affair was an academic tiff. In reply to Erasmus' desire to keep the controversy from reaching the ordinary man, Luther pointed out that it was too important to laymen for them to be kept ignorant of it, and that Erasmus wanted many to know about the contest or he would not have written a book. If the evangelical doctrines were creating disturbances, Luther reminded Erasmus that Christ came to bring not peace but a sword.

In the beginning Luther called attention to a basic contradiction in Erasmus' book, probably due to the author's confusion of justification with sanctification. Throughout the book Erasmus maintained freedom of choice, but in conclusion said that the "will without the grace of God is powerless." Luther flatly declared that such inconsistency left him ignorant of how much he could do, and consequently of how much God could do.

Luther took his stand solidly on Paul. If man can choose to do right, if man can accumulate enough merits to claim salvation from God, then Christ died for nothing. God, Christ, the gospel, and faith are then no longer needed, he argued, if we can really earn our way into paradise. But man is a slave of sin. In outward things man has a semblance of freedom of choice; he can choose to marry or not to marry, to eat or drink, but in matters of his salvation, he is a slave to sin, controlled by something bigger than he.

Only God has free will, Luther continued, for only he is truly independent. According to God's will the universe unfolds, and everything, even evil, is only relatively free, for everything eventually must work out according to God's ultimate purpose. This is divine determinism, within which there is only an appearance of freedom. Luther said Judas was not forced to betray Christ, but the betrayal was necessary in the eternal, unfolding plan of redemption. God foreknew. Whenever men act, they fulfill God's purposes. Metaphysically, then, men are not free, for they are unable to accomplish any purpose except that which God has ultimately willed. If anything else were the case, then one could not trust God's promises.

Within a year seven Latin and two German editions of Luther's reply appeared. Luther regarded it as one of his most important works, and for

its influence on Calvin it has been judged the most important book of
the century.[20]

The subject was vital to Luther; the essence of his religious experience
was involved. With Erasmus it was largely an intellectual endeavor.

Erasmus protested loudly. He claimed that he had been treated like a
Turk, that Luther had unjustly subjected him to the same admirable
ferocity he used against the papalists. He said he would wish Luther a
more amiable disposition if Luther were not so marvelously satisfied with
the one he possessed.[21]

The following year Erasmus published *Hyperaspistes,* a vindictive
attack on Lutheran doctrines, which he said would never prevail because
the leaders were rebellious, arrogant, and insolent. In this denunciation he
included Melanchthon. Philip had hoped for better things, as he wrote
to Camerarius:

Did you ever read anything more bitter than Erasmus' *Hyperaspistes?*
It is almost venomous. How Luther takes it, I do not know. But I have
again besought him by all that is sacred, if he replies, to do so briefly, simply,
and without abuse. At once after Luther published his book, I said this
controversy would end in the most cruel alienation. It has come, and yet I
think Erasmus has reserved something more offensive for the second part
of his work. He does me great wrong in imputing to me a part, and that, too,
the most offensive part, of the work. I have decided to bear this injury in
silence. Oh that Luther would keep silent! I did hope that with age, experience,
and so many troubles, he would grow more moderate; but I see he becomes
the more violent as the contests and the opponents exhibit the same charac-
teristics. This matter grievously vexes my soul.[22]

Melanchthon worried. "Will there be no end to this controversy? If
only God would give us the grace to teach only those things in the church
which serve to build, rather than those things that stir up hate and division!" [23]

When the second part of *Hyperaspistes* appeared in 1527, Melanchthon
begged Luther not to reply. The discussion had become too intricate and
tedious, and the expressions too bitter, he said.[24] Melanchthon was seeking to snatch a brand from the burning, but the fires of hate had caught
too well. Luther henceforth regarded Erasmus as an enemy of all religion,
an atheist, a follower of Lucian and Epicurus. Erasmus regarded Luther

as an enemy of letters, an ally of barbarism.[25] When Luther did not reply to the second and third diatribes, Erasmus boasted victory!

The controversy prodded Melanchthon to examine determinism, which he rejected as a stoic madness contrary to Scripture. In faith he accepted providence or predestination, but neither meant the complete determination of man. He did not pretend to be able by reason to explain this paradox; neither did he regard reason as the final arbiter. Man could not be the author of his salvation and could not finally thwart the plan of God for the world, but Melanchthon after the controversy with Erasmus came more and more to believe that man has the power to accept or reject God's gift of salvation. Otherwise it would not be a gift, and man would not be ethically responsible. In doing so, Melanchthon clung not to Erasmus nor to Luther, but to Scripture.

Perhaps the entire wrangle served further to elucidate the religious foundations of the evangelical movement, but without doubt many humanists were alienated from the Lutheran movement. Erasmus and Melanchthon continued to exchange more or less formal letters from time to time, but they did not discuss theology. The spark of friendship was extinguished.

Unrest was widespread among the peasants in 1524 and 1525. Many of them believed that the astrological predictions of the end of the world were about to be fulfilled, and consequently the rules by which they had been so long bound lost some of their restraining power. The incredibly poor economic conditions of the peasants, and the fanatical preaching of men like Carlstadt and Münzer finally brought open revolt.

The peasants' uprising was one of a series of revolts reaching back to 1476, most of them begotten by the almost beastly poverty in which the peasants lived. Serfdom had made them subject to their lords economically, and the law courts made it legal. Some peasants could not marry without the consent of their masters; some worked with whips cracking over their backs; many had only the holidays and moonlit nights for cultivating their own plots of earth. In contrast the overlords seemed to be living in luxury. While, as some scholars say, the peasants' economic position may have improved by 1525 and their demands may have been a bid for more political power, nevertheless their lives were still wretched.

Contemporary chronicles affirm that the immediate cause of the revolt of 1525 was the Countess of Lupfen, who had an inordinate desire for strawberries and wild cherries and a strange whim for winding yarn on snail shells. The peasants resented working to satisfy this caprice, and complained about irresponsible huntsmen.[26] For centuries the peasants had suffered and chafed under these deplorable conditions.

In the sixteenth century a new peasant spirit began to emerge. The evangelical preaching of the Wittenberg reformers stirred new hope in this segment of society. The evangelical protest against the tyranny of the papal Antichrist was understandably transposed and applied to the peasant's overlord. Luther's tracts on the freedom of the individual, Christian vocation, and the priesthood of all believers had given men a new sense of their worth. They thought of themselves as the innocent poor to whom the gospel was addressed. "Blessed are the poor, the hungry, the persecuted . . ." They recalled the story of Lazarus and the rich man. They made much of the fact that Jesus and the apostles were poor and that farming was pleasing to God.[27] H. S. Beham's famous woodcut, "The Sheepfold of Christ," shows Christ inviting the peasants into his house while nobles, priests, nuns, and bishops are trying vainly to enter the windows and locked doors.[28] The peasants began to feel that they had a spiritual right to some of the material goods of this world.

Fanatical preaching like that of Carlstadt and Münzer was the spark that made the general discontent a social revolt. After the Wittenberg disturbances of 1521 and 1522, Carlstadt married a local girl, Anna von Mochau, moved to the country, and assumed the garb and manner of the peasants. Dressed in peasant rags he administered the communion in both kinds.[29] He continued to berate education, and whenever opportunity presented he dramatically destroyed pictures and other reminders of Roman Catholicism. Inasmuch as he had not bothered to resign his post as archdeacon of the Castle Church at Wittenberg, he increasingly irritated the reformers. Finally in June of 1524, he officially relinquished the post of archdeacon and also gave up the vicarage of Orlamünde. He said he could no longer tolerate his name being associated with the idolatrous worship of the mass.[30] Because of the general confusion that Carlstadt was creating, the Elector finally exiled him from Saxony. But Carlstadt did not stop. He continued his inflammatory preaching from Strassburg and throughout South Germany. His commemorative view of the Lord's Supper precipitated a pamphlet war between the theologians of South Germany and the Wittenberg divines. Carlstadt instigated insurgence among the peasants, but he did not openly preach bloodshed and revolution.

The same could not be said for Thomas Münzer, who fanatically exhorted the peasants to rebel. He believed he was divinely called to inaugurate the kingdom of God by force.[31] He had had visions telling him to do so; the written Word of the Bible was inferior to his "living Word." He claimed that the Holy Spirit had commissioned him to institute a classless society in which all property would be owned communally, but it was to be a society for the "Elect of God" only. His revelations told him that unbelievers were to be mercilessly expulsed and even exterminated. In opposition to the luxury of the clergy he preached an ascetic denial of the world, saying he would abolish the old rituals of worship and make the old-time Mosaic law the rule of the land. Many laymen who boasted similar visions gathered round him, saying those who had a single vision knew more than all the educated doctors and professors about the will of God.

Münzer journeyed through south and southwestern Germany, proclaiming the deliverance of Israel and the establishment of a heavenly kingdom upon earth. His preaching culminated in violence when a group of insurgent peasants led by Hans Müller, Stühlinger peasant, armed themselves with crude weapons, hoisted a black, red, and white flag, and marched on the town of Waldshut, on August 24, 1524. General pillage was the consequence, for neighboring peasants joined the disorders. Banditry, attacks on local chapels, and assaults on nobles, monks, and priests became commonplace.[32]

Münzer returned to Thuringia, the hotbed of the social unrest of the times, and preached blood-red revolution. He wrote letters and signed himself "Münzer with the hammer," and "Thomas Münzer with the sword of Gideon." He scorned the "fabulous gospel" and the "honey-sweet Christ" proclaimed by the Wittenberg reformers who said the Word alone would destroy the Antichrist. That time had passed, he maintained; in the harvest the tares should be rooted out with violence. As Joshua smote the dwellers in Canaan with the edge of the sword, so should the ungodly rulers, the priests and monks, be smitten in order to establish the kingdom of God's elect. To the miners at Mansfeld he wrote:

Beloved brethren, do not relent if Esau gives you fair words; give no heed to the wailings of the ungodly. Let not the blood cool on your swords; lay Nimrod on the anvil, and let it ring lustily with your blows; cast his strong tower to the earth while it is yet day.[33]

PEASANTS MURDERING A KNIGHT

In March of 1525 the peasants published a manifesto of grievances— their Twelve Articles.[34] They said they would give a "Christian excuse for the disobedience and revolt." Many of their twelve demands were just. They wanted the right to choose their own pastors and to dispose them for improper conduct, the right to administer the grain tithe for the support of the pastor and relief of the poor, the right to use forest firewood and lumber, hunting and fishing privileges, emancipation from serfdom, investigation of excessive feudal services, pay for extra work, readjustment of rents, legal security under the old laws, elimination of the *Todfall* or death tax, and the right to present new claims based on Scripture. They demanded social equality, saying, "Christ has delivered and redeemed us all, without exception, by the shedding of his precious blood, the lowly as well as the great."

The Wittenberg reformers were not aware of the extent of the social storm nor of its depth among the peasants until Melanchthon, Luther, and Agricola journeyed to Eisleben to set up an evangelical school for Count

Albert of Mansfeld.[35] This was in April, 1525. They were shocked by
the obvious destruction of property, banditry, assaults, and disregard for
authority. Evidence of the excesses of the peasants was on every hand.
Luther and Melanchthon were heckled and completely unable to restore
order. They feared they might not get back to Wittenberg alive.

Reports poured into Wittenberg about the spread of anarchy. In
Thuringia, it was reported, 35,000 peasants were posed ready to strike,
inflamed by the blood-thirsty preaching of Münzer. Smaller bands pillaged
and robbed throughout the countryside. Believing that all semblance of
order was about to go, Luther wrote his infamous tract *Against the
Murderous and Plundering Bands Among the Peasants*.[36] He called on
the princes to "stab, smite, and strangle, as among mad dogs."

Melanchthon was equally alarmed. Astrological configurations omened
a great conflict in which the kingdom of Satan would try to overthrow
religion, civil order, and morals! When the elector of the Palatinate

PEASANTS ATTACKING KNIGHTS AND MONKS

asked that he come to Heidelberg to do what he could as a native of the
Palatinate to stem the growing danger, he made known his views.[37] He
was different from Luther in that he depended more on Scripture for his
stand; he was neither as sure of his reasoning, nor as dogmatic in his
understanding of revelation. Melanchthon believed he was right; but he
would not make his view absolute.

Early in June Melanchthon completed his *Confutation of the Articles
of the Peasants*. In general he sympathized with the demands therein,

but he felt that peace and order must be restored through the princes. Seizing upon the statement of the peasants that they stood ready to be instructed out of the Bible, he penned his reply to their articles.

No doubt there are many who sin from ignorance, who, it is to be hoped, if they are properly instructed, will forsake godless practices and consider the judgment of God, their own souls, and their poor wives and children. Many, however, are so wanton, and blinded by the devil that they do not and cannot abide peace.

Referring to I Tim. 1:5, Melanchthon pointed out that the love which springs from a pure heart and acts with good conscience and true faith is the essence of law. "In faith we act toward God, and in love toward our neighbor." In faith we know that our sins are freely forgiven through Christ and that we can expect all things from him; he has his eye on us in life and in death. This is the gift of the love of God, un-earned by us, and we are to show our gratitude by keeping the commands of his Word.

What is commanded?

The Gospel especially requires obedience to authority. . . . Because the Gospel requires obedience to civil rulers, and forbids rebellion, even though the rulers may do evil; and because the Gospel further requires that we en-dure wrong; they go against the Gospel when they arise against the govern-ment and use force and violence. . . . It is the devil instigating them, desiring to destroy their bodies and souls. Be the outcome whatever it will, such wickedness will be punished at last, for as St. Paul says in Romans 13:2, "Those who rebel against authority will be punished."

Melanchthon agreed that governments should provide for the preach-ing of the pure gospel; but, he said, if rulers blinded by Satan forbid this, we must not create anarchy by rebelling, for God has forbidden it. If the government is hostile, each person must profess his faith and suffer such hostility. Christian faith is of the heart, and gives rise to all virtues, among which are love and obedience to rulers. If the princes provide unchristian preachers, they are to be shunned, not revenged.

Serfdom should not be eliminated by violence, neither should ordinary freedom be confused with the inward freedom that Christ brings. Spirit-ual freedom can belong to one even under oppression.

Philip thought hunting and fishing disputes could be settled by the courts, and that the forests might be used for the general good.

The Todfall, although proper in serfdom, should be abolished by the government for the sake of widows and orphans. The peasants should not, however, act against God by overthrowing the existing laws which the rulers have a right to impose, but on the other hand the princes should concede what is right, before taking the sword, for they have done much evil.

Melanchthon concluded with a warning to the princes to purify the church and provide pure preaching. The mass should be modified, marriage of ministers allowed, and ecclesiastical properties appropriated for the establishment of schools and charities for the poor. Realizing that the princes would prevail, Philip pleaded for the peasants. "Princes should take care that the innocent are not harmed, and also should show mercy to the poor people, some of whom sinned through fear and others through ignorance." At the proper time David punished, and at the proper time he showed mercy.

The civil rulers should see that the Word of God is preached in the proper manner, and that the rules of the church which are contrary to the Word of God be altered. Then God will grant peace and prosperity to the rulers in their governing, as he did to Hezekiah and the other pious kings who abolished abuses in the service of God. For he has said: "Whoever honors me, I will honor; whoever despises me shall be brought to shame."

At Frankenhausen, on May 15, Münzer had drawn up his army of faithful in an exposed position, protected only by a thin barricade of wagons. He had failed to provide powder for his cannon. Because a colored circle appeared round the sun at noon, he confidently expected a miracle. When the first volley of artillery from the combined armies of Philip of Hesse, Duke George, Duke Henry, and the Elector of Saxony struck the peasants, they replied by lustily singing a hymn. But there was no miracle that afternoon. The peasants were routed and wretchedly butchered.[38]

Münzer was captured and taken to Mühlhausen where he was executed after excruciating torture. He was beheaded and his head placed on a stake as a warning to others.[39]

Readers living in the age of the common man find it difficult to understand the attitude of the Wittenberg reformers. However, at least two points
should be kept in mind. First, Melanchthon thought of religion primarily
as an inward matter, as faith, which was not dependent on outward circumstances. While faith was the basis for love which might bring about
change, it could not be used to make demands. In protesting the revolt,
Melanchthon and Luther were objecting to a misuse of evangelical teachings. When the papists and humanists accused them of having originated
the tumult, they were aghast. The second point is that the reformers accepted the *status quo* as the ordination of God. Any disturbance of the
social order was either the punishment of God, or the work of Satan, and
knowing the wild preaching of Münzer they concluded the latter. Against
the devil and his agents they could sanction force! They seemed to forget
that Satan has many guises.

Melanchthon's confutation of the peasants was at the same time severe
and moderate, severe in that he legalistically applied Rom. 13, and moderate in that he did not preach a crusade against the revolters. Whether
the reformers were right or wrong, sensitive or insensitive, their stand
cost them the support of a large number of laymen, and probably prevented
the Lutheran reform from becoming a mass lay movement.

Just before the peasant disorders reached a climax, Elector Frederick
died, on May 5. In view of the disorders he was remarkably calm toward
the last. He said he did not think it was God's will that the peasants should
become masters, and if not His will, then impossible. From his deathbed
he said to his servants, "If I have ever offended any of you, I pray you to
forgive me for the love of God; we princes do many things to the poor
people that we ought not to do." Both Melanchthon and Luther were
absent, but Spalatin consoled the Elector in his final hours and administered to him the sacrament in both kinds; thus symbolically at least he
confessed the teachings of the Reform. At the funeral Luther preached
a sermon in German, and Melanchthon delivered a funeral oration in
which he praised the Elector for many things, but called special attention
to his efforts to keep peace. "He kept his people in peace during the most
turbulent times." In religious matters he "neither approved nor condemned
anything with haste!" [40] Did Melanchthon call attention to these charac-
teristics because subconsciously they were his own ideals?

The death of Frederick the Wise was only a temporary shock to the
Reformation, for his brother John who assumed control in Saxony aggres-
sively supported the evangelical reformers.

Luther's sudden marriage to Katherine von Bora in 1525 was a
bonanza for the gossips. Foes of the reformer circulated malicious stories
saying Luther had ravished the escaped nun and had to marry her. Melanchthon thought the marriage was exceedingly untimely in view of the
peasant situation, but he defended Luther's integrity and Christian right
to marry. The action weakened the immediate progress of the Reformation, but it laid the foundation for family living in the German pastorate.

Martin Luther and Katherine von Bora were married on June 13, 1525.
Bugenhagen, the town pastor, officiated at the quiet evening ceremony in
the Black Cloister. Lucas Cranach and his wife, Prior Jonas of the Castle
Church, and Law Professor Apel were the only witnesses; Melanchthon
was not present.[41]

Why he was not invited, no one knows. When he heard about it, he
was shocked. Two extant letters record Melanchthon's feelings. The exact
relation between these letters is unknown, but possibly one was written on
June 16, but not sent, and the other on July 24 in answer to an inquiry—
both to Camerarius. He probably wrote the second letter with the first
before him. This is the first:

Greetings. Since dissimilar reports concerning the marriage of Luther will
reach you, I have thought it well to give you my opinion of him. On June 13,
Luther unexpectedly and without informing in advance any of his friends
of what he was doing, married Bora; but in the evening, after having invited
to supper none but Pomeranus and Lucan the painter, and Apel, observed
the customary marriage rites. You might be amazed that at this unfortunate
time, when good and excellent men everywhere are in distress, he not only
does not sympathize with them, but, as it seems, rather waxes wanton and
diminishes his reputation, just when Germany has special need of his judgment and authority.

These things have occurred, I think, somewhat in this way: The man
is certainly pliable, and the nuns have used their arts against him most
successfully; thus probably society with the nuns has softened or even
inflamed this noble and highspirited man. In this way he seems to have
fallen into this untimely change of life. The rumor, however, that he had

previously dishonored her is manifestly a lie. Now that the deed is done, we must not take it too hard, or reproach him; for I think, indeed, that he was compelled by nature to marry. The mode of life, too, while, indeed humble, is nevertheless, holy and more pleasing to God than celibacy.

When I see Luther in low spirits and disturbed about his change of life, I make my best efforts to console him kindly, since he has done nothing that seems to me worthy of censure or incapable of defense. Besides this, I have unmistakable evidences of his godliness, so that for me to condemn him is impossible. . . . I have hopes that this state of life may sober him down, so that he will discard the low buffoonery which we have often censured.

I know that you are concerned about Luther's reputation, which is imperiled. I exhort you to bear it meekly, since marriage is said in the Scriptures to be an honorable mode of life. It is likely that he was actually compelled to marry. God has shown us many falls of His saints of old because He wants us, pondering upon His Word, to be bound neither by the reputation or the face of man. That person, too, is most godless who, because of the errors of a teacher, condemns the truth of the teaching.[42]

If Melanchthon was offended, by June 20 his resentment subsided. Only seven days after the marriage Philip wrote to Link urging him to come to Luther's post-wedding celebration and praying good fortune and blessings on the reformer in his new life.[43] On June 27 a special service was held in the Town Church proclaiming the marriage of Luther and Katherine. Afterwards most of the university took the day off to celebrate.

The years 1524 and 1525 weighed heavily on the Reformation. The conflict with Erasmus, the peasant uprising, the death of Frederick, and the marriage of Luther placed in jeopardy the progress of the evangelical reform. The humanists drew back, the common people shrank in disillusionment, the government wavered momentarily, and the critics fired their ovens with hot rumors. But the Reformation was to rebound and recover much prestige through Melanchthon's work in the schools.

Golden Fruit, Silver Bowl

HE EDUCATIONAL ENDEAVORS OF MELANCHTHON HELPED to recover much of the ground lost during the crisis years of 1524-25. Education was for Philip the silver bowl carrying the golden fruit of the gospel. He was superstitious, believed in astrology, countenanced palming, and saw signs in dreams, but as much as any other man of his century he promoted education and earned the title "Preceptor of Germany," a title bestowed on him by his own generation and those who came afterwards. Through him the first public schools were founded and the university system in Germany completely reorganized. Hundreds of teachers were trained in his methods and through his textbooks thousands of students were instructed.

Under his immediate instruction and influence were brought forward all the great and model instructors of the times; such men as a John Strum in Strasburg; a Valentine Trozendorf in Goldberg; a Michael Neander in Nordhausen; who, attaching themselves closely to his ideas and methods in training and teaching, became in a wider circle the founders of a permanent method in the science of instruction.[1]

At the time of Melanchthon's death there was hardly a city in Germany which did not have a teacher who had been trained by him. "The influence thus exerted by Melanchthon on the secondary and higher education of Germany is beyond all estimate." [2]

Melanchthon began his educational endeavors in 1524, the very year he was so unnerved by the victory-dancing crows, the very year for which astrologers had predicted momentous events. In that year Melanchthon laid the ground work for the school at Nürnberg; in 1525 he supervised the organization of a Latin school in Luther's hometown of Eisleben; in 1527 he visited the schools of Thuringia; and in 1528 he published the basic school plan which was enacted into law in Saxony, thus creating the first public school system since the days of the ancient Roman emperors.

For a while it appeared that the Reformation would lead to obscurantism and that its effects would be hostile to culture. In the fearful tumults of the 1520's the universities and schools came to a standstill, and with the fall of the old institutions of papalism came the fall of those centers of learning which they had brought forth. Many humanists forsook the reform, and Erasmus wrote, "Where Lutheranism reigns, knowledge perishes!" [3] However, in the person of Melanchthon those inner principles of the movement combined with the educational attainments of the Renaissance to inaugurate a new era in German education. For forty-two years he planted and fostered humanistic studies in the German universities, and under his direction Wittenberg came to its zenith. "Long after his death he controlled, through his method and textbooks, the instruction in the Protestant schools and universities." He won for the Protestant half of Germany its ascendancy over Catholicism in education and culture. "German philosophy and science, German literature and culture grew up in the soil of Protestantism, and they may be described as the result, although perhaps remote, of that spirit of freedom and independence of thought which the Reformation called into being." [4]

Nascent in the Reformation were two principles which made mass education mandatory: the appeal to Scripture as the final authority and the priesthood of all believers through justification by faith. The first made it necessary that people be able to read the Bible to know what things pertain to eternal welfare and to participate intelligently in the church services. The second took the responsibility for education out of the hands of the priestly hierarchy and, practically speaking, at the time placed it upon the rulers and ultimately upon the people.

With monks leaving the cloisters where much of the education had been conducted previously, with men like Carlstadt advocating a return to the simplicity of the uneducated, with humanists criticizing the Lutherans as antirationalistic and barbaric, with the general chaos that accompanies any major upheaval of the bases of society, the need to create a school system in keeping with the principles of the Reformation became urgent.

In 1524 Luther made his appeal for general education in a "Letter to the Mayors and Aldermen of all the Cities of Germany." Melanchthon, who had discussed this with Luther and was in complete agreement with him, prefaced the Latin edition of this letter with an appeal of his own. "Anyone who stands in the way of education for the youth of this land should have his tongue cut out." [5] At the request of the Count of Mansfeld, in 1525, Melanchthon, assisted by John Agricola, organized a school at Eisleben. Although it was no jewel sparkling in the darkness of the times, the Eisleben school furnished Philip with some basic patterns for his famous 1528 school plan. Nicholas Amsdorf, perhaps a little earlier, established a Lutheran school at Magdeburg, but neither of these schools embodied or greatly carried forward the reform ideals.[6]

On October 17, 1524, the Nürnbergers called upon Melanchthon to become the rector and professor of rhetoric in the school they hoped to found. Melanchthon was tempted, for he had not yet received his expected raise in salary, but he did not want to appear ungrateful to the Elector of Saxony, nor did he think he was right for the task. He described himself as a poor speaker, and said that a professor of rhetoric should not be scant and devoid of sap, but rich and full in his expression.[7] But the Nürnbergers did not take Melanchthon's self-depreciation seriously and said it would be his fault if the opening of the school was delayed. In December Philip decidedly declined but suggested others for positions—Hessus, Camerarius, Gelenius.[8]

Nevertheless, Nürnberg waited and after the lapse of a year Melanchthon visited the city, accompanied by Camerarius, and laid the initial plans. In the spring of 1526 he joined with the ministers and people in the inaugural ceremonies. His speech was brief. He praised the Nürnbergers for having done something which would outlast and outshine many of their other noble accomplishments. Indeed, he said, without education, religion and the arts will decline and mankind will be reduced to animality. Without learning, love and virtue will suffer, and the proper notions of religion will not be fostered. Some rulers, too ignorant or too selfish to see this, have allowed the schools to waste away. "In this perilous age, your zeal merits peculiar applause, because amidst the general storm that agitates the empire, literature and learning are in danger of being wrecked entirely." [9]

Melanchthon compared Nürnberg to the city of Florence, and added:

If you proceed to cultivate these studies you will not only be illustrious in your own country but renowned abroad. You will be regarded as the authors of your country's best defense, for "no walls or bulwarks can prove more durable memorials of cities than the learning, wisdom and virtues of its citizens." . . . In my opinion wisdom, moderation and piety make better protection than stone and iron walls.[10]

When a person refuses to exert himself for the proper instruction of his children, he is not only sinning but betraying a brutal mind. One great distinction between the human race and the brute creation is that animals do not care for their offspring when they grow up, but man by nature is enjoined to nourish his children not only during their infancy but as they become more mature to cultivate their moral powers. . . . I pray that Christ will bless this important work and look with favor upon your counsels and the diligence of those who study here.[11]

Melanchthon's work with the Nürnberg school demonstrated his genius for organization. The principle which he set forth in that speech and which he followed subsequently was simple: "Only through the maintenance of learning can religion and good government endure, and God demands that children be brought up in virtue and piety." [12]

For a month Melanchthon stayed at Nürnberg enjoying the company of Pirkheimer, being entertained at the St. Aegidius Convent. The noted Albrecht Dürer painted his picture and engraved it on copper; he met the preacher Osiander of St. Lorenz Church with whom he was later to have a bitter controversy; and he was entertained at dinners. Luther attested the success of the Nürnberg school when he described it saying, "It shines like the sun, moon, and stars in all Germany." [13] Melanchthon told Camerarius that he would gladly have stayed the entire summer at Nürnberg enjoying the city's hospitality.

That summer in Wittenberg was one of discontent. The exact nature of the trouble remains a mystery, but Melanchthon spoke of "wolf-friendships full of cares and anxiety," complained that there was no one like Michael Roting with whom to converse, and said he was working like a slave in a mill and never seeming to accomplish anything.[14] In August he became critically ill, and for twelve days his friends feared he would not recover.

Before he was fully well, an urgent request came from Philip of Hesse for advice on how the reformation should be introduced in his domains. Having heard reports of violence and disorder, Melanchthon rallied to make an answer and cautioned Philip of Hesse to move slowly. Abolish all masses except the Eucharist, he suggested. Celebrate the Eucharist every festival day according to the old rites. To avoid disputes and violence, change the ceremonies only gradually; retain those rituals that the people seem reluctant to relinquish, for they do not make one either good or bad. The essence of religion is in the fear of God, faith, love, and obedience. "Christ himself did not desire vengeance, instead he willingly offered himself as a lamb for slaughter. Therefore, your highness should hesitate before rushing to arms in defense of the Church." [15] Melanchthon asked the Landgrave not to imitate the ecclesiastics by instigating war. "Your highness, I believe, can do a great deal to terminate contentions by explaining to the princes the points under dispute."

The following year Philip of Hesse invited Melanchthon to take a professorship in the University of Marburg which opened in 1527. Although Melanchthon helped guide the founding of this university, he declined the invitation.[16]

Melanchthon's advice about gradually introducing the Reformation was not followed throughout the domains of the Landgrave. The reform synod of Homberg, led by Francis Lambert, a former barefoot monk, attempted to obliterate all traces of papalism immediately. Cloisters were closed, images removed from the churches and broken or burned, and the worship ritual radically altered. When Philip of Hesse appeared reluctant to quell these disturbances, Melanchthon and Luther both warned the Elector of Saxony against any alliance with one who would force the gospel on people.

Toward the end of September Melanchthon felt well enough to visit the commercial fair at Leipzig, after which he visited friends in Nordhausen, Mansfeld, and Eisleben, returning to Wittenberg in November.

Melanchthon was rested and well but by no means satisfied. He worried about the contentions that had shaken the Reformation—the dispute with Erasmus, the Peasants' Revolt, and Luther's marriage. He could not forget Erasmus' biting quip, "Where Lutheranism reigns, knowledge perishes," nor was he unaware of the professional jealousy on every hand. In February he wrote to Camerarius:

Behold, here I am an exile far from home, far from friends and relatives, among a poeple with whom I could not converse were I ignorant of Latin. Besides, in this place the greatest envy burns in the minds of all. At this time in this city those who have the management of affairs are not at all harmonious.[17]

During the summer of 1527 there were other things to think about. Foreseeing that he would have to give an account of the state of religion in the Saxon lands, and not knowing the extent of the havoc created by Münzer nor the extent to which the reformed doctrines were really being taught and preached in his lands, the Elector John divided the Ernestine territory into five regions, each of which was to be visited by a survey team composed of representatives from the Wittenberg faculty, clergymen, and lawyers. Luther and Melanchthon helped prepare instructions for the visiting commissions. They were to inspect the schools and churches, settle disputes, test the qualifications of ministers, and make recommendations. Reorganization and reconstruction were the general aims.

On July 5, 1527, Melanchthon left for Thuringia, the territory assigned to him. He was accompanied by Frederick Myconius, a pastor at Gotha; Justus Menius, a pastor at Erfurt; Jerome Schurf; John von Planitz; and Erasmus von Haugwitz. For about a month they inspected the churches and schools in the vicinity of Kahla, Jena, Neustadt, Weida, and Auma.

Neither he nor the others expected the deplorable conditions they found. Among the ministers were many misfits and malcontents, priests and monks who had abandoned the Roman fold, and had not the slightest understanding of evangelical faith. Ignorance was rife. Some of those who had charge of the churches and schools knew only the Decalogue, the Apostles' Creed, and the Lord's Prayer. Some did not even know these! One monk was found who thought the Ten Commandments was the title of a new book. Pastors who were ignorant of evangelical thought were mingling various worship forms. Others were teaching justification by faith as if it were a light-hearted matter having no connection with repentance and contrition. Many simply preached that the pope was Antichrist.

Problems of marriage, divorce, and inheritance had to be settled, and widespread immorality complicated the confusion. At least a third of the supposedly "celibate" clergy were living in "wild wedlock." Others had married and deserted their families. Menius reported that all but ten out of two hundred clergymen were living in open fornication. Some congregations complained that their pastors made alcoholic beverages during the week and explained the art on Sunday, and others that their ministers were seen too often in the gambling dens and beer chambers.[18] This was not the fruit of the Reformation; it was the condition the new movement confronted.

I am engaged in a most difficult business, and so far as I see, without result. Everything is in confusion, partly through ignorance, and partly through the immorality of the teachers. . . . What can be offered in justification of these people having been left in such enormous ignorance, and stupidity? My heart bleeds when I regard this misery. Often when we have completed the visitation of a place, I go to one side and pour forth my distress in tears. And who would not mourn to see the faculties of man so utterly neglected, and his soul, which is able to learn and grasp so much, ignorant of its Creator and Lord.[19]

The visitation was completed in August, and Melanchthon returned to Jena where the University had been temporarily transferred on account of the plague. He remained in Jena until the following April, lecturing and studying the reports of the other commissions. To help guide future commissions and to set a goal for the ministers and teachers in Saxony, Melanchthon drew up a set of visitation articles—the first part being a statement of Lutheran faith, and the second part a detailed school plan. It was the first confession of faith in the Lutheran Church, and the first general school plan.

After the visitation articles were approved by the Elector and members of the Wittenberg faculty, the *Unterricht der Visitatoren* was published as "a witness and confession of our faith. . . . Hence we hope that all pious, peaceful pastors who earnestly love the Gospel and desire to be in accord with us will hold it with us." The document was not intended to be rigid, only a guide "until God the Holy Ghost begins through it or through us something better." [20]

In the winter of 1528 Melanchthon again visited Thuringia, and Luther and others visited other parts of the electoral domains. Churches and schools were reformed and reorganized according to the articles, incompetent ministers were removed, and aged ministers pensioned. Melanchthon was thus the organizer of the Saxon schools and churches. Later Luther and Melanchthon wrote catechisms and sent out sermons that could be memorized by those pastors who could not prepare their own. [21]

The plan bore fruit. Within two years Luther joyously reported: "The Word of God is effective and fruitful in the entire land. Your Grace has more and better pastors than any other country in the world. They preach faithfully and purely and live in entire harmony."

The articles were a confession of faith, a norm for doctrine and worship, and as such very significant in the developing Lutheran Church. The school plan was a monumental step in the progress of education in Germany. That the two were published together was significant, for Melanchthon considered the churches and schools complementary parts in the Christian scheme.

Fourteen of the eighteen articles in the first part were devoted to doctrine, and the other four to such matters as worship, discipline, education, and the Turks. Noticeably lacking were direct attacks on the papacy, for Philip sought a positive approach. Throughout the document two principles reign—Scripture alone and justification by faith.

In Christ's name we must preach repentance and the remission of sins, said Melanchthon, for repentance, faith, and good works represent the three parts of the Christian life. The first is begotten in the heart through a preaching of the law, particularly the Ten Commandments. In the demands of the law the individual realizes his own shortcomings. The second is begotten through the power of the gospel promise that we are forgiven our sins for Christ's sake, rather than any merit of our own. The third, good works, is the consequence of the first two. Melanchthon thought the three should go together. Where there is no repentance, there is a painted faith; where there is no good work, faith is dead. [22]

Melanchthon warned that repentance must be stressed so that people would not regard faith as an easy matter and become falsely secure and careless, and he urged that subtle arguments about good works be shunned. It is far better to be chaste, to be neighborly, to help others, to refrain from lying, to pray, and to be obedient to parents and rulers than to argue.

Melanchthon instructed the pastors to teach that tribulations come from God; that baptism takes the place of ancient circumcision, and that in infant baptism God's blessing and protection are bestowed; that the true body and blood of Christ are in the bread and wine of the Eucharist; that only one part of the sacrament need be taken if the better way is offensive; that true confession does not mean the enumeration of all our sins; that repentance is a sacrament; that Christ is the only true satisfaction for our sins; that the saints need not be invoked, since Christ is our mediator; that persons living in open vice despite admonishment should be forbidden the Lord's Supper but not the hearing of the Word; that invectives against the papacy should be used only when necessary to warn the people.

He exhorted the pastors to preach on important subjects—repentance, faith, and fear—rather than on human ordinances and saints' fables, and to hold disputations on holy days rather than the old rituals and ceremonies.

Free will need not promote contentious debate, for we are able, declared Melanchthon, to perform worldly piety and good works by our own strength, given us and preserved for this purpose by God. This is righteousness of the flesh. "But man by his own power cannot purify his heart, and produce divine gifts, such as true repentance from sin, a true and unfeigned fear of God, true faith, cordial love, chastity, an absence of revenge, true patience, earnest prayers, freedom from covetousness, etc." We should pray God to work these gifts in us. Our true liberty is that our righteousness does not depend on our being able to keep the law and ritual.

Throughout the document Melanchthon tried to be practical, for the visitors had previously found that many pastors knew very little about the fine points of doctrine. For this reason he emphasized good works as the proper fruits of repentance and faith, and the sacraments as signs of grace for the good life as well as signs of forgiveness of sins.

The second part, the school plan, embodied Melanchthon's ideal for education: *Beredsamkeit,* a cultivation of all the powers of the human spirit. He would begin with languages and make the fruits of religion his final goal.

Upon the civil authorities Melanchthon laid the responsibility for the establishment and maintenance of the schools for the people. That children may be trained for service in the church and state, Latin schools should be founded, and the best students should be encouraged to study further.

Preachers also should exhort the people of their charge to send their children to school, so that they may be trained up to teach sound doctrine in the church, and to serve the state in a wise and able manner. Some imagine that it is enough for a teacher to understand German. But this is a misguided fancy. For he who is to teach others must have great practice and special aptitude; to gain this, he must have studied much, and from his youth up. . . . Nor do we need able and skillful persons for the church alone, but for the government of the world too; and God requires it at our hands. Hence parents should place their children at school, in order there to arm and equip them for God's service, so that God can use them for the good of others. . . . But in our day there are many abuses in children's schools. And it is that these abuses may be corrected, and that the young may have good instruction, that we have prepared this plan.

Melanchthon said that Latin rather than a variety of languages should be taught, that teachers should concentrate on a few books rather than a great many, and that children should be classified according to ability.

The first group—The first group should consist of those children who are learning to read. With these the following method is to be adopted: They are first to be taught the child's manual, containing the alphabet, the creed, the Lord's Prayer, and other prayers. When they have done this, Donatus and Cato may both be given them. . . . They should be exercised until they can read well. Neither do we consider it time lost if the feebler children, who are not especially quick-witted, should read Cato and Donatus not once only, but a second time. With this they should be taught to write, and be required to show their writing to the schoolmaster every day. Another mode of enlarging their knowledge of Latin words is to give them every afternoon some words to commit to memory, as has been the custom in schools hitherto. These children must likewise be kept at music, and be made to sing with the others. . . .

The second group—The second group consists of children who have learned to read, and are now ready to go into grammar. . . . The first hour after noon every day all the children, large and small, should be practiced in music. Then the schoolmaster must interpret to the second group the fables of Aesop. After vespers, he should explain to them the *Paedology* of Mosellanus, and . . . select from the *Colloquies* of Erasmus some that may conduce to their improvement and discipline.

This should be repeated the next evening and the children given some short sentence before going home at night. In the morning Melanchthon would have the children again explain Aesop's fables and decline words in accordance with their progress. After the children learn the rules of construction, he would have them drilled in diagraming, etymology, syntax, and prosody, until they understand grammar to perfection. "For if there is negligence here, there is neither certainty nor stability in whatever is learned beside. And the children should learn by heart and repeat all the rules, so that they may be driven and forced, as it were, to learn the grammar well."

"If such labor is irksome to the schoolmaster, as we often see, then we should dismiss him, and get another in his place,—one who will not shrink from the duty of keeping his pupils constantly in the grammar. For no greater injury can befall learning and the arts than for youth to grow up in ignorance of grammar."

Melanchthon would set aside one day of each week for Christian instruction.

For some are suffered to learn nothing in the Holy Scriptures; and some masters teach children nothing but the Scriptures; both of which extremes must be avoided. It is essential that children be taught the rudiments of the Christian and divine life, and likewise there are many reasons why, with the Scriptures, other books, too, should be laid before them, out of which they may learn to read. And in this matter we propose the following method: Let the schoolmaster hear the whole group, making them, one after the other, repeat the Lord's Prayer, the creed, and the ten commandments. But if the group is too large, it may be divided, so that one week one part may recite, and the remaining part the next.

After one recitation, the master should explain in a simple and correct manner the Lord's prayer, the creed, and at another time the ten commandments. And he should impress upon the children the essentials, such as fear of God, faith, and good works. He must not touch upon polemics, nor must he accustom the children to scoff at monks as many unskilled teachers used to do.

Simple psalms that contain the substance of the Christian life, such as psalms 34, 112, 125, 127, 128, and 133, should be memorized and simply expounded. To this should be added a grammatical exposition of Matthew, repeated again and again, until the children are advanced enough for the Epistle to Timothy, or the First Epistle of John, or Solomon's Proverbs. Melanchthon warned against trying to introduce such books as Isaiah, Romans, and John at this stage.

The third group—Now, when these children have been well trained in grammar, those among them who have made the greatest proficiency should be taken out, and formed into the third group. The hour after mid-day, they, together with the rest, are to devote to music.

After this the teacher should explain Vergil, Ovid, and Cicero. Grammar exercises should be continued until the students can compose verses, and then the grammar studies should be gradually displaced by logic and rhetoric. All should be rigidly confined to Latin, even the teachers.[23]

Certain aspects of this school plan should be noted for their intrinsic value: Teachers should be well trained and interested in their work, even in routine grammar drilling. They should explain simply and clearly the materials at hand without trying to display their own erudition. The curriculum should be simple, in the Latin gymnasia consisting almost entirely of Latin grammar and literature. Books required of the students should be few in number, so that the students will not be discouraged by too much work. To lighten the activities of the day immediately after lunch music should be given. And the goal of the schools should be clear—to teach all the rudiments of reading and writing, and to train the abler students to use the basic tools to further their education for higher service in the church or government. The three basic groups were to be formed on the ground of ability, progress, and age, and several years were required to cover all three classes. Such literary training came to prevail not only in Germany but also in England and America.[24]

The 1528 plan became a model for other visitations, for it was the "first determined attempt to definitely establish the Lutheran Church in Saxony." By 1555 more than 135 of these plans had appeared, and some were in use well into the seventeenth century. "Of these all have followed the principles of organization and regulation as laid down in the Saxon Orders of Visitation and Instructions," and all the important ones can be traced back to the 1528 plan of Melanchthon.[25] The Visitation Articles "became the model for scores of other imperial territories and resulted in a remarkably large number of Church Orders and Liturgies which continued to be issued to the end of the 16th century. The protocoled data would cover scores of printed volumes." [26]

And so it was that Melanchthon provided the foundation for the evangelical public school system of Germany. His plan was used and copied again and again until the rays of his influence penetrated almost every territory. Records show that fifty-six cities asked his directions for founding their schools; how many more he influenced can only be conjectured. For the golden fruit of the gospel Melanchthon had designed a silver bowl.

That They May Know the Word

ELANCHTHON'S EDUCATIONAL WORK DID NOT STOP WITH the Latin schools. He regarded the universities as the fountainheads of the school system since from these the teachers would be drawn for the lower schools. Of all the universities he considered Wittenberg the center because it was the heart of the religious changes. This was one of the reasons why Melanchthon refused to abandon the university after Luther's death in 1546, although by staying there he risked being called an enemy collaborator. He became the academic guide of the university. In 1533 he wrote the statutes for reorganizing the theological faculty at Wittenberg and gave the curriculum a scriptural-exegetical instead of a scholastic-philosophical emphasis. Twelve years later he composed the laws that governed the faculties of theology and the liberal arts.[1] He set forth each professor's responsibilities, made provisions for declamations and disputes on alternate Saturdays, and established a balance between the humanities and theology. By 1550 Wittenberg was Germany's most popular university.

From all districts of Germany, even from all parts of Europe, young men flocked to hear him [Melanchthon]. When Melanchthon died there can have been but few cities of Protestant Germany in which there was not at least one grateful pupil to mourn the loss of the Praeceptor Germaniae.[2]

In 1545 Greifswald used Wittenberg as a model, officially spoke of Melanchthon as "our highly esteemed and venerated teacher," and made his textbooks the bases of the university lectures.[3] "It is not too much to

[144]

say that the university in all its departments, throughout Protestant Germany, is his creation." [4]

Döllinger, a Roman Catholic historian, credits Melanchthon with enabling Protestants to use the treasures of classical culture by saying he was the literary head of a mighty cause and richly endowed with classical learning, facility of expression, versatility of composition, and untiring industry.[5] In addition to the universities already mentioned, Melanchthon helped found the universities of Königsberg, Jena, and Marburg; he revised the curricula of Cologne, Tübingen, Leipzig, and Heidelberg; and indirectly he reformed Rostock and Frankfort-on-the-Oder.

What was the ideal of this man who so profoundly influenced the development of German education and through the culture of that nation the education of the world? In a word it was the cultivation of all the powers of the human spirit, *Beredsamkeit.* Or it could be called *learned piety,* "learned" referring to the elements of humanism, and "piety" reflecting the evangelical elements. "On earth there is nothing next to the Gospel more glorious than humanistic learning, that wonderful gift of God." [6] The two burning points of his pedagogy were "back to the sources" and "knowledge of Christ." [7] As he stated in his inaugural speech at Wittenberg, he sought to use the fruits of humanism in the service of religion, so as to recover Christ who is the heart of ultimate wisdom and truth. He believed that the progress of the church, the welfare of the state, and the development of individual character depended upon sound education. Piety, discretion, and truthfulness stood side by side in his education scheme.[8]

Melanchthon believed that education is necessary in the church and in the state, for religious darkness leads to desolation and schism, to barbarism and confusion of men, and political darkness leads to animal life without law.[9] In a speech in 1536 he declared that ignorance obscures religion, creates contentions, and leads to the barbaric downfall of the social order. Unenlightened theology, he said, is one of the greatest evils. By confounding doctrines, misconceiving vital truth, holding matters together that should be divided, one is led into contradiction and inconsistency, so that there is no beginning, no progress, and no result, just floundering frustration. From such a condition flow prolific errors, endless disagreements, and, if each person defends his views, then strife and discord. Believers then become doubters, and doubt unresolved becomes disbelief. The church and the state need sound education, for ignorance is a curse and learnedness a blessing.[10] Learning is a means of transmitting the treasure of religion to posterity, and a means of preventing man from returning to animality. "Without schools how could our society flourish?" Since we are commanded by God to cultivate virtue in our children, and since social barbarism flows from ignorance, we have both a divine and human motive for establishing good schools. In our social order they are necessary to religion and good government. Godlessness in church and state generally follow ignorance of man's culture.[11]

However, Melanchthon did not think ignorance was unrighteousness, per se, and learning necessarily righteousness, per se. He regarded learning as a tool needed to recover the Word of God which was in its purest form encased in languages that could be learned only by diligent study of a number of subjects. "Without an understanding of language, one cannot read the Old and New Testaments; and to understand languages one needs all sorts of related knowledge in history, geography, chronology, and other liberal arts." [12] Learning is a blessing to the church, therefore, and ignorance a curse, not on account of learning itself or ignorance itself, but because without learning one loses the fountain of religion—the Holy Scriptures.

Education was for Melanchthon an introduction to the Word of God. "You must take up a school vocation," he told teachers, "in the same spirit that you would take up the service of God in the church, for in the school one is also concerned with godly things." The teacher "performs before God in a most pleasing service and renders a high service to mankind." [13]

Melanchthon put into the curricula of his schools, especially the higher schools, those subjects which would contribute most to an understanding of the Scriptures. The deeper meaning of the Word of God comes through the Holy Spirit, he said, but we must know the languages in which the divine mysteries are embodied, and we must have a broad base in related subjects to learn the languages.[14] This was the basic reason why Melanchthon did not want anyone, not even Luther, to make inroads on the languages and the humanistic classics at Wittenberg.[15] He hoped and believed that government and personal morals would also be served, and he put considerable emphasis on both of these, but learning as a gateway to the Scriptures was always primary.

For this reason Melanchthon stressed grammar. He was convinced that it was absolutely necessary to a good understanding of Latin, Greek, and Hebrew. He devoted much time to the rudiments of languages, wrote clear basic texts on grammar, and became known sometimes with opprobrium as the "little grammarian." But Melanchthon never lost himself in the pedantry of philology; languages were always tools to unlock the treasures of the classics and the sacred writings of Christianity. Too much grammar, he warned, would discourage and warp students, but a thorough foundation is vital.

How important it is to the church, that boys be well disciplined in the languages! Inasmuch as the pursuit of the divine teachings can not be maintained without learning, and weighty controversies can only be settled by a determination of the meaning of words, a wide range of well-chosen expressions is indispensable to a correct construction; therefore, what will a teacher in the church be, if he does not understand grammar, other than a silent mask, or a shameless bawler? He who does not understand the mode of the speech of God's word cannot love it either. *Ignoti nulla cupido* is a true maxim. But how can he be a good teacher in the church who neither loves the heavenly doctrine, nor yet understands it, nor is able to explain it? Neglect of grammar has recoiled upon our heads, in that through this means the monks have palmed off upon the church and the schools spurious wares for genuine. Hence princes should have a care to maintain learning; we observe, however, that very few do it. And cities, too, should strive to uphold and protect these studies, that embellish not only the church but the whole of life.[16]

In a preface to the second part of his grammar Melanchthon addressed a note to the son of Justus Jonas. He decried those who would become philologists merely by reading the classics without thoroughly studying grammar. They will never be grounded, said Melanchthon, and this repugnance for the restraint of rules could lead to a contempt for law and order!

Melanchthon chose carefully the writings he would use for grammar, because he sought to make school training a preparation for real living. He selected those writers who had also produced worthy products of the human mind. For this reason he was especially interested in Terence.[17]

I always endeavor to introduce you to such authors as will increase your comprehension of things while they contribute toward enlarging your language. These two parts belong together, so that one stands and is supported by the other, because no one can speak well if he does not understand what he wishes to say, and again knowledge is lame without the light of speech.[18]

In this respect Melanchthon forecast Elyot, who advocated Greek and Latin for their content and preparation for living, and also Ascham, who criticized the schools of his day for their grammatical grind and neglect of content.

Melanchthon included logic in the curriculum because of its general importance. Some men, if they are blessed with practical common sense, can do without it, but it helps men who have only moderate capacities and controls those who are especially gifted.[19] In religion logic helps in the making of correct statements of doctrine, although at times it may be abused by heretics and sophists. Those who could speak eloquently, but without either learning or logic, Melanchthon called "self-conceited blockheads." To speak well, he said, one must have something to say, must use logic to think it through, and must have the means of expressing it.[20]

Melanchthon justified physics, saying the church benefited from such studies. Physics, he said, elucidates the harmony of creation, the derangement of this harmony, and the evils which God has visited upon man in consequence of the Fall.[21] In a preface to his *Initia doctrinae physicae,* dedicated to the mayor of Nordhausen, he wrote:

Although the nature of things cannot be absolutely known, nor the marvelous works of God be traced to their original, until in that future life we shall ourselves listen to the eternal counsel of the Father, Son, and Holy Spirit, nevertheless, even amid this our present darkness, every gleam and every hint of the harmony of this fair creation forms a step toward the knowledge of God and toward virtue, whereby we ourselves shall also learn to love and maintain order and moderation in all our own acts. Since it is evident that men are endowed by their Creator with faculties fitted for the contemplation of nature, they must, of necessity, take delight in investigating the elements, the laws, the motions, and the qualities or forces of the various bodies, by which they are surrounded. . . . The uncertainty which obtains with regard to so much in nature should not deter us from our search, for it is none the less God's will that we trace out his footsteps in the creation.[22]

He admonished those who studied physics to read the very best authors, and to take pains to express their own thoughts in faultless Latin. This will be an aid to clear thinking and sharp description, whereas slang and anomalous words will but lead to vague shadows of truth.[23]

Melanchthon regarded astronomy in much the same way. When he wrote a preface to John Sacrobusto's book on the spheres, he declared, "The perdurable harmony of the starry heavens bespeaks a God." He thought that knowledge of the heavens was necessary for chronology and for the conduct of life. "It was to gaze upon the stars that eyes were given to men. For to look at it, the eye itself would seem to bear an affinity with the stars."

Philip would not tolerate sophistry in the curriculum. "The right spirit in the quest of truth is the love of truth!" He burned with hatred toward those who played with truth for their own aggrandizement, men who were

not seeking to bring the truth to light, but only to prove or to disprove in perpetual rotation whatever they have happened to conjecture possible. And this legerdemain they have taken to be the true element of genius. Such men were those universal doubters, the academics and sophists of Plato's time. These undisciplined, lawless spirits were very dangerous; whatever pleased their fancy, this they never ceased to magnify, but everything disagreeable to them they rejected as of no account; that which looked plausible they insisted upon as true; they united things which did not belong together, and things which were manifestly related to each other they put asunder; they employed clear and well-defined terms to express nothing; and threw around sober realities an air of irony.

Against this kind of sophistry all well-meaning persons must wage an implacable warfare. Plato was very earnest to exhort men in their speech to seek not the applause of men but the approbation of God. And accordingly we ought with our whole soul to aim at this one point, namely, to find the truth, and to set it forth with as much simplicity and clearness as possible. Men who, in matters of science, sport with the truth, are blind guides likewise where revelation is concerned. Sophistry has by means of its false precepts occasioned religious dissensions and religious wars. The dispositions of men are easily warped, and it needs great wisdom to keep them in the right way; and Christ calls down the severest judgment upon those by whom offenses come.[24]

Melanchthon implemented the curriculum through his numerous textbooks. The Greek grammar which he published at the age of twenty-one, for example, was used in the schools of Germany for one hundred years. His Latin grammar went through more than fifty editions and was used in all the schools of Saxony until the beginning of the eighteenth century. Melanchthon wrote other texts for theology, rhetoric, logic, ethics, history, physics, and psychology.

But he was never quite satisfied with these manuals. He was constantly revising. In the preface to the 1542 edition of his Greek grammar he disclosed that he had often wished it had perished, because he wrote it when he was only a boy for the use of boys in his charge. But the book-sellers persuaded him to repeat his "foolish" action and to rebuild on the old ruins. Accordingly, he critically revised and altered the entire book. The syntax part of his grammar, however, was not printed.[25]

Originally Melanchthon wrote his Latin grammar for a boy named Erasmus Ebner of Nürnberg, and it was published in 1525, against Melanchthon's will. Two of Philip's noted disciples—Joachim Camerarius and Michael Neander—revised this basic text. Neander shortened it to 130 pages, and Camerarius enlarged it to 507! Melanchthon had said that he did not want to discourage students with too much grammar, and on the other hand that he wanted to be thorough. When Camerarius asked for permission to have the bookseller Papst in Leipzig bring out a larger edition, Melanchthon approved in advance whatever changes Camerarius might make. When Schenk, a Latin teacher at Leipzig, saw this enlarged edition, he exclaimed that the little book had at last been brought to perfection.[27] Neander thought otherwise and published a shortened edition with a longer title: "The Latin grammar of Ph. Melanchthon, delivered with brevity, ease, and clearness, in the compass of a few pages, yet in such a manner as not only to give Melanchthon's language, but his method in the smaller grammar and smaller syntax, that first and oldest manual, which is most admirably adapted to the learner, and which more than any other has been used in all our German schools." If Camerarius' edition was more complete, Neander's was more practical, and popular, for it was used even in the Catholic schools until 1734.[28] Von Raumer remarked that its influence can be traced to modern times through the *Grammatica Marchica* of 1728, which strikingly coincides with Melanchthon's grammar in arrangement, treatment, phraseology, and rules, and through the work of Otto Schulz, who in 1825 said he was following the *Grammatica*

Marchica, whose main features, he said, nearly all teachers concur in approving.[29]

Melanchthon's manuals on logic met with similar success. He first published a logic textbook in 1520, enlarged and improved it in 1527, and brought out a third edition in 1529. In 1547 he dedicated *Erotemata Dialectices* to John, son of Camerarius. This last edition was an immediate success; it was published on September 1 and by October 18 had sold eighteen thousand copies.[30]

This renewed interest in logic reflected a renewed desire to aid in understanding Aristotle. Melanchthon fully explained that the logic he condemned in 1521 in the *Loci* was not genuine logic. In 1547 he wrote that true logic is a preface to all necessary art.

> Even as there are many men of unbridled passions who hate the restraints of moral law, so there are those who cannot abide the rules of art. Dialectics, as hitherto taught by the schoolmen, had, to be sure, fallen into contempt; however, this was because it was not true art, but only the shadow of an art, and entangled men amid endless labyrinthine mazes. But I present here a true, pure and unsophisticated logic, just as we have received it from Aristotle and some of his judicious commentators.[31]

Melanchthon considered logic necessary for differentiating theological doctrines.

Philip's manuals on rhetoric went through numerous editions, and made an impact as far away as England.[32] In the 1531 edition of his manual he stated that rhetoric had not been corrupted by sophistical writers as had logic, but that one should beware of blockheads who conceitedly considered themselves rhetoricians when they could dictate a letter.[33]

Official acts, laws, and manuals never make teachers. Of this Melanchthon was fully cognizant. To the citizens of Antwerp who invited him to guide their school he wrote that the good teacher must know how to teach, speak, and act at the same time. "If you know such a man, get him at any price; for the matter involves the future of your children, whose tender youth receives with the same susceptibility the impress of good and of bad example." [34]

Melanchthon never forsook the personal touch in his teaching. Evidence of his fatherly love for his students abounds. Melchoir Adam described him as a teacher at heart and by nature a friend of children. He was always available for personal conferences. "I can assure you that I have a paternal affection for all my students and am deeply concerned about everything that affects their welfare." [35]

Camerarius related that it was a part of Melanchthon's household arrangement never to deny himself to anyone.

Many came to him for letters of recommendation; many for him to revise their essays. Some sought his counsel in their embarrassments; others told him of incidents that had befallen them, either in private or in public, provided they were such as merited his attention; others again brought this or that complaint before him.[36]

Melanchthon strove to make his lectures interesting, by using the Socratic method, anecdotes, short stories, and current expressions.[37] Often hundreds of students attended his classes, occasionally as many as two thousand. An unpopular subject, however, might reduce the number of hearers considerably. In 1531 Philip announced he would lecture on Homer:

I shall, according to my custom, read gratis. But as Homer in his lifetime was needy and a beggar, so the same fate follows him now that he is dead. For this noblest of poets is compelled now to wander about imploring men to listen to him. He does not, however, seek out those groveling souls, bent only on gain, who not content with resting in ignorance themselves, delight in crying down all noble learning, but turns rather to those free spirits who aim after perfect knowledge.[38]

When Philip lectured on Demonsthenes in 1533 he also expected few hearers:

I had hoped, by disclosing to my hearers the grace of the second Olynthiac, to have allured them to a nearer acquaintance with Demosthenes. But I perceive that this generation has no ear for such authors. For there remain to me but few hearers, and these have not forsaken me lest I should be wholly discouraged; for this courtesy, I thank them. But I shall, nevertheless, continue to discharge the duties of my office. I shall commence these lectures tomorrow.[39]

Melanchthon's lectures on Ptolemy likewise suffered.[40] "I exhort all who began with me these lectures on Ptolemy to come back. To those who have not deserted me, I offer my tribute of thanks."

Sometimes the educational system seemed quite discouraging, for others did not see as much value in education as Philip. This is reflected in a 1536 speech:

Learning is in this day of the utmost consequence to the church, because ignorant priests are growing ever bolder and more careless in their office. Learned men, who have accustomed themselves to thorough investigation in every thing they undertake, know but too well how liable they are to fall into error, and thus diligence itself teaches them modesty. But what great disasters ever befall the church, from the recklessness of ignorance, this, the present condition of things will teach us.[41]

Enemies had been trying to poison the friendship between Melanchthon and Luther. This was the "present condition" to which Philip referred in 1536.

Melanchthon's advice was not always followed. He believed a knowledge of arithmetic was necessary to a liberal arts education, yet he had difficulty keeping it at Wittenberg. A letter to Camerarius is very revealing:

I can only laugh over your anger that my recommendation of mathematics has been condemned. In it I had no other aim, than to restore to the schools the right use of this science, and to allure youth to the study of it. This I have desired, and for this will I labor, so long as any opportunity is left to me to help forward the cause of sound learning.[42]

Apparently mathematics was not highly regarded at Wittenberg, and Melanchthon was not able to do much about it.[43]

Melanchthon often spoke of the woes of teachers, but these were never greater than the joys. Three days before his death he wrote to Camerarius:

My dear Joachim, we have been good friends for forty years, not on account of the good we could do each other, but out of the free choice of our hearts. We have both been schoolmasters and true comrades, each one in his own place. And it has been our hope before God that our work will not be forgotten but will bring forth much fruit.[44]

Melanchthon placed great stress on the training of teachers, academically and morally. But there was much to overcome. Moral standards were often very low. Almost all the school laws specifically required God-fearing, respectful, upright men, simply because there were men who were not. The Breslau law of 1570 indicates that teachers were probably a bit wild:

They shall stay at home, especially at night, since unseasonable absence is rarely without the suspicion that they are engaged in wrong-doing. They shall stay away from houses of prostitution and places of illfame. They shall not wander around nor promenade. They shall not have family quarrels nor stir up strife. They shall not break the commands of the master nor leave home without consent.[45]

There is evidence for saying that neglect, lack of diligence, too much fondness for beer, fighting, gambling, and questionable money-making schemes were among the worst faults of the Latin school teachers. Like some ministers, some teachers made and sold alcoholic beverages on the school premises.

Financial insecurity was apparently at the bottom of most of the school ills. Both Melanchthon and Luther tried to raise salaries and to have teachers supported out of the public treasury, but they were not too successful. Lack of money made it necessary for teachers to engage in questionable activities. Salaries were often paid in goods and in money from many sources. Here is a notation about the teacher's salary in Pretzsch in 1555:

INCOME OF THE SCHOOLMASTER

10 florins from the marshall;
4 loaves of bread and 8 denarii from each landowner;
5 bushels of grain;
1 piece of land across the Elbe, where the schoolmaster may at his own expense sow two bushels of grain and reap the harvest;
⅓ of a piece of meadowland at Brisitz, yielding two loads of hay;
20 denarii for every corpse for which the bells are rung three times;
4 denarii for each christening;
1 groschen tuition for each pupil per quarter.[46]

The prospect of getting twenty denarii for ringing the bells for every corpse might put a strain on one's ethics! Paying teachers' salaries from the public treasury was a practice that developed slowly. Poor children and sons of professors and pastors were usually given school training without any fee.[47]

Melanchthon said teachers should have salaries large enough to make outside work unnecessary, but not large enough to encourage idleness or prodigality. There was little danger of the latter. In writing about the woes of teachers, Melanchthon noted that common laborers were often better paid, that schoolmasters sometimes had hardly enough to eat, that teachers often go in rags while booksellers at fairs dress themselves in gold and parade like maharajahs. Nicodemus Frischlin complained that swine and cattle herders received more pay.[48]

The coarseness of the times inevitably expressed itself in the schools. In 1533 Melanchthon complained saying, "The barbarity of some is so great that they even think that a contempt for discipline and law is a part of true bravery." [49] In 1537 he exclaimed:

Never were our youth so impatient of laws and of discipline, so determined to live after their own wills. . . . It is the part, not of men, but of Cyclops to make public tumults at night; to fill whole neighborhoods with furious outcries; to make bacchanalian and even hostile assaults upon the unarmed and innocent able citizens; to break in their doors and windows, destroy the slumbers of women in childbed, and of the wretched, the sick, and the aged; to demolish the booths in the market-place, carriages, and whatever else comes in the way.[50]

But Melanchthon was patient enough to wait for good fruit, which he believed would come.

I know not of what opinion others may be, but for myself I can boast that I view with the greatest satisfaction these our incorporations of schools. For it is a source of joy to see these supports of the state. . . . What is more profitable, or I may add, more praiseworthy, than to fill the hearts of the youth with the saving knowledge of God, of the nature of things, and with good morals? [51]

The *Schulordnung of Mecklenburg,* 1552, gives a summary of Melanchthon's attitude toward education and expresses the tone of the times:

God, the Almighty, out of his compassion toward men and for the sake of His dear Son, has revealed himself through faithful witnesses and has given gracious promises and has had these his revelations and teachings, which were given through the prophets and apostles, expressed in certain writings. He Himself wrote the Ten Commandments on tablets of stone and commanded that the books of the prophets and apostles should be read and learned. . . . Since it is from these books that doctrine is to be learned, it is highly necessary that there be those who can read. And whoever is to teach others must himself be familiar with the entire substance of the doctrine and must know where and how all the articles in the Holy Scriptures support and explain one another. . . . In order that there may be certainty in the interpretation of Scripture, . . . those who teach others must understand the language of the prophets and apostles and must be prepared through the arts which are of service in that work. I Tim. 4 expressly commands, "Give attendance to reading, to exhortation, to doctrine," a passage which, not without purpose, mentions reading first, for the Gospel is very different from all other knowledge, religion, and sects. Other knowledge, such as computation and measuring, would be developed by the natural understanding of man, even though they were not found in the Scripture. But the divine promise of grace is not a light that is born in us, as is computation or law; but it is the wonderful counsel of God, above and beyond the understanding of all creatures, given by special revelation, set down in the Scriptures by the prophets and apostles. Consequently, reading is the beginning of Christian doctrine. . . .

From many passages it is evident that it is God's will that there be men who shall teach others reading, writing, the languages, and the arts.[52]

Melanchthon concluded by citing biblical and ancient examples of churches and schools working together.

Unfortunately, however, when Lutheranism became narrowed and formalized in the second half of the sixteenth century, education followed suit and severely suffered. In a sense the Württemberg Church Code of 1559, to which Melanchthon's influence is directly traceable, was the climax of his educational endeavors. This epoch-making document was the first co-ordination of state education from the elementary school to the university, and it was widely used as a model for other regions. But the code aimed at uniformity in doctrine and conduct. During the doctrinal struggles of the latter half of the century this tendency became more pronounced. At the end of the Thirty Years' War in 1648, the schools were left in a very sad condition. The dogmatic reaction in the schools could only be regarded as a decline.[53]

Squeezed between Catholicism and Calvinism, the intellectual life of the German universities after Melanchthon's death suffered greatly. Protestantism relapsed from the freedom of a biblical theology to a new kind of scholastic dogmatics, brought about largely by the ultra-Lutherans. In large measure this was the bitter fruit of the condemnation of Melanchthon during the same period. It was not until the basic principles of Melanchthonianism were reasserted in their essential freedom that education again flourished in Germany. The spirit of freedom slowly withered, until by the end of the seventeenth century the schools seemed no longer to be in touch with reality. University life became coarse; brawls with even the faculty taking part became common. Queen Christine of Sweden spoke of the Germans as stupid brutes, and their university doctors as no better than her carriage horses.[54]

It was not until the classics, sciences, and philosophy united with the religious and moral powers of Christianity in the foundations of university education that the universities again became great. And these were the foundation stones laid by Melanchthon.[55]

12

From Protest . . .

HE GROUND RECOVERED FOR THE REFORMATION THROUGH the visitation program afforded little immediate cause for rejoicing. After 1526 political tension mounted steadily until by 1530 the evangelicals, split among themselves, stood facing a determined emperor free at last to deal with the "schismatic pests."

Many of the evangelical princes looked with dismay toward the imperial diet to be held at Spires in May of 1526, for they felt that they would have to account for religious innovations and failure to execute the Edict of Worms against Luther and his supporters. To prepare himself for questions at the diet, Elector John requested from Melanchthon and Luther statements about the right of the princes to reform the church in their territories. This was the first step toward the climactic defensive confessional at Augsburg four years later.

Sometime before the end of 1525 Melanchthon set down his opinion.[1] He spoke first of the right of the reformers to preach their doctrines even though the bishops might disagree. "Without being able to deny our doctrine," said Melanchthon, "the bishops apparently want to condemn us on the technicality that we have exceeded our jurisdictional authority." By arguing that they alone should command, that the practices of the inerrant church should not be abrogated, that it is better to be obedient than to cause schism and insurrection, and that dissension which could lead to war should be avoided, the bishops parade under a pretense of great authority. "But," wrote Melanchthon, "ministers of the Gospel are bound to preach the principal Christian doctrine, faith in Christ, and must not conceal this for any reason whatsoever. Christ said, 'Whoever confesses me before the world, him will I confess before God; whoever denies me, him will I deny.' " Since monks, priests, and bishops promote themselves rather than Christ, "the command of God compels us to struggle against their heathenish, human errors. Pastors must preach the truth, especially when the bishops neglect their duty, and when persecuted, they must say as did the primitive disciples, 'We ought to obey God rather than men.' " Denying that the pope and clergy constitute the true church, Melanchthon upheld those who have the Word and are sanctified and cleansed as the ecclesia and pointed out that Paul predicted that the Antichrist would come as man sitting in the temple of God, in the church.

We are not departing from the church, therefore, in contending against the errors of Antichrist, nor in altering external ordinances, for the unity of the church does not consist in these things, and whoever affirms it does ought to be opposed. The pope and the bishops, by demanding an obedience which amounts to nothing short of a renunciation of the Word of God, have been the real cause of insurrection and tumult.

After appealing further to biblical and historical examples, Melanchthon concluded that the doctrine of justification by faith ought to be maintained, even at the risk of persecution and every kind of distress.

"The second question," said Melanchthon, "is this: Have the princes done right in authorizing the reformation of abuses in their colleges and monasteries?" Since the princes have done right in receiving the gospel, it follows, Philip declared, that it is no less right to remove the abuses which corrupt it.

The question really is whether the reformed doctrines are true or not; if true, then the princes ought to protect them. They are no more under an obligation to obey the persecution edicts of emperors and rulers than Jonathan was to kill David, or Obadiah to kill the prophets. Nor ought they to be stigmatized with the name of schismatics, because they do not separate themselves from the church of Rome out of mere hostility and petulance of disposition, but because they are compelled to it by the express command of Scripture.

The Elector of Saxony and Philip of Hesse toward the end of February, 1526, met at Gotha to form a common evangelical front against any machinations of the papists. They were soon joined by others.

When the deferred Diet of Spires opened on June 25, with the Emperor's brother Ferdinand presiding, the evangelicals were ready for any eventualities. Fortunately, the vicissitudes of politics, contrary to expectation, were auspicious for them. The outbreak of war with the French, new dissension between the pope and the Emperor, the spring advances of the Turks in Hungary, and an acknowledgment on the part of some Romanists of the necessity of purifying the church, tilted the scale of power toward the evangelicals. Several preachers were allowed to explain reform doctrines, and the deputies presented a memorial on the abolition of abuses. After considerable debate the reformers secured a recess decree which recognized the need for a general council to settle religious differences. They also obtained a decree saying each prince should be left free to conduct religious matters as he saw fit, knowing, of course, that in the future he would be responsible to the Emperor and to God. Melanchthon called it a "bulwark of public peace." [2]

During the interim between the first diet of Spires and the second one in 1529, the Elector of Saxony sought to determine the status of religion in his lands and conducted the school-church visitation previously described. It was during this interim also that impetuous Philip of Hesse pushed the Reformation in his lands, sometimes with violence. Melanchthon cautioned him not to rush changes, but this solicited advice was not followed.

Scarcely two years had passed before a Roman Catholic reaction set in. It was occasioned by the notorious Pack Affair and by renewed cooperation between the pope and Emperor. The ease with which the Pack incident fired suspicions and set off persecutions indicated the strength of underlying animosities.

In February, 1528, Dr. Otto von Pack, ex-chancellor of Duke George, sold to Philip of Hesse for the sum of 10,000 gulden a copy of an alleged document in which several Catholic princes and bishops bound themselves to restore papalism in Germany. The document, even though it was not genuine, had all appearances of being authentic. Philip of Hesse, already suspicious because he had heard of some meetings between certain Catholics and King Ferdinand at Breslau, May, 1527, did not for a moment doubt the authenticity of the Pack paper. According to Pack's document the electors of Mainz and Brandenburg, the dukes of Saxony and Bavaria, and the bishops of Salzburg, Würzburg, and Bamberg were to join King Ferdinand in an attack on the Elector of Saxony. If he refused to surrender Luther, they were to partition his territory, and then dethrone Philip of Hesse and give his lands to Duke George. Even the details of the attack were set forth.

Philip of Hesse rushed to Weimar to inform the stunned Elector of Saxony. Immediate counteraction seemed imperative. By March 9 they had 26,000 men ready for battle. The Hessian troops began to assemble near Herrenbreitungen, and the Saxon troops in the Thuringian forest.

The Elector then hesitated. Should force be used in behalf of the gospel? On May 15 he summoned Melanchthon and Luther to Torgau to ask their advice. Though not doubting the genuineness of the document, they both objected to taking the military offensive. Self-defense, they declared, might be justified, but not offense. Three days later Melanchthon wrote to the Elector pleading that he avoid war for the sake of his own soul's salvation, his children, his country, and his people. Aggression would alienate God, he said.[3] The Landgrave argued that the sword had already been taken by the Catholics and that sudden attack would be advantageous. But the Elector held back.

Philip of Hesse finally sent a copy of the Pack paper to Duke George, belligerently asking whether he intended to keep it. The astonished Duke George pronounced it a forgery and called Pack a knave. Others involved in the matter denied any such conspiracy. Luther thought Duke George's explanations were ambiguous.[4] Melanchthon believed Pack was the culprit and was one of the first to recognize the thieving trickery of the incident.[5] After much squirming and rationalizing, even Pack admitted that the affair had been contrived by him.

Before the forgery was revealed, Philip of Hesse attacked the bishoprics of Würzburg and Bamberg and compelled them to pay indemnities of 40,000 and 20,000 gulden.[6] This precipitous move caused the Catholics in papal territories to retaliate against evangelicals. In Austria the evangelicals were punished not simply as heretics but as criminal malefactors of the highest order, and vendors of Protestant books were treated like poisoners and threatened with death by drowning. In Bavaria the streets were watched; evangelicals were seized and fined; nine were put to death by fire in Landsberg, and twenty-nine by water in Münich. In Cologne,

Adolf Clarenbach was condemned to death because he would not say the pope was the head of the holy church. The Pack incident may not have been entirely responsible for the many violent outbreaks, but it increased tension between Catholics and Protestants. Melanchthon regretted the precipitancy of the affair. "It almost consumes me when I reflect with what stains our good cause is covered by the Pack affair. I can only sustain myself by prayer." [7]

Against this dark background, on November 3, 1528, the Emperor mandated the second Diet of Spires for February 2, 1529. It was later deferred to February 21, and finally opened on March 15. In his mandate the Emperor commanded the princes to assemble

to advise and resolve matters pertaining to the Estates. And if you do not appear within ten days after the day appointed, our envoys and Commissioners will, notwithstanding, discuss and determine affairs with the Estates then and there present, in all respects as if you and others who absented yourselves on slight and frivolous grounds had been present.[8]

This mandate, the Pack Affair, and the renewed friendship between the Pope and Emperor caused anxiety among the evangelicals.

Elector John chose Melanchthon and Agricola to accompany him to Spires. Thus, Melanchthon at the age of thirty-two began his activity as an "international" spokesman and negotiator for the Reformation. But his qualms were almost overpowering. "I was so terrified at first," he wrote to Camerarius, "that I almost passed out; it was as if all the miseries of hell would engulf me." [9]

The Wittenbergers journeyed leisurely to Spires. At Weimar they stopped to watch a tournament, and when the opening of the diet was postponed, Melanchthon visited his mother and brother George at Bretten. It was the last time he saw his mother alive. After returning to Wittenberg he learned of her death. It was during this visit that she asked Philip just what she should believe, in view of the various disputes. After listening to her prayers, he told her to continue as she was without being disturbed by the arguments. At this time she had a daughter, born of her second marriage, who was a nun at Nürnberg; her son George, who had become mayor of Bretten, was an ardent Lutheran.[10] Her third marriage was to Burger Melchoir Hechel.

Two days after the Saxon party arrived in Spires, the diet officially opened, on March 15. Almost immediately the 1526 recess decree which ravored the evangelicals was nullified and all religious innovations forbidden. The Edict of Worms was once more in force! And this arbitrary action by a bare majority of the delegates present filled the reformers with consternation. Melanchthon realized that the move had been planned well in advance, for he noted that an extra large number of bishops were swarming all over the place. Hurriedly Melanchthon expressed himself in a letter to Camerarius:

Two days after we arrived, the commands of the Emperor were made known; they are quite terrible. The decree of the convention at Spires of two years ago has been abrogated, and many heavy penalties are appointed for those who do not observe the new edict. The rest concerns the Turkish war. From this summary of what has been done so far, you can easily perceive in what danger we are. There has never been so large an attendance of high ecclesiastics at any other diet as at this one. Some of them show in their very faces how they hate us and what they are plotting against us. But Christ will have regard to His poor people and save them. In this city we are indeed dregs and offscouring. You know that I have felt that our people are not all they ought to be, but what is done here is not for the correction of our faults, but for the suppression of a good cause. I hope Christ will hinder them and bring to nought the counsels of the nations who long for wars.[11]

The Emperor's throne speech referred to the "evil, grave, perilous, and pernicious doctrines and errors" that had arisen and caused "pitiful revolts, tumults, war, misery, and bloodshed." Because imperial mandates and edicts had been little regarded, the Emperor announced that he was no longer in a mood to tolerate disobedience. He would now urge his Holiness the Pope to summon a general council, and he would forbid anyone to oppose "the ancient usages and customs, or go over to any wrong or strange creed, or attach himself to any new sect." [12]

Melanchthon was even more concerned on account of the unusual signs of nature. A great northern light appeared in January, and he believed it meant trouble. Afterwards Philip observed an unusually strange conjunction of stars which he could not explain. "I am greatly excited by these things!" When the Emperor repealed, revoked, and annuled the

Diet of Spires, Melanchthon believed astrological omens were about to be fulfilled.[13]

The Romanists had elected to be aggressive, and none was more aggressive than John Faber, bishop of Vienna, who publicly declared that the Turks were better than Lutherans, because Turks at least fast and Lutherans do not. "If the alternative were required, I would rather reject the Scriptures than the venerable errors of the Church." Melanchthon said it would take a book as long as the *Iliad* to recite Faber's blasphemies! [14]

The evangelicals did not accept the abrogation of the Diet of Spires without objection. They argued about the throne speech in committee, and debated it on the floor of the diet, but in the final voting the Catholic majority prevailed. The resolution of the Emperor was forced through, on April 6 and 7.[15] The resolution not only reinstated the Edict of Worms, but also forbade further innovations, forbade those who denied transubstantiation to preach in public, and said no one anywhere should be forbidden to celebrate or hear the mass.[16]

Six princes and fourteen cities joined together to present a protest in the name of freedom of conscience and rights of minorities. From this action the term "Protestants" has been derived. This April 19 protest declared that the evangelicals could not abide by the will of the majority, inasmuch as each man is responsible to God. King Ferdinand, presiding in the absence of the Emperor, refused to accept the protest and adjourned the diet on April 24. The evangelicals then sent their protest with an appeal to the Emperor, only to have the bearers of the documents imprisoned.[17]

Melanchthon's part at this diet is not clear. On April 8 he dedicated to Ferdinand an exegesis of Daniel and sent to Ferdinand a poem depicting troubled Germany. In both he pleaded for defense against the Turks and peace in the church.[18] In his commentary on the angels in ch. 10 of Daniel he included a story about Faber, whom he apparently thoroughly disliked.[19] He told how Simon Grynaeus dispatched Faber in an argument, and then related that a strange-looking old man appeared at the door where Melanchthon and Grynaeus were staying and warned Grynaeus to flee. With the help of Philip and a few others, Grynaeus escaped across the Rhine, just moments before a party of the king's henchmen came to seize and imprison him. Melanchthon believed throughout his life that the old man was a supernatural messenger.

Commenting on the necessity of the protest, Melanchthon said:

You see it is a horrible business. There are two factions in the Empire which Faber and Eck, by their foolish and wicked advice, are arming against one another, but it seems to me that the antagonists are afraid of each other and equally sorry for the whole shameful business. They are now trying to get our people to stay here, saying that they will moderate the harshness of the decree. What will come of it I do not know. We should be in no danger if our people would be a little more accommodating and would be fairer about other matters—raising money for the Turkish war and for the expenses of the imperial government.[20]

Melanchthon objected vigorously to the statement about the body and blood of Christ in the Eucharist, which the Catholics included in the imperial resolution. He believed that it was aimed at Zwingli, and forcefully declared no man should be condemned unheard.[21] Melanchthon knew also that it was an attempt to drive a wedge between the Zwinglians and Lutherans and thus localize the Reformation. Although he disagreed sharply with Zwingli, he insisted that Zwingli be allowed to present his case.

On the sixth of May Melanchthon returned to Wittenberg, only to find that perparations were under way for a new meeting to establish an evangelical military alliance with the Zwinglians. He and Luther insisted that such an alliance would have to be based on doctrinal agreement.

While these political manipulations were going on, Melanchthon experienced a wrenching bereavement. His son George, who had been born in Jena on November 25, 1527, died on August 15, 1529. Two days after the event Luther described Melanchthon's feelings in a letter to Jonas:

Last Sunday the Lord took from our Philip his son George. You may imagine how we are trying to console this man, whose heart is so exceedingly tender and easily touched. It is wonderful how hard he takes the boy's death, for he has never before been tried with such a grief. Pray for him all you can, that the Lord may comfort him, and write him a consoling letter with your well-known skill. You know how much depends on this man's life and health. We all grieve and are sad with him, beside my own cares and daily troubles. But the God of the humble and afflicted is not yet conquered, though he is, as always, very weak. Of other things again, when our grief has somewhat abated.[22]

Melanchthon's references to the death of his child are few, and filled with deepest emotion: "I cannot say anything to you about my bitterest grief, except that I have lost my greatest joy, my son George." To Myconius he wrote, "My little son has been taken from me, and I am afflicted with an incredible sorrow." "During the entire summer I have not been without grief and tears, for lately my son who was born in Jena, a most delightful boy, was taken from me." [23] How short the days of man!

Union with the Zwinglians had been suggested as early as 1526, at Spires, by Jacob Sturm and Philip of Hesse, and Duke Ulrich of Württemberg had seconded the move, but theological differences on the Eucharist balked all progress. For several years the Zwinglians and Lutherans had been carrying on an acrimonious pamphlet exchange. Melanchthon saw no possibility of change. However, the concerted moves of the papalists against the evangelicals at the second Diet of Spires bestirred Philip of Hesse to seek a federation.

In March, 1529, John von Minkwitz, a trusted Saxon court counselor, wrote to Elector John at Weimar that a plan was under way at Spires to have Luther and Melanchthon meet Zwingli and Oecolampadius at Nürnberg to work out an agreement to end the schism on the sacrament.[24] While at the diet Melanchthon received a letter from Oecolampadius earnestly entreating him not to cast off the Swiss. As if wanting to justify the bitterness of the past pamphlet war, Oecolampadius said, "You must certainly know that we are not happy when everyone says that we like Judas and the cattle eat nothing in the Lord's Supper except bread." [25]

A secret, temporary, tentative alliance was actually effected on April 22 between the Landgrave Philip of Hesse, the Elector of Saxony, and the cities of Strassburg, Nürnberg, and Ulm. Agreement on the Eucharist was all that was needed to make the alliance binding. Desirous of cementing a solid front against the Roman Catholic bloc, on that same day, the Landgrave wrote to Zwingli saying an attempt was being made to bring the Zwinglians and Wittenbergers together "so that if a merciful and almighty God grants us His favor, they may come to some Scriptural agreement about that doctrine and live in harmony, as becomes Christians . . . for the papists say that we who profess the entire and clear Word of God do not agree among ourselves on the doctrines of our religion." [26]

Despite the tentative alliance Melanchthon told the Elector personally and then in writing that he opposed meeting with the Swiss. He did not think the time was propitious for a discussion and suggested a postponement so as not to alienate the Landgrave with a direct refusal. However, he expressed willingness to confer, should the Elector so command.[27] Melanchthon and Luther still remembered the Pack Affair and feared the Landgrave might be leading up to some impetuous action which would bring disgrace on the cause, and possibly war. He was not ready finally to alienate the Roman Catholic political forces, and felt that reliance on God was better than running down to Egypt or up to Assyria.[28]

In spite of Luther and Melanchthon, the Elector consented to the holding of a colloquy and chose Nürnberg as the proper place. Melanchthon and Luther acquiesced reluctantly. "I have no fear of considering this thing with Oecolampadius or any others," Melanchthon wrote, "but I know that the Zwinglian doctrine of the Sacrament of the body and blood of Christ is not true, and can in no way be justified before God. I am deeply grieved that so many people have fallen so hastily into such error; one can almost trace the anger of God in this." [29]

Landgrave Philip of Hesse changed the meeting place to Marburg and did not bother with Melanchthon's suggestion that some neutral Roman Catholics be invited so as to dispel rumors that a political conspiracy was brewing, for that was precisely Philip's object. Disagreement on the Eucharist was simply a snag. Philip of Hesse sent invitations to Zwingli of Zurich, Haller of Berne, Oecolampadius of Basel, Hedio and Bucer of Strassburg, Brentz of Swabian Hall, Urban Regius of Augsburg, and Schwebel of Zweibrücken. Melanchthon and Luther in a joint note formally accepted the Landgrave's invitation, saying they hoped unanimity would be achieved.[30]

The principal opponents at Marburg had radically different views of the Eucharist. Zwingli believed that Christ was not physically present in the supper, that the entire sacrament was a memorial. "Do this in memory of me." He did not understand how Christ, who was supposedly in heaven at the right hand of the Father, could be in two places at once. Luther believed that Christ was physically present in the Supper, that when Christ spoke to his disciples, saying, "This is my body," that he meant the words literally, that the body and blood of Christ were truly in the bread and wine. Luther carved *"Hoc est corpus meum"* on the conference table to remind him of this. He could not accept papal transubstantiation, but he could not reject physical presence.

Melanchthon's views were by no means set, but one thing he knew: he did not agree with Zwingli. He found much support for Luther's views in Scripture and in the ancient fathers, and while he did not regard this as final, he said, "I would rather die than see our cause polluted by a union with the Zwinglians." [31] Although there are many learned men among the adherents of Zwingli, wrote Melanchthon, "I know that what Zwingli and his followers write about the sacrament is not true . . . and it is not a good thing that the Landgrave should have much to do with the Zwinglians." [32]

Melanchthon regarded the Lord's Supper as a mystery. He did not understand *how* Christ's body and blood could be in the bread and the wine, but "in some way this holy body takes on the shape of bread." [33] In this Melanchthon was closer to the Roman Catholics than to the Zwinglians, and this was a major factor in preventing union with the left wing of the Reformation.

When the Lutherans and Zwinglians first began quarreling over the nature of Christ's presence in the Supper, Melanchthon foresaw a wrangling over mere phrases, and for himself said, "I commit the matter to Christ that he according to his wisdom may care for his glory." He would say only that Christ was mysteriously present according to his divine-human nature. [34]

Until 1527 Melanchthon appeared to agree with Luther, but he nurtured secret doubts. In December, 1527, he expressed some doubts about the doctrine of the Lord's Supper, but Luther reassured him for the time being. [35] Unable to go along with either Zwingli, the Catholics, or Luther, in March of 1528 Melanchthon resorted to the mystery of divine appointment:

That Christ gives us his body and blood does not depend upon the prayers of the priest or of the people, for that would be magical. I prefer that it should be referred to the institution of Christ. For as the sun rises daily by the divine appointment, so the body of Christ is in the Church wherever the Church is. No sufficient proof is offered that the body of Christ cannot be in many places. Christ is exalted above all creatures and is everywhere.[36]

But Melanchthon was not satisfied. "The strife about the Lord's Supper troubles me so much that in my life I have not found anything so painful . . . but I find no reason to separate from Luther." [37] For several years Melanchthon struggled with the problem. In 1537 he wrote a letter in which he said "not a single day nor night has passed for ten years in which I have not thought on this subject." [38]

At Spires Melanchthon defended the right of the Zwinglians to be heard, but he himself did not go to Marburg with an open mind, as his letters show:

I am not willing to be the author or defender of a new dogma in the church. . . . Instead of theologians the Zwinglians seem to me gradually to have become sophists, for I see that they rationalize and philosophize about the doctrines of Christ. It is on this account that I have not mixed in the controversy on the Eucharist. But so soon as I shall have leisure, I will express my view. They represent Christ as sitting in one place, as Homer does his Jove living with the Aethiopians. To deny the presence of Christ in the Eucharist seems to me most contrary to the Scripture. . . . It is not right to defend an impious doctrine or to confirm the power of those who maintain an impious doctrine, lest the poison spread.[39]

On September 29, 1529, Zwingli, Oecolampadius, Bucer, Hedio, and Jacob Sturm arrived in Marburg. The next day, Luther, Melanchthon, Jonas, Cruciger, Menius, Brentz, Osiander, and Stephen Agricola arrived. They were all royally entertained in the castle of the Landgrave.

In anticipation of the discussion with the Zwinglians, sometime during the summer of 1529 Melanchthon and Luther, aided by court lawyers, drew up a preliminary set of beliefs. These articles were probably used as a guide by the Wittenbergers at Marburg.[40] These came to be known as the Schwabach Articles because they were carried to Schleiz, to a meeting of the princes on October 5 or 6, and were presented by representatives of the Elector and Margrave George of Brandenburg at a convention held at Schwabach, on October 16. Later Melanchthon incorporated them in the Augsburg Confession.

On October 1, at 6:00 A.M., the Marburg Colloquy began. Knowing that Zwingli and Luther were easily roused to anger, the prince paired Melanchthon with Zwingli and Luther with Oecolampadius for the initial discussions. Bucer reported the meeting between Zwingli and Melanchthon, saying they discussed the divinity of Christ, original sin, the Scriptures, the Trinity, and the Eucharist, but came to no conclusions.[41] In a report for the Elector, Melanchthon said that he found Zwingli poorly informed as a theologian and in error on many points. Among other matters Melanchthon gathered that Zwingli believed a sin was committed only when one actually transgressed, and that he did not believe in original sin. He also said that Zwingli denied the Holy Spirit was given to sinful man in the Word and in the Sacraments, and that Zwingli was inclined to work righteousness in the plan of redemption. In another report Melanchthon added that he and Zwingli disagreed on the Eucharist as well as on the ministry of the Word and the Sacraments. He did not say he acquiesced in reading "This signifies" for "This is" in Christ's words of institution as Zwingli later claimed.[42]

The meeting between Luther and Oecolampadius was equally unproductive.[43]

The next day, again at six o'clock, they gathered for discussion. Although there were about fifty people present, the meetings were not open to the public. After a word of welcome and explanation of the purpose of the colloquy, Luther delivered the opening address. He explained that the Wittenbergers were present by request rather than by choice, and that they did not expect any real agreement. The Swiss, nevertheless, expressed their willingness to consider doctrinal unity and said their views were already in print. At Zwingli's suggestion they immediately began discussing the Eucharist, and more specifically the location of Christ's body. Could it be in more than one place? Whether Christ was or was not actually present in the Lord's Supper depended on how this question was answered. Luther and Melanchthon on the basis of the Trinity and the Incarnation said yes; Zwingli on the basis of Christ's exaltation to the right hand of God said no. At the end of the day it was clear that the different approaches to the problem precluded agreement.

In the afternoon of October 3, the colloquy was terminated with apologies all around. Although the talks had been relatively calm, Luther said he was sorry for speaking harshly. Oecolampadius pleaded for continuation of the discussions for the sake of church unity. Zwingli, with tears in his eyes, said he would rather be on friendly terms with Luther and Melanchthon than with any other two men.[44]

Anxious that the meeting not be a complete failure, Chancellor Feige called a private session the evening of October 3. Luther proposed that they issue a joint statement declaring their recent pamphlet arguments were against those who *totally* rejected the presence of the body and blood in the Supper. The Zwinglians, however, could not subscribe to this.[45]

The disputants did draw up fourteen points on which they agreed and added a fifteenth on which they said they still disagreed. It later developed that the fourteen points were altered by Zwingli when he presented his *Fidei Ratio* to the Augsburg Diet in 1530.[46] The fifteenth point read in part:

Although we are not at this time agreed, as to whether the true Body and Blood of Christ are bodily present in the bread and wine, nevertheless the one party should show to the other Christian love, so far as conscience can permit, and both should fervently pray God Almighty, that, by His Spirit, He would confirm us in the true understanding.[47]

But matters were not as harmonious as this fifteenth article indicated. "When it was all over," said Melanchthon, "the Zwinglians asked to be considered brethren, but this we were not willing to grant by any means. They have attacked us so severely that we wonder with what kind of a conscience they would hold us as brethren if they thought we were in error."[48] This antagonistic attitude points to Melanchthon's real role in this colloquy which was an attempt to unite the Lutherans with the "left wing" of the Reformation. Luther at one point was apparently willing to be ambiguous enough to accept the Zwinglians until Melanchthon pointed out that this would close the door to any agreement with the "right wing." Union with the Roman Catholics was attempted at Augsburg the following year without success.

With the failure of the Marburg Colloquy the first step of the Reformation toward ecumenicity had failed. Whether it was the result of political interests or the inevitable outcome of the individual interpreting Scripture according to right reason can only be conjectured.

. . . To Confession

HE PROTESTANT OUTLOOK AT THE BEGINNING OF THE YEAR 1530 was far from hopeful. In the preceding year attempts to unify evangelical Germany had miserably failed. Ambassadors John Eckinger, Alexius Faventraut, and Michael Kaden, who carried the Protestant appeal of Spires to Emperor Charles V, had not only been imprisoned in Italy but under threat of death were forbidden to communicate with their rulers in Germany. The Emperor had finally concluded his conquests in Italy, and after nine years' absence from Germany was at last in a position to do something about religion. The Emperor and the Pope had composed their differences in a treaty concluded at Barcelona, June 29, 1529, and the two were actually living together in the same palace in Bologna, each having a key to the door connecting their quarters. The Emperor had pledged himself to bring the Protestant dissidents back to the fold and "to avenge the insult offered to Christ."

When the Emperor was crowned, on February 24, 1530, in the Church of San Petronio in Bologna, the German electors were snubbed; they were not even summoned to the ceremony. Only Philip of the Palatinate was present, and he arrived by chance. Spanish nobles performed the functions ordinarily performed by the electors. Although the wooden gallery connecting the palace and the church collapsed just after Charles crossed it and some regarded this as an omen that he would be the last emperor to be crowned in Italy, Charles himself saw in this a sign of benevolent protection. In receiving the crown from Pope Clement VII, Charles swore to defend the pope and the possessions, dignities, and rights

of the church. In the eyes of the world once again the spiritual and
temporal realms were united, but neither the Pope nor the Emperor felt
secure.[1]

With the king of France temporarily subdued, only the unresolved
questions of religion in Germany seemed to bar the way to political and
ecclesiastical unity. Campeggio and other papal representatives, therefore,
urged Charles to fulfill his promise to unify Christendom by the use of
sword and fire, if other means should fail to "exterminate the poisonous
plants." In a formal speech, May 9, 1530, Campeggio warned that if firm
action were not quickly taken, "there is cause to fear that this devilish
pest will not only spread over the rest of Germany but contaminate the
whole Christian world." [2] Campeggio went on to name the leading
evangelicals and to charge them with corrupting the true faith and under-
mining imperial authority for their own ends. He referred to them as
"murderers," "thieves," "rapacious wolves," "malicious and perverted
persons," and "cursed ones." If they refused to obey, Campeggio called
for the Emperor to use interdict, excommunication, confiscation of
property, and forfeiture of life.

However, Charles's former confessor, Garcia de Loaysa, now cardinal
of Osma, advised Charles to proceed more diplomatically. "One must use
flattery, then forceful threats; next presents and worldly goods; in this
way you must take God from the Cross." [3]

Meanwhile, Ferdinand, under false pretenses, was attempting to negotiate with Elector John of Saxony. His object was to gain time to allow
the Emperor to make plans, and to give the Elector a false sense of
security.[4]

To make matters even worse, the evangelical princes appeared to be
hopelessly divided. The Protestants met at Nürnberg on January 6, 1530,
to formulate a common course of action. Instead they had quarreled over
principles and had separated without reaching any conclusion. Melanchthon and Luther insisted that the gospel should not be defended by force.
Melanchthon wrote to the Elector: "It is not lawful to take arms against
the Emperor even though he come with violence. Everyone must profess
the Gospel at his own peril." [5] Other evangelicals did not agree. The failure of the January meeting clearly indicated that the princes were not all
willing to submit to the Emperor.

Among these ill winds was one strange crosscurrent. Suleiman II, the Ottoman Turk, whose victorious army had swept across southern Europe, was already at the gates of Vienna, challenging the army of Ferdinand, brother of Charles. Victory for Suleiman meant that all Europe might become Mohammedan. Charles, recognizing this imminent possibility, desired a unified Germany as an ally, and also felt that the Germans who were in danger would welcome union.

EMPEROR CHARLES V

THE TURKISH MENACE
(*Woodcut by Hans Huldenmundt*)

In January of 1530 Charles V mandated a diet to meet at Augsburg on April 8. The imperial rescript invited all to participate in a discussion of religious differences so as to allay divisions and antipathies. Every care would be taken, the rescript said,

to give a charitable hearing to every man's opinion, thoughts and notions, to understand them, to weigh them, to bring and reconcile them to a unity in Christian truth, to dispose of everything that has not been rightly explained or treated of on the one side or on the other, to see to it that one single, true religion may be accepted and held by us all, and that we all live in one common church and in unity.[6]

This imperial mandate aroused varied reactions among the German princes. The Elector of Saxony was greatly pleased by the conciliatory tone of the mandate and by the fact that Charles addressed him as "Dear Uncle." He wrote exuberant letters to his fellow princes.[7] Philip of Hesse remembered that Charles had imprisoned the "protest" commission, and that he himself had been charged with treason for attempting to put an evangelical book into the hands of the Emperor. The cities of Strassburg and Ulm doubted that the council would be impartial. Others, like Nürnberg, supported the move but hoped for little.[8] These reactions to the Emperor's invitation indicated clearly that there was neither political nor religious harmony among the Protestants.

Feeling that he would have to justify his confiscation of church property and his departure from papal practices, the Elector summoned his "learned counselors"—Luther, Jonas, Melanchthon, Musa of Jena, Agricola, and Spalatin—and asked them to come immediately to Torgau, bringing with them statements about doctrines and evangelical practices, so that "it may be fully decided, whether, or in what manner, or how far, we who have received the pure doctrine, may and can enter upon negotiation before God and with a good conscience." The following week, March 21, the Elector again urged them to come to Torgau in all haste to attend to the many things demanding attention.[9] The Diet of Augsburg would convene within a few weeks.

On March 27 Melanchthon quickly rode the thirty-five miles to Torgau. He took with him a document that has been referred to as the Torgau Articles, but to this day these articles have not been definitely identified. It is believed that Melanchthon with the aid of Jonas and Luther had spent the preceding two weeks in writing a document called *Judgment of the Learned at Wittenberg on Ceremonies and What Is Therewith Connected, To Be Presented to the Emperor,* and that he took this to Elector John on March 27.[10]

Apparently the Wittenbergers thought that a statement about ceremonies would be enough, but they were also ready to present doctrines to show that the gospel was being preached.[11]

Sometime between March 27 and April 3 Melanchthon returned to Wittenberg, and immediately left with Luther, Veit Dietrich, and Jonas for Torgau. On April 4 they joined the electoral party which left for Augsburg. The entourage numbered 160 persons, including such dignitaries as the young John Frederick, Francis Duke of Lüneburg, Wolfgang Prince of Anhalt, Albert Count of Mansfeld, and seventy lesser nobles. George Spalatin, John Agricola, and Kaspar Aquila joined them on the way.

By Friday, April 15, this electoral party reached Coburg. Here they all observed a solemn Easter Sunday and rested for a week. Inasmuch as Luther was under the ban of the Empire, the Elector thought he and Veit Dietrich should be left behind at Coburg. After wending its way through Bamberg, Forscheim, Nürnberg, Roth, Weissenburg, and Donauwörth, the Elector's party arrived in Augsburg on May 2.

While at Coburg Melanchthon was commissioned to write a vindication of the way in which the Elector had fostered religion in his lands. He was still working on this vindication on May 2 when the electoral party finally entered Augsburg. On May 4 Melanchthon wrote a letter to Luther in which he said, "I have made the preface of our Apology somewhat more rhetorical than I had written at Coburg. But in a short time I will bring, or if the Prince will not permit this, I will send it." He wrote similarly to Dietrich.[12] No one knows the exact form of this first draft of the Augsburg Confession but the evangelicals had to alter their original plans simply to defend the Elector's innovations in religion, for the basic Protestant doctrines had been dramatically and unexpectedly attacked as heretical. A sensational book, compiled by none other than John Eck, had just hit the streets of Augsburg.

This new attack on the evangelicals, which threatened to frustrate all attempts to be impartial in the diet, started on January 12 when Ferdinand asked the college at Vienna to survey Luther's writings for old and new heresies, changes in the sacraments, alterations of ceremonies, seditious language, and so forth.[13] To facilitate the research he listed the categories under which the passages might be filed, and to be sure that the research was extensive, he extended the request to other universities.

When the Bavarian dukes William IV and Louis X received a copy of Ferdinand's request, they instructed their papal theologians at Ingolstadt "at once to make a complete summary and catalogue of all such heresies, wrong doctrines and slanderous statements, and to indicate how these views may be refuted so that we may obtain the list from you when we need it." [14]

The final task of editing and arranging was given to the theologians at Ingolstadt, principally Eck, under whose name the *Four Hundred and Four Articles* "extracted from the writings of those who are causing schism in the church" were published. Eck with his intellect, memory, eloquence, pugnacity, sophistry, and boldness was admirably fitted for the task and did not hesitate to claim credit for the finished product.

In the 404 articles were passages from the writings of Luther, Melanchthon, Carlstadt, Zwingli, and others—passages which were frequently cited out of context, labeled heretical and schismatic, and arrayed with quotations from the writings of Hubmeyer, Denk, and others who were commonly regarded by both Protestants and Catholics as heretics. [15] In the published preface Eck characterized himself as the well-known, victorious defender of the faith, and offered to debate his points with any "assailant of the Catholic truth."

Articles 1-41 were those doctrines of Luther previously condemned by the papal bull, Exsurge Domine; 42-54, the articles drawn by Eck for dispute at Leipzig; 55-61, articles written by Eck for public debate at Baden in 1526; 62-65, articles published by Eck for dispute at Berne in 1528; 66-169, a variety of statements pertaining to dogma, drawn from the writings of the reformers; 170-332, a collection of statements touching on ecclesiastical matters; and 333-404, citations alluding to political affairs. Eck did not follow Ferdinand's outline, nor did he indicate how the errors were to be refuted, for he hoped to make a dramatic public refutation at Augsburg. Eck quoted from a score or more of writings, but he singled out Luther for special vilification and named Melanchthon, Bugenhagen, Jonas, Lange, Jacob Strauss, Antonius Zimmermann, and Carlstadt as the inner circle of the "brood of vipers." A great number of items were aimed at Melanchthon. Cited out of context and left unexplained, many of these articles made the reformers appear unchristian, malicious, carnal-minded, and lawless. The following are some that were culled from the writings of Philip:

84. Reason pretends to give Christ honor by reflecting and meditating upon his death, but this is nothing to Christ. (Melanchthon, Super Ioan. 142.)

86. The opinion is certain that all things are done by God, both good and evil, . . . the adultery of David, the betrayal of Judas, the call of Paul, i.e., God wills sin. (Melanchthon, Super epistola ad Rom. 29.31 Floriani.)

133. Jerome superstitiously extols virginity . . . (Melanchthon.)

156. The reason why the Mosaic Law was abrogated is that it was impossible for it to be kept. (Melanchthon.)

162. The Gospel commands nothing whatever (Melanchthon), neither does it prohibit (Luther).

167. Just as circumcision is nothing, so also baptism and the partaking of the Lord's Supper. (Melanchthon.)

176. The commandments of God are impossible. (Melanchthon.)

198. All the works of man, however praiseworthy in appearance, are altogether vicious and are sins worthy of death. (Melanchthon.)

235. In the Eucharist, the substance of bread and wine remains; because transubstantiation is a figment of sophists and Romanists. (Pirkheimer, Melanchthon, Luther.)

396. The word of Christ that many false prophets shall arise and deceive many, I verily think was spoken with reference to the public universities. (Melanchthon.)[16]

Eck sent a copy to the Emperor, saying he was ready to substantiate all his charges before the Imperial Diet. In an unpublished dedication, sent only to the Emperor, Eck extolled Charles as the God-sent saviour of the Christian church and empire, and accused Luther of creating in Germany a "whirlpool of godlessness." "He calls the bishops 'worms and idols'; the schools of theology 'synagogues of Satan'; theologians 'bats'; secular princes 'louse's eggs, fools, and insane drunkards.' . . . He is arming the Germans in order that they may bathe in the blood of Pope and Cardinals. He has produced a vast offspring, much worse than himself, bringing forth broods of vipers." [17] Eck called upon the Emperor to wipe out the despoilers of the church. He dated the dedication, March 14, 1530, and signed it, "Your most worshipful and Catholic Majesty's obedient servant John Eck."

Eck's 404 Articles were translated into German and widely circulated among the people. When the Wittenbergers upon their arrival in Augsburg saw this new attack, they were amazed and alarmed. Melanchthon penned a letter to Luther on May 4 in which he said: "Eck, the repetition of whose name sounds like the cackling of crows: Ek, Ek, Ek, Ek, has compiled a big batch of inferences. He requests the rulers to appoint a disputation against the Lutherans." [18] Until Eck's book appeared the Protestants thought only of defending their ceremonial practices, but the 404 Articles made mandatory a clear statement of their doctrines. Eck maliciously classed them with the Sacramentarians, Anabaptists, and fanatics, and the Lutherans felt compelled not only to state their beliefs but to condemn the positions of others so that subversive rumors might be stopped. New plans had to be formulated; not simply a vindication, but a confession of faith had to be prepared. [19]

Through the diplomatic channels of Elector John, Melanchthon learned that the Emperor would not have time for a long discussion, and so he resolved not to answer the voluble accusations of Eck but to present a positive, clear confession of faith. [20] Significantly, after May 4, no mention is made of the "long and rhetorical preface."

This new turn of events cut short the influence of Luther on the composition of the confession. There was little time for consultation, hardly enough time to have the document finished before the arrival of the Emperor, and so Melanchthon had to fall back on his own resources. Using the Schwabach and Marburg Articles which he had helped compose, Melanchthon drew up a set of doctrines to fit the changed situation. The extent to which Melanchthon expanded these previous documents is indicated in the fact that of the 1,682 German words in the first 17 articles of the Confession only 438 originated in the Schwabach and Marburg Articles.

By May 11 the new work was ready to be sent to Luther. Philip wrote:

> Our apology is sent to you, though it is more truly a confession, for the Emperor does not have time to hear long discussions. Nevertheless I have said those things which I thought to be either specifically profitable or proper. With this design I have brought together about all the articles of faith, because Eck has published the most diabolical slanders against us. Against these I wished to oppose a remedy. Do you in accordance with your spirit judge of the whole writing. [21]

The Elector wrote to Luther the same day:

> After you and our other learned men at Wittenberg, according to our gracious purpose and desire, had brought into a summary statement the

articles which are in controversy about religion, we will not conceal from you that now Philip Melanchthon here has further revised them and has brought them into a form which we herewith send you. It is our gracious desire that you should not hesitate further to revise and consider them. And if they please you, or if you think to add or subtract anything, note it on the margin, and in order that we may be ready at the arrival of his Imperial Majesty which we expect soon, send back the same, well secured and sealed, immediately by this messenger.[22]

At this time the Confession probably consisted of the preface which was later abandoned, some articles of belief, and a section of articles justifying the Lutheran removal of religious abuses. Articles 20 and 28 on faith and good works and ecclesiastical power were not yet written.

Four days later, on May 15, Luther sent his reply:

I have read over M. Philip's Apology. It pleases me very well, and I know of nothing therein to be improved or changed; nor would it become me, for I cannot move so softly and lightly. Christ our Lord grant that it may bring much and great fruit, as we hope and pray.[23]

Apparently two copies of the Confession, one in German and one in Latin, were sent to Luther.[24] It is commonly assumed from the May 15 letter that Luther returned the copy or copies with his approval. However, definite mention of such a return is not made until May 24. Is it possible that the messenger on his return from Coburg was delayed? On May 22, Melanchthon wrote to Luther, apparently assuming that Luther still possessed a copy:

In the Apology we change many things daily. I have taken out the article *On Vows,* because it was too brief, and have supplied its place with another on the same subject somewhat longer. I am now also treating of the power of the keys. I wish you would run over the articles of faith. If you think there is nothing defective in them, we will treat the rest as best we can. For they must be changed and adapted to circumstances.[25]

Possibly this letter was merely delayed; possibly Luther did not receive it at all. From May 15 to June 29, the extant letters of Luther make not one allusion to the Confession. Neither do the letters of Melanchthon to Coburg from May 22 to June 25. Why? Luther had not received his mail. He began to complain bitterly that he had been forgotten by his friends at Augsburg: "Three full weeks of continued silence," "a whole month." When letters did finally arrive, Luther was so enraged that he refused to read them.[26]

Luther did not see the completed Confession until after it had been presented to the Emperor. This evidence, while it shows that Luther had little to do with the actual writing of the Augsburg Confession, should not be taken as an indication that Luther was deliberately snubbed or that Melanchthon was proceeding heedlessly onward.

As the days advanced, the significance of the coming Diet seemed to fill the very atmosphere. With the arrival of more and more imperial, papal, and princely delegates, the city buzzed with rumors and predictions. In deepest anguish Melanchthon began to realize that the future of Protestantism might depend on the wording that he put into the apology, and that the apology might tip the scales for war or peace. He did not relish the task nor the acid criticisms of his fellow theologians. Throughout May and June, Melanchthon endured mental and physical agony. To his brother he voiced his torment:

> I could almost believe that I was born under an unlucky star. For what distresses me most has come upon me. I could easily bear poverty, hunger, contempt, and other misfortunes, but what utterly prostrates me is strife and controversy. I had to compose the Confession which was to be given to the Emperor and the Estates. In spirit I foresaw insults, wars, devastation, battles. And now does it depend upon me to divert such great calamity? O God, in whom I trust, help thou me. . . . Dear brother, I dare not drop the matter so long as I live. But not by my fault shall peace be destroyed. Other theologians wanted to compose the Confession. Would God they had had their way. Perhaps they could have done it better. Now they are dissatisfied with mine, and want it changed. One cries out here, another there. But I must maintain my principle of omitting everything that increases the bitterness. God is my witness that my intentions have been good. My reward is that I shall be hated.[27]

Many assailed, none assisted, sighed Melanchthon. He sweated over every portion of the Apology, for he wanted to state the core of evangelical doctrine without alienating the Roman Catholics. War with all its horror and destruction, he believed, would be the result of his failure.[28]

Emaciated, exhausted, nervous, and anxious, Melanchthon spent many moments in tears.[29] At times he felt the Apology was too mild and pacific, made so by his earnest desire for ecumenical peace; and at other times he was convinced that the Confession was too severe and polemic, made so by his keen understanding of the implications of the Protestant-Catholic differences.

An early letter of Luther's written on May 12 shows that he understood the turmoil and the labor of Melanchthon, and felt impelled to warn him against overexertion. "I command you and all your company that they compel you, under pain of excommunication, to take care of your body, and not to kill yourself from imaginary obedience to God. We serve God also by taking holiday and rest." [30]

The composing of the Confession moved slowly; nobody seemed satisfied, least of all Melanchthon. He consulted incessantly with assembled Protestant theologians, added words, omitted phrases, and reconstructed sentences. He worried over each preposition, verb, and noun. On May 28 a report of the Nürnberg delegates Kress and Volkamer indicated the progress of the Confession: "The counsellors and theologians of the Elector are holding daily sessions on the Confession of faith, with the purpose of giving it such a form that it cannot be passed over, but must be heard." [31]

Three days later another letter of the Nürnberg representatives related that they had received a copy of the Confession, in Latin, without a preface and epilogue, and that the German copy was daily being rewritten.[32] On June 3 they wrote home saying the Latin preface had been written, but that the epilogue and some articles were still being worked over by the Saxon theologians.[33] Five days later the Nürnberg delegates reported, "The Saxon Confession of faith which we last sent you [the Latin] has been laid before the preachers and jurists for examination." Later they wrote, "The Saxons are not yet done with it." [34]

The May 31 copy of the Confession which the Nürnberg representatives sent home showed that the changes still being made, while important for a detailed study of the Confession, were not vital. Far more important was the preface, now in its third revision. In it Melanchthon affirmed his faith in the Emperor's justice and mercy, praised the Elector's merits and loyalty, and detailed the well-regulated church affairs in Saxony. He omitted the statements that the Scriptures were to guide in matters of faith and that one had a religious duty to protest abuses. This diplomatic approach indicated the Saxons still hoped the Emperor could be convinced of the truth of their doctrine and the rightness of the changes in ecclesiastical practices. Melanchthon's letter of May 22 to Luther also indicated that the Saxons expected the Emperor to be impartial.[35] But even more important the records show that the Saxons were not thinking of a common confession, only of a Saxon confession. As late as June 8 the chancellors of Brandenburg and Kress of Nürnberg objected to this exclusiveness; they thought that other princes and estates should be included.[36]

By June 15 a change was evident. Although the document was still referred to as the Saxon Confession, a sense of unity and mutual distress impelled the Protestant princes to present a common statement of faith. A noted Lutheran writer, Schmauk, later spoke of this change as "the hand of God in the formation of the Augsburg Confession." The Nürnberg delegates' letter of June 15 revealed the change:

> The Saxon Confession of faith is finished in German. We herewith send it to you. It does not yet have the preface and the conclusion, and as Philip Melanchthon has stated, he has not put any part of those into German, because he thinks that this same preface and conclusion may probably be presented not alone in the name of the Elector, but in common in the name of all the Lutheran princes and estates.

The Nürnberg delegates asked that the document be carefully studied and an opinion given on joining with the Saxon to present a common confession.[37]

By June 19 the Confession still needed an epilogue, a careful examination, rearranging, but apparently no more articles. However, the work on the Confession was temporarily suspended. June 15 marked the arrival of Emperor Charles V.

A Cause Committed to God

OLLOWING THE CORONATION AT BOLOGNA, CHARLES V journeyed toward Augsburg, "accompanied and preceded by the usual hangers-on and court dalliers, each with his own cause to further or favor to seek." [1] Papal legate Campeggio went ahead to prepare for the Catholic case. His dispatches to the Emperor were filled with accounts of plots, deals, and schemes at Augsburg.

The Elector John, with a gesture to diplomacy, sent advance representatives to the Emperor to pay his respects, but these did not fare very well. The Elector thought the Emperor had prejudged the very thing to be considered, and Charles accused the Elector of flagrant disregard of the Edict of Worms. Also just prior to the Emperor's arrival in Augsburg copies of Luther's *Admonition to All the Clergy Assembled at the Diet of Augsburg* were being circulated and creating much comment, for in fighting words Luther called for drastic reforms. The bowstring of tension could hardly have been pulled tighter. Melanchthon believed that all the basic decisions already had been made at meetings at Innsbrück, one of the places where the Emperor stopped on his way to Augsburg. [2]

Augsburg was extravagantly prepared for the royal arrival. The imperial baggage train arrived a week ahead and created an enormous din in the city. At 5:00 A.M., June 15, the electors and princes assembled in the city hall. As soon as dust clouds from the Emperor's entourage appeared on the horizon, cannons began to boom. About one o'clock virtually the entire city awaited the Emperor near the Lech River bridge, and princes great and small wrangled about precedence and rank. After about an hour's wait the imperial soldiery rode forward and then the Emperor himself. A great shout went up. Charles dismounted and shook hands with each prince. Considering this an opportune moment to further papal interests, Campeggio blessed the entire group. With the conspicuous exception of Elector John and Landgrave Philip of Hesse, the company knelt for the rite. Following an official welcome by the Archbishop of Mainz, the royal procession formed in order of rank.

First marched two companies of newly recruited *landsknechts,* guards of the imperial city. Behind these came the mounted soldiers of the six electors, with the 160 horsemen of Elector John leading, followed by cavalry of the electorates of the Palatinate, Brandenburg, Cologne, Mainz, and Trier. All were magnificently arrayed. The red-coated Bavarian cavalry, though without legal rank, also marched. Then came the Spanish, Bohemian, and German lords in their velvet and silk uniforms. Two rows of trumpeters heralded His Majesty. The Elector of Saxony rode immediately in front of the Emperor and as lord high marshall bore the gleaming sword of authority. King Ferdinand and Cardinal Campeggio rode behind the Emperor, followed by German cardinals, bishops, prelates, and ambassadors. The militia of Augsburg marched last.

Several hours later, between eight and nine o'clock in the evening, this colorful procession entered the city and was met near St. Leonard's Church by the town clergy lustily singing *"Advenisti desiderabilis."* In the cathedral an impressive "Te Deum" ceremony was conducted, during which the Emperor twice knelt on the bare stone floor. But again the Elector John and Landgrave Philip conspicuously did not even uncover their heads during the blessing. As the delegates sensed rebellion, excitement began to mount.

Following the cathedral service the entire procession marched to the Emperor's quarters in the bishop's palace. Although it was past 10:00 P.M., the Emperor asked for a private meeting with Elector John, Margrave George, Duke Francis, and Landgrave Philip. In his private quarters they were vehemently harangued by Ferdinand, who spoke for his brother Charles. He demanded that the Protestants join in the Corpus Christi scheduled for the next morning and that they not have any gospel preaching in Augsburg.[3] The Elector was too stunned to speak, but

Margrave George and Landgrave Philip boldly stepped forward to say that the Emperor had no jurisdictional right to dictate to their consciences and that Christ did not institute his Eucharist for adoration in the Corpus Christi procession. George declared that gospel preaching, far from being heretical, was in complete harmony with the early church, as seen in Augustine and Hilary.[4] The Emperor's face betrayed his mounting anger, but George, looking directly into the eyes of Charles, said: "Before I let anyone take from me the Word of God and ask me to deny my God, I would rather kneel down here before Your Imperial Majesty and let you cut off my head." The Emperor quickly stammered in broken German, "Not cut off head! Not cut off head!" The princes were given until the following morning to make their final decision.[5]

Those Protestant delegates who had not been present at the meeting were roused out of bed and informed of the new situation.[6] Spalatin and Melanchthon and a few other theologians, sensing the importance of the proposed Corpus Christi procession, stayed up the rest of the night working on a statement saying why the Protestants could not participate. In the Corpus Christi the bread, believed by the Roman Catholics to be the actual body of Christ, was carried aloft; and the Lutherans considered this elevation of the Host idolatrous. In their statement they said: "The Sacrament was not instituted to be worshipped like the brazen serpent of the Jews. We are here to confess the truth and not to confirm abuses." [7]

At 7:00 A.M. the Protestant princes, with Margrave George designated as their spokesman, gathered before the Emperor. "My ancestors and I have always supported you," said the Margrave, "but in the things of God, the commandments of God compel me to put aside the command of man. If, as we are told, death is to be the fate of those who persevere in the true doctrine, I am ready to suffer it." Handing the Emperor the Protestant reply, he stated, "We will not countenance with our presence these human traditions, opposed to the Word of God; on the contrary, we declare unitedly that we must expel them from the church, lest those in it who are still sound should be affected with the deadly poison." [8]

Elector John was not present; the strain of the previous day had been too much. For three hours the Emperor harangued the princes, but they steadfastly refused to participate in the Corpus Christi festival. Charles, a few Catholic princes, and less than a hundred townsmen took part.[9]

Charles, infuriated, threatened to disband the diet and was prevented from doing so only by his counselors, who warned that the action would result in civil war!

The Protestant princes called on the indisposed Elector and resolved to send a formal reply to Charles concerning gospel preaching and godless ceremonies. Chancellor Brück wrote a long legal opinion on why the Protestants could not interdict gospel preaching, and the Saxon theologians, led by Melanchthon, prepared a considered opinion on "whether the princes without violation of conscience can take part in the procession of Corpus Christi." On the following morning, June 17, the Protestant princes formally told the Emperor that they could not forbid preaching or participate in the Corpus Christi. To ratify their actions, Adam Weiss preached before the Elector, and John Rurer with instructions from Margrave George conducted evangelical services in St. Catherine's Church.[10]

On the afternoon of June 17 a much discussed series of meetings began between Melanchthon and the imperial secretaries Cornelius Schnepper and Alfonso Valdes. For his part in these meetings, which lasted four days, Melanchthon has frequently been labeled a cowardly betrayer of the evangelical reform, and has been accused of trying to subvert the entire Lutheran movement.[11] This condemnation has been so general that even a careful scholar like Reu, after detailing evidence exonerating Melanchthon of every humiliating charge, concluded with the sly remark that Melanchthon *probably* did begin the negotiations and therefore should not be excused.[12]

In 1903 Theodore Brieger opposed the traditional views, saying that the imperial secretaries opened the negotiations, that Melanchthon was acting under orders from the princes, and that the "short summary" which was mentioned referred to a short form of the Confession. The picture did not become clear until J. v. Walter presented material from the Italian archives drawn from Sanuto's diary, the report of the Venetian ambassador Bagaroto. This diary shows that Melanchthon was acting with the knowledge and approval of the princes who, if they did not set up the four points for the negotiations, in any event knew about them.[13]

We are now able to reconstruct what happened. Shortly after the arrival

of the Emperor, probably June 17, Melanchthon approached the imperial
secretaries. Nobody knows exactly why, but it was probably to speak about
the death of the Lord High-Chancellor Mercurinus Gattarina, whom
Melanchthon respected and who had died as recently as June 4.[14] Of all
the imperial secretaries only Alfonso Valdes, the Spaniard, an Erasmian,
was approachable. Their conversation turned to Lutheranism, and Melanchthon asked why Spanish writers continued to paint Lutherans as
rejecting the Trinity and ignoring Christ and Mary. He sought to show
Valdes that the Lutheran doctrines were not heretical and that the difficulties had arisen over flagrant abuses.[15]

Convinced by Melanchthon's arguments, Valdes reported to the Emperor that the Lutherans did not believe anything that was contrary to
Roman Catholic doctrine;[16] and the Emperor, impressed by the determination already shown by the Protestant princes, decided to explore this
avenue further. On June 18 he summoned the Roman Catholic princes to
a private conference and asked advice. Some Catholics proposed radical
action against the Protestants, but Charles was in a conciliatory mood.
He decided to learn more about the specific abuses which stood in the
way of harmony. Valdes acted as mediator and requested Melanchthon to
state the specific points. Melanchthon then presented four items, saying
that if agreement could be reached on them, all other difficulties could be
worked out: marriage of the clergy, both forms in the Eucharist, the
mass, and church property.[17] Melanchthon was not acting independently;
he was a spokesman for the princes.

Valdes consulted with Campeggio about the four points, and the
Catholic legate seemed favorably disposed to permit the cup for the laity
and to allow marriage for priests, since the Lutherans would concede
the existence of purgatory. Campeggio, however, withheld judgment on
private mass.[18]

On June 18 when Charles summoned the Protestant princes, a peaceful
settlement of the long-existing differences appeared possible. After a discussion of three hours' duration, the Protestants agreed to further talks
and to an interdict of preaching if it applied equally to the Roman Catholics. That evening the royal interdict of evangelical and papal preaching
was proclaimed; no preaching, only the reading of the Scriptures would
be allowed.[19]

Melanchthon and Valdes, as the chief negotiators, were instructed to carry on the talks. The Emperor formally requested Melanchthon to draw up those articles which the Protestants desired to have granted. June 19 the Nürnbergers reported that there was some doubt about making the Confession.[20]

Melanchthon's own letters show that he thought a settlement might be reached, but the Confession was by no means abandoned, for united action was still being discussed. The Elector John seemed uncertain, not knowing how the current negotiations would end. Nevertheless, the evangelicals were planning to act concertedly, as the June 19 report of the Nürnberg delegates indicated.

That same day the Emperor met with the two sides separately, then jointly. He allowed the Protestants to believe that the religious differences might be resolved without breaking the unity of the church. As a token of mutual good intentions, Charles asked both sides to attend the opening mass of the Diet.[21]

Melanchthon's letters that Sunday afternoon, June 19, to Myconius, Luther, and Camerarius show that he thought the entire dispute might be settled by correcting abuses.[22] Melanchthon believed that the evangelical movement in Germany was a product of the vital spirit of the old Latin church, that the fundamental doctrines of justification by faith were not anything new but a reassertion of the heart of the Christian gospel, which in the centuries of church development had become obscured by ecclesiastical observances. In casting these aside Melanchthon believed the evangelicals were adhering to the pristine practices of the church, as reflected in Scripture and the early fathers, particularly Augustine. To Valdes he was trying to show that the reformation practices were in accord with the old canonical rules and compliant with genuine catholic Christianity, and ought, therefore, to be tolerated and encouraged by the Emperor.

But something happened. Although the evangelicals attended the early morning mass, June 20, as requested, and even though the Elector John carried the imperial sword, not a single evangelical representative participated in the ancient, mysterious rites. Charles showed his displeasure, but the Protestants seemed to have determined upon another course of action.[23]

When the Diet formally opened in the Rathhaus, the imperial mandate about considering religion and other matters was solemnly read in both German and Latin. Then wrangling over the order of procedure ensued, with the Protestant delegates succeeding in having religious matters separated from such items as the Turkish war and old business. When, in view of the invitation to the Diet, the Protestants insisted that the Catholics prepare a confessional statement, the latter replied that they represented the "true" church and needed no such statement. The evangelicals then asked for a general council on religion, only to have this countered with a proposal that a committee of twelve examine the Lutheran views and recommend imperial action. Campeggio had already contrived to have the committee two-thirds Roman Catholic. Thinking their cause would be unfairly treated or allowed to die in committee, the Protestants rejected this proposal and belligerently demanded a public hearing for their confession.[24]

That evening, as the Protestants gathered in various groups, tense uneasiness predominated. The Elector was deeply disturbed. Melanchthon realized that war might very well be the outcome of the evangelical stand, a war in which people and property would be ruthlessly destroyed. The Elector called together those whom he could count as allies and urged steadfastness.[25] That night neither he nor Melanchthon nor the other Protestant princes slept well.

Elector John spent the first few hours of the morning of June 21 reading the Psalms and praying. Afterwards he summoned his son John Frederick, Chancellor Brück, and Melanchthon for a serious, confidential talk. At this time the four definitely decided to have nothing more to do with Valdes and to take no action without the consent and counsel of the other Protestants. They were all in the same predicament and so resolved to make a public, common confession. "If God be for us, who can stand against us?"[26]

During these days, obviously, Melanchthon was not acting on his own. The princes knew about the four points of discussion with Valdes. Equally apparent were Melanchthon's efforts not to betray the Lutherans. He had not overnight become a sniveling coward. The negotiations were suddenly terminated because the Protestants became suspicious of the good faith of the papists. When Pimpinella called them "heretics" and Frederick of the Palatinate implied they were seditious and lawless, they knew they could not expect impartiality, only delay and subterfuge.

A report from the Nürnberg delegates recorded some of the activity of the Protestants that June 21st.

I, Kress, was called to the Elector's residence. His Electoral Grace, Margrave George, and the counsellors of Hesse and Lüneberg were there. In the presence of the Elector and of Margrave George, they declared simply, that, inasmuch as the Elector had already prepared a confession of faith, a copy of which your Excellencies have received, they, through us, have offered to join the Elector. At this time they are holding a session over the articles, and are further revising, stating and finishing them. It is the desire also of the Princes that your Excellencies should immediately send your preachers, or whom you will, but especially Osiander, and would instruct them to help us to consider and deliberate over these articles, and whatever is needed in the transaction.[27]

Melanchthon met with various representatives and theologians and feverishly worked to perfect the Confession as a mutual document. Their common danger had united them in the struggle. But time was running short. On June 22 the Emperor curtly notified the Protestants to have their Confession ready to present not later than June 24. Melanchthon and a few others now worked night and day to bring the Confession to a satisfactory completion. Melanchthon spent June 23 revising the entire text, while Brück and Jonas rewrote the preface and conclusion. The Nürnbergers reported:

Last Thursday early we and the delegates from Reutlingen were summoned before the Saxon, the Hessian, Margrave George, and Lüneburg. There, in the presence of all their princely graces, their counsellors, and the theologians, of whom there were twelve, besides other scholars and doctors, the aforesaid Confession was read over, examined and considered in order to present the same . . . to his Imperial Majesty.[28]

Landgrave Philip insisted on several final changes. Articles 20 and 21 were added and the article on justification was revised. For political reasons, no mention was made of the Zwinglians or Sacramentarians in the rewritten preface.

Presenting the Augsburg Confession (*Koenig*)

The Elector and Friends Visit Luther During an Illness (*Koenig*)

Although the Latin text was still in Melanchthon's handwriting, it was at this meeting that the signers affixed their signatures: Elector John of Saxony, Margrave George of Brandenburg-Ansbach, Duke Ernest of Brunswick-Lüneburg, Landgrave Philip of Hesse, Prince Wolfgang of Anhalt, and the cities of Nürnberg and Reutlingen. Prince John Frederick of Saxony and Duke Francis of Lüneburg probably signed at this time.[29]

When the afternoon of June 24 came, the Protestants were prepared. Two copies of the Confession were in readiness: a Latin translation in the hands of Chancellor Brück, a German copy in the hands of Dr. Christian Beyer.[30] But the entire afternoon passed without an opportunity to present the Confession, for during the afternoon Roman Catholic partisans delivered long harangues on the Turkish menace, and the papal legate connived to use up the time. At last, when it was too late for the document to be read, Chancellor Brück was finally recognized. Charles suggested that, because of the lateness of the hour, the Confession be handed to him without being read publicly. But the evangelicals were not to be frustrated by a parliamentary maneuver. The astute Dr. Brück reminded the Emperor that a public reading had already been promised, and he further requested that the reading be allowed in German. Eck strongly objected to this public reading, and indeed two years later still talked about it. Ferdinand protested that the mixed audience could not follow the German; but after Elector John reminded them that on German soil the German language would be more fitting, permission was granted. The actual reading was postponed until the next day's session.[31]

To prevent a larger crowd from hearing the Confession, the meeting place was suddenly transferred from the Rathhaus to the "lower large room" of the Episcopal Palace where not more than two hundred people could be seated. Many more came. The room filled to capacity and those who could not get in overflowed into the corridors and the courtyard.

At three o'clock in the afternoon the Emperor Charles V entered and officially opened the session. When Chancellor Brück and Dr. Beyer stepped forward to present the Confession, every Protestant delegate rose to his feet! Dr. Beyer read the Germany copy so clearly that every word could be heard even by those standing in the Castle Court. The reading required two hours. As the German and Latin copies were handed to the Emperor, Brück reportedly said, "Most gracious Emperor, this is a confession which, with the grace and help of God, will prevail even against the gates of hell." The Emperor gave the Latin copy to his secretary Schweiss to translate into French and the German copy to the Elector of Mainz for safekeeping, but both copies have been lost.[32]

Many stories have circulated about the reception of this Augsburg Confession. Justus Jonas said the Emperor listened with interest; Brentz said he fell asleep. According to another report the Emperor exclaimed, "Would that such doctrine were preached throughout the whole world!" [33] Duke William of Bavaria, realizing he had been misinformed about Lutheran beliefs, leaned over to Eck and asked how it could be refuted. Eck replied that it could be refuted out of the Fathers but not out of Scripture. The astonished William then asked, "Do I understand that the Lutherans stand on the Scriptures and we outside of them?" Melanchthon reported the Bavarians were very subdued.[34]

Deeply impressed by the document, the free cities of Heilbronn, Kempten, Windsheim, Weissenburg, and Frankfort-on-the-Main immediately added their names, and still others followed later.[35] "Today," exclaimed Spalatin, "occurred one of the greatest events that has ever happened on earth!"

The following day brought Melanchthon into a public clash with papal legate Campeggio. In an assembly of the clergy, Campeggio vehemently denounced the Protestants! He "hurled thunderbolts like an angry Jove." In a fearless display of evangelical conviction Melanchthon replied, "We cannot yield, nor can we desert the truth, and we pray that for the sake of God and Christ our adversaries will concede to us that which we cannot with a good conscience relinquish." Campeggio shouted, "I cannot, I cannot, for the keys do not err."

Rejecting the infallibiilty implied in Campeggio's remark, Melanchthon exclaimed, "To God we will commit our cause and ourselves! If God be for us, who can stand against us? . . . We have forty thousand wives and children of pastors whose souls we cannot desert. We will toil and fight, and die, if God so will, rather than betray so many." [36]

Melanchthon, concerned to know what Luther thought of the transactions, dispatched a letter to Coburg: "Our defense has been presented to the Emperor. I send it to you to read." To Veit Dietrich he wrote, "Write me back the Doctor's opinion of it." [37]

Luther was happy that the Confession had been presented, and "rejoiced that he had lived to see the hour when Christ was confessed by such great confessors in such a glorious Confession." But Luther was also angry, angry because he had not been consulted, angry that Melanchthon had not been more bold, and angry because he thought the Augsburg representatives were trusting too much in the rationalizations of men. "You will not accomplish anything by being overly careful. What more can the devil do than to kill us?" [38]

The same day Melanchthon wrote again to Luther and the letters crossed en route. "Here we are constantly in the greatest trouble. . . . The sophists and the monks are running daily, and making every effort to excite the Emperor against us."

Melanchthon was anxious to know Luther's reaction and what he thought about further negotiations. "At no time," he wrote on June 27, "have we stood in greater need of your advice and encouragement than at this time."

Luther's reply was far from calm, for he was still irritated that for three weeks he had received no news about Augsburg, and he was fearful that a trap might be sprung by the papists. He said:

I have received your Apology, and I am wondering what you mean when you say you desire to know what and how much we may yield to the Papists? According to my opinion, too much is already conceded to them in the Apology. . . . You are troubled about the beginning and end of this matter, because you cannot understand it. If you could understand it, I should not like to have anything to do with the matter. . . . God has set it in a place which you can neither reach by your rhetoric nor by your philosophy. That place is called Faith. . . . I am ready, as I have always written to you, to yield up everything to them, if they will only leave the Gospel free. But whatever opposes the Gospel I cannot allow. What other answer can I give? [39]

On June 30, Luther sent another letter which referred to Melanchthon's "exceedingly wicked and perfectly useless cares."

If we fall, Christ will fall with us, and He is the great Ruler of the whole world. And if it were possible for Him to fall, yet I would rather fall with

Christ than stand with the Emperor. . . . You are killing yourself and utterly fail to see that the matter lies beyond the power of your hand and counsel, and that it will be carried on regardless of any concern which you may feel.

"I pray for you," said Luther in closing, "have prayed, and will pray, and I doubt not that I am heard, for I feel the Amen in my heart. Your Martin Luther." [40]

Delivered from Hell

FTER JUNE 25 ALMOST EVERY ACTION OF CHARLES WAS dictated by the Catholic majority at the Diet. Fortunately for the Protestants, the Catholic princes were not united in their opinions. The Archbishop of Salzburg wanted to proceed with violence, if necessary, to bring the Protestants into line; but the Archbishop of Mainz, with one eye on the Turkish menace, cautioned patience.[1]

For two days there were clandestine meetings behind closed doors. Campeggio suggested that a committee of qualified theologians study the Confession and specify the heresies. If the Protestants, when confronted with such a report, did not immediately recant, counseled Campeggio, then the Emperor aided by the Catholic estates should forcefully extirpate this heresy with his "temporal arm."[2]

Leading the committee of "qualified" theologians was John Eck. Named to assist him were Cochlaeus, Usingen, Wimpina, Faber, Paul Haug, John Burkhard, and Conrad Colli. Eck was considered the most "qualified" for he had already edited the 404 articles. He worked with amazing speed, and in less than two weeks completed a confutation numbering 351 pages![3] When this voluminous document, together with a pile of books to support it, was presented to Charles on July 8, he was greatly disappointed. He easily detected the bitter theological scorn. Thinking either to strengthen the confutation or to conciliate the Protestants, he sent the document back to the committee with instructions to confine the discussion to points raised by the evangelicals' confession, to use answers based solely on Scripture, and to omit the preface and the conclusion.[4]

Several factors influenced Charles. He desired to win the aid of the Lutheran princes against the Turks and to win their support to have his brother Ferdinand crowned king of the Romans. It was also privately rumored that Landgrave Philip of Hesse was quietly fashioning a political league to withstand the Emperor, if necessary.[5] Also the religious opposition was growing. Zwingli and Bucer had not been included in the Confession on account of their views of the Lord's Supper, but they sent their own bold confession to the Diet.

Ulrich Zwingli's *Ratio Fidei* came to the Emperor in printed form. It was dated July 3, and officially presented July 8. Piqued because he was treated as a heretic by both the Roman Catholics and the Lutherans, Zwingli described himself as being between the "victim and the knife." After declaring his confession to be biblical and that he would change it only if someone demonstrated that Scripture taught otherwise, Zwingli said no one will dare to overthrow it, for "we will produce the arms we have in reserve." Zwingli clearly meant a resort to war. He called upon the Emperor "to desert Rome with her rubbish," and to use the force formerly directed against the pure gospel against the "criminal attempts of the ungodly Papists." [6]

The Lutherans were offended by the Zwinglian views on original sin and the Lord's Supper. Zwingli thought of original sin as a state into which we are born but for which we are not guilty; and he looked on the Eucharist as a memorial, a sign, a public testimony of what God has already done for man. "In the Eucharist," he wrote, "the true body of Christ is present only by the contemplation of faith," contrary to what the "papists and some who long for the flesh-pots of Egypt assert." [7]

Melanchthon was singularly unimpressed. In a letter to John Brentz, on July 12, he termed it "silly" and "contrary to Scripture." [8] In a letter to Luther two days later, he remarked:

Zwingli has sent hither a printed confession. You would say he was altogether out of mind. Concerning original sin and the use of the sacraments he renews the old errors. Concerning ceremonies he speaks very Helvetically, i.e., most barbarously, that he wants all ceremonies abolished. He earnestly urges his cause concerning the Holy Supper. He wants all bishops abolished.

I will send a copy when I can get one; the one which I had is going the rounds of the princes.[9]

Hedio and Wolfgang Capito presented the Tetrapolitan Confession on July 11. These Strassburg theologians were joined by representatives from Constance, Memmingen, and Lindau.[10]

The Emperor had reason to be concerned with the growing atmosphere of defiance. Melanchthon's letter of July 25 indicated that a union to resist the Emporor was a possibility.[11]

In the meantime the papal theologians—Eck, Granvella, Valdes, Cochlaeus, and others—labored over their reply to the Augsburg Confession. Four times they revised the massive initial reply and finally reduced the 351 pages to 31. After a month of such work, on August 3, the revised document was ready.[12] In the same room where the Confession had been read the delegates heard Alexander Schweiss read the *Confutatio Pontifica*. Several of the Protestant articles were entirely approved, others qualified. However the Roman Catholics made no substantial concessions, even though the articles on justification came so close to the evangelical view that Roman Catholics later accused the framers of the Confutation of hypocrisy. The Confutation did recognize a difference between a good work done with grace and one done without grace, so that to some extent the idea of merit in the mere performance of a sacramental act was relinquished. But, essentially the Confutation reflected the established papal system. The seven sacraments, transubstantation, the Eucharist in one kind only, and the divine origin of the hierarchy were insisted upon. Many of the abuses to which the Protestants so strenuously objected were defended as good. The only hints of compromise were the rationalizations for a return of the Protestants to the "one true church." The writers assumed that the Catholics were entirely right and that the evangelicals had strayed into the supreme error of breaking the unity of the church. Hence, schism must first be healed. Concessions would appear to be sanctions. The Confutation closed with a promise and a threat. If the Protestants would heed the Emperor's fatherly advice, he would graciously reward them; if not, as the defender and steward of the church he would proceed against them. The papacy in union with the empire had spoken.[13]

The Lutherans asked for a copy of the Confutation, only to be told two days later that they could have one on the condition that they promise to accept its provisions and not to publish a reply. Campeggio engineered these incredible terms. Brück likened these conditions to those of the fox who invited the stork to lunch and then set food before him in a wide, flat dish. Forty-three years passed before the Confutation appeared in print.[14] Fortunately, however, Camerarius had taken extensive notes during the reading of the Catholic reply, and on the basis of these notations and what could be remembered, Melanchthon undertook later to write a reply, known as the *Apology to the Augsburg Confession*.[15]

Protestant reaction to the Confutation was generally disdainful; some of them even laughed. Melanchthon wrote:

All good men in our party seem calmer and firmer . . . . They know that among our adversaries there is no acquaintance with religion. The Confutation was childish and silly. . . . Our rulers could easily obtain peace if they would court the Emperor and the more moderate princes. But there is a marvellous indifference, and, as I think, a quiet indignation that withholds them from such business.[16]

Brentz' opinion was similar: "The entire document smacks of Cochlaeus, Faber, and Eck. It is absolutely stupid, so that I am ashamed of the Roman name, because they do not seek out men who can reply to us heretics in a prudent and decorous way." [17]

When the Emperor announced that he would abide by the Confutation and commanded the Protestants to do likewise, all previous overtures for peaceful settlement seemed completely doomed.[18]

Every possible pressure was now brought to bear upon the Lutherans to compromise their stand in religion. Charles threatened to withhold the investiture of Elector John. Margrave Joachim of Brandenburg warned Elector John that his lands might be confiscated and he himself sent into exile. Margrave George was offered imperial favor in his claims on Silesia. Eck freely predicted war, if the Protestants rejected the Confutation. In disgust Philip of Hesse requested permission to leave Augsburg. When permission was denied, he left anyway, on August 6, and then wrote to the Elector of Saxony that he would stake himself, his people, and his possessions behind him and God's Word. Erasmus wrote, "Do anything rather than allow war to be undertaken." In the background, a threat to both sides, loomed the Turks.[19]

Alarmed over the situation, the Protestants made a last desperate effort to keep negotiations going. Chancellor Brück and Melanchthon wrote revealing letters. In his note of August 3, Brück declared that the Protestants were not satisfied with the mere reading of the Confutation. He asserted Protestant loyalty to the church and empire and put the blame for disunity on careless bishops. He rejected charges of immoral marriages among the evangelicals, and pointed a finger at priests who were living with harlots, treating the mass frivolously and practicing simony. He declared that the Protestants stood ready to accept episcopal rule and to unite with others as far as Scripture and conscience would permit. Furthermore, he proposed a small committee to consider the disputed articles, with the aim of effecting agreement. He pledged that the Protestants would act in good faith.

Melanchthon's letter to Campeggio, written the following day, represented not obsequiousness, as has been charged, but rather the final limit that he could go in setting up the agenda for discussion. The desire for peace and unity which this letter illustrates was a part of the very fiber of Melanchthon's character. If there was a mistake, it was to suppose that it would affect Campeggio, who had for several weeks been urging the Emperor to "extirpate the poisonous plant by fire and sword." Melanchthon complimented Campeggio on his wisdom and learning and added that he had been led to believe that Campeggio would be a promoter of peace:

For this reason I have often shown that if a few things were kept in the background, these divisions could be healed. In my opinion it would contribute very much to the quiet of the Church and to the dignity of the Roman See to make peace on the conditions which I have mentioned. . . . It is our earnest desire to be freed from these contentions that we may give our whole attention to the diligent improvement of doctrine.

He alluded to the evangelicals' willingness to accept the bishops, pointed out that the Confutation was not an admirable document, spoke briefly of the real possibility of greater commotion, and said:

You see, we cannot dissolve the existing marriages, nor have other priests. Nor could the change in regard to both elements cease without contempt of the Sacrament. It does not belong to the papal clemency to make war for such reasons, since there is nothing which is injurious to good men or to piety.[20]

The letter was polite in tone, for Melanchthon was addressing the representative of the greatest sovereign of the time; politeness showed good taste. Philip was not abandoning the evangelical principles when he held out the olive branch on the basis of the sacrament in both kinds and marriage of priests. To have conceded these in their evangelical understanding would have upset the foundation of the Roman papacy, breaking down the ascetic barrier between laity and clergy and sanctioning the doctrine of the priesthood of all believers. These had been granted in the past and Melanchthon thought they might be accepted as points for further discussion. Episcopal rule as a human administrative device was not difficult for the Protestants to accept. Melanchthon's letter presupposed that the bishops would act properly and would promote sound doctrine. "It was not a truckling spirit nor personal fear that inspired the letter, but a sincere desire to avert impending ruin, and to preserve the freedom of the Gospel in fundamentals." [21]

These two letters, the fear of a costly civil war, and the menace of the Turks influenced the Emperor to appoint a committee of fourteen, with equal Protestant and Catholic representation, to consider doctrine. The Lutherans felt that they could convince the Roman Catholics of the orthodoxy of evangelical teachings, inasmuch as some of the papists were already favorably disposed. "Anything contrary to Scripture cannot be accepted." This was the principle which guided the Protestants in these negotiations.[22]

The work of this special committee began on August 16, and several tentative agreements were reached, but the committee could not agree on the Eucharist in both kinds, clerical marriage, private masses, canon rules, and monastic vows.[23] That clerical marriage and the Eucharist were not the only points up for discussion is indicated not only by the scope of the committee's deliberations but also by the fourteen points which Melanchthon presented on August 21 and the letter which he wrote on August 22 to Luther. Melanchthon's fourteen points show that he was not forsaking evangelical truth, for they contain the very heart of the Protestant reform: [24]

1. Faith justifies us before God, not the works that precede, nor those that follow. For Christ's sake we are justified. 2. Good works are necessary although one cannot thereby earn grace or justification before God. 3. It is not necessary to name the sins in confession. 4. Although contrition must and should be present in repentance, sin is not forgiven on account of contrition but on account of faith. 5. It is not necessary for remission of *poena* that special satisfactions be laid upon man in repentance. 6. The holy Sacrament does not justify, *ex opere operato* without faith. 7. For a true unity of the church and of faith unity of human ordinances is not necessary. 8. Church services for the purpose of thereby obtaining merit are contrary to the Gospel and obscure the merits of Christ. 9. The monastic vow and life, when instituted to merit grace, are contrary to the Gospel. 10. Human ordinances, which may be kept without sin and are beneficial to good order in the church, should be observed in love for the sake of avoiding offence. 11. To call on the saints is an uncertain and dangerous matter and obscures the office of Christ. 12. Those who forbid both forms in the Sacrament act contrary to Christ's institution and Scriptures. 13. Those who forbid matrimony do so contrary to God's command. 14. The mass is not a work which *ex opere operato* merits grace.

The Protestants could not forsake these articles nor could they concede that the Confession had been refuted by the Roman Catholics. Luther was especially suspicious of the papal movements and anxious lest Melanchthon in his earnest desire for peace concede something in good faith that would be used for self-gain by a foe smiling behind a mask.[25] Melanchthon's letter of August 22 depicts the wrangling in committee and the Protestant concern with the wily manipulations of the papal representatives:

Yesterday we ended the Conference, or rather the Strife, which was conducted in the presence of Judges. At the beginning the Judges were Henry of Brunswick, the Bishop of Augsburg, Eck, Cochlaeus. Later Duke George took the place of Henry of Brunswick, for Brunswick was required to follow the Macedonian [Philip of Hesse] who, they fear, is mustering an army. In regard to the doctrines, things are about as follows: Eck found fault about the word *Sola,* when we say that men are justified by faith. Yet he did not condemn it, but said that the unsophisticated are offended. I forced him to confess that the righteousness of faith is correctly taught by us. Nevertheless, he wanted us to write that we are justified by grace and faith. I did not object, but that fool does not know the meaning of the word grace. There was another dispute about the remission of penalty and about satisfactions. There was a third about merits. On these two subjects there was no agreement. Though he did not assign such to merit, we did not accept that even. Then we took the subject of both species. We regarded it as absolutely indifferent whether we take one or both. And if we should teach this, he would cheerfully allow us both species. I could not accept this, and yet I excused those who hitherto by mistake have taken one, for they clamored that we are condemning the entire Church. What think you? The appointment of Christ refers to the laity and to the clergy. Hence, when we are forced to use the sacrament, minds ought to retain the form of the entire sacrament. If you think thus, write it unequivocally. In regard to the Mass, Vows, Marriage, there was no dispute. Only some propositions were made. These we did not accept. I cannot divine what the end will be. Although our opponents also need peace, some seem not to consider how great will be the danger if war should come. We propose very moderate conditions. We render obedience and jurisdiction to the bishops, and we restore the common ceremonies. What weight this will have I do not know. You will pray Christ to preserve us.[26]

Luther's reply, dated August 26, showed that he was very anxious about the negotiations:

It is not in our power to place or tolerate anything in God's church or in His service which cannot be defended by the Word of God, and I am vexed not a little by this talk of compromise, which is a scandal to God. With this one word "mediation" I could easily make all the laws and ordinances of God matters of compromise. For if we admit that there is a compromise in the Word of God, how can we defend ourselves so that not all things become compromises. . . . In short, I am thoroughly displeased with this negotiating concerning union in doctrine, since it is utterly impossible except the Pope wishes to take away his power. It was enough to give account of our faith and to ask for peace. . . . And since it is certain that our side will be condemned by them, as they are not repenting, and are striving to retain their side, why do we not see through the matter and recognize that all their concessions are a lie? [27]

Historians writing on the Augsburg Confession usually criticize Melanchthon as childish if not traitorous for his activity during this period. The last part of Luther's letter is frequently quoted. In the letter, however,

Luther actually praised Melanchthon for not accepting anything from the Catholics; but he was careful to point out that Eck should not be trusted and that the smallest loophole in any compromise would be an open gate for hierarchical abuses and aggrandizement. Luther did not claim that Melanchthon had altered doctrine or that he had become a traitor or that he had acted in a cowardly fashion. Luther, however, did see clearly that the basic difference was one of authority, and that there could be no genuine compromise as long as the papacy remained. Luther noted that Melanchthon recognized this basic difference and that Melanchthon asserted this in demanding freedom of the gospel, but Luther felt that this was not enough, for he distrusted the papists, believing that they only appeared to consent. It is intriguing to note that Luther felt Melanchthon had acted rightly in regard to the Lord's Supper, episcopal jurisdiction, and ceremonies, and that Luther did not object to the concessions on justification by faith alone but only to Eck's monumental perfidy. Luther objected to the negotiations, not to Melanchthon's conduct. Melanchthon was, after all, acting under appointment by the Emperor and assent by the Elector. Luther did not want either Melanchthon or the Elector to be fooled by mere words; "Campeggio," he said, "is a perfect devil." [28]

In another letter Luther asked Spalatin not to try to unite Christ and Belial. On August 28 he called upon Melanchthon to stop the negotiations, for he feared a gross intrigue was under way to beguile the evangelicals: "My dear Philip, . . . you could do nothing more right in my opinion, than to free yourself from these gross intrigues by saying you would give to God what belongs to God and to the Emperor what belongs to the Emperor. . . . Deal in a manly way, and let your heart be comforted." [29]

While Luther was writing these letters, the committee of fourteen was reduced to six, either to facilitate discussion or to manipulate a small group of Protestants more easily. The evangelicals objected strenuously and instructed their three delegates to concede nothing to the Catholics and to confine the discussions to the mass, Communion in both kinds, marriage of priests, monastic vows, and episcopal power. Catholic representatives were Bernhard Hagen, chancellor of Cologne; Hieronymus Vehus, chancellor of Baden; and John Eck. Representing the Lutherans were Gregory Brück, chancellor of Saxony; Sebastian Heller, chancellor of Margrave George of Brandenburg; and Philip Melanchthon.

The Protestants said they were ready to consider reasonable proposals, that they had no intention of yielding to abuses, and that they would wait for the decision of a free council if necessary. In the meantime they would seek to promote peace and administer their affairs, remembering that they would have to give account to the Emperor and to God.[30] The meetings continued for several days but with little hope of agreement. Melanchthon's letter of September 1 to Luther indicated that the conferences were near an end.[31] Rising suspicion and fear among the Protestant princes that unacceptable concessions might be made to the Roman Catholics caused the negotiations to falter. Some even rumored that the Lutherans had been bought off with papal gold.[32] Melanchthon was bitterly criticized for making unwarranted concessions, even though he was not acting on his own initiative. He repeatedly complained of the utter lack of courage on the part of the princes.[33] About the middle of August dissension had begun to spread among the Protestants who were not taking part directly in the negotiations, and it now grew worse.

On September 13 Baumgartner wrote a letter to Spengler at Nürnberg in which he painted the situation as dark and hopeless. He said Melanchthon was acting childishly and subserviently toward the papists and arrogantly toward the evangelicals. He feared everything would be lost to the wily intrigues of the Romanists.[34] While Baumgartner was understandably irritated by the negotiations which had dragged on and on, and was fearful lest the discussions be maliciously used against the Protestants, it was hardly true that Melanchthon and the others were ready to agree with the Roman Catholics, nor were they childish, clumsy, confused, or fainthearted, as Baumgartner implied. Actually during this time Melanchthon was working on an answer to the Confutation, an answer which showed not the slightest evidence of weak concession, and it was Philip who presented the fourteen articles which the evangelicals could not abandon.

All the negotiations came to a sudden halt when the Emperor tentatively ordered an imperial recess on September 22. Politely but forcefully Charles said that the purpose of the diet had been fulfilled, that both sides had been heard, and that he after careful consideration had found the

Protestants thoroughly refuted "by means of the Gospel and other writings." In manifest leniency and for the sake of peace and unity, the imperial mandate granted the evangelicals until next April 15 to confess the same beliefs as the Roman Catholics until a general council could be convoked. The Protestants were told they could not print, sell, or retail any new books dealing with religion; that they were not to proselytize any Catholics, nor interfere with Catholic worship, nor introduce any innovations whatsoever; and that they were to assist in dispersing the Anabaptists and others who persisted in rejecting the "blessed and holy Sacraments." The pope would be asked to summon a general council.[35]

The conference had failed. And the time had come to present the Protestant reply to the Confutation, for it could not be granted that the Confutation had refuted the Confession.

Relying on notes taken during the reading of the Confutation by Camerarius and on the memory of those present at the time, Melanchthon had set about preparing an answer early in August. When the committee negotiations were being conducted, this reply was pushed into the background, but Melanchthon worked on it intermittently, as did the Nürnberg theologians and lawyers who were ordered to do so by their city council. The theologians handed their opinion to Melanchthon on August 18, and the lawyers gave theirs to Melanchthon only a short while afterwards.[36] When it was obvious that the special committee would not establish concord, the reply to the Confutation was again taken up. On August 29, "Chancellor Brück and other Saxons" were officially commissioned to prepare a reply. The task was turned over to Melanchthon, although he modestly acknowledged help from others. Early in September the special committee of six began to hold meetings which limited the time that Melanchthon could give to the defense. However, when an unfavorable recess of the diet was rumored, the answer was rushed to completion. In a letter written to Camerarius on September 20, Melanchthon referred to his writing the defense of the Confession, and he implied that he had not used the arguments of the Nürnbergers.[37] As late as September 20 no one knew whether the evangelical reply would be permitted before the diet.

When the imperial recess was read on September 22, the Lutheran estates hurriedly decided that Chancellor Brück should present Melanchthon's reply. There was little time for an extended consultation among the evangelicals, so Chancellor Brück, with an excuse for the incomplete form of the document, offered it to the Emperor. However, on the whispered advice of Ferdinand, the Emperor refused to accept it.[38]

This reply is known as the *Prima Delineatio Apologiae,* a cursory document compared to the extended Apology which Melanchthon wrote the following year. This first, short apology clarified the Lutheran stand at the diet, and made no unseemly or weak concessions to the Roman Catholics. Melanchthon successfully rejected the Confutation attacks on Articles 2, 4-6, 7, 10-15, and 21, and defended the evangelical practices of both elements in the Eucharist, marriage of ministers, voluntary masses, vows, and church government. In a defense of the basic doctrines of justification, Melanchthon scorned the papal practice of work-righteousness with unmistakable sarcasm.[39] In defending the evangelical practices Melanchthon firmly stated that responsibility for the discord in Christendom rested with the Roman Catholics.

Here at the diet we have, for the sake of peace and love, offered to retain such common usages as far as we could and dared to do without sin. But this moderation and offer, which we hope, is pleasing and acceptable to God, helped us little with our enemies who, contrary to all fairness, have demanded that we, against our conscience, accept and retain all the former abuses. . . . We have at all times been obedient and are yet willing to live in humble submission to his Imperial Majesty in all things that are compatible with God and our conscience. But now we cannot, if we are not to deny Christ, go back to the old abuses.[40]

In conclusion Melanchthon apologized that a copy of the Confutation was not available for more accurate references and said that the Lutherans would be willing to give an extended reply. Already he had such an answer in mind.

The day after the recess, September 23, the Elector, without having received his coveted investiture, and with the future still very uncertain, decided to leave the diet and go home. The diet itself continued with other affairs into October.[41]

For six long months Melanchthon had wrangled with the opponents. The anguish he suffered can never be known. Criticized by impatient friends, perjured by dissembling enemies, Melanchthon nevertheless confessed truth. His attempts at moderation and conciliation were but the bending of an honest man genuinely seeking truth and peace. His work at Augsburg is a monument of patience. Luther dared; Melanchthon endured.

At Coburg the electoral party tarried a few days. Luther thanked God that they had all confessed the gospel and had been delivered from hell.[42]

16

Defending the Confession

HE INTELLECTUAL DEFENSE OF THE AUGSBURG CONFESSION was Melanchthon's Apology; the political defense was the Smalcald League; nor were these defenses completed before the clouds of war threatened.

For months after the Augsburg Diet, Melanchthon occupied himself with enlarging, revising, and perfecting his reply to the Catholic confutation. Although the long, grueling conferences at Augsburg had been physically exhausting, Melanchthon could not rest. He was so engrossed in his work, even while returning to Wittenberg, that he wrote on Sundays and during meals. Luther once snatched the pen from his hand, saying, "Dear Philip, we can serve God not only by work but also by rest." [1] Melanchthon's letters show that during the fall and winter of 1530 he persisted in the completion of this task almost to the exclusion of all other work.[2] In February he wrote to Brentz:

I am revising the Apology. It will be much larger and more fully substantiated. At the present time the article that men are justified by faith, rather than by love, is being copiously treated. If Christ is our atonement, then it is necessary to understand that we are justified by faith, and that justification by love is justification according to the Law and not according to the Gospel. The Gospel sets forth one kind of righteousness, the Law another. When I have finished it, I will send it.[3]

Two months later he wrote to Bucer: "My apology is published. In it I think I have treated the articles on justification, on repentance and some others in such a way that the opponents will understand that the burden of proof is placed upon them." [4]

The finished product scarcely resembled the short document which had been presented at Augsburg. The first writing was hurriedly done from notes taken by Camerarius and others; the completely rewritten work was based on a copy of the Confutation which Melanchthon obtained through his Nürnberg friends.[5]

Although a group was originally assigned the task of writing the Apology, Melanchthon issued it under his own name in order to avoid a charge of anonymity. Along with it he issued a copy of the Augsburg Confession, for already seven unauthorized editions had appeared, six in German and one in Latin. In the spring of 1531 the Apology and the *Editio Princeps* of the Augsburg Confession were published. This Latin edition came to be known as the authoritative, unaltered text of the Augsburg Confession, in contrast to the altered editions that Melanchthon himself subsequently published. The later changes did not attract much attention until 1540 when Eck noted some alterations in the doctrine of the Lord's Supper. After Luther's death Melanchthon was falsely charged with altering the public Confession to infiltrate his heretical teachings. He did alter the Confession, from 1531 on, but only in order to make some of the passages clearer.

The Apology exhibited a firmness of belief that astonished those who thought Melanchthon had weakly acquiesced at Augsburg. In the Confession Melanchthon had tried to justify to the Emperor the aspects of worship and belief as they were being taught by the Lutherans. Such phrases as "it is taught" and "our churches teach" and this or that opinion is "falsely imputed to us" occurred frequently. Passages beginning "we reject" and "we condemn" the views of certain heretics and sects were intended to show the orthodoxy of the evangelicals, especially in comparison with the early Latin church. When the Confession was presented, the situation called for diplomacy. A number of basic items like the divine right of the pope, predestination, the number of sacraments, and character *indelebilis* were not discussed, for in the Confession Melanchthon wanted to explain the grounds on which certain changes had been made. His object was not to convert, but simply to defend. He maintained that the evangelical party had not deviated from the genuine principles of the catholic church, and that consequently the emperor might well consent to tolerate the new organization of the church.[6]

When Melanchthon came to write the Apology, the situation had changed; the diplomatic soft-pedaling or *Leisetreterei* was no longer necessary. The attempt to unite with the Roman Catholics had failed. Melanchthon paid slight heed to those articles which were not attacked by the Catholics, but the articles which they had attacked he carefully explained. With consummate skill he rejected one by one the opponents' arguments. He supported the evangelical doctrines and practices with scriptural references and diligently traced the origin and development of the opposing views to expose them as human, scholastic additions. He showed that the Lutheran practices were not innovations at all but in complete conformity with the ways of the primitive church. For all the polemic in the writing, it was also dignified and respectful. A sense of deep feeling permeated the entire book, as if Melanchthon had experienced everything about which he wrote. Justification by faith keyed the contents, for not only was this itself copiously treated, but every topic was inevitably brought back to this central doctrine. No other document of the time affords a better view of the theology of the Reformation nor a better explanation of the Augsburg Confession than the Apology of Melanchthon.

Inasmuch as the Confutation was supposed to be a complete scriptural refutation of the Augsburg Confession, Melanchthon could not refrain from occasional snide remarks about the sophistry of the "blockheads" at Rome, but for the most part he developed a deliberate, discerning, and devastating treatment of the central issues: original sin, justification by faith, good works, the church, the Eucharist, marriage, and ceremonies.[7]

In the introduction Melanchthon reminded the readers that His Imperial Majesty demanded that the evangelical princes assent to the Catholic confutation although no copy was furnished them for careful study. In the negotiations for peace, continued Melanchthon, "our princes declined no burden, however grievous, that could be assumed without offence to conscience." He pointed out that the princes could not agree to abuses and errors nor to a confutation which they were not allowed to examine carefully. The adversaries "seek neither truth nor concord, but to drain our blood." In order that others might see that the evangelicals were upholding the gospel, Melanchthon proposed to explain the evangelical doctrines and expose the opponents' sophistry. "Discord does not delight us; neither are we indifferent to our danger, the extent of which, in such a bitterness of hatred wherewith the adversaries have been inflamed, we readily understand. But we cannot abandon truth that is manifest and necessary to the Church." [8]

Melanchthon concluded his lengthy treatment of Protestant doctrines by fixing upon the Roman Catholics the responsibility for the schism in Christendom. "Those who in the beginning condemned manifest truth, and are now persecuting it with the greatest cruelty, will give an account for the schism that has been occasioned." The devil and those who set themselves against God's Word are the causes of dissension and want of unity. [9]

In upholding justification by faith, in appealing to scriptural authority, and in unmasking the pretenses of the papists, Melanchthon struck a mighty theological blow for the Protestants. When the princes struck a corresponding political blow through the formation of the Smalcald union, the Emperor was forced to work out with the Protestants a treaty that kept the peace for fifteen years.

Melanchthon's Apology was an immediate success. Alongside the Augsburg Confession it became a part of the confessional symbol of the Lutheran Church. In 1532 at Schweinfurt it was recognized as a part of the confession of the Lutherans. [10] At Smalcald in 1537, the Lutherans officially placed it beside the Augsburg Confession and the theologians assembled at Smalcald signed it as a confessional document. The Formula of Concord officially stated, after the death of Melanchthon, that it was always received as the unanimous judgment of the churches. [11] Brentz considered it worthy of canonization. [12] In 1533 Luther exhorted the Leipzig Christians who were being persecuted by Duke George to "hold fast to our Confession and Apology!" [13]

The reaction of the Roman Catholics also testified to its significance. The Archbishop of Mainz forwarded a copy to Emperor Charles to show him how the Christian religion was being *destroyed*. In Italy it was so well received that Cochlaeus himself was asked to write an answer. [14] Today, the Apology is regarded as the most scholarly of all the Lutheran symbols, and yet it is so practical and spirited that it would serve as a devotional book as well. [15]

No document is more important in the theological writing of the Reformation than the Apology of the Augsburg Confession. "Seldom has a man shown greater strength of conviction, or more transcendent skill as a theologian. . . . He who would read the theology of Melanchthon at its best must read the Apology." [16]

But an intellectual defense of the evangelical stand was not enough, for underneath the powder keg of religious controversy was the question of political power. Melanchthon knew that thousands of lives depended on keeping the peace; he knew also that a shift in the balance of power among those vying for control could loose a holocaust of destruction. One can almost feel Melanchthon's despair as he wrote to his friend Silberboner:

The history of the Convention is a long drama of tragedy. Yet our confession will show until the end of time that we piously and conscientiously thought about and sincerely endeavored to set forth the doctrine of the church universal and to extend the glory of Christ. True, reasonable service to God, pleasing above all else to Him is this: His Word purely to teach and to use. If we are suppressed by ungodly means, our writings will show generations to come that our opponents, under the pretext of honoring Christ, stirred up the prince against us, and did not concern themselves with either the upbuilding of the Church nor the Gospel nor the glorification of the name of Christ. The matter now rests with God alone. We pray, therefore, that He will for the sake of the Glory of Christ come to our aid and allow the pure doctrine of the Gospel to perish not.[17]

Repeatedly Melanchthon spoke of the wives and children who would be the real casualties in the event of war. His own family would be endangered. Melanchthon wept as he agonized prayers for the peace of the church: "In our time, O Lord, give peace!" As the years passed he despaired of human counsels.[18] Significantly, after 1530 his known prayers increased in number, and he later added an essay on prayer to his *Loci Theologici*. This trend marked a deepening recognition of human finiteness and inability to order the world.

When the final, imperial decree of the Diet of Augsburg was published on November 19, 1530, two months after the Elector left, Melanchthon's anxiety was not lightened, for the proclamation cast all guilt on the evangelicals. The final decree of Charles granted the Protestants until April 15 to set their houses in order and warned that those who were still obstinate in defying constituted authority would after that date be dealt with according to the laws of the Empire. With his loyal estates the Emperor served notice that he would "stand by the true and ancient faith and protect the same" against errors and innovations. After enumerating so-called Lutheran errors, the Emperor decreed that only preachers approved by bishops would be admitted to pulpits; that all married priests would be suspended until they got rid of their wives and received holy absolution; that printers could publish nothing without proper sanction; that confis-cated and plundered churches, cloisters, and bishoprics would have to be restored; that monks, nuns, and priests must be given back any posses-sions wrested from them; and that "no one whether he belong to the law or to the clerical order shall do violence to another, or oppress him, or make war upon him, on account of his religious beliefs; nor deprive him of his lawful rents, fines, tithes, or other possessions." [19] Charles pledged himself to arrange with the pope for a general council, but reiterated that meanwhile all the old Catholic forms were to be retained, and measures were to be taken against all Sacramentarians and Anabaptists.

On November 12, just a few days before the decree, the few Protestants still at Augsburg clamored that the Emperor had no right to command in matters of belief. When, in spite of this, the November 19 decree appeared, the evangelicals saw that military measures were mandatory.[20]

Indeed, the feeling had been growing among the Lutherans that force would finally be decisive. Elector Joachim of Brandenburg had boasted that the Protestants would either unite with the Roman Catholic estates or be destroyed. But other Catholics, like the Elector of Mainz, the Elector of Trier and Pfalz, Duke Heinrich of Braunschweig and Duke Ludwig von Baiern, assured the Elector of Saxony that they would never consent to an offensive war, even though they felt compelled to appear to go along with the war-minded legates and bishops of the papacy.[21] Warlike threats and rumors of violence were in the air.

When the Wittenberg theologians were consulted under these circum-stances, they no longer were so positive that all resistance was wrong, and they also implied that protective measures against the outrages of the Emperor were warranted. Even though Melanchthon and Luther did not give an outright answer about defending the gospel by force, the princes met on December 22 in the convent at Smalcald on the southwest frontier

of Saxony to form a military league. The Elector of Saxony, the Duke of
Lüneburg, the Landgrave of Hesse, the Prince of Anhalt, two Counts of
Mansfeld, delegates from Magdeburg and Bremen, and representatives
from Strassburg, Constance, Memmingen, and Lindau agreed to oppose
the election of Ferdinand, to protest the legal procedures being prepared
against the evangelicals, to vindicate their actions for the kings of France
and England, and to assist each other if attacked on account of the gospel.

Melanchthon, always the spokesman for the Reformation, wrote the
explanatory statements of the evangelical stand for the kings of France
and England. He reminded these kings (who could so easily become
friends or enemies) that in the past many good Christians had complained
of the abuses prevalent in the church and had vainly tried to correct them.
He cited cases in Germany where Christian truth had been obscured, and
situations where even papal adherents recognized the need of reform. At
Augsburg, he said, the Protestants stood united in their opposition to
inequities, and now they would defend their position. They would preserve the church from robbery; they would defend the suffering! [22]

A few weeks earlier Melanchthon had written to Camerarius:

Many necessary and righteous reasons for defense in case of peril can be
drawn up. The evil of our opponents is so great that they would not hesitate
for a moment to mount an invasion if they thought we were unprepared.
Their burning souls would not let them rest if it were not for our strong
defenses. Our theological doubts about this we would raise up in vain. I condemn none, and do not criticize the foresight of our side, if we can only
see that nothing evil is undertaken. [23]

Melanchthon was reluctant to alter his former position that the gospel
must not be defended by force. However, in the face of the realities of the
moment, he resorted to the just-war theory of the early church. Under
properly constituted authorities, with just rules, and for a right cause,
Christians could take up arms.

In the meantime Charles was playing his diplomatic cards—bribes,
promises, and threats. He wanted enough Protestant support to ensure
Ferdinand's election as king of the Romans. This would strengthen
Ferdinand's legal claim to the imperial succession and would bestow
enough executive dignity upon him to manage affairs in Germany when-

ever Charles had to be absent. A united Germany would also be a buffer in the event of a Turkish advance through the Balkans. On account of the plague the actual voting took place at Cologne, January 5, 1531. Although Melanchthon and Luther both urged the Elector to attend the session, inasmuch as refusal might be construed as an unfriendly act, he consented only to send his son John Frederick with a formal protest against the choice of Ferdinand. Nevertheless, Ferdinand was elected.

The Protestants then moved quickly. By the end of March, 1531, they concluded and signed a formal treaty of mutual assistance, and in the months that followed, this Smalcald League became a bristling reality. With the princes of Saxony and Hesse acting as chiefs of the alliance and nearly all of northern Germany solidly in the league, the Smalcald union had enough strength to be reckoned as one of the powers of Europe. Other nations soon sought to join. The Emperor's political maneuvering for military advantage had been checkmated, but the threat of war had not been lessened.

Believing Germany to be rent by internal dissension, the Turkish sultan chose this time to advance against Charles. His armies marched through the Balkans, and, if the Protestants had refused to aid the Emperor, western Europe might have been overrun by the Turks. But patriotism and religious hatred of Islam impelled the evangelicals to put a large number of well-equipped troops in the field. John of Saxony and Philip of Hesse rendered such noteworthy service that the Emperor gave them assurances he would not take extreme measures against the Lutherans.

Early in 1532, then, at Schweinfurt, the Protestants and Catholics again met to iron out their differences. In view of Charles's changed attitude, Melanchthon and Luther urged the Elector to modify some of his demands, but not too much as it might all turn out to be papal beguiling. The Romanists will "knit away the time," he said, and if one can judge from their past actions, they will by intrigue and subterfuge seek four things: (1) To prevent us from entering new territories with our doctrine; (2) to prohibit others joining us; (3) to bring us by legal maneuvering to judgment before the *Kammergericht,* a thing which in principle would mean that a human court has the right to judge both the church and doctrine; and (4) to entrap us with a council dominated by the pope instead of the Word of God.[24]

Melanchthon believed that the opponents were secretly preparing for war, and he openly accused Elector Joachim and Duke George of desiring to set Germany on fire for their own selfish gains. Nor was he altogether sure that all the Protestant princes were above feathering their own nests. In a letter to Camerarius he hinted that all was not well in the evangelical camp. "The papists have in the past suppressed the Church by their tyranny, and the coming struggle will not be less injurious. Wherever this thing may lead, I have no hope that we will ever be free to express our opinion about doctrine, and this is absolutely necessary if there is to be concord." When war breaks out there will be no chance for discussion; conformity will be the great motto. "These thoughts torture me, and all that I would I may not say." [25]

Melanchthon was clearer in a letter to Brentz: "I see that many profane things are mixed with the Gospel." He feared an unholy alliance of politics and religion! He thought the Protestants, for the sake of politics, might actually work out a compromise with the Catholic forces. He reproached the evangelicals for this apostasy, saying, "These negotiations for peace will not help in the securing of religion; terror will make a union only for a time." [26]

After lengthy negotiations both sides agreed not to do violence to anyone on account of his faith. The Emperor agreed to urge the convening of a council within a year and a half, and if a general council failed to materialize, to call the Estates together for consultation. Lawsuits against the evangelical princes by the imperial fisc were to be suspended, thus postponing if not settling the important question of confiscated church property.

But this treaty so favorable to the Protestants was definitely unacceptable to the Catholics. They thought that the Emperor had been too generous and refused to ratify this agreement. The Emperor, anxious to make peace, offered the same terms on his personal pledge, and the evangelicals accepted. On August 2, 1532, the Peace of Nürnberg became operative. Even though this was only a private understanding, it brought a shaky peace to Germany and gave the evangelicals time to consolidate.[27]

Charles had bowed, his motive a commingling of gratitude and political sagacity, but he had not changed his ultimate plans to suppress the Protestant movement. He probably never understood the real theological basis behind the German upheaval, but he knew that the defiant evangelicals weakened his imperial authority, and that the time would eventually come when the sword would decide to what extent Protestantism had to be tolerated.

Melanchthon, too, saw that the cold war could not go on forever. He wanted only spiritual weapons to defend the gospel, but he recognized the right of necessity, even though he feared that it might be used by the princes as an excuse for lust and destruction. Philip finally advocated defense for the Protestants on the basis of the priesthood of all believers, namely, that we are all Christians through the same Spirit, and that those who possess worldly powers have the duty to correct abuses and to curb evildoers, be the evildoer the Emperor himelf!

A cloud settled over the political truimph of the evangelicals on August 16, with the unexpected death of Elector John. A ruptured brain artery brought sudden apoplexy, and before Luther and Melanchthon could arrive he lost consciousness. The Elector was entombed two days later in the Castle Church at Wittenberg, Luther preaching a sermon in German and Melanchthon giving a Latin oration.[28]

Melanchthon praised the Elector's efforts to establish peace; extolled his piety, firmness, and unselfishness; and recounted his paternal justice and mercy—all of which helped to bring harmony not only to Germany but throughout the Empire. Significantly, however, Melanchthon said war is sometimes necessary and preparedness is mandatory, for he did not expect the Elector's efforts at peace to prevail. He looked forward not to peace, but to "dangers and misfortunes," "miseries which may yet await us," and future "agonies of a painful disorder." We grieve, therefore, he said, for one who strove to keep the peace, and we ask God's mercy and preservation.

Melanchthon's elegy, full of tribute to the Elector, was engraved on a brass plaque and placed on John's tomb.[29]

John Frederick succeeded his father to the electorate. Though youthful, dogmatic, and often impetuous, the new Elector faithfully promoted the Protestant cause, nor was it long before he had an opportunity to prove his mettle.

17

Intrigue of Kings

Y THE SPRING OF 1533 MELANCHTHON LONGED TO ESCAPE the chaos of the last times. In his own mind he was convinced that the apocalypse was about to break upon the world; there were wars and rumors of wars, evil in high places, omens of disaster, and strange astrological configurations! But constant demands bound him to the present. One of his children became dangerously ill, and at the same time a report began circulating that a general council was at last to be called.

Emperor Charles V had indeed tried to stir the papacy into calling together the representatives of the church. In March, 1533, an imperial ambassador came to Saxony to discuss preliminaries for a council to establish doctrine. Melanchthon and Luther were both skeptical; neither thought the pope wanted a genuinely free discussion. "The pope will not be guided by a general council," observed Melanchthon, "for if one does come, he will use cunning and power against us. Would to God that our electors and estates might effect a council in which no one would be browbeaten for his convictions! Truly the church is in a miserably deplorable state!" [1]

Charles nevertheless continued to try to bring about a council. In response to Charles's personal request Pope Clement VII asked his nuncio, Hugo Rangonus, to accompany the Emperor's ambassador to Germany to talk about a council. They arrived in Weimar near the beginning of June, 1533, and laid before John Frederick their impossible terms, namely, that the Elector accept the pope as the final authority. Melanchthon advised his prince not to reject the council outright, lest such a refusal be used as propaganda against the Protestants, but to insist that the Word of God be the final authority. Melanchthon was often as wise as a serpent! (He also dedicated his edition of Romans to Archbishop Albert of Mainz, saying, "What unfeeling souls are those who are not moved by the dangers of war!" The Archbishop sent him a handsome present.)[2] "It is my firm opinion," he wrote to the Elector, "that the Roman Pontiff is practicing a piece of dissimulation to induce us to agree to the decisions of a general convention of his own arrangement. Be wary." [3] Melanchthon wanted a council, but one in which Christ would be the Pontifex.

On June 30, after a meeting at Smalcald, the Elector officially explained to the legates of the Pope and the Emperor that they could not sanction a council bound by anything less than the Word of God. In a foreword to the official transcript of the meeting, Melanchthon wrote an opinion saying the Emperor ought to be thanked for desiring a righteous council and prayers ought to be offered to God to enlighten the pope and the princes that once again truth and unity may come to the church.[4] Nothing more was heard about a council. Pope Clement VII had not been in earnest.

The unstable Nürnberg Peace seemed once more threatened in 1534 through a misunderstanding that developed between Elector John Frederick and King Ferdinand, who resented the fact that the Elector had not supported his election. Cooler heads stopped the brewing danger by calling for a committee to talk over the differences. Six representatives met, very casually, on April 29, 1534, in the priests' cloister at Leipzig. Brück and Melanchthon represented the Elector of Saxony.

Carefully, point by point, the group went over the Augsburg Confession. They paused for special discussion of justification, the Lord's Supper, and grace, and could not agree, primarily because the Roman Catholics insisted on the principle of meritorious works. The negotiations were friendly enough and that might be called progress, but nothing was achieved. Brück reported that it was all a matter of words spoken in such a manner as to allow each side to save face and keep its own views.[5] Melanchthon was the spokesman at scores of such meetings. Toward the end of his life he said, "I have lived in councils and it looks as if I will die in one."

Meanwhile, Melanchthon's fame spread throughout Europe, so that he received invitations to visit France, England, and Poland.[6]

The King of France was one of the first to recognize the political value of a man like Melanchthon. Believing that he might curry the favor of the German evangelicals, and, at the insistence of the Queen of Navarre, Francis made overtures to Melanchthon. A personal ambassador, Chelius, bore the king's invitation to Wittenberg. At the same time William Bellay, brother of the Bishop of Paris, went to Strassburg to talk with Bucer about unifying Christendom. Bucer and Melanchthon promptly noted their views.[7]

Melanchthon, only thirty-eight years old, felt highly honored; he looked forward to championing the evangelical faith in France. The religious controversies might be relieved, he noted, if thoughtful men would really try to achieve peace. For the sake of harmony he would be willing to overlook some abuses but none which might destroy the truth about faith or lead to idolatry or impel men to sin. He could accept the episcopacy and the canons of the church if they were not made into absolute rules. He could regard fasts, holy days, clerical garbs, and tonsures as indifferent. But he could not accept righteousness by human works, for we are justified by trust in Christ. He would have to reject the private masses that require an enumeration of sins and the performing of masses as a work of merit. He could not condone the withholding of the cup from the laity, since the early church gave the bread and the cup to the laymen. If a union is to be achieved, said Melanchthon, the Pope must remove human restrictions on the sacraments.

Melanchthon added that saints might be honored and studied, but that they should not be worshiped. Vows taken by children should not be considered irrevocable, as this only increases the misfits who live in the monasteries. Clerical celibacy, like other human rules, should not be made binding.[8]

While Melanchthon was willing, even eager, to bring about church harmony, he was not willing to sacrifice any of the basic evangelical doctrines. Human rules, he said, may be compromised, but not the Word of God.

The papal prelates at Paris were not at all pleased with Melanchthon's opinion, and they looked about for some means to alienate the French ruler and the Lutherans. Their golden opportunity came when a few pro-reformers used violence in a demonstration against the mass and the pope. Even Melanchthon was unwilling to condone the irresponsible incitement.[9] Many of the French evangelicals suffered punishment.

Despite this outbreak, the conferences with Chelius continued, only now it began to look as though Melanchthon was too friendly with the forces of Satan. The Catholics circulated copies of the opinions of Melanchthon and spread the rumor that the Lutherans were prepared to submit to the Pope again.[10] Melanchthon and Bucer became objects of bitter barbs of censure. Many criticizers claimed that thousands would strangle themselves before they would tolerate being put under the papal tyranny, and in vain Melanchthon and Bucer wrote letters of explanation and made public disavowals. Bucer finally went back home to exonerate himself. The invitation from the King of France proved abortive.

In spite of a sense of disappointment and anger, Francis soon sought again to cement friendship with the German Protestants through Melanchthon. Politics, not religious fervor, dictated his decision.

To bear the second invitation King Francis chose Barnabas Vore, Lord de Lafosse, an admirer of Melanchthon. He was to urge that Philip come in the king's name to the court of France at once. Vore also carried a letter from Jacob Sturm to Melanchthon urging him to answer the call of those in distress and the voice of God and Christ.[11] The appeal was powerful, but rumors were already spreading that his going to France was a desire to desert the Reformation. Recalling his controversy with the mighty Sorbonne and feeling distrust for Francis, Melanchthon hesitated.[12] In May, 1535, he wrote to Sturm that any plan short of a synod to restore the church would be both futile and pernicious and that his coming to France would result in nothing.[13] In May, Vore returned to Paris. A short time later Francis himself wrote to Melanchthon. After mentioning Bellay and Vore, Francis said:

I wish you to come the very first opportunity, and fully confer with some of our most eminent doctors on the reconciliation of opinions, and on other things susceptible of improvement in the government of the church, for which I feel the greatest solicitude and anxiety. I will send Vore de Fossa to you immediately with these letters for a safe conduct, imploring you not to be dissuaded by any one from this pious and holy undertaking. Your visit will be most grateful to me, and you are at perfect liberty to come either in a private or public character, and be assured you will find me, as indeed I always have been, most desirous of promoting your glory, reputation, and comfort, both at home and abroad.[14]

A little later King Francis anxiously proposed through Jacob Sturm a secret conference in order to avoid needless difficulties.[15]

In addition to the King's letter, Vore carried messages from Cardinal John Bellay and Sturm, and also one from Margaret, the queen of Navarre, and her preacher, Gerhard Roussel.[16]

Urged so fervently and halfway hopeful for Protestantism in France, Melanchthon formally sought the Elector's permission to travel as a private person. Luther joined in the request.[17] Melanchthon journeyed to the court at Weimar for a direct word with the Elector. He found the Elector extremely reluctant and wary, for the Elector knew instinctively that Francis' motives were political. Melanchthon's going to France would look as if the Elector were interested in an alliance against the Emperor. The Elector even suspected that Vore was an agent of the papacy. John Frederick also feared that Melanchthon might concede too much in his desire to be conciliatory and that the Catholics would again use the occasion to promote false gossip.[18]

In the background darkly loomed an "incident" in France, the posting of some handbills in public places by Lutheran partisans. Infuriated by this decrial of the Roman faith, King Francis sent out a decree against all heretics. To allay any suspicion that he might be anti-Catholic, the King ordered a solemn procession through the city with the Holy Ghost carried in a brazier. He himself walked behind bareheaded and barefooted, and the queen and other court dignitaries attended. Six Lutheran heretics were condemned by the parliament to be burned, and the decree was executed with brutal barbarity before the procession ended. Other heretics were put on the to-be-ferreted-out list.

That the French realized the "incident" would weigh heavily with the evangelicals in Germany is attested by the fact that William Bellay was sent to the German princes to explain. He was to assure them "that the persons proscribed and punished were guilty of seditious practices, that the king wished for an accommodation on the subject of religion, and that he was particularly desirous of a visit from Philip Melanchthon." [19]

MELANCHTHON'S ORATION AT THE FUNERAL OF LUTHER (*Koenig*)

Translating the Bible (*Koenig*)

In France, however, Roman Catholic Cardinal Tournon and the Sorbonne were publicly criticizing the invitation to a heretic. Francis was obviously playing both sides, dissembling for political advantage, panegyrizing the Protestants on the one hand and persecuting them on the other. Melanchthon, nevertheless, desired to go to France. Luther urged the Elector, saying the very expectation of Melanchthon's arrival had caused the persecutions to abate. But John Frederick was not without worldly wisdom. In an ultracourteous note he told the King of France that Melanchthon simply could not be spared, inasmuch as the university had been forced once again on account of the plague to transfer its classes to Jena.[20]

MELANCHTHONIAN DOODLES AND HANDWRITING

The Elector sent a firm, blunt note to Melanchthon. Temporarily hurt by the sharp refusal, Melanchthon nevertheless accommodated himself to the Elector's desire, and Luther later rejoiced that the evangelicals did not get mixed up in the affairs of France.[21]

On August 28 Melanchthon replied to the ruler of France. "I wanted to come," he said in effect, "but as Vore will explain to you, certain circumstances stand in the way of a visit." [22]

Another king, also behind a mask of religion, had his eye on Melanchthon—King Henry VIII of England. As early as 1531 Henry asked Melanchthon to prepare an opinion on divorce, inasmuch as the vigorous Henry wanted to divorce Catherine of Aragon in order to marry Anne Boleyn with whom he was already amorously involved. But Melanchthon found nothing wrong in Henry's marriage to Catherine, and could see no scriptural grounds for divorce. For the sake of an heir to the throne, however, he advised Henry to contract a second marriage without abrogating the first, "because polygamy is not forbidden by law and is not without precedent." [23] "If Henry wants a divorce, he can get it without me." [24] The other Wittenberg theologians joined Melanchthon in this advice, adding that they would not countenance divorce. Henry, however, acted on the advice of other theologians; he divorced his queen on November 14, 1532, and married Anne Boleyn. Two years later he broke with Roman Catholicism and declared himself the head of the English church. This made his political position precarious. Desiring to strengthen himself with allies, Henry sought to woo the Smalcald League. He sent Anthony Barnes, his chaplain, to Saxony to invite Melanchthon, religious spokesman for the league, to come to England, assuring him he would be free from danger, and offering hostages if they should be required.

Melanchthon wrote an exceedingly complimentary letter to Henry, praising him for his literary interests and exhorting him to use his offices to abolish abuses and either to introduce simple, specific doctrine or none at all.[25] At the suggestion of Barnes, Melanchthon dedicated a new edition of the *Loci* to Henry. The preface was so heavily scented with perfumed phrases that scholars have wondered about Melanchthon's motives, but the flattery was not for his own aggrandizement; Melanchthon hoped Henry would think seriously about evangelical doctrines and would be broad-minded enough to read some Protestant writers. Henry was indeed flattered; he wrote Melanchthon a personal letter which he signed, "Your Friend, King Henry VIII," and sent him a present of two hundred florins.[26]

At the request of the Smalcald League, Melanchthon drew up Thirteen Articles which were signed by Henry's envoys, the Landgrave of Hesse, and Elector Frederick. If Henry was to enter the Smalcald League, the Lutherans wanted to be sure his religious views were the same as theirs. The first article provided:

That the Most Serene King shall promote the Gospel of Christ and the pure doctrine of faith in the manner in which the Princes and confederated Estates confessed it in the Diet of Augsburg, and have guarded it in the published Apology; unless perhaps with the common consent of the Most Serene King and the Princes themselves, some things should seem to need correction or change in accordance with the Word of God.[27]

In the meantime Henry enlarged the English delegation to the Smalcald League. Edward Fox, bishop of Hereford, and Archdeacon Nicholas Hethe joined Dr. Barnes. They enthusiastically reported that Henry had abolished papal indulgences and abuses, designated papal rule no better than Babylonian tyranny, and had called the pope the Antichrist. With these men Melanchthon discussed the Thirteen Articles, but he was not greatly impressed by the envoys.[28]

When the Elector astutely surmised that Henry's motives were political, he again refused to let his famous teacher leave the university. After the death of Henry's queen, this time the unfortunate Anne Boleyn, Melanchthon wrote to Camerarius, "I am now freed from anxiety about going to England. Since the occurrence of such tragedies in England, there has been a great change of views. The late Queen, accused rather than convicted of adultery, has been executed." [29] (Anne Boleyn died on May 19, 1536.)

Diplomatic overtures continued, but with less hope of success. Despite Henry's matrimonial difficulties, the Smalcald League seriously considered an embassy, which would have included Melanchthon. The group would have gone to England to secure Henry's subscription to the Augsburg Confession as a condition for entering the Smalcald League. But other German estates opposed the plan. In September, Melanchthon, in the name of the evangelical princes, wrote to Henry asking for his views on the Thirteen Articles to which his envoys had already agreed and announcing that the Lutherans would postpone their drive for a general council until Henry's stand in religion was clear.[30]

Communication delays and new concerns caused a suspension of negotiations with England. It was just as well, for a series of English documents revealed Henry's political motives, even in the invitation to Melanchthon.[31]

Even though Melanchthon did not journey to England in 1535, his

ideas did, especially in the person of Alexander Aless. Aless, a refugee
from Scotland since 1532, carried copies of Melanchthon's *Loci* to England in August and presented them to the King and the celebrated Archbishop Cranmer. Aless, highly recommended by Melanchthon, became an
intimate friend of the Cromwell family and a close consultant of Henry,
who called him "my scholar." It was he who accompanied Cromwell
to the convocation in 1536 when Cromwell insisted that only two sacraments, baptism and the Lord's Supper, had Jesus' original appointment.
He also penned a treatise on *Schism* which supported the evangelical
view. Both the matter and the argument were Melanchthonian. Later
Aless served as a professor at Leipzig.[32]

In the following year Melanchthon rejoiced that the plague which
had forced the university of Jena had abated and that the faculty was
again home on the banks of the Elbe.

Sign of the Bread

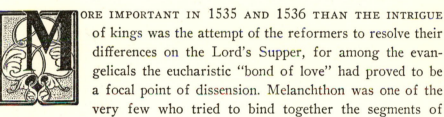ORE IMPORTANT IN 1535 AND 1536 THAN THE INTRIGUE of kings was the attempt of the reformers to resolve their differences on the Lord's Supper, for among the evangelicals the eucharistic "bond of love" had proved to be a focal point of dissension. Melanchthon was one of the very few who tried to bind together the segments of Reformation Christianity and was one of the first to realize the unitive significance of the Eucharist. The title "Father of Ecumenicity" is not inaptly applied to him. In his efforts, however, he modified Luther's famous "This-is-my-body" literalism, for which many have never forgiven him. Others have seen in his change, which came after ten years of struggle with the problem, an assertion that the Christian's experience of grace and love cannot be dogmatized.

In the sixteenth century, arguments about the Lord's Supper were not academic tiffs; a man could be deprived of his job, or be exiled, or lose his life. At Rostock participants in communion could not have beards; licking the blood of Christ from one's beard meant instant death! At Frankfort, when Musculus accidentally spilled some wine, Elector Joachim declared that prison, exile, and deposition would be punishment too mild for such an offense; whoever spills Christ's blood, he said, must have his own spilled. Three of Musculus' fingers were chopped off! Supt. Kongius of Hildesheim was expelled from his office because he picked up a wafer. Melanchthon's son-in-law, Peucer, went to prison for twelve years for seeming to deny Christ's physical presence in the bread. If some wine accidentally spilled on a suit, it had to be cut out immediately and burned. If some fell on the ground, it had to be licked up by the priest. If the linen altar cloth became wet with wine, it had to be washed three times and the water drunk by the priest. Fear that wine might be spilled was one reason prompting the Roman Catholics to deny the cup to the laity.

Such practices grew out of the superstition centering around the priest, who according to official doctrine had power to change the bread into the flesh of Christ and the wine into blood—transubstantiation!

After ten years of grappling with the problem in all its complicated aspects, Melanchthon came to a decision, and by 1544 he was ready to depart from Wittenberg rather than accept the semitransubstantiation still held by Martin Luther.

Political expediency was not the basic factor in Melanchthon's change. On the contrary, he came to realize that Christian truth may be more than any one individual can state. Oneness in Christ was to Melanchthon more essential than divisions begotten by scholastic interpretations. But it was not easy to change. "For more than ten years not a day nor a night has gone by without my thinking over the Supper." [1]

There is little doubt that the Marburg Colloquy of 1529 saddened Melanchthon. The this-is-my-body stand of Luther was a reaction in the direction of Roman Catholicism, probably brought on by the personal animosities in the pamphlet warfare between the Zwinglians and the Lutherans preceding the colloquy. Earlier, in the ninety-five theses of 1517, Luther asserted that faith in the forgiving grace of God must be present in the partaker before the sacrament of the Lord's Supper is effective, and that absolution by a priest is not necessary since spiritual blessing comes by faith. In 1519 Luther spoke of the mass as an external sign of an internal grace. But Luther never completely relinquished the old Roman view. As late as December, 1519, he still accepted transubstantiation, although he had condoned Melanchthon's rejection of the Roman Catholic dogma in September. Early in 1520 Luther spoke of *infused faith* as the chief thing necessary for the sacrament. In the *Babylonian Captivity* Luther decisively undercut priestly sacerdotalism and the theory that there is merit in a mechanical act. But the Marburg Colloquy evidenced a partial return to the papal doctrine, for Luther emphasized the physical presence of Christ in the bread and wine. This was what troubled Melanchthon! Could Christ be *physically* present in the bread, in a hundred communion services? Would this not be *true* presence? For more than a decade Melanchthon investigated and pondered the question. Gradually he drifted away from the hardened position of Luther.

Melanchthon began to have doubts about Luther's position when he read a dialogue by Oecolampadius of Basel. After reading it at Augsburg in 1530 he wrote to Luther: "Oecolampadius has written a dialogue against me. Inasmuch as it is better than he usually writes, I will bring it with me when God gets me out of here." [2]

Melanchthon was struck by the evidence that Oecolampadius brought forth to show that the ancient church subscribed to both mystic and symbolic views of the Eucharist, four centuries before the doctrine of the physical transformation of the elements was expressed.

Nevertheless, throughout 1530 Melanchthon continued to say why he could not unite with Oecolampadius and the Zwinglians. He objected to Zwingli's idea that the risen Christ bodily occupies one place and cannot be present in a multitude of eucharistic observances and to Bucer's idea that Christ is present in the Lord's Supper only to believers. What he could not tolerate was a memorial view; it was too far from the scriptural words. Zwingli still held that when Christ said, "This is my body," he pointed to himself. Melanchthon, driven by faith and reason, had come to the mysterious barrier between the infinite and finite. The Presence he could not deny in the Supper, neither could he explain or express it.

Before the end of 1530 Bucer, the opportunist, capitalized on the widespread desire among the princes for a union of the German and South German evangelicals. Through the Strassburg magistracy he sent to Landgrave Philip of Hesse and Duke Ernst of Lüneburg a compromise view of the Lord's Supper, saying Zwingli and Oecolampadius could agree with Luther that Christ's true body and blood are present in the Supper and are offered with the *Word* to the *soul* for strengthening of faith. Philip of Hesse sent word of the compromise to the Elector of Saxony, and the Wittenbergers rejoiced, but Melanchthon wondered if the Swiss would really go so far. He remembered the perfidy of Bucer in falsely translating some of Luther's works and in introducing "corrective" notes in others, and he could not so easily forget the bitter pamphlet exchanges a few years previously. But the Wittenbergers could not afford to ignore the obvious concession and Melanchthon "seized the opportunity to unite the Church and to bring variant views into harmony." [3]

Melanchthon wrote to Bucer:

I am exceedingly happy that you acknowledge the presence of Christ as to his soul; I do not understand why you should deny his presence as to the signs. Try to comprehend and come to an agreement on what remains in controversy. If Luther were positive that he knew Zwingli's and Oecolampadius' view fully, that they really taught as you write. . . .

But here was the rub. Bucer was an opportunist; he had promised too much for the Swiss; he was more interested in a unity of hearts than in a theological union. [4]

The effort to unite was without success. In April of 1531 Melanchthon wrote Bucer about his prayers and hopes for union and his unhappiness over the strife between Luther and the Swiss. [5] The turn had come; quite the opposite had been expressed at Marburg and Augsburg. In a letter to Thomas Blaurer, Melanchthon admitted that he was more and more suspicious of the bodily presence of Christ. Christ may be in the bread and everywhere as Luther contends, he said, but this is hard to conceive bodily inasmuch as Christ is everywhere only on account of his Godhead. Melanchthon wrote, "I will not speak against Luther's doctrine, but I will not object if Blaurer does." [6]

Melanchthon realized more and more that the *presence* of Christ in the sacrament is a mystery, analogous to faith. "This is my body" came to mean a spiritual allusion to the presence of Christ at all times and in all places, not a physical presence, not simply a memorial. The form of the union of Christ with the bread and the wine posed a mystery, the mystery of faith. To the Rev. Rothmann, preacher at Münster, Melanchthon wrote, December 24, 1532:

Why spread profane speculations about whether Christ is anywhere except in heaven, or whether he sits at a definite place. The Scripture orders us to call upon him. We must confess that he is truly with the Word and signs, and that he promised to be with us and to comfort us. I know well that able minds brood over how Christ can be present and that learned people subscribe to Zwingli's teachings, for which they have apparent grounds. But reason is not everything. The Presence, as I state it, has for it the analogy of faith.[7]

Bucer continued his efforts, despite the abortive bid earlier, and Melanchthon tended to favor the none-too-reliable expediter of union. With Zwingli and Oecolampadius deceased (1531), more South Germans looked to Bucer for guidance. In 1533 Bucer sent Melanchthon a book which he had written, *In Preparation for Union*. The report had circulated that a general church council was about to be announced by the pope and the emperor, and Bucer hoped his plan would help bring Protestants and Catholics together.[8] The book made a favorable stir in Wittenberg. Melanchthon replied:

I shall write you later about your book. I only wish now, as you will see, to say how truly and wholeheartedly I love you. You are taking the steps necessary for a sound union of the Churches, and to the best of my ability I promise to stand by you on this. I am not at all pleased that one question should separate us. I do hope that as we confide in one another, means will be found to make an end of division. That sudden meeting [at Marburg] of men who would not give an inch, did not help in this enormous evil. Would to God that you and I at least could talk together about this doctrine.[9]

Later Melanchtohn wrote, "There is nothing I wish more than that the horrible scandal of schism which hinders the progress of the Gospel be wiped out." [10]

But Melanchthon did not want to waste his time in a fruitless barter. Before meeting Bucer at Cassel, where Philip of Hesse had arranged the conference, he first sought reassurances from Bucer about the presence of Christ, according to his divinity, in the Supper.[11]

Receiving the reassurances, Melanchthon turned for words of instruction from Luther, for without Luther's consent there could be no union. The reply was crass. "The heart of our doctrine is this, that in the bread or with the bread, the body of Christ is really eaten, so that all motions and actions which are attributed to the bread, are attributed also to the body of Christ, so that the body is actually torn with the teeth and eaten." [12] Luther spoke of Christ's flesh being "eaten and bitten with the teeth." "From this view I cannot deviate even if heaven should fall on me." [13]

The presence of Christ in a spiritual sense Melanchthon looked upon as a *via media* between the realism of Luther and the memorialism of the Zwinglians, but Luther's statement furiously rejected any middle way. Luther's ill health contributed to the irritability that begat such a sharp statement. This Melanchthon knew, but he felt only disheartenment as he looked forward to Cassel. "I go," he said, "as the bearer of another's view, not my own." [14]

Inasmuch as Luther was the titular head of the German evangelicals, Melanchthon had to present his instructions at the interview with Bucer in December of 1534. Luther's crude formula about the true body being bitten and eaten, placed before Bucer, was forthwith rejected. Bucer and his friends were ready to agree to the Augsburg Confession, but not to any such private opinion of Luther.

The leader from the upper Rhine, and the preachers of his territory, willingly confessed that the body and blood of Christ are essentially and truly received in the Supper, and that the bread and wine are signs by which the body and blood are given and partaken. They would not confess to a natural union.[15] They felt that the union was sacramental.

After a further exchange of views, Melanchthon abandoned Luther's crude statement and reached agreement with Bucer,

That the body of Christ is really and truly received, when we receive the Sacrament; and bread and wine are signs, *signa exhibitiva,* which being given and received the body of Christ is at the same time given and received; and we hold that the bread and body are together, not by mixing of their substances, but as a sacrament, and are given with the sacrament. As both parties hold that bread and wine remain, they hold that there is a sacramental conjunction.[16]

This was as far as the compromise could go. After the long journey back from Cassel, Melanchthon laid the results before Luther. Even though the idea of sacramental union did not please Luther, he agreed to it for the sake of peace. The statement was given to other theologians for consideration.[17] The following July, with a delegation of Swiss leaders, the Wittenbergers closely examined Bucer's *Report* against the Anabaptists and *Ten Articles* which he had drawn up for the reformed cities of the South. Luther and the others were so pleased that they spoke as if agreement were virtually accomplished.

Melanchthon was intent on preserving the mystery of the sacrament as he believed it to have prevailed in the early church. Oecolampadius had strongly influenced him. In 1535 he had come to believe that Zwingli and Luther both represented extreme views. Zwingli's view bordered too closely on rationalism; Luther's view swung too close to sacerdotal transubstantiation. Melanchthon regarded transubstantiation (official papal doctrine since 1215) and Zwingli's memorialism as late developments in the Christian community. "I will not be a starter or defender of any new dogma," Melanchthon wrote to Brentz. "Investigate this yourself to see whether you defend the teaching of the ancients. I earnestly wish the Church would decide the matter without sophistry or tyranny." [18] His study of the church fathers convinced him he had been wrong in his earlier views of the Supper. And so, in 1535, Melanchthon was ready to change not simply for the sake of unity but for the sake of religious conviction born of study and experience. In changing, Melanchthon displayed the courage of deep belief.

Inward, spiritual communion with Christ was for him essential in the Eucharist. From this view, which might be called the spiritual view of the Supper, Melanchthon was never to depart. The 1535 *Loci* contains Melanchthon's beautifully expressed spiritual blessing of the indwelling Christ:

As I have said before, the word *sacrament* means an external sign which God has joined to his promise, through which he offers grace. The external sign (bread) is a sacrament. One should understand and take it for an external divine pledge and seal of the whole Gospel. . . . When we believe the divine promise that we are offered consolation and the forgiveness of sins through Christ, this external sign is to be received. And the external sign God places before our bodily eyes, and lets us eat, drink and partake, so that we may be awakened in faith and become the more certain and strong in the knowledge of Christ. For when Christ gives us his body, he takes us as members of himself, and shows very comfortably that grace and treasure are for us. . . . When one offers in the Supper bread and wine, there is truly offered to us the body and blood of Christ, and Christ is truly there, and is powerful in us, as Hilarius says: This eating and drinking makes it that Christ is in us and we in him. And it is truly a wonderfully dear great pledge of the highest divine love toward us and the highest mercy, that the Lord in the Supper shows that he truly gives himself to us, that he truly gives us to enjoy his body and blood, that he makes us members of himself, upon which we know that he loves us, takes us up, protects and upholds us.[19]

After more than a year's preparation following Cassel, Bucer arranged for the Oberlanders and Wittenbergers to meet at Eisenach, May 14, 1536. Luther's illness necessitated changing the place to Grimma and the time to May 21. After waiting a few days at Eisenach the Oberlanders journeyed on. When Bucer and his party arrived at Grimma, Melanchthon and Cruciger met them with a formal invitation to proceed to Wittenberg. They arrived on Sunday, May 21, at three o'clock in the afternoon. On the following day, the conference began in the home of Luther, who was still too ill to be about. Luther's obvious suspicions —on account of a recently published preface by Bucer—threatened the entire conference, even though Bucer explained that the preface had been written years before.

At the beginning of the second day Luther insisted that the South Germans renounce their earlier teaching, and confess that independently of the faith of the recipient the body and blood of Christ are truly present in the Supper. The Bucer party agreed, even agreeing that the body and blood are received by worthy and unworthy communicants, but they maintained a further distinction, e.g., the wicked cannot receive. This fine point threatened the success of the colloquy. Only after Melanchthon's diplomatic maneuvering did Luther finally declare, in the name of all the Wittenbergers:

We have now heard your answer and confession, viz. that you believe and teach, that in the Lord's Supper the true body and true blood of Christ are given and received, and not alone bread and wine: also, that this giving and receiving take place truly and not in imagination. Although you take offence in regard to the wicked, yet you confess with St. Paul that the unworthy receive the Lord's body, where the institution and word of the Lord are not perverted;—about this we will not contend. Hence, as you are thus minded, we are one, and we acknowledge and receive you as our dear brethren in the Lord.[20]

It was a joyous moment. The doctrinal differences had been bridged; union was assured. In a burst of mutual feeling they shook hands with each other, and tears came visibly to the eyes of Bucer and Capito.[21]

Discussions continued on other matters, but they all knew that the crucial point had been settled. On Sunday there were three services—Alber preached in the morning, Bucer in the afternoon, and Luther at vespers. They communed together. The Oberlanders winced at certain vestiges of Roman Catholicism—candles and pictures, elevation of the elements—but Bugenhagen assured them that these practices, continued only for the sake of the weak, were being changed gradually, that he and others often omitted them. Melanchthon finally brought about the official abolition of the elevation of the host in 1544.[22]

Friday morning, May 26, the formal articles, drawn up by Melanchthon, at the request of both sides, were laid before the Oberlanders. On Monday morning, after three days of formal and informal discussions, the conferees officially signed the *Wittenberg Concord*.

When the document was circulated among the local Swiss preachers, they quickly called attention to the fact that it committed the Lutherans to nothing but the hope that all might agree. The Eucharist is both earthly and heavenly, said Melanchthon in the concord agreement, and "with the bread and wine the body and blood of Christ are truly and substantially present, offered and received."

And although they deny that transubstantiation occurs, and do not hold that a local inclusion in the bread occurs, or any lasting connection without the use of the sacrament, yet they concede that, by the sacramental union, the bread is the body of Christ; i.e., they hold that when the bread is held out the body of Christ is at the same time present and truly tendered. For, apart from use, when it is laid by in the pyx or displayed in processions, as occurs among the Papists, they hold that the body of Christ is not present.

Since, however, only a few of us have met, it is necessary on both sides to refer this matter to other preachers and superiors. . . . Since, however, all profess that in all articles they want to hold and teach according to the Confession and Apology of the princes professing the Gospel, we are especially anxious that harmony be sanctioned and established. And we have the hope that if the rest, on both sides, would so agree, there would be thorough harmony.[23]

Twenty-one theologians signed. A statement about favoring baptism for infants and one about allowing private absolution were added and "subscribed as above."

But all was not well. Despite the jubilation of the participants, many theologians had doubts. On the very day that the concord was signed, Melanchthon wrote to a friend saying that there were still basic differences between the two parties which would occasion censure of the agreement and that he had no hopes for any permanent good. He was right.[24] Melanchthon did not doubt the sincerity of either Bucer or Luther, but he knew smooth words would not displace deep disagreement. "Sacramental union" meant one thing for Luther, another for Bucer; and the term "unworthy" remained unexplained.

Earlier Melanchthon had said, "If I could purchase union by my own death, I would gladly sacrifice my life," but from the day that he carried Luther's demand to Cassel he had not been fully in favor of the negotiations.[25] Bucer tried earnestly to convince his cohorts back home; but uneasiness persisted. Bucer's friends thought he had conceded too much and received too little.

Although the *Wittenberg Concord* has gone down in history as one of the great ecumenical events in Protestantism, it was abortive. Lasting concord was not achieved, not even among the Lutherans. The sign of the bread became the sign of dispute.

Worn out by the constant drains on his energy, in July of 1536 Melanchthon sought permission from the Elector to visit his brother and Camerarius. But he had hardly left Wittenberg before the tongues of rumor began to wag. This time the venom was that a great rift had grown between the "quiet scholar" and the "boar in the vineyard," and that the scholar was not really leaving to visit his brother but to escape the thrust of Luther's tusks. Melanchthon's teachings were no longer pure, they said; he had fallen from the heights of Augsburg to the rocks of Sacramentarianism. Never again, the rumorers surmised, could there be harmony at Wittenberg. It might even be necessary for the university to investigate![26]

By the time Melanchthon rode into Nürnberg, the rumors had overtaken him. Incensed and indignant he wrote a sharp letter to his colleagues:

Never have I meant to sever my teaching from yours, but if I am to be loaded with the suspicions and calumnies of certain men, and must be in

dread of alienations, I would rather go to the ends of the earth. I complain
of these things to you rather than to others. I am unwilling to be the cause
of any dissidence between us. Heartily do I love and cherish each one. Also I
am devoted to the public welfare. If my labours and a fair amount of diligence
in every duty do not witness for this, then in vain do I cry out in this matter.
But I hope you thoroughly understand me. I have never refused admonition
and friendly conference. Each one had his own gift. I have taken nothing
upon myself, nor have I ever wished to offer anything new. I have read your
writings and to the extent of my ability, I have wished to expound them in the
most simple manner.[27]

The rumormongers received a mortal broadside. By the time November 5 came and Melanchthon returned to the university, general approbation had choked the vicious whispers. The affair passed.

However, when once a man is vilified, others for reasons all their own find excuses to add to the character assassination. Jacob Schenk, a Freiberg preacher, raised a question about administering the communion in one kind only. Was this papal practice ever to be condoned? Would it be all right in some circumstances to give out the bread alone? Melanchthon answered affirmatively. If a devout, faithful Catholic has not been instructed and does not understand the underlying principles of the evangelical mass, he said, then it is permissible to use only the bread.

Misconstruing the scriptural basis for Melanchthon's words, and perhaps seeing an opportunity to attract attention to himself, the Freiberg sycophant (as Melanchthon called him) sent a copy of the letter to the Elector. Thinking this might indicate a deviation toward Catholicism, of which Melanchthon was often suspected, the Elector hurriedly forwarded the letter to Luther and Bugenhagen for their immediate judgment. "I will share my heart with Philip," said Luther; "I will pray for him."

A letter from Catholic Cardinal Sadolet coming in the wake of such suspicions threatened for a while to wreck the friendship of Wittenberg's two great professors. Sadolet's letter brimmed with praises for Melanchthon's moderation and learnedness. A short time later another letter of the Cardinal was printed and circulated in Wittenberg; it was filled with complaints about Luther's needless violence. Luther wondered, and the wonder became a doubt about Melanchthon. Many Wittenbergers began

referring privately to Melanchthon as a popish traitor. Amsdorf, a fiery
Magdeburg preacher who thrived on professional rivalry, wasted not a
moment in trying to arouse Luther against Melanchthon. When Luther
discovered, however, that Melanchthon had never answered the Cardinal's
letter, he saw in the matter just another trick of the papists to sow seeds
of discord. "The Catholics would like to win over our Philip," Luther
declared. "If Philip would consent, they would readily make him a
Cardinal and let him keep his wife and children."

There were other disputes with Osiander and Agricola, and one
wonders if these peripheral outcroppings were portents of some central
trouble. Was there an unspecified feeling that Melanchthon had deviated?
He had indeed deviated from Luther's semipapal view of the Eucharist!

In the Corpus Christi the Roman Catholics paraded the bread with
elevation, adoration, and worship. Luther did not give up the practice
until Melanchthon persuaded him to do so. It was not eliminated from
Protestant worship in Wittenberg until 1544.[28]

In 1538 the practice of elevation occasioned strife in Nürnberg. One
preacher wanted to abandon the practice, but Veit Dietrich, with a high
view of the local presence of Christ, sharply protested. Both Dietrich and
Osiander wrote Melanchthon. After consultation with Luther, who saw
no reason for quarreling about unimportant things, Melanchthon wrote
to Dietrich:

> In order not to separate myself too far from the ancients, I set the sacra-
> mental presence *in use* (not simply in the signs), and they say that *with the
> offered bread* and wine Christ is truly present and effective. That is certainly
> enough. I add nothing as to an inclusion or union, according to which the
> body attaches to the bread or is mixed with it. What more do you want? [29]

Dietrich was not satisfied with an indirect answer. So Melanchthon
answered to the point: If one believes in the physical presence, then elevation is proper; if not, then elevation ought to be omitted.

> Sacraments are signs that something else is present. Adoration is not
> necessary, or in any event adoration should not be made to the bread. . . .
> There is a real union, like the union of fire and iron. I believe in a real union,
> an inclusive one, a sacramental union, which means that with the given signs
> Christ is truly effective.[30]

In 1540, when Germany was making overtures to Calvin, Philip published a new edition of the Augsburg Confession, known now as the *Variata* because of the many changes in phrases and sentences. The changes in the article on the Lord's Supper demonstrated the change in Melanchthon's thought.

Article X of the Augsburg Confession, 1530, read, "Of the Supper of the Lord, they teach that the Body and Blood of Christ are truly present, and are distributed to those who eat in the Supper of the Lord; and they disapprove of those who teach otherwise."

Then years later, 1540, Melanchthon altered the wording of Article X. "Of the Supper of the Lord, they teach that with the bread and wine the body and blood of Christ are truly tendered to those who eat in the Lord's Supper." Melanchthon left out "they disapprove of those who teach otherwise," and he substituted "tendered" for "distributed." These changes marked Melanchthon's departure from the near-Catholic view of Luther to a view that could be accepted by many liberal Protestants in the twentieth century. Melanchthon had come round to a belief in the *real, spiritual presence*. A desire to unite the segments of Protestantism brought the change of thought into the open, but it was not an alteration to satisfy Calvin, whom Melanchthon had the good judgment to admire. Melanchthon's view had changed before Calvin came into the picture. On the other hand the new wording, which did not *deny* Luther's view, *allowed* for a spiritual interpretation which Calvin could accept.

In 1543 a dispute arose in Eisleben over what to do with the bread and wine that remains after communion. In sermons and public discussions the furor permeated the entire community. What should be done with the unused elements in the Eucharist? Should they be carried about, honored, and worshiped as the papists did in their Corpus Christi? Should the wine be poured on the ground? Should it be mixed with ordinary wine? Should one of the priests drink it? Should it be used again? The real question, however, was how long are the body and blood of Christ present in the elements? The disputants finally laid the entire matter before the Wittenbergers.

Luther was reluctant to answer; he saw in the dispute an overtone of scholasticism. He did not want to advocate transubstantiation, for that

might encourage adoration of the elements. On the other hand he wanted
to suggest a physical presence that lasted beyond the ordinary use. He
could not conceive that afterwards the elements reverted to ordinary bread
and wine. The elements, he said, had to be treated *sacramentally*. The
wine might be poured with other wine and drunk. Luther could not shake
off the Roman view.

Melanchthon made no such reservations.

> God is not to be bound to bread and wine apart from the purpose for which
> the communion was instituted. It would be wrong to portray the union in a
> manner which at the words of consecration would make Christ's body so united
> with bread as to be perpetually there. Only while the visible signs are being
> received is Christ present and effective.

There had been debates formerly about a mouse's sanctification after eating bread following communion. Melanchthon's opinion allowed for no
such question. After the act of communion, the elements are no longer a
sacrament. If taken by a noncommunicant, they are as ordinary bread and
wine. The remains, he said, can be handled as ordinary bread and wine,
but if this seems abrupt and irreverent to some, let the leftover bread
and wine be consumed.[31]

Melanchthon had appropriated the spiritual view of the supper. Some
evangelicals could not or would not distinguish this from the memorial
view of Zwingli, a view which was generally outlawed in Lutheran
circles, and so Melanchthon's stand came to be more and more obscured
in a rash of rumors and charges and deliberate misinterpretations. Luther
had ears and he heard. In 1543 and 1544 communication seemed to break
down between the two reformers; suspicion and unfriendliness grew.

The personal relations between Melanchthon and Luther were further
strained when a small book on the Eucharist appeared in Cologne. Melanchthon helped edit some of the worst features out of the book, and for
this attempt to improve the book he was charged with joint authorship.

In January of 1543 Melanchthon received an invitation from Archbishop Herman of Cologne to come to the assistance of Bucer, who had
been invited to set up a program of reform for the Lower Rhine. Luther
favored this "godly and Christian work," Camerarius rejoiced, and the
Elector gave his warm consent to Melanchthon along with a hundred

gulden and an escort. On May 4, in the company of Justus Jonas, Jr., and Jerome Schreiber, Melanchthon entered Bonn. The religious situation was almost as bad as that found in the Saxon domains during the 1528 visitation. Melanchthon spoke of the "barbarism" and "heathenish superstition" and the worship of images, but observed that the people were at least responding to pure teaching and preaching.[32]

One plan, that of John Gropper, the archiepiscopal chancellor, had already been submitted, the plan of the "painted articles" as Melanchthon described it. Bucer had already submitted a plan, also, but it needed drastic revision. Melanchthon spent three days rewriting various doctrines, filling in necessary gaps, smoothing the language. The statements on the sacraments he left untouched as he believed them to be a fair approximation of the views in the Wittenberg Concord. The results of his work and that of Bucer were put forth in a little book called Herman's *Consultation,* which later became a Lutheran church order, but the immediate results were explosive.

The papal clergy of Cologne raged. They voted to reject the *Consultation.* Gropper, piqued, because his own plan was discarded, attacked it in a book called *Antididagma.* Billich, a Carmelite monk, whom Melanchthon described as a "matted priest of Bacchus and Venus," added his abusive lampoonery. The clergy of Cologne then turned on Herman and had him deposed, April 16, 1546.

Melanchthon did not see that anything could come of so much wrangling. "I have attended many conventions, yea, battles; but I have never happened among more rabid and impudent sycophants."[33] Never before had he been so wretchedly accommodated.

I am living here the life of a sailor. My lodgings are by the Rhine just where the boats land, whence comes the foul stench of the bilge-water. In the house everything, the table, the bed, the fireplace, are crowded together just as in a boat. The wine is wretched; the cooking is Westphalian. The cleanliness is far from that of France, or of the Upper Rhine. It is also expected that the imperial army will pass through these parts.[34]

Melanchthon's answer to Billich's satire is a masterful defense of evangelical reform over against superstitions of the papal clergy, the corruptions of monasticism, and the evils of celibacy. He refuted charges of innovation, sedition, and self-interest.[35] But Melanchthon had had enough of the controversies on the Lower Rhine. In July, he turned once more toward Wittenberg, not knowing exactly what to expect, for disturbing bits of information had been reaching him. But Melanchthon had nothing to fear. He paused momentarily at Frankfort to adjust a ceremonial dispute about the Supper, reported to the Elector's court at Weimar, and on August 15 entered Wittenberg. A crowd of students and professors met him outside the city walls and escorted him home in triumph.

But the Cologne incident was not over. Archbishop Herman sent a copy of the *Consultation* to the Elector of Saxony, who noticed and frowned on the spiritual interpretation implied in the statements on the Lord's Supper. He turned to Amsdorf, a professional rival of Melanchthon's and more extreme than Luther on the Eucharist, for a judgment. Amsdorf's reaction was unfavorable and he sent a copy of the book to Luther along with his hostile comments. Unduly prejudiced by Amsdorf, Luther reacted very negatively. "The book talks about the usefulness, the fruit, and the honor of the sacrament," he exclaimed, "but it mumbles about the substance." "It says not a word against the fanatics" and it does not mention "the oral reception of the true body and blood." [36] "I trace in its long pages," said Luther, "the work of that Klappermaul Bucer! It is more comforting to the Zwinglians than to us."

Luther attacked the book in sermons, lectures, and letters, and he let it be known that he was preparing a new book on the sacraments that would set the Sacramentarians back on their heels. The implication was that he would attack Melanchthon, even though Philip was not the author of the disputed passages. The two of them no longer ate dinner together. The garden retreat behind Melanchthon's house where they had conversed so often was deserted.

Agonized over the dissension that seemed imminent, Melanchthon wrote:

If this new strife breaks out, it will cause much worse and more tragic confusion than anything hitherto. I am sorry that this tragedy should begin again, more for the sake of public welfare than for my own. I do not know what will happen to me. Perhaps I shall have to wander forth in this my old age. Is there anything more sorrowful, more deserving of tears than that that holy pledge of love [the Lord's Supper] should be used as a subject of strife and division? [37]

Word spread in Wittenberg that Luther planned a devastating criticism of Melanchthon and Bucer in the book he was writing, and the rumor circulated that he had drawn up a formula which he was going to demand that Melanchthon sign or suffer the consequences. Melanchthon seriously contemplated taking himself and his family into exile. On August 28, 1544, he penned a note to Bucer:

I wrote you by Milich that our Pericles is about to thunder most vehemently on the Lord's Supper, and that he has written a book, not yet published, in which you and I are beaten black and blue. Amsdorf, whom he recently visited and consulted on the matter, is applauding the assault. Tomorrow, as I learn, he will summon Cruciger and me. I pray God to grant the Church and us a salutary result. Perhaps it is God's will that the subject be agitated again, that it may be further explained. I am calm and will not hesitate to withdraw from this penitentiary should he attack me.[38]

In October of 1544 the much heralded book appeared, *A Short Confession on the Holy Sacrament, Against the Fanatics*. Melanchthon thumbed through the pages. He and Bucer were not even mentioned!

But Luther did attack "the fanatics and enemies of the sacrament— Carlstadt, Zwingli, Oecolampadius, Stenkefeld [Schwenkfeld] and their disciples in Zurich and wherever they are." "Before I die," he said, "I want to bear witness against them." The twaddle about spiritual eating and the unity of the participants are fig leaves to cover up the sins of "blasphemers and liars." The common people can be excused, but the masters cannot. He accused Zwingli of having a false heart at Marburg. One sentence must have stood out, "He who does not want to remain, let him go." [39]

Although Luther's irritable, passionate nature showed throughout the book, Bucer and Melanchthon were spared. Was it because Luther discerned a difference between the spiritual and the memorial views? Was it because he wanted no ill feeling? Had he ever intended to attack Melanchthon?

Cruciger wrote Dietrich, October 5, 1544, that the tirade against Melanchthon and Bucer which everyone took for granted was nowhere to be found. Brück informed the worried Elector, "I notice that Philip and Martin are still quite good friends. The Almighty send his grace." Luther himself spoke words that are somewhat difficult to fathom, "I have absolutely no suspicion in regard to Philip." [40] Luther also wrote to the Venetians that if they should hear that either he or Philip had succumbed to the Sacramentarians, they were not to believe an iota of it. [41]

The Zurichers were furious when they saw the book. Bullinger immediately put out a sharp answer. He would honor Luther, he said, as a servant of God, forgetting neither his fine virtues nor his glaring weaknesses! Calvin wrote to Melanchthon about his respect for Luther and the distress he felt on account of the entire situation. If Luther were only more moderate!

Realizing that a new pamphlet warfare was likely to break forth, Philip of Hesse appealed to Chancellor Brück to use his influence to quench further outbursts.

For the honor of Christ ponder this matter truly and with all diligence. Luther as well as the Zürichers are somewhat rough in this controversy, but there is no need of their getting heated and making others suffer; they should act as more reasonable men and exercise a Christian patience. For should disunion once grow between Luther and Master Philip, God help us! What would come of it? How the papists would glory and say, If a kingdom is divided in itself, it will go down. It would without doubt cause many Christian people to become offended and scandalized and many would fall away from the Gospel. O, Almighty God, what is the matter with people that they get up such hurtful and angry disputes. It is not a true apostolic spirit that does this, but a spirit as seeks a quarrel, division and brawl. [42]

When Philip of Hesse learned from reliable sources that Luther was planning to answer Bullinger, he urged the Elector to forbid it, saying only the Romans would profit. John Frederick sent Brück to consult with Melanchthon. With tear-filled eyes Melanchthon told Brück that he feared a dispute between Luther and the Zurichers would destroy the Wittenberg Concord and destroy what little hope there was for unity among the evangelicals. Knowing that the Zurichers were coarse and restless and that Luther could easily control his vehemency, Melanchthon advised that the Elector suppress the controversy in Saxony and forbid the sale of Bullinger's book. Melanchthon went directly to Luther and asked him to draw up some simple statement that might be subscribed by both sides, but he would not. Cruciger wrote to Dietrich, "If Philip were not here keeping unity among us with his moderation and good will, the University would fall to pieces." [43] The Elector, keenly aware of this, as well as Melanchthon's value to the university, forbade Luther to attack Philip.[44]

Misunderstanding begat misunderstanding until Luther felt that he was not wanted at Wittenberg. The climax came in a quarrel between Luther and the law school. Jurists on the law faculty engineered a rule that approved secret weddings. Believing that this was against the Decalogue injunction to honor father and mother and therefore an "upsetting of the divine law," Luther objected. He became increasingly morose and irritable. Finally, in disgust and despair, Luther left Wittenberg with no intention of returning.

Melanchthon prepared to leave also, for he declared that he would not live at the university without Luther. Realizing the crisis, the Elector begged Melanchthon to stay and to persuade Luther to return, whereupon Melanchthon journeyed to Merseburg, found Luther, and brought him back. The long years of friendship nullified the breach between the two leaders of Wittenberg. Luther celebrated his birthday, November 10, 1544, by inviting Melanchthon, Cruciger, Bugenhagen, Jonas, and Major to dinner.

If he felt any fundamental difference between himself and Melanchthon, Luther could hardly have spoken as he did of the 1545 edition of the *Loci:*

He who desires to become a theologian has the Bible, and after that he can read the *Loci* of Philip. When he understands both, he is a theologian, and to him all theology will stand open. You can find no other book under the sun where the whole of theology is so excellently explained as in the *Loci*. Philip is more moderate than I; he defends and teaches; I am a talker, a public speaker. If people will follow me, they must print only those books of mine which teach doctrine, such as the commentaries on Galatians, Deuteronomy, and John. Let the other books be only for history, so that one can see how it all began, for at first it was not so easy as now.[45]

After the death of Luther (February 18, 1546), extremists once again asserted Luther's "physical" view of the Lord's Supper, and Melanchthon denounced this as bread idolatry. Once again Wittenberg resounded with strife. The sacrament of grace and the bond of love externally, at least, was little more than a figure of speech.

An Unending Web

OPE PAUL III WAS FAR FROM FEVERISH IN HIS DESIRE FOR a general council, but for political and economic reasons just two years after he ascended the papal chair he announced that he would convene a council in May of 1537 at Mantua.

The evangelicals had long pleaded for an impartial council, but in the pope's summons they were prejudged as "heretics." Realizing, however, that they would have to say why they would not attend such a council, the Protestants called for an assembly of all the Lutheran estates at Smalcald, February 7, to decide on a common course.

Luther was asked to formulate a statement expressing the evangelicals' attitude. Instead of revising the Augsburg Confession, he prepared new articles. When the Confession was written in 1530, a faint hope still lingered that the churches might become reconciled. Melanchthon, therefore, had emphasized agreement and had underplayed the points of dissension. As the years passed, the Roman Catholics took advantage of Melanchthon's "light-stepping" to pervert the underlying evangelical point of view.

By 1537 the irreconcilable differences between the two divisions of Christendom had become evident. Instead of making an indirect claim for toleration Luther felt impelled to show "open and uncompromising hostility to the hopelessly corrupt papacy." [1] By arraigning the Roman church for the errors in which it had become hardened, Luther drew a sharp line between Catholicism and Protestantism. In doing so, he had the sanction of his colleagues. Before the new articles were sent to the

[249]

Elector they were approved by Melanchthon, Jonas, Cruciger, and Bugenhagen, as well as Amsdorf, Agricola, and Spalatin who had been summoned to Wittenberg.

By January 3, the Smalcald Articles, as they came to be called, were on their way to the Elector for perusal. Convinced of their truthfulness and basic agreement with the Augsburg Confession, he openly declared he would confess them in council and before the whole world, and would petition God to keep him, his relatives, and his subjects from vacillation.[2]

The Smalcald credo was almost a declaration of war on the papacy. Part I stated the evangelical belief about the Trinity and the Incarnation. Part II discussed redemption through Christ, and the abuses which originated through relics, pilgrimages, and like works. Part III set forth some doctrines the evangelicals were still willing to discuss. Actually, these were quite a few, but the antipapal note throughout the articles was unmistakable, for Luther spoke of the pope as Antichrist.[3]

Toward the end of January, 1537, the Elector, Melanchthon, Luther, Spalatin, and Bugenhagen mounted horses and wagons bound for Smalcald. Forty theologians and almost as many civil rulers converged on the city. When the cold wintry blasts proved too much for Luther's health, the Elector loaned him his personal wagon for the return home. As he went through the city gate, he shouted to Melanchthon, "May God fill you with hate for the Pope!"

The brunt of a strained situation fell on Melanchthon, for in attendance at the meeting were Vorst, the papal nuncio, and Held, the vice-chancellor to the Emperor. As at so many previous meetings, there were threats and talk of war. And as usual there were long, protocol-filled deliberations which consumed time and energy. It is not clear why the princes hesitated to accept Luther's articles, but they did delay, and even asked Melanchthon to discover what articles of faith the evangelicals would sustain at all hazards. Melanchthon complained that attempts to compromise would lead to apprehension and disharmony.

When Luther's articles were laid before the theologians, they signed, because they recognized the document as a powerful statement of their convictions. The princes, however, needed something else to present at Mantua, since it was generally conceded that the Protestants should not attend a council where they would be considered heretics.[4] When Melanchthon subscribed to Luther's articles, he added:

I, Philip Melanchthon, regard the foregoing articles as right and Christian. But of the Pope I hold that if he will permit the Gospel, the government of the bishops which he now has from others, may be *jure humano* also conceded to him by us, for the sake of peace and the common tranquillity of those Christians, who are or may hereafter be under him.

This willingness to accept the pope's control of bishops rested not simply on a desire for peace. Melanchthon saw in the *human* control of the pope a realistic solution to a situation which was neither black nor white. He carefully qualified his statement so as to safeguard the gospel, which for him meant justification by faith. In the tractate which he penned a few days later, he did not hesitate to excoriate the papacy for its corruptness and to demonstrate that its claims to divine sanction were unbridled pretensions. Melanchthon knew that no one, be he pope or Luther, is absolutely right, that no human system is final or without flaws, that limited human beings always devise relative goods.

Cognizant also of the increasing control of the evangelical churches by the princes, Melanchthon thought some means should be devised for keeping church polity independent of the state. In the urgency of the historical situation, others unfortunately did not see likewise. Melanchthon's qualification aroused considerable feeling among the evangelicals, but this did not deter the so-called acquiescent Philip nor prompt him to erase the note added to his signature.[5]

While still at Smalcald, Melanchthon, at the request of the princes, composed one of the sternest and ablest apologies for rejecting the papacy that has ever come out of Protestantism. With characteristic skill he refuted the papal claim of supremacy and asserted the right of churches everywhere "to ordain for themselves pastors and other church officers." He forcefully brought out the grounds on which the proposed council had been refused. Using Luke 22:25, John 20:21, Gal. 2:7 ff., I Cor. 3:6, and similar passages, Melanchthon showed that Scripture does not place the pope by divine right above other pastors, and that the same is true in early church history. He then systematically refuted the scriptural passages used by the opponents.[6]

Melanchthon composed the essay in Latin and Veit Dietrich made the German translation that was signed by thirty-four ministers and theologians. It was just what the princes needed to accompany their rejection of the proposed general council. In the recess statement the princes expressly mentioned and approved the Augsburg Confession and the Apology and this new writing which was called the *Appendix on the Papacy.* The essay thus received an immediately symbolical authority among the evangelicals. For many years it superseded Luther's articles which were privately published by Luther in 1538, 1543, and 1545. By the time of the Book of Concord in 1580, Luther's Smalcald Articles and Melanchthon's essay had acquired solid symbolic authority.

After composing several other items for the princes on how to handle miscellaneous religious problems, and after requesting the princes to use the papal church and school properties which they had confiscated for Protestant religion and education, Melanchthon departed for home. He was worried about Luther's health, wondering if Dr. Sturz of Erfurt had helped the pain of the stone, wondering if the prayers he so earnestly offered had been answered. At Weimar he rejoiced to see Luther, who had recovered considerably, and the two rode together to Wittenberg. He wrote to Agricola:

I was seized by a peculiar sorrow when I saw Luther's danger. I was moved to it by the loss of the Church, but also by my love for this man, and my admiration of his distinguished and heroic virtues. I could not but be greatly troubled at the danger of such a man. Therefore, I heartily thank God and our Lord Jesus Christ, that he has looked upon our tears and sighs, and has restored Luther to health.[7]

After a week's travel, Melanchthon, exhausted, again set foot in Wittenberg. He thanked God for the quiet of his home, and exclaimed, "I shudder when I think of conventions! These unlearned affairs draw me away from my studies into I know not what fate and they upset the routine which I prefer above all others. And I do not see just how they will be useful to us."

During the following year uneasiness reigned throughout Germany with distrust as the chief minister. The Roman Catholic princes, meeting secretly at Nürnberg, on June 10, 1538, formed their Holy League to counterbalance the Protestant League of Smalcald. When the evangelicals heard of the Roman deliberations, outright conflict appeared inevitable. Philip of Hesse called for war, but the Elector, remembering the Pack affair, did not let his anxiety sweep him into precipitous action.

When electors Joachim of Brandenburg and Louis of the Palatinate offered to mediate for the leagues and to set up a conference at Frankfort, both sides agreed to talk. And so, on February 1, 1539, Melanchthon left his home and family to journey with his Elector to Frankfort. The Elector's brother and nephew Henry (called Maurice of Saxony) and four hundred horsemen joined them. Trampling down the frozen roads, they resembled a small army. Landgrave Philip made an equally pompous entry with about four hundred *Lanzknechts*. Delegates from the free cities and the foreign representatives and the usual tradesmen made Frankfort look like a convention city. But the Duke of Lüneburg, Ernest, made almost no show of circumstance with his arrival, and the Duke of Württemberg, who lived only two days' journey away, did not even come. He went hunting.

There was not much calm in Frankfort; each side accused the other; and talk about war increased.[8] By March 4 the negotiators on both sides seemed to reach an impasse, and hopes for general peace dimmed. Melanchthon wrote to Brentz:

The matter has almost come to that point, that, as the Emperor said, the time for arms, and not for deliberations, seems to have arrived. Yet, although I tremble when I think what a very serious matter this is, I am sometimes surprised that our friends, who are so greatly irritated, do not break forth more violently.[9]

To make the evangelical position perfectly clear, Melanchthon wrote three essays in German. In the first he developed the evangelical right of defense in case the enemy attacked; in the second he demonstrated that upright persons could not take up arms against the Protestants; and in the third he called on all godly men to assist the Lutherans.[10] There was little doubt that the evangelicals would wage war on the Emperor if they had to do so. By April 5 matters were still unsettled, and Melanchthon wrote to Camerarius:

We have been here weaving the veil of Penelope. If we have rejected one form of peace, another is laid before us, which merely differs from the preceding one in words, but not in sense. Some maintain that they are treacherously procrastinating this matter, but this has not frightened us yet. I hope that the Empire may remain undisturbed, although no fair conditions could yet be obtained from the Imperial orator. He demands that we should not receive any new confederates. This shameful condition is introduced again and again, with new sophistries, although it has been rejected repeatedly. In this you have the entire history of the Convention. In the beginning, I disputed concerning a number of points; but when the Imperial ambassador made such unreasonable demands, I ceased; and if no truce is made, we shall publish the reasons which induced us to reject those demands.[11]

Melanchthon was not the only one who keenly felt the tension of war. John Calvin, who had come as a representative of the Swiss, spoke of the ominous threats hanging over the conference. He made frequent references to the danger of war, hasty evangelicals who actually voted for war, fear of the Turks, resignation to violence on the part of the Saxon elector, an attack on Lüneburg, and the many speculations about conflict.[12]

Calvin noted the desire of the evangelicals to be free to administer their own churches and dispense ecclesiastical property and the desire of the Emperor on the other hand to maintain authority in his hands, although he was bending toward the evangelicals out of fear of the Turkish menace. "Thus," wrote Calvin, "all as yet is in suspense, nor are we out of danger of war, unless the Emperor makes further concessions." [13] When the Roman Catholics proposed annulment of former agreements and a static status quo until arrangements could be made for a general German church reform, the Lutherans considered the move a bit of subterfuge and passed a sharp decree,

by which they declared, that they would sooner see their wives and children put to death before their eyes; that they would incur the loss of all their privileges; see their city ploughed up and utterly destroyed, and themselves cut off to the last man, rather than they would admit those laws by which the progress of the Gospel of Christ should be interrupted.[14]

Calvin, who had come to Frankfort not only as an official but "to exchange thoughts with Melanchthon about religion and the concerns of the Church," has left a portrait of Melanchthon. Having heard reports about Melanchthon's "soft disposition," Calvin was surprised. "I wish that our excellent friend N. could behold how much sincerity there is in Philip. All suspicion of double-dealing would entirely vanish!" [15] Melanchthon so much desired a peaceful union of the church and had so often expressed his hopes, that many people believed he was deflecting toward Rome.

Calvin admired Melanchthon for his obvious candor and he noted the dogmatic tenacity of the German evangelicals. Some of the latter were so obstinate and despotic

that for a long time he [Melanchthon] seemed to be in actual jeopardy, because they saw that he differed from them in opinion. But although he does not think that a solid agreement can be come to, he nevertheless, wishes that the present concord, such as it is, may be cherished, until at length the Lord shall lead both sides into the unity of his faith.[16]

This observation of Calvin points up an important factor which lay at the bottom of what seemed to many of Philip's contemporaries and later interpreters to be "wavering weakness." Melanchthon believed that neither he nor Luther nor Calvin had grasped final truth, nor would they in this world. Consequently, he was willing to negotiate, willing to appear weak, that all possible human light might be shed on the situation. He was conscious of limited human machinations, at Frankfort as elsewhere, and so wrote to Camerarius, "We sit here and work as Penelope did on an unending web." [17] When the emotional tempest comes, Calvin reported, Melanchthon is apt to advise delay.[18]

After lengthy discussions, the convention ended in a truce, April 19, 1539, each side binding itself to keep the peace for fifteen months. "We thank God," Melanchthon wrote from Saalfeld four days later, "that no one is permitted to start a war, and that the peace of Nürnberg has again been established and renewed. But this was gained only by great exertions." [19]

Melanchthon found time during the convention to write a letter to Henry VIII of England, who was still trying to induce him to come to England.[20] The Elector had sent two seasoned diplomats to England in the place of Philip: Vice-Chancellor Burkhart and the Hessian Marshall Ludwig of Baumbach. Melanchthon wrote not only to Henry but also to Cranmer.[21] But the evangelicals suspected that all was not well in England. Reports began reaching them of Henry's arrogance and atrocities and his burning a man for not subscribing to the physical presence of Christ in the Lord's Supper.[22] On July 28, 1539, their suspicions were confirmed. Henry issued his Six Articles establishing transubstantiation, private masses, auricular confession and vows, and forbidding the marriage of priests under pain of confiscation of goods and loss of life. Persecutions followed.

Melanchthon then penned a harsh letter to Henry which was published a few years later in England under the title *The truth will have the victorie*.[23] He decried what appeared to him to be a mere shuffling of papal practices, and added that the king had probably been ill-advised by self-seeking bishops.

I hear that certain excellent men in learning and godliness, as Latimer and others are kept in prison, for not consenting unto what is decreed. . . . Although there can nothing happen unto them better or more glorious, than to suffer death in so plain a confession for the truth; yet I would not have your grace to be sprinkled with the blood of such men.

In religious strifes, warned Melanchthon, the wrong often seems right, because the "devil disfactions himself into an angel of light and garments false opinions with all fained colors possible." Very craftily, Melanchthon observed, the bishops say auricular confession is "needful." Why do they not say plainly that God requires us to enumerate all our sins in confession? They speak in generalities in order to "cast a mist before the people's eyes," and the article requiring private masses is "bewitched with sophistry."

A like sophistry is it when they say that the wedlock of priests is against the word of God, they not unknowing that plain text of Paul saying, a bishop must be faultless the husband of one wife. Besides that what shamefulness and tyranny add they when they command them to be killed that will not break their wedlock and part from their wives. . . . O shameless bishops, and O wicked Stephin Gardiner bishop of Winchester, which thinketh to deceive the eyes of Christian people, and the judgment of the godly the whole world through.

Surely it is the influence of Antichrist that countermands the gospel for the sake of making money, garnering worldly splendor, and acting the tyrant, said Melanchthon. The "wiles of the devil" stir up "ungodly opinions" that mankind may suffer "wrongful slaughters and baudry."

Again therefore, I pray you, for our Lord Jesus Christ's sake, that your grace will suage and amend the bishops' decrees . . . and serve the glory of Christ and take heed to your own salvation and wealth of your church. . . . All the godly pray and entirely beseke your grace that ye prefer not the wicked and cruel sentences, and sophistical cavillation of these your bishops.

During the summer following the Frankfort convention Melanchthon introduced the Reformation in the lands of Duke George. After the death of George on April 17, his brother Henry came into control and he favored the evangelicals. Although hindered by papal intransigence, Melanchthon introduced the evangelical principles into the law of the land, reformed the Leipzig University, and conducted a church visitation. He had hardly finished this work when the Elector of Brandenburg, Joachim II, asked him to come to Berlin to introduce the Reformation in his territory.

Finally returning to Wittenberg in October of 1539, Melanchthon found the plague raging. His brother-in-law Sebald Münsterer and Frau Münsterer had just died, leaving their children homeless. Melanchthon took them into his own house, even though he himself was burdened with many cares. He wrote Dietrich in Nürnberg that he was going through a climacterical year and that he was tired, partly because of the despondency he felt and partly because of excessive labors.

Although I might wish to live somewhat longer, on account of my children, also on account of my books, yet I shall follow God with resignation, whenever it pleases him to call me away from this place. I am very glad that you so kindly offer your assistance to my son [Philip, then fourteen], and I commend him to you; for he will need the kindness of his friends, when I am gone. His moral character is good, but I cannot praise his temperament; and I also believe that he does not possess sufficient talent to study.[24]

Despite the plague, Melanchthon resolved to stay in Wittenberg. "I will bear this cross, as I have borne many other things; God will put an end to it." Nevertheless, Melanchthon believed that he, too, might succumb to the plague and drew up his last will and testament, November 12, 1539. To his heirs he left his religious convictions.[25]

In the name of God the Father, Son, and Holy Spirit.

The chief purpose apparently for which wills were first made was that fathers might leave to their children a sure testimony of their views in regard to their religious faith, that they might obligate their children to retain and conserve the same views, as we see by the wills of Jacob and David. Therefore, I have desired to begin my will by reciting my confession. . . .

In the first place, I return thanks to God the Father of our Lord Jesus Christ who was crucified for us, the Creator of all things, because he has called me to repentance and to the knowledge of the Gospel; and I pray him for the sake of his Son, whom he wills to be a sacrifice for us, to pardon all my sins, to receive, justify, hear me, and to deliver me from eternal death. This I believe truly he will do. For thus he has commanded us to believe. And it is impiety to magnify our sins above the death of the Son of God. This latter I magnify above my sins. Moreover, I pray God for the sake of his Son our Redeemer, by the Holy Spirit to increase in me these beginnings of faith. I am indeed distressed by my sins, and by the scandals of others; but I magnify the death of the Son of God, that grace may abound over sin.

In the second place, I declare that I truly embrace the Apostles' and the Nicene Creed; and in regard to the entire Christian doctrine, I hold as I have written in the *Loci Communes,* and in the last edition of the *Commentary on Romans,* in which, article by article, I have striven to say without ambiguity what I hold.

In regard to the Lord's Supper I embrace the Form of Concord (the *Wittenberg Concord*) which was made here. Therefore I unite myself with our churches, and I declare that they profess the doctrine of the Catholic Church of Christ, and that they truly are churches of Christ. I also enjoin upon my children to abide in our churches, and to flee the churches and society of the Papists. For the Papists in many articles profess the most corrupt doctrine: they are absolutely ignorant of the doctrine of Justification by Faith, and of the Remission of Sins; they teach nothing about the difference between the law and the Gospel. In regard to the worship of God they hold heathenish and Pharisaical notions. To these errors they also add many others, besides manifest idolatry in their Masses and in the worship of dead men. Therefore I beseech my children on account of the command of God to obey me in this matter and not to join the Papists.

And since I see that posterity is threatened with new commotions of doctrines and of the Church, and that there will probably be fanatical and trifling spirits who will overthrow the articles of the Son of God and of the Holy Spirit, I wish to warn mine to adhere to the views which I have professed with the Catholic Church of Christ in the *Loci,* where I condemn Samosatenus and Servetus, and others who dissent from the received Creeds.

It is also probable that new sophistries of a seductive nature will come after a while, when the old errors, somewhat changed in colour, will be re-established, and these conciliatory measures will corrupt the pure doctrine, as it is now taught. I also admonish mine not to approve these sophistical attempts to conciliate.

The learned also are to be exhorted to watch, lest under the semblance of peace and public tranquillity they accept such doctrinal confession as was promulgated at the Syrmian Synod. This I can truly affirm, viz., that I have striven truly and properly to explain the doctrine of our Church, that the young may rightly understand our views and transmit them to posterity. If this form is profitable, as I think it is, I request *Caspar Cruciger* and others who have been my pupils, to conserve it in the schools.

I know that certain persons have at times suspected that I have done some things to favour the adversaries. But I call to God to witness that I have never wished to favour the adversaries; but I have sought accuracy in explanation in order that these things when freed from ambiguity might be better understood by the young. How difficult it was for me to attain to such order and method in explanation, many know, who know that in explaining, I often changed the form. It is evident that the Augustinian form is not sufficiently explicit. Hence I declare that with a pure motive I studied the method which is employed in the *Commentary on Romans,* and I desire to leave behind me distinct views, without ambiguity, because ambiguity afterwards produces dissensions. Nor has it been my purpose to present any new opinion, but clearly and properly to expound the Catholic doctrine, which is taught in our churches, which by the special blessing of God I declare to have been revealed in these recent times through *Doctor Martin Luther* in order that the Church which had almost perished might be cleansed and restored. Therefore so long as we can, let us preserve this light. And I pray God the Father of our Savior Jesus Christ, the Creator of all things, to promote the studies of the pious, and to preserve the Church, and especially to bless our churches which on account of the Gospel are daily attacked.

Melanchthon concluded with words of thanks to Martin Luther, John Frederick, Chancellor Brück, his bother George, and nine other close friends.

The *Loci* to which he referred was the 1535 edition and the *Commentary on Romans* was the 1532 printing. Since Luther endorsed both of these after Melanchthon made his will, this document is also a testimony to the spiritual harmony of the two reformers.

Bigamy!

HE BIGAMY OF PHILIP OF HESSE IN 1540 CREATED A scandal which threatened the entire Reformation, for both Luther and Melanchthon gave their tacit approval! The evangelical leaders enjoined secrecy on Philip of Hesse, which was enough to arouse suspicion, but on top of that Luther denied the affair and circulated a lie on the ground that a confessional is to be safeguarded, and Melanchthon published an equivocal letter which raised more questions than it answered. All Europe began talking. To maintain his position in politics, Philip of Hesse was forced to dissolve his military alliance with the evangelicals and prostrate himself before Charles V. Ironically, Charles had sired illegitimate children all over Europe, children who were eventually legitimatized by the pope that they might hold offices of state, but that did not matter.

It all began in 1523 when Philip of Hesse, then only nineteen, married Christina of Saxony, the daughter of Duke George, Luther's formidable enemy. It may have been a political marriage, but three sons and three daughters were born to the couple.[1] From the beginning Philip was unfaithful, and as early as 1526 he contemplated bigamy as a halter for his adulterous lechery. Condemned by his own conscience, he abstained from the Lord's Supper, but he could not control his sex drives. To justify his adultery and probably to lay the foundations for annulment of his marriage, he accused his wife of moral and physical infirmities. In 1539 Philip resolved to take a second wife and to justify it on the basis of Scripture, for he realized that his father-in-law, Duke George, would never tolerate a divorce, and that annulment, the usual procedure in

such cases, was out of the question since he was Lutheran rather than
Catholic. In the Old Testament he found many examples of polygamy
and concluded that he, too, could have two wives.

The Landgrave decided on bigamy when in the court of his sister, the
Duchess Elizabeth of Saxony, he met seventeen-year-old Margaret von
der Saale. After wooing Margaret, he began negotiations with her
mother, the "Hofmeisterin" Anna von de Saale. Anna insisted on having some scholarly opinions that such a union would not violate divine
law, and she wanted the ceremony to be semipublic with nobles and
theologians of note present.

In an effort to fulfill the demands of Anna and also to bolster his own
decision, Philip consulted Bucer and then dispatched him with a confessional for the theologians at Wittenberg. The Landgrave then obtained the consent of his first wife and had a document drawn on December 17, 1539, in which he made her children the legal heirs to his titles
and estates.[2]

The situation was explosive with political possibilities. Categorically
to deny Philip might drive him to the Roman Catholics, who could be
counted on to annul his first marriage in order to win him from the
evangelical cause. To give permission for divorce would be contrary to
Matthew's teachings that only adultery is a ground for divorce.[3] The
only course apparently was to assure Philip that bigamy was not condemned in the New Testament, was practiced in the Old, and in special
cases of "necessity" had been condoned by the church.

This line of thought was not new for Melanchthon. He had previously
suggested bigamy as a substitute for divorce or adultery. The advice
was given to Henry VIII when he was contemplating the divorce of
Catherine of Aragon in 1531. In writing to Henry, Melanchthon refuted the arguments urged in favor of divorce and then added:

But what if the public good render a new marriage advisable for the sake
of the succession, as is the case with the King of England, where the public
benefit of the whole kingdom would be promoted by a new marriage? Here
I answer, if the King desires to provide for the succession, how much better
it is to do so without throwing any stigma on his previous marriage! And
this may be done without peril to any one's conscience or reputation by a
second marriage. For although I would not concede polygamy generally,—

for I said above that we are not laying down laws,—yet in this case, for the great benefit of the kingdom, and, it may be also, for the sake of the King's conscience, I hold that the safest course for the King would be to marry a second wife, without casting off the first; because it is certain that polygamy is not prohibited by Divine Law; nor is it unprecedented. Abraham, David, and other holy men had a number of wives. The Emperor Valentinian enacted a law allowing two wives, and himself married Justina, without casting off his prior wife Severa. The Popes, too, have formerly granted such permissions, as to one George, an Englishman.[4]

Luther joined Melanchthon in the advice to Henry, and the stand was not new for Luther either. But Luther and Melanchthon both regarded monogamy as normal and had no thought of making polygamy generally legal. Melanchthon had previously written to Bucer that he would rather in this matter strain the authority of the magistrate than sanction divorce.[5]

The reformers were, of course, criticized by the Catholics, and every effort was made to link the Wittenbergers with the excessive Anabaptists who introduced polygamy in Münster, July 23, 1534. Nevertheless, many Catholic leaders held views similar to those of the reformers. Cardinal Cajetan thought the Pope should have given Henry VIII a dispensation for bigamy, and the matter was discussed seriously before the consistory of cardinals before a negative answer was given, for canon law condoned bigamy under certain circumstances.

What then made the Philip of Hesse affair so sensational? Why did it attract so much unfavorable attention? The answer is twofold: People became aware that Philip's "necessity" was only his lust, and the "pure" reformers who had denounced the corruption of the clergy of Rome appeared to be condoning immorality for political advantage.

Melanchthon and Luther were unsuspectingly dragged into the matter. Bucer, after receiving the confession of the Landgrave, hurried to Wittenberg to obtain the approval of Luther and Melanchthon for the projected bigamy. He pictured the situation as one of necessity. Philip wanted to make use of the means provided by God to free himself from the immoralities conditioned by his unhappy marriage, Bucer said. The Landgrave wanted "a testimony for his personal use" showing that bigamy is not contrary to God's holy ordinance. Actually, Philip of

Hesse wanted the testimony because Anna demanded it. He himself had already made up his own mind and had already ordered wine for the nuptials, and had virtually completed arrangements for the wedding. In this, he deceived the reformers.

In a letter dated December 10, 1539, Melanchthon gave his ill-fated appraisal of the matter. It was meant as confessional advice, but the Landgrave regarded it as a quasi dispensation. Luther added his signature as joint author, and seven others signed: Bucer, Antonius Corvinus, Adam Fulda, J. Lemingus, Justus Winther, Dionisius Melander, and Balthaser Raid. The letter was not clandestine compromise; Melanchthon and Luther were honestly trying, as spiritual advisors, to lay before the Landgrave their opinions. Under confessional seal they admitted a qualified dispensation for bigamy in case of necessity.

Since your princely Grace has through Master Bucer laid before us a certain longstanding trouble of your conscience,—although it is difficult for us to answer it in such haste, we would not let Bucer ride off without a letter. And first, we are heartily rejoiced and thank God that He has helped your Grace out of your dangerous sickness; and we pray that He will strengthen and preserve your Grace in soul and body to his praise. For, as your Grace sees, the poor miserable Church of Christ is small and forsaken, and verily needs pious lords and princes; as we doubt not God will preserve some, although every kind of temptation befall.

With regard to the question, of which Master Bucer spoke with us, firstly, this is our opinion. Your Grace knows and understands this yourself, that it is a very different thing to make a general law, and in a particular case to use a dispensation, out of weighty reasons, and yet according to divine permission; for against God no dispensation has force. Now we cannot advise that it be openly introduced, and thus made a law, that each be allowed to have more than one wife. Should anything of this get into print, your Grace may conceive that this would be understood and adopted as a general law, whence much scandal and trouble would ensue. Therefore, this is by no means to be adopted; and we pray for your Grace to consider how grievous it would be, if it were charged upon anyone that he had introduced this law in the German nation, whence endless troubles in all marriages might be feared. As to what may be said against this, that what is right before God should be allowed altogether, this is true in a measure. If God has commanded it, or it is a necessary thing, this is true; but if it is not commanded, nor necessary, other circumstances should be taken into account. Thus with regard to this question: God instituted marriage that it should be the union of two persons alone, and not of more, unless nature had been corrupted. This is the meaning of the saying, *They two shall be one flesh.* And this at first was so retained. But Lamech introduced the example of having more than one wife at once, which is recorded of him in Scripture as an innovation contrary to the first rule. Thenceforward, it became customary among the unbelievers, till at length Abraham and his descendants took more than one wife. And it is true that afterward this was allowed in the Law of Moses, as the text says, Deut. xxi. 15, *If a man have two wives,* etc. For God gave way somewhat to the weakness of nature.

But since it was according to the first beginning and the creation that a man should not have more than one wife, this law is praiseworthy, and has thus been adopted in the Church: nor should another law be made and set up against it. For Christ repeats this saying in Matt. xix. 5, *And they twain shall be one flesh,* and reminds us how marriage was to be at first, antecedently to man's infirmity. That in certain cases, however, a dispensation may be used,—as if a person taken captive in a foreign land should marry there, and on gaining his freedom should bring his wife with him,—or if long continued sickness should supply a cause, as has been held at times with regard to lepers,—if in such cases a man takes another wife with the counsel of his Pastor, not to introduce a law, but as a matter of necessity, such a man we could not condemn.

Since then it is one thing to introduce a law, and another to use a dispensation, we humbly entreat your Grace to consider, first, that care should in every way be taken that this matter be not brought publicly before the world, as a law which everybody may follow. Next, since it is to be no law, but merely a dispensation, let your Grace also consider the scandal, namely, that the enemies of the Gospel would cry out, that we are like the Anabaptists, who take several wives at once, and that the Evangelicals seek the liberty of having as many wives as they please, according to the practice in Turkey. Again, what Princes do gets abroad much further than what is done by private persons. Again, if private persons hear of such an example in their lords, they desire that the like should be allowed to them; as we see how easily a practice spreads. Again, your Grace has an unruly nobility, many of whom, as in all countries, on account of the great revenues which they derive from the Chapters, are violently opposed to the Gospel. Thus we know ourselves that very unfriendly speeches have been heard from divers young squires. Now how such squires and the country folks will behave toward your Grace in this matter, if a public proceeding be adopted, may easily be conceived. Again, your Grace, through God's grace, has a very illustrious name, even among foreign kings and potentates, and is feared on account thereof, which credit would be impaired hereby.

Seeing then that so many scandals are combined, we humbly entreat your

Grace to consider this matter well and diligently. This, however, is also true, that we by all means entreat and exhort your Grace to avoid fornication and adultery; and in truth we have long had great sorrow from hearing that your Grace is laden with such distress, which may be visited with punishments from God and other dangers; and we entreat your Grace not to esteem such matters out of wedlock a light sin, as the world tosses such things to the wind and despises them. But God has often fearfully punished unchastity; for it is recorded as a cause of the Deluge, that the rulers practiced adultery. Again, the punishment of David is a solemn example: and Paul often says, *God is not mocked: adulterers shall not enter into the Kingdom of God.* For faith must be followed by obedience, so that one must not act against one's conscience, nor against God's commandment. *If our conscience condemn us not, then we have confidence toward God:* and *if through the Spirit we mortify the deeds of the body, we shall live; but if we live after the flesh,* that is, against our conscience, *we shall die.* This we say, because it is to be considered that God will not trifle with such sins, as many people now grow bold to entertain such heathenish thoughts. And we have heard with pleasure that your Grace has seriously mourned on account thereof, and feels sorrow and repentance for them. These great and weighty questions press for your Grace's attention. Moreover, your Grace is of a slender and far from strong constitution, and sleeps little; wherefore your Grace should reasonably spare your body, as many others are forced to do. . . .

Again, even if your Grace had another wife, and did not seriously resist the evil practice and inclination, it would not avail your Grace. It behooves man in his outward walk to bridle his members, as Paul says.

Be also pleased to consider that God has given your Grace fair young Princes and Princesses with this Consort. Be content with her and avoid offence. That we should excite or urge your Grace to an offensive innovation, is far from our mind. For your country and others might reproach us on account thereof, which would be intolerable to us; because we are commanded in God's Word to regulate marriage and all human matters according to their first divine institution, and, so far as possible, to keep them therein, and to avert whatever may offend anyone. The way of the world is now such that people like to throw all the blame upon the preachers, if anything unpleasant fall out; and men's hearts, among high and low, are unsteady: and all sorts of things are to be feared. We would rather that your Grace stood in better case before God, and lived with a good conscience, for your Grace's happiness, and the good of your country and people.

If, however, your Grace should at length resolve to take another wife, we think this should be kept secret. Your Grace, and the Lady, with some confidential persons, should know your Grace's mind and conscience through confession. From this no particular rumor or scandal would arise; for it is not unusual for princes to have concubines; and although all the people would not know the circumstances, the intelligent would be able to guess them, and would be better pleased with such a quiet way of life, than with adultery and other wild and licentious courses. Nor are we to heed everything that people say, provided our consciences stand right. That which is permitted concerning marriage in the law of Moses is not forbidden in the Gospel, which does not change the rule of outward life, but brings in eternal righteousness and eternal life, and kindles a true obedience to God, and would set our corrupt nature straight again.

Thus your Grace has not only our testimony in case of necessity, but also our advice, which we beseech your Grace to weigh, as an illustrious, wise, Christian Prince; and we pray that God may lead and direct your Grace to His praise and to your Grace's happiness.[6]

Although the legal penalty for bigamy was death, Philip now went ahead with arrangements. On some pretext he lured Melanchthon to Rothenburg, on the Fulda, and there in Melanchthon's presence with Bucer and a few others looking on he married Margaret.

Luther and Melanchthon were both uneasy. They both exhorted Philip to keep the matter secret and to strive to improve his life as he promised.[7] They both received Rhenish wine for their advice!

However, secrets are seldom kept. At the insistence of his ambitious mother-in-law, Philip consented to a public repetition of the ceremony with several nobles present. The storm of gossip followed.

Believing that he had done untold damage to the cause of the evangelical church, Melanchthon became despondent. "The weakness of my body increases more and more," he wrote Luther, "for with every new day I hear mounting evils about the Hessian affair. . . . Ask God to turn away the monstrous danger and scandal." Thinking thus, and believing that his dream of death was about to be fulfilled, he became dangerously ill. At Weimar, while en route to a convention at Hagenau, Melanchthon broke down. The Elector summoned his own physician from Erfurt and asked Luther and Cruciger to ride immediately from Wittenberg. Solomon Glass graphically described what took place when Luther arrived:

He found Melanchthon apparently dying. His eyes were dim, his understanding almost gone, his tongue faltering, his hearing closed, his countenance fallen and hollow; he knew nobody; he could eat and drink nothing. At the sight of him Luther became alarmed, and turning to those present, he exclaimed, "Behüt Gott, how the devil has assaulted this man!" Then Luther facing the window prayed fervently. "Our Lord God could not but hear me," said Luther, "for I threw my sack before His door, and wearied His ears with all His promises of hearing prayers." After this he seized Philip's hand: "Be of good courage, Philip, you shall not die. God has reason to slay, but He willeth not the death of a sinner, but that he should be converted and live. God received into his favor the greatest sinners that ever lived on earth, Adam and Eve, and he will not reject you, Philip, or let you perish in sin and despair. Do not succumb to this dejection and murder yourself, but trust in the Lord, who can slay and make alive again, can wound and bind up, can smite and heal again." Luther knew well the burden on Philip's heart and conscience. Thus addressed, Philip began to stir, but for a long while could say nothing. At last he turned straight toward Luther and began to beg him for God's sake not to detain him any longer,—that he was now on a good journey,—that he should let him go,—that nothing better could befall him. "By no means, Philip," said Luther; "you must serve our Lord God yet longer." Thus Philip by degrees became more cheerful, and let Luther order him something to eat; and Luther brought it himself to him; but Philip refused it. Then Luther forced him with threats, "Philip, you must eat, or I excommunicate you." With these words he was overcome, so that he ate a very little: and thus gradually he gained strength again.[8]

On the wall Melanchthon read a quotation from Ps. 118, "I will not die, but will live and publish the Word of the Lord." It was a good omen.[9] The Elector wrote Melanchthon to take heart, to trust in God, and to come to Eisenach with his friends when he felt better.[10]

Luther's letter to Melanchthon in June showed that the Landgrave, in seeking advice, had not made a full confession:[11]

You know it was told us in that matter that it was a case of extreme necessity, to which a law does not apply, or which at least requires a modification of it. Wherefore, I beseech you for Christ's sake, be of a calm and quiet mind; and let them whose concern it is do something, and bear their own burdens, and not throw the whole weight on us, whom they know to be candid and faithful. . . . Why then do you torment yourself? Our ultimate cause is sure to stand, that is, Christ's victory, although our formal and intermediate cause is somewhat disgraced by this scandal. We, who love you sincerely, will pray for you diligently and effectually.[12]

By July 7 Melanchthon felt strong enough to journey to Eisenach for a discussion of the developments with the Hessian theologians. It was here that Luther upbraided Philip and the Hessians for their duplicity and their breaking of the confessional secret.

Melanchthon's recovery was slow. Not until September 1 did he write his well-known words to Camerarius:

I cannot possibly describe for you the terrible pangs that I suffered during my illness, some of which return even now. I could see that Luther was in agony of mind, but he repressed his anxiety, lest he should increase mine. He tried to raise me up with the greatest magnanimity, not only by comforting me, but often by reproving me severely. If he had not come to me, I would have died.[13]

Others involved in the affair were neither as honest nor as dismayed as Melanchthon. Bucer and the Landgrave deliberately deceived the reformers by not saying anything about negotiations with Anna or about the concubine that Philip had kept earlier, and by pretending *necessity*. When the scandal became widespread, Bucer urged the Landgrave to make a public denial of the entire matter![14] Luther, on the basis of the inviolability of the confessional, also counseled giving an ambiguous answer. Philip of Hesse did neither. One of his preachers, Lenning, under the name of Huldreich Neobolus, published a pamphlet justifying polygamy. Luther was furious and blamed Bucer. The essay in which he planned to blast Philip and Bucer was abandoned because John Frederick did not want to prolong the scandalous affair.[15] Two letters of Melanchthon, one dated April 5, 1542, and one March 28, 1543, showed that the scandal was still smoldering after four years. Luther's final expletive was fitting: Let the devil bless future bigamists with a bath in hell!

Although the Landgrave prostrated himself before the Emperor asking forgiveness and although he lost political prestige, he continued to live with both wives. His first wife bore him three children after his bigamy, and by his second wife he had seven sons and one daughter, the last born in 1554!

The adverse effect on the evangelical church reform can hardly be assessed. Roman Catholics, who winked at worse affairs in their own bailiwick, advertised the incident as the kind of fruit that could be expected of a heretical schism. Annulment would have been the Catholic solution; divorce the Protestant solution a few centuries later. Luther and Melanchthon would countenance neither, inasmuch as they were committed to a literal interpretation of Scripture. Kolde's judgment was right: "It is highly probable that the beginning of the decline of Protestantism as a political power coincides with this marriage of the Prince of Hesse."

As the official theological spokesman for the Lutherans in the 1540's, Melanchthon had more than his share of conferences, colloquies, and diets. He keenly sensed the inadequacy of such gatherings and was continually conscious of the hypocrisy, the striving for worldly place, and the sophistry in caucus-room haggling.

When the Hagenau conference floundered, the delegates resolved to meet at Worms on October 28, 1540, but there seemed to be little hope that the Lutherans and Catholics could come to unity in necessary things, liberty in doubtful things, and love in all things. Melanchthon arrived in Worms on the last day in October, and two days later wrote to Camerarius about the "shameless hypocrites" who had been sent to the conference by the Catholics.

Not until January 14 did the diet open officially, and even then for another whole month Morone and other papists managed to frustrate the proceedings by arguing about agenda, rules, and order.[16]

The weeks of wrangling over procedure were but a preface to the main event of pettifoggery. When Melanchthon presented the Augsburg Confession as a basis for the discussions, Eck protested that it was not the same as had been read at Augsburg in 1530—not that he would have any more readily accepted the 1530 document! Eck claimed he had examined the original at Mayence. Melanchthon did not deny having changed the Confession; he had done so to make the meaning plainer, not different. The most important change was on the Eucharist allowing for a spiritual interpretation. Unable to slip a cog in the conference wheels by this maneuver, Eck allowed the matter of *Variata* to drop.

Melanchthon was never more skillful, more sincere, and more devastating than he was in the ensuing debates with Eck. In flawless Latin

and with biblical and historical acumen, he argued the basic views of
the evangelical reform.

After debating original sin for four days, the conference suddenly
ceased. Granvelle, commissioner for the Emperor, and presider over
the conference, received an order from Charles to transfer the proceedings to Regensburg. Melanchthon hurried home for a few days, and on
March 14, 1541, again rode out of Wittenberg. Two days later he joined
other delegates at Altenburg. While going through Bavaria the carriage
in which he was riding overturned, hurling him headlong on the half-
frozen ground. The wrist of his right hand was severely sprained. For
months he had to write with his left hand, and, although he learned to
write with his right hand again, the pen strokes were heavily scrawled.

The Diet of Regensburg, with Emperor Charles present, opened on
April 5. The Emperor promptly appointed a committee to discuss religious issues: John Eck, Julius von Pflug, and John Gropper to represent
the papal side; Philip Melanchthon, Martin Bucer, and John Pistorius to
represent the evangelicals. He charged them to forget animosity and seek
the glory of God.

When the appointed committee began its public debates, on April 27,
the Emperor presented to the members *The Regensburg Book*. He hoped
it might be a basis for harmony, but the book's half-Catholic, half-
Protestant views rendered it unacceptable to both sides. The authorship
of the *Regensburg Book* is uncertain. John Gropper may have done it.
Eck apparently believed that Melanchthon did, for he declared before
an assembly of the princes that he never would approve the book because
it "Melanchthonized" too much. Melanchthon disclaimed any connection with it and surmised that Eck wanted to insult Gropper by his
insinuation.[17] Acting on the Emperor's request, the conferees examined
each article in the book. They obviously disagreed on transubstantiation,
the mass, divine right of the pope, infallibility of general councils, and
minor matters. They agreed on the Fall, free will, and original sin, and
came to agree to some extent on justification.

When the Catholics in this meeting attributed justification to faith in
Christ's merits, they undercut the sacerdotal power of the Roman priesthood and undermined the medieval principle of ecclesiastical authority,

for this made the mass unnecessary as a meritorious work. Rome later reprimanded Contarini for his part in this compromise.[18]

After an eight-hour debate with Eck on the Lord's Supper in which Melanchthon said, "Nothing has the nature of a sacrament apart from the divinely appointed use," and "Christ is not present for the sake of the bread, but for the sake of the recipient," Eck seemed greatly confused. Melanchthon wrote that "Eck became sick, having become too excited, perhaps, and drinking so excessively afterwards, that a fever followed."[19] He never returned to the meetings.

An official letter to the Emperor accused Melanchthon of being stubborn in carrying out the suggestions of Luther and the Elector. In defense Melanchthon made it plain that he was not just the mouthpiece of Luther or anybody else, that even the Elector had not given him definite guidance. "I have sought to find truth according to Scripture," he said, "and I wish your Imperial Majesty could see my heart so that you might judge truthfully what my endeavors in regard to these disputes have been for many years." Asserting that he could not sanction the recently developed corruptions of saint-worship and private masses, Melanchthon asked to be dismissed.[20] Elector Frederick and Luther were highly pleased that Melanchthon had called the hand of his accusers. "May God Almighty graciously sustain him in his course."[21]

In his report of June 24 on the *Regensburg Book* Melanchthon said he could not receive the book because of what he believed:

I conclude upon the Word of God and with a good conscience that I cannot and will not receive this book. . . . And that everyone may know what I believe, I will here declare that I hold the doctrine of our churches as it is set forth in our Confession and Apology, and by God's grace I intend to abide in it. And I thank God that he has enlightened his Church, nor do I wish to give occasion for obscuring the pure doctrine again. No one can truthfully charge that I have pleasure in useless strife. For it is manifest from my writings that with the greatest diligence I have sought and maintained mildness and moderation. I also pray God for peace and Christian unity; and *I am ready for a further declaration.* May God, the Father of our Savior Jesus Christ, help us.[22]

Melanchthon's willingness to reconsider was not begotten in cringing fear, as has so often been charged against him. He knew that men behold truth only in spots, that they see through a glass darkly, and that he had no monopoly on divine light, but he also knew that he must stand in such light as he had until further illumination.

The Regensburg Diet represented a great degree of conciliation, but it was conciliation based on a mature consciousness of what the Reformation meant religiously and politically. It was conciliation coming out of a sense of strength. Those at Regensburg realized that the evangelical movement had reached dogmatic consciousness, confessional dignity, and political power. Rome regarded Germany as lost. Melanchthon had done his work well.[23]

During the next three years Melanchthon's health became increasingly poor. He mentioned insomnia and worldly cares in many of his letters. But his work did not slacken. The letters that he wrote in 1542 would make a large volume and in December an edition of his works came out in Basel. His energy appeared to have no end. "He is doing more than all the rest," Luther observed. "He is the Atlas who sustains heaven and earth." [24] Nevertheless, Melanchthon buckled under the strains of the time and the poor health which seemed to be his lot. In 1543 there were the tensions and suspicions in Wittenberg over Luther's expected attack on the Sacramentarians. And in 1544 Melanchthon sustained repeated onsets of the stone and internal infection. On July 1, 1544, he wrote to Dietrich: "Dearest Veit, while I am writing this, I am suffering severely from an infection of the spleen, which has been caused by the afflictions which have weighed upon me the past two months. If my spleen ulcerates, I shall die." [25] Camerarius became alarmed about Melanchthon's health and hastened to Wittenberg. In the space of two days, with great pain, Melanchthon passed three stones, yet he continued to lecture at the university! [26]

When an affair at Mansfeld developed and when representatives had to be chosen for another meeting at Regensburg, Luther asked that Philip be excused from both, even Regensburg. "As it will be a useless and ineffectual council, of which we can hope nothing, Philip, who is indeed very ill, should be spared." Luther spoke to Brück, saying Melanchthon's life should not be risked in a fruitless venture. "If we should lose this man from the University, it is likely that half the University would leave on his account." The Elector excused him.[27]

Acute pain from the stone and constipation prevented Melanchthon from accompanying Luther to Mansfeld to settle matters between the counts there. Luther left on January 23, 1546, accompanied by his three sons. Melanchthon never saw him alive again! He worried lest Luther and his sons be caught in the swollen Saale River, but Luther died suddenly of other causes.

On February 19 Melanchthon received a letter from Jonas telling the news of Luther's short illness and death. At nine o'clock that day Melanchthon was to lecture on Romans, but he could think only of Luther. With tears in his eyes he spoke:

I intended to explain to you the Epistle to the Romans, because in this is contained the true doctrine of the Son of God, which God in special mercy has revealed to us, in this our day, through our venerable father and dear teacher, Dr. Martin Luther. But I have this day received a sad letter which troubles me so much that I doubt whether I shall be able in the future to discharge my duties in the University. What this is I will now relate to you so that you may not believe other persons who may circulate false reports in regard to the matter.

On Wednesday, February 17, shortly before supper, Dr. Martinus was attacked by a pain in the pit of the stomach, with which he was several times afflicted here. This returned after supper, and as it did not cease he went to his chamber, and laid himself down for about two hours, until the pains had become much worse. He then called Dr. Jonas, who slept in the same room, and asked him to request Ambrosius, the tutor of his sons, to make a fire in the room. He then went in, and was soon surrounded by Count Mansfeld and his lady, and many others. . . . On the morning of February 18, before four o'clock in the morning, he commended himself to God in this prayer, "My dear heavenly Father, eternal, merciful God! Thou hast revealed unto me thy beloved Son, our Lord Jesus Christ; him have I taught and confessed, him I love and honor as my dear Saviour and Redeemer, whom the wicked persecute, despise and revile. Take my soul to thyself!" He then thrice repeated the words: "Into thy hands I commend my spirit, thou hast redeemed me, O God of Truth!" and then said: "God so loved the world. . . ." This prayer he repeated several times, and while thus praying was taken by God into the everlasting school and eternal joy, where he is now enjoying fellowship with God the Father, Son, and Holy Ghost, together with all the prophets and apostles. Alas! Gone is the Chariot of Israel which ruled the

Church in this last age of the world. For assuredly this doctrine of forgiveness of sin, and of faith in the Son of God, was not invented by the wisdom of man, but was revealed by God through this man. . . . I beseech Thee, O Son of God and Immanuel, who wast crucified for us, and didst rise again, to rule and protect thy Church. Amen.[28]

The students wept.

About noon, on February 22, Luther's corpse was brought back to Wittenberg. All the bells tolled and a vast crowd moved alongside the coffin. Bugenhagen preached a deeply moving funeral sermon, and Melanchthon delivered a Latin oration.[29]

Melanchthon set Luther's work in relation to God's providential care for the church. He spoke of Luther as "a minister of the Gospel raised up by God" to establish true worship, expound Holy Scripture, preach the Word of God, and proclaim the Gospel of Jesus Christ. He placed him in the succession on Adam, Abraham, Moses, David, Elijah, the Apostles, Augustine, Tauler, and many others. The world has had great leaders who ruled over vast empires, he said, "but far inferior were they to our leaders, Isaiah, John the Baptist, Paul, Augustine, and Luther."

Luther brought to light the true and necessary doctrine. He showed what true repentance is, and what is the refuge and the sure comfort of the soul which quails under the sense of the wrath of God. He expounded Paul's doctrine, which says that man is justified by faith. . . . Many of us witnessed the struggles through which he passed in establishing the principle that by faith are we received and heard of God. Hence throughout eternity pious souls will magnify the benefits which God has bestowed on the Church through Luther.

Melanchthon was not blind to Luther's faults, nor did he let the faults blind him to Luther's greatness:

Some have complained that Luther displayed too much severity. I will not deny this. But I answer in the language of Erasmus: "Because of the magnitude of the disorders, God gave this age a violent physician." . . . I do not deny that the more ardent characters sometimes make mistakes, for amid the weakness of human nature no one is without fault. But we may say of such a one, "rough indeed, but worthy of all praise!" If he was severe, it was the severity of zeal for the truth, not the love of strife, or of harshness. . . . Brave, lofty ardent souls, such as Luther had must be divinely guided. . . . God was his anchor, and faith never failed him.

In conclusion Melanchthon warned that confusion often follows the death of an illustrious man:

Yonder, the Turks are advancing; here, civil discord is threatened; there, other adversaries, released at last from the fear of Luther's censure, will corrupt the truth more boldly than ever. . . . That God may avert these calamities, let us be more diligent in regulating our lives and in directing our studies . . . for God has not revealed himself by such splendid witnesses and sent his Son in vain, but truly loves and cares for those who magnify his benefits. Amen.

The Important Nonessentials

N 1530, DUE TO POLITICAL DIFFICULTIES, THE EMPEROR had found it impossible to enforce the conclusions of the Augsburg Diet on the Protestants. Accordingly, in 1532, he concluded a peace pact with the evangelicals until a general council could decide the multifarious religious disputes. Frankfort, Worms, and Regensburg were all attempts to bring this about. By 1545 the Nürnberg Peace was nearing an end, and both the Pope and the Emperor were free to "exterminate" the German heretics. The Council of Trent, set for 1545, was to be the test. If the Protestants would not subscribe, then war.

The evangelicals realized that conflict was imminent. In April of 1546 Melanchthon, Bugenhagen, Cruciger, and Maior declared that resistance against the Emperor under the prevailing circumstances was a duty:

If it is true that the Emperor intends to persecute these states on account of religion, then it is undoubtedly the duty of these states to protect themselves and their subjects, for the magistrate is a minister of God and shall punish those who do evil as murderers. Such resistance is the same as when a man repels a band of murderers, whether the Emperor or another commands. This is a public tyranny. We know how the Spaniards, Italians and Burgundians will act in these lands, for we know how they acted in Julich. Therefore, every father should offer his body and life to repel this great tyranny.[1]

Melanchthon and others believed the Emperor was in league with the pope to overcome all Lutherans:

It is certain that the Emperor Charles is preparing to wage a terrible war against the Elector of Saxony and the Landgrave. Already huge armies are gathered in the vicinity of Gelders, and troops from Italy which the pope is supporting are expected. Charles does not try to hide his intentions, for he called representatives of the cities to Regensburg and exhorted them not to aid the Duke of Saxony, but the cities repeatedly declared that they would not forsake their ally.[2]

Comparing the times to those of Herod, Antiochus, and Daniel, Melanchthon summoned evangelicals to defend their doctrines.[3] On July 10, 1546, he reprinted Luther's *A Warning to My Beloved Germans* and in a preface again called on all men who feared God to resist, "according to the position and means of each," those who try to reintroduce papal idolatry by means of murder and destruction of royal families.[4] The passive resistance to authority which Luther had in his early years advocated, and then modified, was now completely abandoned.

The Emperor's ban against the evangelicals appeared on July 20, 1546. It was a declaration of war. Before the fighting really began, Duke Maurice of Saxony, ambitious for power, turned traitor against the Elector of Saxony. This created confusion. When the forces of Charles attacked at several points, the evangelical leaders of the Smalcald League weakened their striking power by returning home to defend their own domains. Duke Maurice had entered the Elector's lands and had created havoc among his subjects. While John Frederick was turning back Maurice and gaining control of the Elbe, the Emperor conquered South Germany, Swabia, and the Danube![5]

That the ravage of war might be avoided, the University of Wittenberg was dissolved. Melanchthon with his family and a few hastily gathered possessions fled to Zerbst. All seemed lost.[6]

The Elector succeeded in driving Maurice out of Saxony, but Charles joined forces with Ferdinand and the remainder of Maurice's army at Egra, and these combined armies defeated the Elector at Mühlberg, April 24, 1547. It was a black day for the Protestants.

Melanchthon immediately took up his pen and entreated the Emperor to withhold further destruction.[7] The Elector and the Landgrave were imprisoned; further resistance was futile. Melanchthon expressed his grief in a series of letters.[8] Most of all he feared that Maurice would root up Protestantism by destroying the schools and forcing ministers to preach Roman Catholicism.[9] From Zerbst he traveled to Magdeburg and then to Nordhausen. Rumors reached him that pastors were being murdered near Wittenberg, and he longed to return to be with the sufferers.[10]

In a letter from Cruciger, dated June 8, 1547, Melanchthon learned that Duke Maurice had announced his intention of restoring Wittenberg University as a Lutheran school and that he desired to have all the former professors reinstated.[11] Word also reached Melanchthon that the sons of John Frederick were planning to set up a university at Jena, but these plans were inchoate. On June 16, Melanchthon told a friend that he would go to Wittenberg, despite the confusion, if there was a possibility of gathering the remnants of the faculty.[12]

Then came an invitation from Maurice to come to Leipzig to consider with other theologians the possibility of restoring Wittenberg.[13] Melanchthon wanted to return to the banks of the Elbe, but he did not trust Maurice. However, when Maurice solemnly assured the theologians of his desire to have pure doctrine preached and taught at Wittenberg Melanchthon felt he ought to venture. The theologians drew up a statement of what they thought "pure doctrine" meant, and Maurice publicly avowed his good intentions. Melanchthon's decision was made. He would return to Wittenberg, trusting God to be his guide.[14] He did not know that the Emperor had repeatedly demanded his arrest and deliverance, nor did he fully realize that Maurice's defection from the Elector was a bid for political power and that Maurice needed him in order to have standing with his subjects.[15]

The rebuilding of Wittenberg was difficult, reminding Melanchthon of the rebuilding of the walls of Jerusalem, and the task was not made any easier by the ill will of those who hoped to start a school at Jena. Melanchthon could have gone to Leipzig, Königsberg, or England, but he felt that Wittenberg was a vital symbol of the entire Reformation. If the university is not restored, he said, barbarism will engulf the churches.[16]

Melanchthon's troubles increased when critics began saying he had deserted Frederick to serve the "treacherous" Duke Maurice. In a letter to a pastor in Salfeld, Melanchthon admitted that he might have hoped for too much, but it seemed as though God in his special mercy preserved our city from utter destruction. . . . Although I know that many speak ill of me on account of my return, I do not reply, but simply pray that my sorrow may be forgiven me. . . . In my loneliness I perhaps longed too much for my old friends . . . and it is possible that in these perilous times that I had too much hope for restoring the University, the accomplishment of which is dubious. Certainly, I did not seek pleasure or gain for myself, for I live here at my own expense, as a stranger, in constant grief and prayer, and days do not pass without my shedding tears. If the restoration succeeds, I hope the churches in these areas will be blessed. If it does not, then I will go into exile again. . . . Those who magnify my error saying I have rejected doctrine do me an injustice. If they could only see their own errors!

By the grace of God the voice of the Gospel is heard as unanimously in Wittenberg as it was before the war. Almost every week, ministers of the Gospel are publicly ordained and sent into the nearby districts. I therefore beseech you not to believe those who slander us. . . . I myself reverently honor the imprisoned prince, and daily commend him to God. I will beseech God to deliver us from slanders in this time of tribulation.[17]

As the opponents of Melanchthon had so freely predicted and then rejoiced when the prediction came true, in January of 1548 Charles asked for a colloquy to unify doctrine. Maurice's position became precarious, for he was caught between two forces—his Lutheran subjects without whom he would have no real power, and the Emperor Charles who could unseat him and who was demanding that papal Christianity be established.

Emperor Charles commanded John Agricola, a Protestant; Julius von Pflug, an Erasmian; and Michael Helding, a medieval historian; to prepare a document which would unite the Catholics and Protestants until a general council could make a final decision. This was the Augsburg Interim, May 15, 1548.[18] The general principle of the Interim was to secure agreement in essential matters and let the government dictate in nonessentials, or adiaphora, but the document was decidedly Roman Catholic in tone. Although it granted the cup, marriage of priests, and confiscated property, it demanded episcopal rule, seven sacraments, recognition of the pope as the interpreter of Scripture, transubstantiation, and works of supererogation, besides invocation of saints, festivals, and various rites.[19]

Maurice was worried. He sent a copy of the Interim to Melanchthon for an opinion. Melanchthon answered that the evangelicals could accept the rule of bishops only if they would promote the gospel, and that they could not accept auricular confession, supererogation, transubstantiation, masses for departed souls, or saint invocation. If the Interim is enforced, he warned, trouble will ensue and many people will abandon religion altogether. He prayed that God would impede the "evil and ruinous" negotiations afoot.[20]

When Melanchthon had time to study the Interim closely, he denounced it as an insidious and fraudulent document, especially since it made faith a mere preparation for works of love, just as if good works *really* justified a person before God. Such works as the sacrifice of Christ in the mass, and masses for the dead, said Melanchthon, "are all terrible lies, and therefore these articles should not be agreed to." [21] Other theologians concurred.

Maurice was desperately using his theologians to gain time. He summoned Melanchthon, Cruciger, Maior, and Pfeffinger to Celle to determine the attitude of the people of his domains, so he said. On April 24 they sent their studied opinion to him. Quoting scripture to support their views, they emphatically rejected the Interim article on justification as a camouflaged reiteration of papal work righteousness. With qualifications they said they could accept episcopal rule, confirmation and extreme unction if practiced as in the early church, nonauricular private absolution, and certain rites. But they rejected masses for the dead, meritorious works, and saint invocation.[22]

Melanchthon feared that the Interim would be enforced, no matter what he and the other theologians did. In a letter to Camerarius he said he was resigned neither to assent to nor impede the action of the authorities, for he thought resistance would only increase the turbulence, persecution, and ruining of the church.[23] What comes from God does not perish, he said, and what does not come from God is not worthy of preservation.

Carlowitz, a Roman Catholic bigot anxious to appear zealous, wrote to Melanchthon *demanding* that he approve the Interim and conciliate the Emperor, or suffer the consequences of war. Melanchthon replied:

When the prince has come to his conclusions, I will not make any disturbance, although I may not approve of things in them. I will either remain silent, depart, or bear whatever ensues. In previous days I bore an almost unseemly servitude to Luther when he acted according to his pugnacious nature rather than in accord with his dignity and the public welfare. I know that we must silently and modestly bear and cover many defects of the affairs of State, even as we must bear the evil effects of a storm. But you say that I am not merely required to be silent, but to approve the Interim. Now I doubt not that a wise man like you understands the natures and dispositions of men. I am not controversial by nature and I love peace among men as much as anyone. Neither did I start the controversies which distract the states, and I have taken part in them with a sincere desire to arrive at the truth. . . . Gladly will I promote the harmony of the churches; but I am not willing either that they shall be disturbed by a change in doctrine, or that worthy men shall be driven away.[24]

Carlowitz published the letter, and the evangelical enemies of Melanchthon excerpted the phrase "unseemly servitude to Luther" and loudly proclaimed that Melanchthon had at last shown his true colors. Melanchthon denied that this phrase connoted a basic doctrinal difference between himself and Luther. In the Greek, he explained, the term implies accepting a great man despite his faults.[25]

Melanchthon was not about to accept Catholic doctrine! On April 29, 1548, he warned Maurice that any patched-up peace would be like that between wolves and sheep. While Catholic bishops can be accepted if they adhere to true doctrine, the churches have good reasons for fleeing idolatry, abuses, and false doctrines of the present Catholic bishops.[26]

But Melanchthon was not hopeful; he foresaw the horrors of war. His only comfort, he confessed, was in the belief that he had acted to the best of his ability and had trusted God. "In the consciousness of having desired what is right, we shall suffer what may fall upon us. For, in obedience to divine command, we have sought the truth, which indeed was buried in thick darkness, and we have brought many good things to the light . . . but we have experienced the uncertainty of the help of man." [27]

Repeatedly during this period Melanchthon declined invitations to go to England, for he felt duty bound to restore the university.[28]

On May 15, 1548, the Emperor issued the Augsburg Interim. The

Elector of Brandenburg signed; margraves Wolfgang and Custrin and the prisoner John Frederick refused. The Emperor compelled the Protestant cities in South Germany where he held sway to accept; hundreds of evangelicals were killed, and four hundred ministers were banished. Nevertheless, many northern cities refused to abide by the Interim, especially Magdeburg, which called itself the "chancery of God." Maurice hedged, probably because he felt that he could not enforce the Interim in his Lutheran territories without violence.

Hoping for something from his theologians, Maurice requested a fourth opinion of the Interim. It was composed by Melanchthon and signed by Bugenhagen, Pfeffinger, Cruciger, Maior, and Froshel.[29] Melanchthon declared that despite the threat of war God's Word would not be denied. The commandments of God are greater than the commandments of men. What could be accepted, would be, wrote Melanchthon in his judgment, but the errors would be openly condemned, especially the articles on justification, transubstantiation, and work righteousness. We are justified before God and please him through our Saviour and Redeemer Christ Jesus. Love is the fruit not the basis of justification. A man may hardly have true faith, however, and still live in evil and have no love. Truly, "he that loveth not abideth in death."

Evangelicals and Catholics both howled. The former thought Melanchthon left the door open for papal works of merit, and the latter believed their whole system had been attacked.

In desperation Maurice summoned the theologians to Meissen in July and begged them, in view of the existing situation, to set forth all those things that could be conceded for the sake of harmony and peace. Maurice feared the Emperor might descend on him. The assembly at Meissen, however, only reiterated the previous stand of the Wittenberg professors, and entreated the Emperor not to enforce the Interim.[30] In response to Maurice's frantic plea that they at least yield on nonessentials, the theologians said those ceremonies conducive to discipline or learning could be kept for the sake of good order.

Melanchthon called the Interim a "harsh servitude" and declared to Casper Aquila that he would preach incorruptible doctrines insofar as he was able, regardless of the imperial confusions and threats. He had decided definitely to suffer a servile burden.[31]

The second phase of the paradoxical importance of the nonessentials began when on August 22, 1548, Maurice summoned Melanchthon and a few others to a conference in Pegau. He told the group that he wanted to give to Caesar what was Caesar's and to God what was God's, and he saw no reason for obstinancy in nonessentials. Since the evangelicals had not been obstinate about adiaphora, Maurice wanted either to extend the nonessentials or to stall for time to be able to tell the Emperor that he was taking the necessary steps.

Melanchthon wrote a "scriptum" for Maurice, saying the evangelicals wanted both unity and propagation of the gospel, provided these could be had without idolatry and persecution. He then linked transubstantiation with idolatry.[32]

Virtually the same thing happened at Torgau on October 18 and 19. Acceptance of the ambiguities in the Interim document, the Protestants maintained, would open the way for papal interpretations.

When Melanchthon received an order to go to Celle in November, he had grave fears that the constant discussions were a prelude to some yielding. If more than unity in nonessentials is desired, Melanchthon said to Maurice, then the Interim should be stated in such a manner that the evangelicals may leave the country.[33] Melanchthon thought the Emperor would not be satisfied with concessions in nonessentials, but he resolved not to give up basic doctrine. But the princes at Celle, without the theologians, drew up a document. They had decided to act without the theologians!

Their Celle document, which Melanchthon called a "botch," conceded authority to the church to determine doctrine, interpret Scripture, and regulate ritual. The mass was to be performed with lights, vessels, singing, costumes, and other regalia; pictures of Christ and the saints were to be allowed in the churches. Canonical hours were to be maintained as well as special days including Corpus Christi and many others—all to be celebrated with mass and preaching. On Friday and Saturday during Lent there was to be no eating of meat. Penance was to be practiced with confession, absolution, and works of satisfaction. However, marriages of priests were not to be abolished.[34]

Melanchthon said the Celle Interim was polluted with errors and could not possibly be regarded as scriptural, especially since the statement on justification was but a mask for work righteousness.[35]

But Maurice felt that he had to satisfy the Emperor. Having gained the support of the local princes, he believed he could act without the theologians. So, on December 17, the princes issued the *Decretum Interbocense,* which was the Celle Interim with a prologue and epilogue.[36]

Realizing that all was near to being lost, Melanchthon sought to rewrite the article on justification, believing that the preservation of this one doctrine would keep the heart of Protestantism.[37] He felt that he must now try to obtain anything which would be justified in the fundamentals in order to keep the university and the evangelical views alive in Wittenberg and the surrounding territories. He knew the price was high, but he knew also that the desolation of the churches, as in Swabia, would be even costlier.[38]

After seemingly endless disputes, Melanchthon salvaged justification and felt he could accept the other matters as adiaphora. His opponents, however, cried out that justification had been relegated to one of the nonessentials! This was a malicious and false interpretation, for Melanchthon worked strenuously to have the evangelical doctrine of justification included precisely because this was the heart of the Lutheran Reformation, and without it all the other matters in both principle and practice would have been overwhelmingly Catholic. He could do no more. Out of Celle came the Leipzig Interim, the acceptance of which Melanchthon thought would be a lesser evil than abandoning the schools and churches. He resigned himself to acceptance, trusting God to bring good even out of evil.

The Leipzig Interim provided that: men receive what the church teaches "as she shall and cannot command anything contrary to the Holy Scriptures"; ministers obey the bishops; baptism be administered according to the ancient rites; confirmation and extreme unction be allowed as in the early church; repentance, confession, and absolution be taught without auricular enumeration; ministers be examined before ordination; the idea of meritorious sacrifice be omitted from the mass;

bell-ringing, lights, vessels, costumes, and other ceremonies be retained; ministers be allowed to wed or not to wed; pictures be permitted in churches but not worship of them; singing be allowed; certain holidays be observed; meat not be eaten on Friday and Saturday during Lent; and clergymen wear distinctive dress.[39]

With meritorious sacrifice eliminated, Melanchthon could regard all the other ceremonies as nonessentials, but his opponents vigorously denounced him. These should not be accepted for the sake of order, discipline, and example, they maintained, for these ceremonies will cause the common people to believe that papal doctrines have everywhere been revived. Melanchthon wrote to Paul Eber saying he regretted that some things were not done differently but that he thought doctrine would be preserved.[40]

Within a few days, January 7, 1549, the theologians of Berlin addressed a long letter of inquiry to the Wittenberg professors.[41] They asked sarcastically if adiaphora included such trifles as holy water, herbs, salt, censing, flags, palms, torches, consecration of the unleavened bread, unctions at baptism and sickbeds, pageant-laying of the cross in passion week, and so forth. Bugenhagen and Melanchthon emphatically answered no, and in their reply they stated the principle on which the Wittenbergers finally accepted the Leipzig Interim: "Since great devastations are occurring in other places, we believe that it is better to endure a hard servitude, if it can be borne without impiety, than to leave the churches." [42] It was a fact that where concessions had not been made, the churches were being ruined and ministers banished.

Christian liberty, Melanchthon replied to his critics, is not a matter of nonessentials. Liberty lies in the free confession of truth and not in rejection of externals. Faith, prayer, and a pious life are the essentials of the worship of God. We are bearing a yoke in Wittenberg, he admitted, so that the physical existence of the churches may be maintained; we are not sacrificing pure doctrine, only adiaphora.[43] On this basis, at Torgau and at Leipzig, Melanchthon publicly defended the Interim so far as essential doctrine was concerned.[44] Yielding on adiaphora neither helps nor reasserts the papacy so long as evangelical essentials are maintained. The violent persons who want to compel everybody to hold the opinions they hold are instituting a new kind of popery, he retorted.[45]

Actually Melanchthon never fully accepted the Leipzig Interim; he simply tried to mitigate a bad set of circumstances.

To the Hamburg theologians who said that the reintroduction of the inane Roman Catholic scenic spectacles and gesticulations would cause the people to think Catholicism was flooding back into Germany Melanchthon pointed out that in Saxony the gospel was still being preached, in spite of the few who were craftily taking advantage of the situation.[46] It is better to endure a harsh servitude, he again asserted, than to desert the church on account of nonessentials.

The most persistent opponent of Melanchthon was Matthias Flacius Illyricus (1520-75). At the age of twenty-one, after having studied for the priesthood at Venice, Basel, and Tübingen, he enrolled at Wittenberg. Melancthon extended him a personal welcome. While at Wittenberg he went through a period of spiritual despair followed by an experience of justification by faith alone. He manifested his conversion in a violent hatred for everything pertaining to the papacy and a passionate defense of the purity and involability of what he had newly found.

In 1544, at the age of twenty-four, he was appointed to the chair of Hebrew at Wittenberg; in 1546 he received his M.A. During the dispersion of the university in 1547 he fled to Brunswick, after which he returned to Wittenberg only to leave again on account of the Interim.

Flacius fiercely opposed the Augsburg Interim, and the "compromise" of Melanchthon in the Leipzig Interim. From Magdeburg where he was the acknowledged leader of the strict Lutherans—Amsdorf, Gallus, Judek, Faber, Wigand, Aurifaber, Schnepf, Otto, Strigel, and Stolz— he carried on a literary attack against Melanchthon personally and the interimists generally. He set himself up as the true teacher, defender, and prophet of the Lutheran faith, and called the Wittenberg theologians Baalites, knaves, belly-servers, Samaritans, and traitors. He charged that Melanchthon colluded with the papists, brought calamity on the churches, and reinstated papal domination. He even published many of Melanchthon's private letters and copies of the Leipzig Interim with additions, changes, and omissions. His attacks were so malicious that Melanchthon refused to answer, firmly believing that the exaggerations would destroy the venom of the *"alumnus in sinu serpentem."* [47]

Flacius' first writing, *Wider Das Interim,* was aimed particularly at the Augsburg Interim, although it came out in 1549 after the Leipzig Interim had been accepted.[48] Ironically, because of this lapse of time Melanchthon—who could have agreed with everything Flacius said about the Augsburg Interim because he, too, had objected to it—was regarded as the target of this essay. Flacius aided the irony by pretending that there was no difference between the two "godless" interims.

After expressing astonishment that so many people had "apostated divine truth and accepted false doctrine and ritual," Flacius came to his main point: ceremonies, no matter how unimportant, if they are germane to the mass, are idolatrous because the mass is contrary to the Word of God. Against the Word of God, declared Flacius, the priest takes common bread and supposedly *sacrifices* the Son of God again. This cannot be derived from any portion of the Bible, regardless of how much "slobber drivel" the interimists mouth. Since the ritualism of the mass and the sacrifice of the mass cannot be supported in Scripture, the entire "Intermass" ought to be condemned, for the Lord orders us not to go astray from his Word, neither to the left nor the right!

Melanchthon, too, had sharply rejected the Emperor's Augsburg Interim, but Flacius chose to ignore this.

In other writings, Flacius turned his vituperative contempt directly on Melanchthon. In one tirade after another Flacius called on all good Christians to avoid the contagion of leprous adiaphora. The hope of peace is not sufficient reason to admit so many potentially evil practices, he said, for Christ came not to bring peace but a sword, even the sword of truth which the interimists have buried in impious ceremonies. Belial and Christ are at war, and this is no time for concessions.[49]

How can the interimists ask us to be silent in order to preserve at least a little doctrine, asked Flacius, when papal rites everywhere proclaim the reinstitution of papal abuses? To be silent is to deny truth. Flacius' general rule for nonessentials was stated in many pamphlets: All ceremonies, regardless of how unimportant they are ordinarily, cease to be adiaphora when they become compulsory. When constraint is attached to them, they become an occasion for scandal and impiety. To the extent that they are compulsory, they destroy rather than build the church of God.[50]

In an essay called *True and False Adiaphora,* 1549, Flacius declared that preaching, baptism, the Eucharist, and absolution have been commanded by God, and that suitable ceremonies have also been commanded, *in genere.* If the evangelical doctrines are correct, then evangelical forms and ceremonies should be maintained inviolate. Cultus reflects doctrine; therefore, Catholic ceremonies cannot be accepted as adiaphora because they reflect Roman doctrines and stand for such in the eyes of the people.[51]

The views of Flacius and Melanchthon were directly opposite. Melanchthon regarded nonessentials such as ceremonies as if they were static. Thus he could keep justification by faith and allow many papal rites. Flacius thought ceremonies were directly and dynamically connected with doctrines, and in this he showed genuine insight into the nature of rites, but the personal abuse, calumny, and hatred that he sent forth from his "chancery of God" caused him to step out of bounds. He was so positive that nothing should bind Christian liberty that he *demanded* rejection of adiaphora in time of crisis! This, Melanchthon observed, was fomenting "a new, violent popery," contrary to the Christian idea of liberty: He who forbids circumcision errs just as much as those who demand it.[52] Unwittingly, in preserving "pure" Lutheran views on adiaphora, Flacius fell into a type of legalism that has been called "Protestant scholasticism."

Flacius understood the connection between a man's supposedly adiaphoristic actions and his beliefs better than did either Luther or Melanchthon, but the latter understood that Christian love must be manifested in whatever situation prevails, for faith acts through love, and that actions expressing love cannot absolutely be condemned, for to condemn them is to imply that love must be expressed in a particular way. Melanchthon knew the love that a Christian must by inward compulsion display; he knew that love cannot be bound by rules and that circumstances dictate whether a person shall for the public good accept or reject certain external regulations. In this Interim Melanchthon was manifesting the principle that one should endure human traditions, for the sake of peace, love, and order, if they do not obscure faith, nor give offense, nor destroy one's sense of true doctrine. In every situation the justified man must choose according to what he believes will be the best expression of his love, and this may be keeping or refusing to keep external regulations, as when Paul refused to have Titus circumcised but not Timothy. Flacius' demands that adiaphora be rejected were just as much a denial of Christian liberty as the demands of the pope that they be kept. Melanchthon thought the Leipzig Interim did not encroach on Christian liberty and would under the circumstances help promote peace and order. Flacius thought just the opposite.

On September 9, 1549, Melanchthon explained his position in a letter to Moller,[53] insisting anew that nonessentials should not become a cause of war. While not entirely convinced that the Emperor would be satisfied with a few concessions in rites, Melanchthon gambled. He maintained that the Interim actually did not change either doctrine or essential ceremonies for the evangelicals, and that the "fountain of misery, transubstantiation" had been rejected.

On October 1, 1549, Melanchthon finally replied to Flacius. He had become convinced that the whole church was being harmed by Flacius' fanaticism.[54] Evangelical doctrine has not been destroyed, Melanchthon declared. The present teachings agree with the *Loci Communes* and the Augsburg Confession, and Luther himself did not object to these! We are bearing the present servitude, he said, that our churches and schools may not be wantonly destroyed; we have not departed from justification by faith; and we have not reinstated papal abuses. He closed the letter with an expression of trust in the God of all events.

In the fall and winter of 1549 the self-appointed defenders of Luther demanded the blood of Melanchthon. Melanchthon did not desire the same for them and even advised the princes at Dresden not to take any drastic action against Flacius.[55] When Flacius collected and published some of Melanchthon's letters, Philip was shocked that they had been changed and so many misleading notes added. He became excessively tired of the continual bickering and seriously thought of going to England to escape the "rage of the theologians." [56] The letter which he received from Calvin condemning him for the part he took in the Interim did not make matters any easier.[57]

In 1552 politics again affected the entire controversy. Maurice turned against the Emperor and asserted his independence. On August 2, 1552, the treaty of Passau was formally concluded between Maurice and King

Ferdinand. Legally, the Leipzig Interim was at an end. The Elector and the Landgrave of Hesse were liberated. Whether Melanchthon was right or wrong in principle, he did preserve the university from devastation. Three years later, 1555, the Protestants and Roman Catholics concluded the famous Peace of Augsburg which established the principle of *cuius regio, eius religio,* that the religion of a land would coincide with the religion of the ruler.

Flacius and his cohorts, however, kept attacking Melanchthon and continued to publish letters which Melanchthon denied ever having written. In the famous Coswig experiment of 1557, Gallus, Flacius, and other opponents from the "chancery of God" tried to force Melanchthon to say he had been erroneous in the past. They asked him to accept the Augsburg Confession and the Smalcald Articles, as if he had not already done so! He was to reject all errors of the papists and interimists, "errors" being determined by Flacius. He was to disavow the "corrupting" doctrine that good works are necessary to salvation, which he had never accepted. He was to say that churches must not depart from the views of the Magdeburg pastors as they had expressed themselves in their 1550 Confession. He was to admit that in time of persecution a sincere confession of truth must be made, as if he had been totally wrong in the Interim. He was also to testify in writing that his views on adiaphora and good works agreed with the teachings of Luther, as if he and Luther had openly conflicted.

"To such strangulation," he said, "I cannot submit." If for the past thirty years I have been wrong, said Melanchthon, then compassion might have been a more Christian attitude on the part of the "guardians of Christ." He could not agree to the humiliation of the Coswig articles, especially when he was not convinced that he had willfully done anything wrong.[58]

Flacius contended not only with Melanchthon but with many others until Duke John Frederick finally was forced to set up a consistory with the power to excommunicate and censor. For objecting to this Flacius was deprived of his position at the University of Jena. The following year, 1562, Flacius helped establish an academy at Regensburg. However, in a treatise on original sin, he maintained that the nature of man is essentially and totally corrupt, that original sin is the very substance of man and not just an accident.[59] For this doctrine Flacius was branded a heretic and forced to leave Regensburg; he had to give up a pastorate at Antwerp; and he could not even be a refugee in Frankfort and Strassburg. The last portion of his life was spent in a Catholic convent at Frankfort. He died March 11, 1575.

The Formula of Concord, 1580, declared that "in time of persecution, when a bold confession is required of us, we should not yield to the enemies in regard to adiaphora." This stands as the basic view of the Lutheran Church today.

The bitter arguments over the importance of nonessentials had come to an end. "In necessary things, unity; in unnecessary things, liberty; and in all things, love" did not become a reality. The adiaphoristic arguments cast a spell of suspicion over Melanchthon and more than anything else caused his name to be obscured in Lutheranism.

The Word, the Holy Spirit, and the Will

THE INTERIMS OF 1548, THE ACCUSATIONS OF THE ULTRA-Lutherans in the "chancery of God" at Magdeburg, and the professional jealousy of men who wanted to lead Protestantism, brought suspicions, misunderstandings, and hatreds which saddened the final years of Melanchthon's life. He longed to hear no more of the "madness of the theologians," but he could not avoid their acrimony. Even after his death their aspersions did not cease, for they set themselves up as the guardians of undefiled evangelical doctrine. They insisted that Philip had departed from the pure teachings of Luther, that he was a follower of Erasmus, a Pelagian, and a Romanist!

One topic of bitter aspersion was conversion. Does man do anything to help or hinder his conversion? Flacius and his cohorts magnified the early Luther and maintained that man is determined; God elects to save some and damn others; man can do nothing in the process of justification.

Melanchthon did not see matters in the same light. Because he could not find determinism in the Scriptures, he objected to this "Stoic fatalism." He could not believe that all things are determined, for he believed that God does not make a man sin, rather that man is responsible for sin. Man is also responsible for accepting or rejecting the promises of God. for God does not force salvation upon a man as if he were a block of wood or a piece of stone.

Luther himself never objected to Melanchthon's understanding of conversion, but the so-called "Gnesio" or "Genuine" Lutherans accused Philip of synergism (co-operation between man and God in achieving righteousness). This was intended as a derogatory label, but in his "synergism" Melanchthon was both evangelical and scriptural! He rejected any declaration that "God snatches you by some violent rapture, so that you must believe, whether you will or not." [1]

Melanchthon had always cherished a considerable doubt as to the exact relationship between conversion and predestination. In the early *Loci* of 1521 he stated: "We can do nothing but sin. . . . Since all things happen necessarily according to divine predestination, there is no freedom of our wills." However, he avoided a discussion of predestination on the grounds that man should not be overly curious about the mysteries of God. "One should not rely on the *secret* decree of God but on the work of Christ, on redemption through Him."

Melanchthon's doubts became more evident in his *Commentary on Colossians* of 1527, when he implied a rejection of predestination.[2] He did not mention predestination at all in the Augsburg Confession, on the ground that any attempt to clarify it would result in more confusion.[3] As he thought about the biblical message of salvation, Philip gave less and less attention to predestination and more and more consideration to the universal promises of God. In the Apology of 1531 he wrote:

> In the courts of men, law and obligation are certain, mercy is uncertain. In the presence of God the case is different. Mercy has the clear command of God. For the Gospel is itself the command which bids us believe that God pardons and saves on account of Christ. . . . He that believeth in Him is not condemned.

Melanchthon felt assured of the promise of mercy to *all*, but he could see no reason why only some should receive mercy and others should not, *unless* man is in some way responsible.

> The question of particularity arises. Because when we hear that mercy is the cause of election, and yet that few are elected, we are even more distressed, and wonder whether there is respect of persons with God, and why he does not have mercy on all. To such temptation ought to be opposed the universal promises of the Gospel, which teach that God for Christ's sake, and gratuitously, promises salvation to all, as is said: "The righteousness of God through faith in Jesus Christ is to all and upon all." And again, "The Lord of all is rich in mercy to all." Again, "Whosoever calleth on the name of the Lord," etc. These universal statements must be opposed to the temptation in regard

to particularity. Then it must be affirmed that in regard to the will of God we must not judge according to reason without the Word of God. As in justification, so in election, we must not judge according to reason, or according to law, but according to the Gospel.[4]

Melanchthon could not resolve the difficulty, nor could he trust completely in the guidance of reason!

In *Catechesis Puerilis,* 1532, Melanchthon emphasized the universal promises of mercy and resolved not to let the contradictions presented by predestination disturb his faith:

As the preaching of repentance appertains to all, so also the promise. Let us not allow our faith to be shaken by unreasonable discussions about predestination; but let us begin with the Word of God, and let us remember that the promises appertain to all, and let us be assured that those things truly belong to us which God has set forth and promised in his Word, because he acts through his Word, and wishes to be found in his Word, according to the passage: "The Gospel is the power of God unto salvation to everyone that believeth." [5]

In a letter to Brentz in 1531 Melanchthon noted that predestination, strangely enough, parallels our faith and works, as if our believing and doing had some bearing on our destiny.

This idea was more fully expressed in the 1532 *Commentary on Romans.* "In conceiving faith there is a struggle in us," and in election, "there is some cause in the accipient in that he does not reject the promise extended." Melanchthon was unwilling to add *alone* to the phrase "justification by faith" if *alone* meant that man was completely inactive. Ethical responsibility would not allow him to admit that man has nothing whatsoever to do with election. "All the old writers, except Augustine, place some cause of election in us." But Melanchthon did not mean that man can make himself righteous.

The promise of mercy cannot be accepted, nor can confidence be conceived except as the Holy Spirit by the Word moves hearts, as is said: "No one comes unto me, except the Father draws him." Moreover, let the will do all that it can, it must never be thought that salvation depends upon the measure or value of our action, but upon the promise, so that justification be not separated from trust in mercy.[6]

In 1535 Melanchthon saw that extreme predestination is contrary to religious experience and morality. The very fact that man preaches the gospel and calls upon sinners to repent implies that the hearer does something. While he does not initiate, create, or in any real sense accomplish his salvation, he does at least cease resistance and make a choice. *He accepts the gift of God.* Any other conception renders the preaching of the gospel meaningless, detracts from moral significance, and utterly vacates the ethical personality of man.

Melanchthon believed that in some sense man is an active concurrent in conversion; if not, he is a beast or a stone without a will. In conversion God helps man, as one would help an invalid into bed, not as one would place a stone in a wall. In conversion, there are always the Word and the Spirit, but the human will is not wholly inactive. It is a *causa concurrens,* not that it is equal to the Spirit and the Word, but it must finally accept the gift freely offered by God. In conversion, "three causes are conjoined: The Word, the Holy Spirit and the Will not wholly inactive, but resisting its own weakness. . . . God draws, but draws him who is willing . . . and the will is not a statue, and that spiritual emotion is not impressed upon it as though it were a statue." [7]

Even though God foresees all things, he does not do away with our freedom. Man does at least accept the gift of God. Man does not earn salvation, because then there would be no gift, only a wage; neither does God force salvation on man, because a gift ceases to be a gift if the recipient is forced to take it.

This moral aspect of Melanchthon's thought again became apparent in the 1535 *Loci,* when he berated those people who refuse to try to live morally and say, "If we are elected, we are elect; if not, then there is no use trying."

To those who excuse their cessation of activity because they think that the will does nothing I reply: On the contrary, it is the eternal and changeless command of God that you should obey the Gospel and hear the Son of God, and acknowledge Him as Saviour. "I cannot," you say? Yes, you can, in a certain sense, sustaining yourself with the Word of the Gospel; you can ask to be helped by the Holy Spirit; then you shall know that the Holy Spirit is efficacious in the comfort given. You shall know that when we strive with ourselves, when, aroused by the promise, we call upon God and resist our distrust and other vicious desires, that that is the very way God desires to convert us. Since the promise is universal, and there are no contradictory wills in God, the cause must be in *man* that Saul is cast away and David is accepted. This, rightly understood, is true, and its benefit in the exercise of faith and the enjoyment of true comfort when the heart rests in the Son of God revealed through the promise, will make clear this joining of causes: The Holy Spirit, the Word of God, and the Will. . . . Pharaoh and Saul were not coerced, but of their own wills opposed God. . . . David was not converted as if he were a stone. . . . The free will of David worked something when he heard the threats and promises. . . . The Gospel is the power of God to salvation to one not opposing but consenting and believing.[8]

In 1554 Melanchthon wrote to Calvin saying that everything happens by divine foreknowledge and human will, but that he did not know how to harmonize the two.[9] God's promises are universal; there is no secret will in God damning some and saving others.

The only cause for rejection is *our* striving against God's Word. Therewith, we should console ourselves and be content. . . . When you hear the preaching of the Word, remember that it applies to you, and do not be puzzled over election or predestination. If you have the beginning of faith, then God will help you farther.[10]

Melanchthon expressed the final form of his doctrine of free will in an official opinion prepared in 1558 for "all the Electors, Princes, and Estates of the Augsburg Confession":

First, it cannot be doubted that the Stoic necessity is a downright lie and is a reproach to God. It is also a lie that there is no contingency.

Secondly, it is incorrect to say in general that in evil works the Will is absolutely passive. David, without compulsion and voluntarily, took the wife of Uriah. He might have retained the Holy Spirit, had he resisted the temptation, in which struggle he might have had the Holy Spirit. The same thing is true of many others. In external morality the Will is not forced to commit adultery, theft, etc. . . . It is true that God very marvelously illumines and works in conversion, and even during the entire life of the saints, which illumination the human will only receives, and is not a co-worker, and is absolutely passive. Also it must be taught that in all temptation we should reflect on the Word of God, and should will to strengthen ourselves by it, and to pray for God's assistance, for God operates through the Word. . . . "God draws, but he draws him who is willing." A person must not persist in unbelief, and think that he shall wait until he is drawn to God, without his own will, by some special Anabaptistic vision or miracle. God works, gives the Holy Spirit, strengthens and comforts by his Word. Faith comes by hearing and hearing by the Word. This rule people can understand and can profitably employ. It also leads man to God's Word, and does not create any confusion in regard to predestination, or other irrelevant disputes about necessity. And although Luther in the *De Servo Arbitrio* wrote harshly, yet in other writings he counsels just as we now have done. Nor do we have from this those pernicious consequences that therefore man has merit, etc., as Gallus of Regensburg and Anthony of Nordhausen have caviled. In a word, could intelligent men in a convention understand this subject, they would, I think, abide by this opinion.[11]

Inasmuch as Flacius and the "Genuine" Lutherans accused Melanchthon of departing from the true teachings of Luther, it is important to note that Luther made no such charge. In 1559 Melanchthon noted that

during the lifetime of Luther and after, I have rejected these Stoic and Manichean errors which Luther and others have written, that all good and bad works must so happen in all men good and bad. For it is apparent that this teaching is against God's Word, injurious to all discipline, and blasphemous against God.[12]

Melanchthon called the attention of Luther to changes in the treatment of Colossians on predestination as early as 1527, and he said he would treat it further.[13] In the *Ratio Discendae Theologiae,* 1530, Melanchthon commanded that his *Scholia on Colossians* be read, but he added, "I would also order the reading of my *Loci,* but they contain much that is yet crude which I have decided to alter. It is easy to understand what displeases me by noting what I have modified in my *Colossians."* [14]

Luther knew about the changes in Melanchthon's 1535 and 1544 *Loci.* It was common knowledge. Brück jokingly said Melanchthon was trying to gain a cardinal's hat. In 1538 Philip wrote to Veit Dietrich: "You know that I write less sternly concerning predestination, the assent of the will, the necessity of our obedience, and concerning mortal sin." [15] Melanchthon seemed to believe that these views were well known.

Luther gave no hint of disapproval of the 1535 or 1544 *Loci;* indeed, shortly before his death he wrote:

I have resisted for a long time those who wanted an edition of my works. I have done so because I do not want the works of the ancients to be neglected and because by the grace of God we have better methodical works, among which Philip's *Loci* is the best. A theologian and bishop can best learn out of that to be strong in holding forth on the doctrine of godliness.[16]

Critics who wished to demonstrate Luther's opposition to Melanchthon often quoted his letter of July 9, 1537, to Capito, in which he expressed a wish that his books would be devoured as Saturn devoured his own children, that they would perish! "For I see that none of my books are right, except *The Bondage of the Will* and the Catechisms." [17]

In answering Erasmus, Luther wished to assert the supremacy of God as the giver of every good gift, to exclude Roman work righteousness, to bring man back to the commands of Christ alone. In later works he put more emphasis on justification than on bound will. Justification was the heart of his Christian doctrine.

Luther never disavowed the early view, but except for that one letter, he seems to have allowed it to drop into the background, for he knew that the heart seeking salvation cannot rest in predestination, but must live by what has been *revealed* of the secret will of God. After the Erasmian controversy, Luther stressed the revealed will, the universality of the call, the preaching of the Word. For all practical purposes, he abandoned his earlier views on predestination. Melanchthon and others heard him console the despondent, saying, "God does not desire the death of a sinner but that he turn and repent. . . . The mercy of God is offered to all; let your heart be comforted."

In the same year in which Luther wrote to Capito, Melanchthon composed some theses for a candidate in theology. These propositions were expounded publicly before an immense crowd at Wittenberg, with no evidence of any objection from Luther:

Our will is not active without the Holy Spirit, but when by the Gospel it arouses and comforts itself, it is assisted by the Holy Spirit.

For it must be truly established that we acquire the benefits of the Gospel, in which also is the gift of the Holy Spirit.

Since we begin with the Word, men must be taught to resist their natural unbelief.

I do not approve the Manicheans, who attribute no activity to the human will, not even when assisted by the Holy Spirit.

Therefore, the blessing of God must be recognized, in that the promise is general, and that it is the will of God to save all. And care and diligence must be aroused in us, so that we do not indulge our natural unbelief, but resist it.[18]

Had Luther disagreed, he would probably have made an objection to this public defense of so-called synergism, or to the "synergism" plainly expressed in the 1540 *De Anima* in which Melanchthon commented on the attempt of Potiphar's wife to seduce Joseph. Had Joseph yielded, he and not God would have been responsible, said Melanchthon, for while the Holy Spirit was assisting Joseph, "the will of Joseph might have shaken off the Holy Spirit." In a moral struggle the will of man is not inactive.[19]

The 1540 edition of the Augsburg Confession, known as the *Variata,* seemed to imply synergism: "Man's will has no power without the Holy Spirit to work spiritual righteousness. . . . Spiritual righteousness is wrought in us when we are *helped* by the Holy Spirit. And we receive the Holy Spirit when we *assent* to the Word of God." Nevertheless, during Melanchthon's lifetime no one objected to this.[20] The *Variata* received official authorization in diets and colloquies from 1541 to 1557. It was revised and approved by Luther, and Melanchthon declared that the meaning was not changed, "though in the later editions some things have been either more mildly expressed or have been better explained." In 1561 the Naumberg Convention of princes approved it as "the same Confession somewhat more stately and elaborate, repeated, and also explained and enlarged on the basis of Holy Scripture." It was called "the Confession delivered to Emperor Charles V at Augsburg, 1530," and was publicly and privately used as Lutheran doctrine for twenty years.[21] The first attack on the *Variata* came after Melanchthon's death when Flacius, in a public debate, asserted that he had heard a man (since deceased) say that Luther objected to Melanchthon's synergism!

If Melanchthon was synergistic, why did Luther not indicate opposition to it? The answer: because Luther agreed. A gradual evolution in Luther met a radical change in Melanchthon, so that the latter never had to defend his views. Melanchthon consciously steered a course between

Pelagius and Augustine because he did not think either had remained true to Scripture or to experience. Referring to the 1535 *Loci,* Luther admonished his students:

Read Philip's *Loci* next to the Bible. In this very wonderful book the pure theology is taught in a quiet and orderly way. Augustine, Bernard, Bonaventura, Lyra, Gabriel Biel, Staupitz, have much that is good; but Master Philip can explain the Scriptures and present their meaning in brief compass.[22]

Melanchthon never was a Pelagian; he never attributed anything *meritorious* to the will's activity. He did not use the word "co-operate," and he did not say that the will acts by its own powers.

In 1578 the theologians of the churches of Pomerania would not accept the Bergic book in which Flacian charges against Melanchthon were embodied. Some of the Pomeranian preachers had been students of Melanchthon and Luther and had heard discussions of free will. They issued a statement, to counteract Flacius' charges against Melanchthon:

The opinion of the cooperation of man's free will in spiritual things by its own natural powers we never heard of or saw a trace of during the lifetime of Luther. On the contrary, we heard and were taught, and by God's grace have taught others, that in conversion to God man's free will by its own powers can do and does do nothing, and can contribute nothing of itself or by itself to his conversion. But also that in conversion to God man is not absolutely like a block or a stone. But when through the instrumentality of the Word of God he is moved and drawn by the Holy Spirit, he then, as a rational being, has a movement in himself. By carnal wickedness he can oppose God. Or by the grace of the Holy Spirit, without whose grace man can do nothing by his natural powers, he can by using his Will submit to God and his Word, and can become obedient to the same, though there is still much weakness in the flesh.[23]

Flacius and the right-wing Lutherans based their entire system upon the bondage of the will. The basis for Melanchthon's views was the gospel promises as revealed in Christ. Philip changed his early views because he saw the moral and psychological dangers of extreme predestinarianism, and because he had seen the actual experiences of anxiety and response of Christians in conversion. Yet he did not wish to detract from the Holy Spirit or the Word, nor to imply work righteousness. "I turn with horror from the blasphemy that man can by his natural powers, without the Holy Spirit, satisfy the law of God by internal and external obedience." [24]

He wanted to eliminate compulsion and vindicate the ethics of conversion. Though he was misunderstood, and caricatured, he never taught a "co-operation of causes." His doctrine was evangelical and biblical, and was eventually to emerge in the evangelical churches, even in Wesleyanism! [25]

Reformer at Home

ELANCHTHON'S LIFE WAS NOT ALL CONVENTIONS, JUDI-cium, and colloquies. Indeed, he knew many joyous moments. He never missed a student social if he could possibly be present, and he often had students present dramas in his own home or sit around the fire and read parts. Urban Baldwin, in 1529, sent a letter to Stephen Roth and added a postscript, "One thing more, I have seen Melanchthon dancing with the provost's wife. It was a strange sight." Another dance episode was mentioned in 1541.[1]

The Melanchthon home welcomed many visitors. One friend reported a supper at which guests spoke twelve different languages. Melanchthon never turned anybody away. Whatever was needed—a recommendation, money, or food—he gave. Camerarius said he often gave away his last groschen, or sold a family cup or spoon to help some stranger. The silver and gold coins which he sometimes received as honoraria for his many services he gave away to the first one who might ask for them. Once when Melanchthon allowed a stranger to choose from his coin collection, the stranger promptly asked for *all* the coins. Melanchthon relinquished the entire collection, with a remark that the man seemed a bit greedy.

When Philip saw the six-month-old child of pastor Melander of Kassel lying in a cradle, he joyously asked permission to read the child's hand. Ascertaining the day and hour of birth, he described a wonderful future. The child, he prophesied, would grow up to be a learned man, honored and esteemed; he would have religious struggles, but he would emerge a great man! Melanchthon elaborated until finally Melander stopped him saying, "That would be fine, except that the child is a girl!"[2]

Melanchthon's own children were a constant source of joy, and he was frequently seen on the floor playing their games. Camerarius reported that Philip told them stories and bits of history and tested their wits with ingenious puzzles. A French visitor, astounded that Philip would be reading a book and rocking a cradle, received a lecture on the duties of parents! He went away "greatly instructed."

Phil , oldest child, Anna, born in 1522, delighted her father. He recorded that she once came to his study, found him weeping, and with her apron wiped away his tears. "This show of her love made a deep impression on my heart." When she was only fourteen, she married George Sabinus, a gifted young poet. On the recommendation of Erasmus, Sabinus had come to Wittenberg to study and had become a close friend of the Melanchthon family. Philip admired him for his ardent study habits and emotional poetic perception, a quality which Anna shared. They were married in 1536. Two years later Sabinus was appointed professor of literature at Frankfort-on-the-Oder, but he soon felt the position was beneath him and sought something that would give more fame and fortune. His poem *"Res gestae Caesarum Germanorum"* won him considerable reputation and some noted patronage, but Melanchthon was disturbed by his son-in-law's excessive ambition.[3] Anna did not share Sabinus' desire for greater recognition, and suffered because of his spendthrift habits and neglect of family responsibilities. Friction developed between them.[4]

On the recommendation of Camerarius, Sabinus was appointed the first rector of the University of Königsberg, August 17, 1544.[5] That summer before the household made the move, Anna and her children stayed in Wittenberg at her parents' home. Melanchthon grew fond of the children and dreaded their departure. He wrote to Camerarius, "This journey of my daughter fills me with constant sorrow." [6]

Three years later, March, 1547, Anna died. Camerarius related that Anna appeared as a corpse to Melanchthon in a dream the very night she died. Melanchthon wrote to him that his daughter had passed gently away—still loving God, husband, and children. From Zerbst, Melanchthon wrote to Paul Eber in Wittenberg:

I send you a narrative of my daughter's death, which, whenever I read it, or even but think of it, so increases my parental sorrow, that I fear it will injure my health. I cannot banish the sight of my weeping daughter from my eyes, who, when she was asked what she would like to say to her parents, replied: "I think of several things, which fill me with anguish!" [7]

After Anna's death Melanchthon wrote to Sabinus:

I wish our friendship to be a lasting one, and am determined to cherish it faithfully. I shall look upon your children as my own, and they are indeed my own. I do not love them less than I loved their mother. Many know how fondly I loved my daughter; and this love has not been extinguished by her death, but continues to be nourished by sorrow and ardent desires. And as I know how much she loved her children, I believe that I must transfer her affections to myself. [8]

Melanchthon rejoiced when Sabinus came to Wittenberg that fall to bring Anna's three daughters and son to live with him and Catherine. As would any fond grandparent, he often spoke of these children in his lectures.

Philip, Jr., was born January 13, 1525. During his early years his parents feared for his life, and he was destined always to be weak. Melanchthon often worried about what would happen to him when no one was around to care for him, but Philip, Jr., lived to be eighty. Although his intellectual attainments were quite ordinary, he served as notary of the University of Wittenberg.

George, born November 25, 1527, died at the age of two. This unusually gifted child was the first of Melanchthon's family to die, and weeks after the child's death Luther wrote to Jonas:

Philip is still grieving. We all sympathize with him, as a man of worth richly deserves it. O that all those proud Timons were humbled by crosses like this, who are so proud of their own wisdom, that they do not know how much this man, sinful and feeble though he be, is exalted above many, yea, thousands like Jerome, Hilary, and Macarius, who are altogether unworthy to unloose the shoe laces of my Philip. [9]

The youngest Melanchthon, Magdalen, was born July 18, 1533. At nineteen she married Dr. Caspar Peucer, a noted physician, who wrote extensively on medicine, mathematics, and theology. After Melanchthon's death he became ranking professor at Wittenberg and physician to the

Elector. Following the death of his father-in-law, Peucer collected Melanchthon's works and actively propagated his ideas, as he understood them. Because Peucer took a decidedly Calvinistic or spiritual view of the Lord's Supper and because the Elector of Saxony, Augustus, was inflamed by the insinuations of the ultra-Lutherans who accused Peucer of crypto-Calvinism, in 1574 Peucer and many others were persecuted. For twelve years he was confined in prison. Penniless and homeless, Magdalen died in great distress and sorrow at Rochlitz, July 18, 1576. When Peucer was finally liberated, it was as if he had been freed to mourn. He retired to Zerbst and was often seen weeping during the public worship services.

John Koch was a remarkable servant in the Melanchthon house, almost a member of the family. For thirty-four years he managed the household affairs and helped the children in their early studies. Melanchthon frequently remarked about John's reading in theology, and sometimes corresponded with him in Latin. "He devoted his mornings to the reading of the Scriptures and prayer, then to the training of my little sons and daughters, and then to household affairs. He accompanied us in all our times of exile, labors and afflictions." [10] Melanchthon invited his university colleagues to Koch's funeral and gave a Latin oration at the grave.

Melanchthon felt warm sympathy with friends when death came to a family. In his letters of consolation there is little sentimentality; what breathes in them is a spirit of trust that in God's hands all is well. When Baumgärtner was captured by a robber-knight in 1544 Melanchthon wrote to his wife:

We pray that God will not permit you to sink in this great distress, but would by his Holy Spirit grant you comfort and strength, as he has often promised. . . . What our Savior said is certainly true, that all our hairs are numbered by God; God regards and preserves us, although we may be in danger. Even as he preserved Daniel among the lions, so he will also comfort and preserve your lord in the midst of the robbers who have captured him. . . . God has promised to be with the troubled and terrified who call upon him. Therefore do not doubt that the Eternal God is with your lord and you, and will strengthen and save you from this great distress. . . . Doubt not that God will hear you, and the many Christians who are praying that the Lord will

EFFIGIES REVERENDI VIRI, D. PHI-
LIPPI MELANTHONIS, EXPRESSA VVL-
TEBERGÆ, ANNO 1562.

1561.

MELANCHTHON AT THE AGE OF SIXTY

restore your husband to you with joy. May the Eternal God, the Father of our Lord Jesus Christ, do this for his own glory, and at all times comfort and protect you and your husband.[11]

A year later Baumgärtner was returned to his family.

When Pfeffinger suffered the loss of his son, Melanchthon wrote:

God has implanted the principle of natural affection in mankind, for the double purpose of strengthening the bonds of human society, and teaching us to realize the ardor of his love to his own son and to us. He therefore approves the affection we cherish for our offspring, and the piety of our grief for their loss. . . . But you are well aware that we are not permitted to mourn unduly. It is certain that these events are under divine superintendence; it becomes us, therefore, to manifest a due submission of mind to God, and quietly to resign ourselves to his disposal in every season of adversity. . . . Wise men have often inquired with astonishment as to why the feeble nature of man is oppressed with such a weight of afflictions; but we who can trace the causes to a divine origin, ought to be resigned to the appointments of God, and avail ourselves of those remedies for grief which divine goodness has revealed. . . . Remember that "In Him we live and move and have our being." [12]

The habits of Melanchthon's daily living were simple and orderly. When he arose in the morning, usually about two o'clock, he said a brief prayer:

Almighty, eternal God, Father of our Lord Jesus Christ, Creator of heaven and earth, and man, together with thy Son, our Lord Jesus Christ, thy word and image, and with thy Holy Spirit, have mercy upon us, and forgive us our sins for thy Son's sake, who thou hast made our Mediator according to thy wonderful counsels, and do thou guide and sanctify us by thy Holy Spirit, which was poured out upon the Apostles. Grant that we may truly know and praise thee throughout all eternity!

After the prayer he read portions from the Bible, then looked at the almanac to see what saints of the past were associated with the day. Then he answered letters. One of his customs was never to read a letter just before retiring in order not to be disturbed in his sleep. Melanchthon avoided a luxurious diet; his meals mainly consisted of soups, fish, vegetables, and eggs. Except when occasions of state demanded otherwise, he ate only two meals, frequently only one a day. "We Germans eat ourselves poor, sick, and into hell." He enjoyed conversation and jest at table. Before each of his two simple meals he returned thanks, never omitting the Apostles' Creed. One table grace is extant:

> O Saviour!
> Bless what thy providential care
> Has for our bodies given;
> Let thy good word (superior fare)
> Sustain the soul for heaven.[13]

Just back of the Melanchthon house was a large court garden with a shaded stone bench where he and Luther often conversed. A doorway in the garden wall opened on a path leading directly to the back entrance of Luther's home.

Most of the day, from about six o'clock in the morning, was spent studying, lecturing, and counseling with students. After a quiet evening with family or students, Melanchthon usually ended his day by nine o'clock. It was his custom to have a glass of wine before retiring. During the evening, he ignored all business and would not even read late mail.

Melanchthon's correspondence reflects the conscientious intensity with which he pursued every subject. His letters fill ten massive volumes. When assisting Luther in the translation of the Bible, he took great pains to obtain exact words. For two months he wrote letters and talked to numerous people in an effort to find German equivalents for Roman and Greek coins. He searched the classics for idioms. He wrote to farmers to find out about grains.[14] After the New Testament was published, Melanchthon planned to get maps of Palestine for later editions and asked the University for the funds.[15] The little Wittenberg group that helped Luther translate the Bible into German gathered once a year in Bugenhagen's house to celebrate the "festival of the translation."

Melanchthon was never ordained to the ministry, but on Sundays he frequently preached in his own home. George Helt reported such meetings in 1544.[16] In these family services he talked about Christian doctrine. In the first half of the meetings, which began at six o'clock, he presented an explanation of some passage of scripture, and in the second half hour gave a dialectical development of the passage. The audience participated with readings, questions, and comments. Students and townspeople, young and old, joined his family in these early morning meetings.[17]

Regular church attendance, said Melanchthon, is something that all people need if they are not to become swine and devils:

> You are not to act in so brutish and impertinent a manner as to think it does not matter if I do not go to church, for it is nothing but popery and superstition. No, but it is barbarism to neglect these privileges. There is no more beautiful sight than orderly and holy assemblies, in which men are instructed of God, and where they unite in prayer and thanksgiving. We have here a type of eternal life, where we shall sit in the presence of God and his Son, and hear the Son of God instructing us in reference to the greatest wonders.[18]

In his eulogy, Heerbrand noted that Melanchthon was anxious to frequent public worship, not only to set a good example, but because he knew that the Holy Spirit exercised his power through the Word of God and that the Son of God was present. "He constantly offered up prayers and supplications for the church and himself. We, who knew him, are all able to testify in regard to this."

Deeply expressive of Melanchthon's life were his prayers, which reflect in miniature his total outlook. Although he prepared a small handbook of religion for children to use in the private school of his own home, 1523-24, and although he included some formal views on prayer in the 1527 Visitation Articles and sent a short explanation of the Decalogue and the Pater Noster to Stephen Roth for inclusion in a prayerbook, his really vital interest in prayer did not come until after 1530, and more particularly after 1540. Beginning with a catechism on the Commandments, the Apostles' Creed, and the Lord's Prayer for his daughter Anna in 1530, revised and enlarged for his daughter Magdalen in 1540,[19] Melanchthon seemed to take an intense interest in prayer. At Augsburg in 1530 Melanchthon became poignantly aware that men do not control affairs. As the years passed, he became weary of the multiple intrigues of men. This, coupled with a series of personal tragedies, fostered a feeling of inadequacy, in anguish causing him to seek divine comfort.

His mother and his small son George both died in 1529. Three years later, Elector John, champion of the Reformation, died. With many people in Wittenberg succumbing to the raging plague of 1539, Melanchthon, overworked and tired, believed his own death was imminent, and in that year he set down his last will and testament. In the following year the bigamous scandal of Philip of Hesse was so depressing that Melanchthon wanted to die and, except for the prayers and solicitude of Luther, might have done so.[20] The death of Luther in 1546 and of Melanchthon's daughter Anna in 1547 climaxed a succession of personal tragedies. He sought comfort in the words of the psalmist: "Call on me in time of trouble and I will deliver you." [21]

But something more positive than personal frustration, namely a living belief and trust in the personal guidance of God, gradually emerged during these years. This is seen in his prayers.

Ministers, kings, and ordinary laymen asked Melanchthon to write prayers for them; and although he wrote many formal prayers, he never wanted prayer to become a "superstitious prattling" or a recitation of empty words. He simply wanted all people to think seriously about giving prayers, to ponder the nature of God, the commandments, the promises. Each person, he wrote, should carefully compose a formal prayer, diligently considering the meaning of every word, so that his prayer might be a witness and a glory to God.

A deep sense of personal worship and reliance on God for completion of his kingdom and fulfillment of his promises pervade Melanchthon's prayers. Throughout the invocations five elements are stressed, the first of which is praise. In order to praise God one must know him as he has uniquely revealed himself in his Word. In Scripture one knows God not only as creator, almighty and eternal, but as the Father of our Lord Jesus Christ, revealing himself as a God of mercy and love and comforting us through the Holy Spirit. Here one knows that God answers prayers. Men properly praise God by acknowledging him as he has disclosed himself. Most of Melanchthon's prayers begin with majestic general praise:

O Almighty God of Truth, Eternal and Only Father of our Savior Jesus Christ, with thy only begotten Son and Holy Spirit, Creator of heaven and earth and all therein; O God of Wisdom and Goodness, Righteousness, Truth, Mercy, and Lovingkindness; with my heart full of thanks I remember thy favors and blessings which are so many and so great that I cannot count them or reflect upon them enough. . .[22]

The second element of prayer is thanksgiving. In giving thanks, Melanchthon stated, man should recall the constant mercies of God and honor him with gratitude and obedience:

I give thanks to Thee, Almighty God, for revealing thyself to me, for sending thy Son Jesus Christ, that he might become a sacrifice, that through him I might be forgiven and receive eternal life. I give thanks to Thee, O God, for making me a recipient of thy great favor through the Gospel and the Sacraments, and for preserving thy Word and thy Holy Church. O that I might truly declare thy goodness and blessings! Inflame me, I earnestly beseech Thee, with thy Holy Spirit that thanksgiving may shine forth in my life. . . . Enlighten my heart, I beseech Thee, that I may be more fully aware of thy favor toward me and forever worship Thee with true thanksgiving.[23]

Confession, said Melanchthon, must be included in prayer, for only upon self-examination before God does one really know what to pray for:

I beseech Thee, Christ Jesus, Son of God, crucified for us and resurrected, have compassion upon me. Intercede for me with the eternal Father. Purify me with thy Holy Spirit. . .[24]

O Almighty, Eternal God of Truth, . . . I confess and I am deeply sorry that I am sinful and have so often sinned against Thee. I implore Thee to forgive me all my sins, be gracious unto me, and justify me for thy beloved Son's sake, whom thou didst decree to be our Redeemer. With thy Holy Spirit purify my heart and guide my soul that I may truly know, adore, and be obedient unto Thee, O God of Truth, Eternal Father, Son and Holy Ghost . . .[25]

In the fourth element of prayer, petition, Melanchthon included supplication for material blessings, as well as for forgiveness; and in the fifth element of prayer, adoration, he sought to ascribe all glory, honor, power, and dominion to God:

O God our Father, guide me with thy unchanging Spirit. Let thy Son, my joy and my life, be always in my heart. And when my brief time on earth is ended, take me to thyself, Lord Jesus Christ, for I am thine and thou art mine, and I long to be with Thee. Lord Jesus Christ, help me. Here on earth let my small service be a part of thy great work in the world, and into thy Kingdom, Lord Jesus, receive me at last.[26]

O Lord Jesus Christ, Son of God, our High Priest, with anxious hearts we implore Thee, for the sake of thy glory and that of the Eternal Father: Destroy all idols, errors, and hatred. Even as thou didst pray, sanctify us in thy truth, and in the hearts of all men kindle the light of thy Gospel and inflame us with true worship. Incline our hearts to serve and please Thee in newness of life, that in all eternity we may gratefully praise and honor Thee. Amen.[27]

Melanchthon keenly felt the littleness of man—his moral weakness, his finitude of thought, his inability to cope with social and political forces, his approaching death. He realized the frustration and despair of man attempting to control affairs, or even his own individual life, when man does not know what an hour will bring forth. In addition, Melanchthon believed demonic forces were actively opposing man and God, seeking to entrap man not in this and that impish act but in a long web of entanglement leading to despair and hopelessness. This reflects Melanchthon's biblical orientation as well as the climate of the sixteenth century. He believed that man without God would be helpless before such demonic powers.

Yet, out of this sense of dependence rise triumphant hope and joy and unusual activity—strong because resting on the rock of faith. "If God be for us, who can be against us!" was the phrase framing his portrait in the 1561 edition of his works. He himself quoted it many times.

Nothing short of this explains Melanchthon's lack of trust in the machinations of man and the height of his courage in God. Without God, the fruit of man's wisdom and effort is ultimately nothing. Abandoned by God, man flounders in a sea of frustration. But with God, "all things are possible."

That God reveals himself in the Bible is a basic presupposition with Melanchthon. Outside the Bible one may know about God, but one does not know him in his love to man, for this is revealed in Christ, a philosophical absurdity. For this reason, Melanchthon believed, true prayer is made only by those who hear the Word. The importance of knowing this biblical revelation and its implications became, of course, the basis of Melanchthon's educational system.

Melanchthon regarded the New Testament as the fulfillment of the Old, the promises of the Old as reaching their bloom in Christ. God moves through the Bible, manifesting his promises, his control of history, his nature. God may be known as he really is through this revelation which is received in faith through the Spirit.

Although Melanchthon sometimes allegorized certain biblical passages in ways strange to a modern reader, his acceptance of the biblical revelation was by no means static, superstitious, or slavish, for he believed in the guidance of the Holy Spirit. Without the Holy Spirit in the heart and mind of man as he reads, the revelation remains hidden, so that man has eyes but sees not, ears but hears not. Because Melanchthon considered the biblical revelation so primary, he repeatedly appealed to biblical passages to substantiate his views.

Is prayer valid? Is prayer answered? Does God control history? Should we pray for material goods? Do hardships come from God? Will the promises of God be fulfilled? Should the unworthy pray to God? To all these questions Melanchthon answered, "Yes." [28]

Melanchthon's prayers show him as one who trusted in the providence, guidance, and ultimate triumph of God, as one who confidently believed that God will richly endow those who call upon him in spirit and in truth.

One of Melanchthon's greatest sorrows, the death of his wife, came when he was attending affairs. In 1557 he met with the Roman Catholics at Worms in an effort to work out a basis of union. From the fruitless disputes about the pope or Scripture as the final authority, Melanchthon was called temporarily to Heidelberg to adjust some matters consequent on changing the Augustinian convent into an academy. There he renewed his friendship with his brother George and conversed with his celebrated son-in-law Peucer. But in the midst of this happy reunion, Camerarius brought the news about Katherine. Upon arriving Camerarius could not bring himself to tell Philip immediately, and he waited a day before speaking. In the prince's garden, Philip learned the truth. He made no tearful display of his sorrow, but simply said, "Fare thee well, I shall soon follow thee."

Two years after the death of Katherine he wrote:

Passionate and sorrowful yearning for a deceased wife is not effaced in the old man as it may be with those who are younger. When day by day I gaze upon my grandchildren, I recall not without a sigh their grandmother, and thus at the first sight of the bereaved little ones my sorrow is renewed. She cared for the whole family; she cherished the infants; she nursed the sick; by her consoling words she lessened my griefs; she taught the children to pray. And so it is that I miss her everywhere. I remember how almost daily she repeated these words of the psalm, "Forsake me not in my old age." And thus I also continually pray.[30]

Melanchthon composed an eight-line Latin verse and placed it on her tombstone—"and I was absent when she died!"[31]

After the death of Katherine, Melanchthon sensed the approach of his own death.[32] The recent controversies with the theologians left him lonely and weary. He thought that he might be driven out of Saxony by his enemies. "If they drive me out, I have made up my mind to go to Palestine, and there in the seclusion of the cloister of Hieronymous, at the call of the Son of God, to record my unclouded testimony to the doctrine, and dying to commend my soul to God."[33]

Shortly before his death, Melanchthon had a vision of himself lying in bed. He was convinced it portended either his death or a terrible scourge. Recalling the reading of his life according to the stars by Johann Virdung von Hassfurt, court astrologer of the Palatinate, who said he would be shipwrecked at sea, and seeing a map of the sea on the wall beside his bed, Melanchthon remarked: "Now I am not far from it, but I think the sea is on the map." The boyhood prophecy about shipwreck caused Melanchthon to fear the sea, and was undoubtedly a factor in his not going to Denmark and England.

On the thirtieth of March, 1560, Melanchthon journeyed to Leipzig on business for the Elector. When he returned on April 4 the weather was unusually cold and a sharp north wind made the inside of his carriage frigid. Back at Wittenberg he became ill. On the eighth of April his fever was so high and his eyes so sunken that his friends became alarmed. Dr. Peucer believed that the stone infection had returned and prescribed a bath and warm poultices.

On the ninth Melanchthon felt better but could not forget that the positions of the planets omened death. Despite obvious weakness he managed to get to his classroom at nine o'clock and to lecture for fifteen minutes. He talked about Christ's ransom.

During the next few days he felt stronger, talked about Easter, conversed with friends, ate a few Hungarian plums, and drank some Rhenish wine. Prince Joachim of Anhalt, hearing of his illness, sent him a moor hen and several partridges. Dr. Peucer applied a cardiac of corals which relieved him for a while so that he slept, but attacks of fever kept recurring.

Melanchthon improved enough on the seventeenth of April that Camerarius thought he might leave for a few days to attend to business. But the pains in his side and back did not leave, and Melanchthon remarked, "If this be not death, it is indeed a very severe scourge."

Though feverish throughout the night, on April 18, Philip arose at 4:00 A.M. He was too weak, however, to stay up. During the day he called his grandchildren to his bedside and blessed them. That night he ate some broth and a few slices of lemon. When he continued to feel alternately hot and chilled, he asked Peucer to tell him his true condition. Peucer said, "God is your life and the length of the days of your life. But as you request me to tell you the whole truth, there is indeed very little hope, as far as I am able to judge from natural causes, for you are very weak, and your weakness is increasing every moment." "Yes," he responded, "I feel my weakness, and understand what it imports very well. I have commended the whole matter to God, whom I pray to deal mercifully with me."

On the nineteenth of April Melancthon was very weak. He asked that his hair be cut; he put on three clean linen shirts, as was his custom. His fever mounted and his feet remained cold. Audibly and fervently he prayed the prayer he was in the custom of using:

Almighty, eternal, everliving God of Truth, Maker of heaven and earth, and Creator of men, together with thy eternal beloved Son, our Lord Jesus Christ, who was crucified for us and raised from death, and with thy Holy Spirit, everliving, pure and true: O God of wisdom and goodness, mercy and justice: O Savior bountiful, righteous, and faithful, through whom life and light are given: Thou hast said, "I do not desire the death of a sinner, but that he be converted and live," and "Call on me in time of trouble, and I will deliver you:" To Thee do I confess myself a miserable sinner, burdened with many iniquities, for I have greatly sinned against thy holy commands, and I am heartily sorry that I have offended thee. For the sake of thy dear Son, have mercy on me, forgive me all my sins, and make me righteous through Jesus Christ, my Lord, thy Son, thy eternal Image and Word, whom thou didst send into the world to be for the world a Sacrifice, Mediator, Redeemer, Deliverer and Savior, according to thy wondrous wisdom and mercy which is past our understanding. Sanctify me with thy holy, living Spirit of purity and truth that through thy Spirit I may truly know thee as the only God, the omnipotent Creator of heaven and earth and men, the Father of our Lord Jesus Christ; that I may know thy beloved Son, thy Word and Image; that I may know thy Holy Spirit of truth and purity, my living Comforter; that I may firmly believe in thee, obey thee, give thanks to thee, reverently fear and call upon thee, and come at last in joy to behold thy face and worship thee forever. In thee, O Lord, do I put my trust; let me never be ashamed. Deliver me through thy righteousness. Turn me, O Lord, unto righteousness and eternal life. Thou hast redeemed me, O Lord God of Truth!

Mercifully preserve and rule our churches, our country, our schools. Give the blessings of peace and order. Direct and protect our leaders and those in authority; gather unto thyself and forever keep a Christian Church in this land. Purify and unite us with thy Holy Spirit that we may be one in thee, truly knowing and calling upon thee through thy Son, our Lord, Jesus Christ, who tasted death on the cross for us and rose again.

Almighty, eternal Son of God, our Lord and Savior, Jesus Christ, thou who art the eternal Word and Image of the Father, our Mediator and Redeemer, who died for us and rose again, with all my heart I give thee thanks, for thou didst take upon thyself the nature of a man and became my Deliverer, didst suffer physical pain, didst die and arise again. And now thou art pleading for me. I beseech thee, look graciously upon me and have mercy, for I am alone and in need. Through thy Holy Spirit increase in me the light of faith, help me to overcome my weakness; guide, protect and make me pure. In thee do I put my trust, O Lord; let me never be ashamed.

Almighty, Holy Spirit of truth and purity, our living Comforter, enlighten me, direct me, and sanctify me. Strengthen the faith in my soul and heart, and grant me a sincere trust. Sustain and guide me that I may dwell in the house of the Lord all the days of my life, that I may see the will of the Lord, that I may forever be in God's holy temple, and with a joyous heart give thanks unto him, and in the assembly of his eternal church honor and praise him forever. Amen.

Toward the close of the day Melanchthon tasted a soup made of Hamburg beer, but was unable to raise himself. Peucer asked him if he desired anything, and he replied, "Nothing but heaven, and therefore do not ask me such questions any more." His friends read passages of scripture. His lips moved in prayer but the words could not be understood. Then for a long while he was quiet. Without the slightest motion, Melanchthon died at seven o'clock, April 19, 1560. He was sixty-three.

As was the custom, Lucas Cranach painted his portrait the next day, and hundreds of people passed by the coffin.

At the parish church Paul Eber preached a funeral sermon. The body was placed by the side of Luther, and Veit Winsheim delivered a moving Latin oration. "At the very time when we are tossed about by the ocean storms," lamented Winsheim, "we have lost our pilot." None before in Wittenberg had witnessed so large a funeral.

The old Wittenberg account of Melanchthon's life closed with a prayer typical of the life and faith of Melanchthon: [34]

Out of the depths of our hearts we beseech God to gather and keep in this land and throughout the world an eternal Christian Church, through his dear Son, our Lord and Savior, Jesus Christ. We beseech him graciously to save us from factions and schisms within and to give us the courage and strength to withstand confidently and fruitfully all opposition from without. And as man is weak in power and wisdom, we pray the eternal Son of God, through his Word, to pour out on all believing hearts his Holy Spirit, to give us understanding and wisdom, to direct and lead us in all good things, that by us and the whole Christian Church his name may be honored and praised in this world and forever in the world to come. Amen.

NOTES

KEY TO REFERENCES

ARG—Archiv für Reformationsgeschichte.
Camerarius—Joachim Camerarii, *De Vita Melanchthonis Narratio.*
CR—*Corpus Reformatorum.*
DeW—*Martin Luthers Briefe.* Wilhelm Martin Leberecht de Witte, ed. (Berlin, 1825-28), 5 vols.
Enders—*Dr. Martin Luthers Briefwechsel,* E. L. Enders and G. Kawerau, eds. (Stuttgart und Leipzig, 1884 ff.), 19 vols.
Erlangen—*Dr. Martin Luthers sämmtliche Werke* (Erlangen, 1826 ff.), 65 vols.
Hartfelder—K. Hartfelder, *Philipp Melanchthon als Praeceptor Germaniae* (Berlin, 1889).
Matthes—K. Matthes, *Philipp Melanchthon* (Altenburg, 1841).
Richard—J. W. Richard, *Philip Melanchthon* (New York, 1898).
Schmidt—Carl Schmidt, *Philipp Melanchthon* (Elberfeld, 1861).
Smith, *Correspondence—Luther's Correspondence and Other Contemporary Letters,* Preserved Smith and C. M. Jacobs, trs. and eds. (Philadelphia, 1913 ff.), 2 vols.
Stokes—*Epistolae Obscurorum Virorum,* F. G. Stokes, tr. (New Haven: Yale University Press, 1925).
WA Br.—*D. Martin Luthers Briefwechsel, D. Martin Luthers Werke, kritische Gesamtausgabe,* K. Burdach, *et al.,* eds. (Weimar, 1930 ff.), 6 vols.
WA, TR—*Tischreden, D. Martin Luthers Werke, kritische Gesamtausgabe,* K. Drescher, ed. (Weimar, 1912 ff.), 6 vols.
ZKG—Zeitschrift für Kirchengeschichte.

INTRODUCTION

1. First annual meeting of the Melanchthon Synod of the Evangelical Lutheran Church, December 1-3, 1857, printed by T. Newton Kurtz, Baltimore, 1857.

2. John Brerely, *Luthers Life . . . with a further shorte discourse, touchinge Andreas, Melanchton . . .* (St. Omers, 1624), pp. 81-88.

3. R. R. Caemmerer, *Concordia Theological Monthly,* XVIII (1947), 321 ff. Cf. J. Pelikan, *From Luther to Kierkegaard* (St. Louis: Concordia Publishing House, 1950), pp. 24 ff.

4. F. Galle, *Versuch einer Charakteristik Melanchthons als Theologen, und einer Entwickelung seines Lehrbegriffs* (Halle, 1840). K. Matthes, *Philipp Melanchthon, sein Leben und Wirken aus den Quellen dargestellt* (Altenburg, 1841).

5. *The Athenaeum,* II (1903), 621. A listing of the source materials in the Bretten House may be found in *Archiv für Reformationsgeschichte,* XIX (1922), XXIV (1927).

6. *Lutheran Quarterly Review,* NS XXVII (1897), 12 ff.

7. *Biographie Universelle,* "Melanchthon," XXVII, 546.

8. *The Confession of Augsburg . . . composed by Luther and Melanchthon. . . ,* printed by James Oram (New York, 1813). Cf. Krauth, *Conservative Reformation and Its Theology,* pp. 219 ff.

CHAPTER 1

1. *Corpus Reformatorum, Melanchthon Opera* (CR), eds. Bretschneider and Bindseil, 28 vols., 1834-60; 1:42, cxlviii. Cf. Joachim Camerarii, *De Vita Melanchthonis Narratio,* ed. G. T. Strobel (Halle, 1777), p. 26.

2. CR 10:260-61.

3. *Tischreden,* ed. Karl Drescher (Weimar, 1912), 6 vols. (referred to as WA, TR), 2:669. Cf. E. G. Schwiebert, *Luther, and His Times* (St. Louis: Concordia Publishing House, 1950), pp. 206-7. Cf. H. Boehmer, *Der junge Luther* (3rd ed.; Leipzig, 1940), p. 49. Cf. Eschenhagen, "Wittenberger Studien," *Luther-Jahrbuch,* IX (1927), 25 n.

4. CR 1:cxlviii.

5. CR 1:52; 10:531. J. W. Richard, *Philip Melanchthon* (New York, 1898), pp. 36, 112.

6. Schwiebert, *op. cit.,* p. 242. Cf. J. Hauszleiter, *Die Universität Wittenberg* (Leipzig, 1903), p. 28 n. Roland Bainton, *Here I Stand* (Nashville: Abingdon Press, 1950), p. 71, calculated 1,902,202 years and 270 days. Other scholars have cited different numbers of relics and rewards.

7. Schwiebert, *op. cit.,* p. 235.

8. P. Kalkoff, *Luther und die Entscheidungsjahre der Reformation Von den Ablassthesen bis zum Wormser Edikt* (München und Leipzig, 1917).

9. CR 11:15-25, *De corrigendis adolescentiae studiis.*

10. CR 11:24.

11. CR 11:22, 23.

12. CR 11:24.

13. K. Hartfelder, *Philipp Melanchthon als Praeceptor Germaniae* (Berlin, 1889), p. 63.

14. Enders and Kawerau, eds., *Dr. Martin Luthers Briefwechsel* (Stuttgart und Leipzig, 1884 ff.) 19 vols., 1:220 ff. (Referred to as Enders.)

15. CR 11:1006.

16. *Der Joeden Spiegel, Der Joeden Bicht, Der Juden Veindt, Hostis Judaeorum. Epistolae Obscurorum Virorum,* tr. F. G. Stokes (New Haven: Yale University Press, 1925), xxii f., xlvii.

17. Reuchlin published *De Verbo Mirifico,* 1494, claiming that the religious mysteries of the world were concealed in the Hebrew tongue. In 1506 he published *De Rudimentis Hebraicis,* the first Hebrew grammar to appear in Germany.

18. *Epistolae Obscurorum Virorum,* i, 22.

19. CR 1:5-6.

20. Stokes, xlvii.

21. Stokes, i.

22. Enders, 1:226-27.

23. CR 10:472-79. In the belief that Melanchthon was the author this was included in his collected works. CR 11:1007. Stokes, xxv. Cf. CR 1:21 for Melanchthon's satire on Hoogstraten. Crotus Rubianus and Ulrich von Hutten stand out as the possible writers of these letters. In 1531 Crotus Rubianus apologized for having broken with the church, and in the following year a Lutheran reformer, Justus Menius, criticized him for not displaying the noble spirit he showed in

writing the letters. Rubianus did not answer. Ulrich von Hutten, literary knight, had won fame with the writing of *Querelen*. Hutten, a close friend of Rubianus, collaborated with him. Cf. Stokes, introduction; also Walter Brecht, *Die Verfasser der Epist. Obsc. Virorum* (Strassburg, 1904).

24. CR 1:cxlvi. Cf. Carl Schmidt, *Philipp Melanchthon* (Elberfeld, 1861), p. 29.

CHAPTER 2

1. Karl Hartfelder, *Melanchthons spätere Beziehungen zu seiner Pfälzischen Heimat*. Studien der evangel-protest. Geistlichen der Grossherzogtums Baden. VIII (1882), 113. Jac. Micylii, *Sylvarum Libri*, V (1564), 141.

2. John Wesley, *Works* (New York, 1831), II, 232.

3. Camerarius, *Vita Mel.*, p. 26.

4. CR 10:255 ff.

5. Anna married Chilian Grumbach and lived her last days at Heilbron. George became a historian and mayor of Bretten. Margaretha married Andrew Stichs, and after his death married the electoral secretary Hawerer. Barbara lived an unhappy, frustrated life as the wife of Peter Kecheln.

6. CR 8:367.

7. CR 1:cxlv; 10:258.

8. CR 25:464; 10:469. Cf. Hartfelder, *Philipp Melanchthon*, p. 4.

9. CR 20:549.

10. CR 28: Annales Vitae. Cf. Schmidt, *Philipp Melanchthon* (Elberfeld, 1861), p. 3. Cf. S. Bierordt, *D. John Unger, Melanchthonis praeceptore* (Karlsruhe, 1844). Cf. CR 25:448; 4:715.

11. CR 25:448-49; 28:2. Richard, *op. cit.*, p. 7. Cf. Hartfelder, *op. cit.*, p. 4.

12. CR 10:258.

13. CR 10:258. Cf. D. Nisard, *Renaissance et Reforme* (Paris, 1877), II, 198.

14. CR 28:1, Annales Vitae.

15. C. L. Robbins, *Teachers in Germany in the Sixteenth Century* (New York: Teachers College, Columbia University, 1912), ch. iii, p. 29.

16. F. V. N. Painter, *A History of Education* (New York: D. Appleton & Co., 1904), p. 143.

17. CR 10:259. Cf. L. Geiger, *Johann Reuchlin* (Leipzig, 1891), s. 79.

18. L. Geiger, *op. cit.*, s. 323. Camerarius, *Vita Mel.*, p. 8. The Wittenberg professors erroneously named Hildebrandt as Philip's Greek instructor, CR 10:259. Both Camerarius and Melanchthon say Simler was his Greek instructor. Cf. Camerarius, p. 9; CR 4:715.

19. Cf. CR 11:1001; J. G. F. Pflüger, *Geschichte der Stadt Pforzheim* (Pforzheim, 1862), s. 292. In 1511 Anshelm went to Tübingen and later to Hagenau. Cf. Pflüger, p. 189; also K. Steiff, *Der erste Buchdruck in Tübingen* (Tübingen, 1881), s. 13.

20. Cf. CR 10:469; 20:765; 1:cxxxi, 9; 2:520, 542, 558; 3:210-11. *Schwartzerd* was also spelled *Schwarzerd, Schwartzerdt, Schwartzert*. Cf. G. Töpke, *Die Matrikel der Universität Heidelberg* (Heidelberg, 1884), I, 472. Roth, *Urkunden zur Geschichte der Universität Tübingen*, s. 591. Cf. CR 1:cxlvi.

21. Among the fellow students with Melanchthon at Pforzheim were Francis Friedlieb of Ettlingen, who did a historico-geographical study of the German Empire; Simon Grynaeus, linguist and theologian of Basel; Berthold Haller, the reformer of Bern; Nicholas Gerbel, a jurist at Strassburg; and John Schwebel,

a reformer of Zweibrücken. It is doubtful that they had any influence on Melanchthon at this time.

22. CR 11:442.

23. Hartfelder, *op. cit.*, pp. 18, 20-21. CR 3:673. Cf. Camerarius, *Vita Mel.*, p. 12.

24. Hartfelder, p. 23.

25. CR 4:715.

26. CR 11:280, 396; 3:674.

27. CR 11:439-42; 4:716, 720.

28. Cf. Leonard Cox, *The arte or Crafte of Rhetoryke,* ed. F. I. Carpenter (Chicago, 1899). Cf. *Zeitschrift für Kirchengeschichte,* IV, 327, n. 7.

29. CR 11:439-42.

30. CR 4:715.

31. Cf. Töpke, *op. cit.,* I, 481.

32. CR 10:469.

33. CR 20:765. *Melanchthons Briefwechsel,* Supplementa Melanchthoniana, von Otto Clemen (Leipzig, 1926), Bd. 1.

34. CR 24:85.

35. CR 10:260; 1:cxlvi.

36. Schmidt, *op. cit.,* p. 11. Camerarius, *Vita Mel.,* p. 23.

37. Camerarius, p. 22.

38. CR 4:718, for reference to Lemp; CR 1:321, 1083, for Occam.

39. CR 24:309.

40. Preface to *Farrago rerum, theolog., Wesselo autore* (Wittenberg, 1521, or 1522).

41. CR 10:259-60. Camerarius, *Vita Mel.,* p. 16.

42. CR 10:192; 20:766; 1:938. Camerarius, *Vita Mel.,* p. 15.

43. CR 11:332. Melanchthon Declamations, Tom. I, *Encomium Suevorum.* Cf. CR 4:720-21; 1:15; 19:271, 272.

44. CR 4:70; 1:87-88.

45. CR 1:13; 10:297. Cf. Richard, *op cit.,* p. 22.

46. Cf. K. Steiff, *op. cit.,* for a long list of humanistic publications from Anshelm's presses.

47. CR 10:260; 1:cxlvi.

48. CR 1:14; 1:cxlvii.

49. CR 1:9 ff., 13, 18, cxlvii; 19:655; 17:1123, 1137.

50. CR 1:15; 11:1, 14.

51. CR 1:24; 18:124; 20:3.

52. CR 1:cxlvi. See Bishop Latimer's *Sermons,* ed. 1635, fol. 124.

53. CR 1:31, cxlvii.

54. CR 1:25. Richard, pp. 36, 112.

55. CR 1:cxlvi, 34 n. C. F. Ledderhose, *Philip Melanchthon* (Philadelphia, 1855), tr. Krotel, p. 26 n. CR 1:23. Ode to Pirkheimer, CR 1:22-23, 27-28.

56. CR 1:27-31.

57. CR 1:32-33.

58. CR 1:34.

59. CR 10:299.

60. CR 1:33 n. Cf. Camerarius, *Vita Mel.,* p. 25.

CHAPTER 3

1. CR 1:75, 203.
2. CR 10:301.
3. CR 10:301. Cf. Richard, *op. cit.,* p. 44.
4. *Ibid.*
5. Enders, 2:280-82; 1:226-27. Cf. DeW, 1:196, 143, 380.
6. CR 10:302.
7. CR 1:44, 50, 52.
8. Smith, *Correspondence,* I, 100-104. Cf. WA 2:23.
9. Smith, *Correspondence,* I, 96-98, 116. Enders, 1:210-13, 239.
10. Enders, 1:244-45. Smith, *Correspondence,* I, 118.
11. CR 1:58.
12. Enders, 1:310-12.
13. WA Br., 1:289-94. Enders, 1:408. Smith, *Correspondence,* I, 160.
14. For the exchange of publications and essays which brought on this debate, see Smith, *Correspondence,* I, 76-77, 90, 85-86. Enders, 5:1-2; 1:402-5. WA Br., 1:415-19, 319. WA 2:155, 157-58, 160-61. CR 1:93.
15. CR 1:81 ff.
16. CR 1:82 n., 83.
17. WA 2:251.
18. CR 1:91.
19. CR 1:91-92, 94-95.
20. CR 1:cxlix, 82, 84.
21. CR 1:85. DeW 1:305. Enders, 2:103-21.
22. CR 1:87-96.
23. CR 1:59. Cf. CR 1:78.
24. CR 1:103.
25. CR 1:105, tr. Cox.
26. CR 1:108-18.
27. CR 1:113-14, 115.
28. Milner's History, IV, 428.
29. Enders, 1:327. DeW 1:214.
30. CR 1:138.
31. *Melanchthons Werke,* ed. Robert Stupperich (Gütersloh, 1951), 1 Bd., pp. 24-25. CR 6:1, 78-79.
32. WA Br., 1:492.
33. Richard, *op. cit.,* p. 59. DeW 1:341. Enders, 2:182.
34. CR 1:cxlix.
35. DeW 1:380. Enders, 2:280-81.
36. CR 1:137-46. *Melanchthons Werke,* 1 Bd., pp. 26 ff. The same themes were discussed by Melanchthon in his June 25 address on Paul, patron saint of Wittenberg.
37. CR 1:149-50, abridged.
38. CR 1:362. March 21, 1521.
39. Cf. Melanchthon to Spalatin, 1523, CR 1:646.
40. CR 1:125 n., 126-27, tr. Richard.
41. CR 10:302.
42. CR 11:728.
43. CR 1:160, 269.
44. Richard, *op. cit.,* p. 42. Preface to Commentary on Colossians.

45. Cox, *op. cit.*, ch. i.
46. *Ibid.*, quoted from M. Baillet.
47. CR 1:141; 10:303; Camerarius, *Vita Mel.*, p. 14.
48. Rothe's address on Philip Melanchthon, *American Theological Review*, III (1861), 281.
49. WA, TR 5:5511, 5647, 5787, 5827, 6439, 6458.

CHAPTER 4

1. Preserved Smith, *Luther's Correspondence and Other Contemporary Letters,* I:332. Used by permission of The Muhlenberg Press. Enders, 2:423.
2. Smith, *Correspondence,* I:345. Enders, 2:456.
3. CR 1:265.
4. CR 1:211-12.
5. CR 1:212.
6. CR 1:cli. Camerarius, *Vita Mel.*, p. 38.
7. Enders, 2:523. Smith, *Correspondence,* I:393.
8. CR 10:552 n, 143, 560.
9. Cf. WA Br., 2:234. Also WA 7:183-86.
10. CR 1:201. Enders, 2:365, 404, 419. Cf. Pastor, *History of the Popes,* VII, 404.
11. WA 6:570-93, 597-612.
12. WA 7:183 ff.
13. CR 1:211.
14. Cf. E. G. Schwiebert, *Luther, and His Times* (St. Louis: Concordia Publishing House, 1950), pp. 466-67. Cf. CR 1:211; Enders, 2:432, 443.
15. CR 1:269.
16. CR 1:212-62.
17. CR 1:284-86. WA 7:259-60.
18. K. Sell, *Melanchthon und die Deutsche Reformation bis 1531* (Halle, 1897), s. 23. CR 1:286-358. WA Br., 2:214. *The Rhadini in Ph. Melanchthonis Luteranae haereseos defensorem oratio,* Rhomae, 1522.
19. Pastor, *History of Popes,* VII, 415. Richard, *op. cit.*, p. 72.
20. CR 1:366-88. WA 8:261. Two other universities had condemned the teachings of Luther—Cologne, October 12, 1519, and Louvain, November 9, 1519.
21. DeW 2:30. WA 8:291-93. CR 1:367.
22. CR 1:399-416.
23. WA Br., 2:365, 357. Erlangen, 27:408.
24. *Opera Lutheri,* 7:78-91.

CHAPTER 5

1. CR 1:389-90.
2. Cf. Smith, *Correspondence,* II:22-23. Enders, 3:148.
3. CR 1:396. Ledderhose, *op. cit.*, p. 44.
4. Enders, 3:162. Smith, *Correspondence,* II, 33-34.
5. Smith, *Correspondence,* II:21-22. Enders, 3:146.
6. Cf. WA Br., 2:370-72. Barge, *Karlstadt,* I, 290-91. Enders, 3:207-8. Smith, *Correspondence,* II, 47-51.
7. Cf. Schwiebert, *Life and Times of Martin Luther,* p. 524. Cf. Barge, *Karlstadt,* I, 265 ff., 289 ff., 475 ff.
8. CR 1:418 n, 420.

9. CR 1:418 n, 422 n.

10. CR 1:419-21.

11. CR 1:421-40. Herman Barge in *Zeitschrift für Kirchengeschichte*, XXIV, 310-18, says Carlstadt was the author of this apology, but his evidence is not conclusive.

12. Cf. CR 1:440-42.

13. CR 1:419 ff.

14. Enders, 3:229. Smith, *Correspondence*, II, 56 ff.

15. *Supplementa Melanchthonia*, VI, 1, 161. Cf. N. Müller, *Die Wittenberger Bewegung*, 16-17.

16. CR 1:456-58. WA 8:398-409.

17. CR 1:459.

18. CR 1:465-70.

19. CR 1:470-74.

20. CR 1:493 ff.

21. CR 1:499-500.

22. CR 1:503, 504-5, 507-8.

23. CR 1:477-81.

24. WA Br., 2:409-11.

25. On Monastic Vows. On the Abolition of Private Masses. A Blast Against the Idol of Halle.

26. WA 8:670 ff. CR 1:484, 488, 504, 506.

27. B. J. Kidd, *Documents Illustrative of the Continental Reformation*, No. 53. Fröschel's Preface, *Tractate vom Priesterthum*, 1565. Used by permission of Oxford University Press.

28. Cf. N. Müller, *Wittenberger Bewegung*, No. 75. Cf. Barge, *Karlstadt*, I, 379-86.

29. Cf. CR 1:512. Roland Bainton, *Here I Stand*, p. 206. Barge, *Karlstadt*, I, 558-59. Cf. Smith, *Correspondence*, II, 47-48.

30. CR 1:546.

31. Cf. Smith, *Correspondence*, II, 81-82. P. Wappler, *Thomas Münzer und die Zwickauer Propheten*, 1908. H. Böhmer, *Neues Archiv für Sächsische Geschichte*, XXXVI (1915), 1-38.

32. CR 1:533. Their first convert in Wittenberg was Martin Cellarius, a private teacher.

33. CR 1:534-35.

34. CR 1:513-15.

35. Smith, *Correspondence*, II, 82-83. Cf. *Archiv für Reformationsgeschichte*, VI (1909), 390.

36. CR 1:535-38.

37. Camerarius, *Vita Mel.*, pp. 51-52.

38. Cf. Müller, *Die Wittenberger Bewegung*, pp. 169, 212. Enders, 3:256 ff. WA Br., 2:471-73, 478-79.

39. CR 1:540-41. Dr. Beyer's report to Von Einsiedel, adviser to the Elector.

40. Cf. Müller, *Die Wittenberger Bewegung*. Pallas, *ARG*, VI, 238-39.

41. CR 1:547. Tr. Richard.

42. *Supplementa Mel.*, VI, 1:179.

43. Smith, *Correspondence*, II, 84-85. Cf. Enders, 3:272.

44. Smith, *Correspondence*, II, 90-93. Cf. WA Br., 2:453-70.

45. Cf. Smith, *Correspondence*, II, 2:93-96.

46. Smith, *Correspondence*, II, 115. Cf. Holman, *Writings of Martin Luther*, 2:391-92.

47. Sermons, Erlangen, 28:202-60.

48. Cf. Smith, *Correspondence*, II, 102. Enders, 3:306-7, 353 ff. Camerarius, *Vita Mel.*, pp. 51, 52.

49. Enders, 5:80, 4:89. Schwiebert, *op. cit.*, p. 544.

50. WA 10, Part III, 352 ff., 371 ff.

CHAPTER 6

1. CR 1:366. Cf. DeW 2:110. Schmidt, p. 74.

2. Cf. Strobel, *Versuch einer Litterär* . . . pp. 39 ff. CR 1:128.

3. CR 1:136.

4. CR 1:158.

5. CR 11:34 ff.

6. CR 1:521.

7. CR 1:122.

8. CR 1:273-75, 266, 301; CR 18:1131.

9. CR 21:50-60. Cf. CR 21:11-48, 82-227, 1-60.

10. Cf. Plitt, *Loci Communes*, p. 1.

11. T. W. Baldwin, *William Shakspere's Small Latine and Lesse Greeke*, 2 vols. (Urbana, Ill.: University of Illinois, 1944), I, 259.

12. *Loci Communes*, tr. C. L. Hill (Boston: Meador Publishing Co., 1944), pp. 67 ff. (*Loci* references are to this translation unless otherwise indicated.)

13. CR 1:50-60.

14. *Loci*, pp. 64-65. Used by permission of Meador Publishing Co.

15. *Loci*, p. 65.

16. *Loci*, pp. 76, 72-73, 74, 108, 109.

17. *Loci*, p. 71.

18. *Loci*, p. 108.

19. *Loci*, pp. 81 ff.

20. *Loci*, pp. 87, 98-99, 101.

21. *Loci*, pp. 113, 116, 112, 115, 117.

22. *Loci*, pp. 117 ff., 154 ff., 166 ff., 170.

23. *Loci*, pp. 172, 176-77.

24. *Loci*, pp. 177, 202 ff.

25. *Loci*, p. 207.

26. *Loci*, pp. 265 ff.

27. *Loci*, p. 267.

28. *Loci*, pp. 84, 165, 129.

29. *Loci*, p. 109. Cf. pp. 72, 74, 227, 108, 86, 96, 98, 196, 197, 210, 104, 188, 210.

30. *Loci*, p. 263.

31. CR 10:303, 305, 293-313.

32. CR 1:667.

33. Richard, *op. cit.*, pp. 101-2.

34. Strobel, *op. cit.*, p. 184.

35. Cf. Strobel, *op. cit.*, pp. 48-49.

36. CR 2:513.

37. E.g. Denifle und Weiss, *Luther und Luthertum* (Mainz, 1909) II, 268.

38. Schaff, *History of the Christian Church*, VI, 369.

39. Plitt, *op. cit.*, p. 1. Strobel, *op. cit.*, pp. 184-85.

40. Strobel, *op. cit.*, pp. 184 ff.
41. Cf. *Deutsche Drucke älterer Zeit in Nachbildungen*, von Dr. Wilhelm Scherer. III. *Passional Christi und Antichristi* (Berlin, 1885).
42. Cf. *Passional Christi und Antichristi*, VI-VII, VIII ff. G. Lechler, *Joh. Wiclif und die Vorgeschichte der Reformation* (Leipzig, 1872), I, 58.
43. *Passional Christi und Antichristi*, XIX. DeW 2:9. Enders, 3:162. As early as December 11, 1518, Luther had suggested that the pope might be Antichrist. DeW 1:198. WA 2:205.

CHAPTER 7

1. Richard, *Philip Melanchthon*, pp. 104-5. DeW 2:238.
2. CR 14:1043.
3. Hartfelder, *op. cit.*, p. 70.
4. Cf. CR 2:550.
5. Cf. CR 1:677.
6. Richard, *op. cit.*, p. 109. DeW 2:217.
7. Smith, *Correspondence*, II, 223. DeW 2:490.
8. CR 1:677.
9. CR 1:729.
10. Smith, *Correspondence*, II, 363. Enders, 5:319.
11. CR 1:593-94.
12. Cox, *op. cit.*, ch. ii.
13. CR 1:593-94.
14. CR 1:575. Cf. Richard, *op. cit.*, p. 108.
15. CR 11:50-66. CR 1:575-76.
16. CR 1:684. Cf. Kawerau, *ARG*, X (1912-13), 281-85.
17. Hartfelder, *op. cit.*, p. 72.
18. CR 1:652, 653-54. Schmidt, *op. cit.*, p. 103. Cf. CR 28: Annales Vitae.
19. CR 10:491. Cf. Richard, p. 114. Melanchthon composed an epitaph for the rhetorician, saying his name would be in the "records of eternal fame."
20. Matthes, p. 61.
21. CR 1:656.
22. Camerarius, *Vita Mel.*, p. 97, Schmidt, *op. cit.*, p. 105. Richard, *op. cit.*, p. 116.
23. CR 1:657-58.
24. Schmidt, *op. cit.*, p. 107.
25. Camerarius, *Vita Mel.*, p. 98.
26. CR 1:703-12.

CHAPTER 8

1. Camerarius, *Vita Mel.*, p. 100.
2. CR 1:684.
3. Cf. G. Hellmann's paper "J. Stöefflers Prognose für das Jahr 1524," *Beiträge zur Geschichte der Meterologie*, No. 1 (1914), 5-102. Cf. Lynn Thorndike, *History of Magic and Experimental Science* (New York: Columbia University Press, 1941), V, ch. XI. Cf. K. Hartfelder, *Aberglaube Philipp Melanchthons*, n.d., pp. 262-63. Cf. L. F. Heyd, *Melanchthon und Tübingen*, 1839.
4. Thorndike, *op. cit.*, V, 379.
5. Thorndike, *op. cit.*, V, 401. Hieronymous Wolf, Camerarius, Achilles Gassar, Vitus Amerbach, Johannes Homelius, J. Schöner, J. Heller, David Chytraeus, Joachim Cureus, Herman Witekind, Jacob Milich, and Caspar Peucer.

6. Cf. C. Meyer, *Der Aberglaube des Mittelalters und der nächstfolgenden Jahrhunderte* (Basel, 1884). Cf. J. Burckhardt, *Die Cultur der Renaissance in Italien,* 3 aufl., von L. Geiger (Leipzig, 1877), II, 279. Cf. Thorndike, *op. cit.,* V, 378 ff.

7. CR 7:952; 8:942, 943; 10:545, 712, 715; 11:261, 817.

8. Cf. Barnard, *Teachers and Educators in Germany,* 270 n.

9. CR 5:292, Annales, July 23, 1523; March 31, April 23, 1538. CR:10:256, 535, 538 ff.

10. CR 8:61-63; 18:1-2.

11. CR 8:942-43. Regiomontanus was the Latinized name for Johann Müller of Konigsberg in Franken, b. 1436. Cf. Melanchthon's speech, CR 11:817. Cf. R. Wolf, *Geschichte der Astronomie* (München, 1877), p. 87.

12. CR 11:261-66. This oration appeared between 1524 and 1533.

13. CR 11:263-64; 2:105-6. Cf. Hartfelder, *Aberglaube,* p. 240. Melanchthon's detailed consideration of astrology in relation to medicine may be found in CR 10:715-17, 887-89. Cf. CR 11:265.

14. CR 11:264 ff. Hartfelder, *Aberglaube,* p. 240. Cf. Schmidt, *Philipp Melanchthon,* p. 684. Cf. Planck, *Melanchthon* (Nordlingen, 1860), s. 149.

15. CR 10:712-15.

16. Cf. Bernhardt, *Ph. Mel. als Math. und Physiker* (Wittenberg, 1865), s. 42. Melanchthon's opinions about days, CR 24:202 ff.

17. *Initia doctrinae physicae.* Cf. Thorndike, *op. cit.,* V, 398, 402-3, CR 7:950-53.

18. CR 20:675-792; 13:99-101. Cf. CR 1:778.

19. CR 1:778 ff.; 20:682.

20. CR 20:682, 688.

21. Cf. Thorndike, *op. cit.,* V, 401. Cf. CR 20:565-66, 567, 571, 579; 6:779.

22. Cf. K. Gödeke, *Grundriss der deutschen Dichtung* (Dresden, 1886), II:2, 562. Hartfelder, *Aberglaube,* pp. 255-56.

23. CR 7:652-54; Hartfelder, *Aberglaube,* p. 259.

24. CR 6:764. Cf. Planck, *Melanchthon,* p. 151.

25. Translated from French into English by John Brooke, London, 1579.

26. Brooke's explanatory letter. Brooke's translation has been slightly altered for the sake of the modern reader.

27. Cf. Grisar, *Kampfbilder der Reformation.*

28. *Reuchlin, sein Leben und seine Werke* (Leipzig, 1871), p. 177. Melanchthon defended astrology and astronomy against Pico della Mirandola in the first edition of the Sphere of Sacrobosco, CR 2:530-37, in 1531.

29. Cf. J. Burckhardt, *Cultur der Renaissance in Italien,* 3 aufl. (Leipzig, 1887), II, 280.

30. CR 7:950-53. Cf. Thorndike, *op. cit.,* pp. 402-3.

CHAPTER 9

1. Allen, *Opus Erasmi,* III, 587.

2. Cf. Smith, *Correspondence,* I, 402.

3. Smith, *Correspondence,* I, 54.

4. Smith, *Correspondence,* II, 123, 190-91. Enders, 3:375.

5. Smith, *Correspondence,* II, 196-98.

6. Smith, *Correspondence,* II, 228-30. Enders, 4:319.

7. CR 20:700. Schmidt, *op. cit.,* p. 115.

8. CR 20:700.

9. CR 1:667-68. Smith, *Correspondence,* II, 294-95.

10. *Ibid.,* 250-51.

11. Münzer, the "heavenly prophets."

12. Smith, *Correspondence,* II, 253 ff. CR 1:674.

13. CR 1:673-74.

14. CR 1:675 ff.

15. Smith, *Correspondence,* II, 265 ff. CR 1:688-89.

16. CR 1:688-89. December 10, 1524.

17. CR 1:667. Cf. Smith, *Correspondence,* II, 251 n.

18. Schmidt, *op. cit.,* p. 117.

19. WA 18:600 ff.

20. Enders, 11:247, July 9, 1537. Smith, *Erasmus,* pp. 353-54.

21. Smith, *Erasmus,* pp. 354-55.

22. Richard, *op. cit.,* pp. 120-21. CR 1:793.

23. CR 1:880.

24. CR 1:893.

25. CR 9:766. Schmidt, *op. cit.,* p. 120.

26. Von Ranke, Leopold, *History of the Reformation in Germany,* tr. Sarah Austin (Philadelphia, 1844), Bk. III, ch. vi, pp. 210-11.

27. Cf. Kurt Uhrig, *ARG,* "Der Bauer," XXXIII.

28. Cf. John 10:1 ff.

29. CR 1:538. *ZKG,* 5:331; 22:125. Cf. Smith, *Correspondence,* II, 222-23, 255-56, 278. Cf. W. Friendensburg, *ARG,* XI (1914), 69-72.

30. Cf. *ARG,* XI (1914), 69-72, for Carlstadt's letter of resignation and the Elector's acceptance, June 10, 11, 1524.

31. Cf. Melanchthon's History of Münzer, *Philip Melanchthons Werke,* ed. F. A. Koethe, I, 201-18. Cf. Smith, *Correspondence,* II, 241 ff., for a description by Luther.

32. Cf. Smith, *Correspondence,* II, 241 ff. Enders, 4:372.

33. Ranke, *op. cit.,* Bk. III, ch. vi, pp., 216-17.

34. B. J. Kidd, *Documents Illustrative of the Continental Reformation* (New York: Oxford University Press, 1911), pp. 174-75. Cf. Böhmer, *Urkunden zur Geschichte des Bauernkrieges* (Bonn, 1910).

35. Enders, 5:157.

36. WA 19:224.

37. CR 1:724-25. May 18, 1525. CR 20:641-62.

38. Ranke, *op. cit.,* Bk. III, ch. vi.

39. Koethe, *Philip Melanchthons Werke,* I, 201-18.

40. CR 11:90 ff. Poem by Melanchthon about Frederick, CR 10:502. Cf. Ranke, *op. cit.,* Bk. III, ch. vi.

41. Cf. Smith, *Correspondence,* II, 322, 264, 257-58. Cf. Boehmer, "Luthers Ehe," *Luther-Jahrbuch,* VII (1925), 40-70.

42. Smith, *Correspondence,* II, 324 ff. Cf. *ZKG,* 21:596. CR 1:754. Boehmer, *Luther in the Light of Recent Research,* tr. Huth (1916), pp. 217 ff. For a translation of the letter by J. A. Faulkner, *The Lutheran Quarterly,* XL (1910), 124-26.

43. CR 1:750.

CHAPTER 10

1. Rothe, *American Theological Review,* III (1861), 278.

2. Friedrich Paulsen, *The German Universities,* tr. E. D. Perry (New York:

The Macmillan Co., 1895), p. 43. F. V. N. Painter, *A History of Education,* p. 169.

3. *Erasmi Epistolae,* 1642, xix, 50. Also *Opera,* 1703, iii, col. 1138-39.

4. Friedrich Paulsen, *The German Universities and University Study,* tr. F. Thilly and N. W. Elwang (New York: Charles Scribner's Sons, 1906), p. 33.

5. CR 1:666.

6. Cf. CR 1:739, 674; Suppl. CR 6, I:258.

7. CR 1:678.

8. CR 1:686, 713, 720. Camerarius, *Vita Mel.,* p. 103.

9. CR 1:789, 796, 713; 11:108.

10. CR 11:109.

11. CR 11:111.

12. CR 11:111.

13. Cf. Schwiebert, *op. cit.,* p. 679.

14. CR 1:804.

15. CR 1:819.

16. Cf. Schmidt, *op. cit.,* pp. 131 ff.

17. CR 1:859. February 26, 1527.

18. Cf. Schwiebert, *op. cit.,* pp. 618-19.

19. CR 1:881, tr. Richard. Cf. Ledderhose, *op. cit.,* p. 70; Richard, *op. cit.,* pp. 160-61.

20. CR 26:7-28, 31, 46, 49-96.

21. CR 23:104 ff.

22. CR 26:51, 52-54. Cf. Luke 24:47.

23. Cf. CR 26:89-95. Tr. from German by Henry Barnard.

24. Painter, *op. cit.,* p. 169.

25. H. C. Paul Schmieder, *Lutheran Church Review,* XXXII (1913), 361, 369 ff.

26. J. O. Evjen, *Lutheran Church Review,* XLV (1926), 237-38. Cf. C. L. Robbins, *Teachers in Germany in the Sixteenth Century* (New York: Columbia University, 1912). Emil Sehling, *Die evangelischen Kirchenordnungen des 16. Jahrhunderts* (Leipzig, 1902-9).

CHAPTER 11

1. CR 10:992-1024.

2. Paulsen, *The German Universities,* p. 43.

3. *Ibid.,* p. 237.

4. Rothe, *Am. Theol. Rev.,* III (1861), 261-83.

5. Cf. Richard, *op. cit.,* p. 137.

6. CR 11:398.

7. Cf. A. Nebe, *Sammlung pädagogischer Vorträge,* Band IX, Heft 7, *Philipp Melanchthon, der Lehrer Deutschlands.*

8. CR 9:605.

9. CR 11:279-80, 489, 107.

10. CR 11:278.

11. CR 11:111, 605, 445, 617; 5:127.

12. CR 11:130.

13. CR 11:298 ff.

14. CR 11:50.

15. CR 1:54; 11:867.

16. CR 3:1119, tr. Barnard. Cf. CR 11:492, and Painter, *op. cit.*, p. 166.

17. CR 1:772, tr. Barnard. Cf. CR 10:101.

18. E. R. Graves, *History of Education, during Middle Ages and Transition to Modern Times* (New York: The Macmillan Co., 1910), p. 243.

19. CR 7:653, 705.

20. CR 2:507.

21. Cf. Barnard, *German Teachers and Educators*, from Karl von Raumer, *Geschichte der Pädagogik*. Barnard, p. 269. Raumer, I, 324 ff.

22. CR 7:472, in 1549. Cf. Barnard, p. 268; Raumer I, 324 ff.

23. *Ibid.*

24. CR 11:266. Barnard, pp. 177-78.

25. CR 1:16, 25.

26. CR 3:1118.

27. Barnard, *op. cit.*, p. 173. Raumer, I, 199.

28. *Ibid.*

29. Von Raumer, *op. cit.*, I, 201.

30. CR 7:653, 705.

31. *Ibid.* Cf. Barnard, p. 176; Raumer, I, 202.

32. CR 1:62; Camerarius, *Vita Mel.*, p. 544. CR 2:507.

33. *Ibid.*

34. Painter, *op. cit.*, pp. 143-44.

35. CR 3:562. Camerarius, *Vita Mel.*, p. 92, Hartfelder, *Philipp Melanchthon als Praeceptor Germanae*, p. 88. CR 11:268.

36. Camerarius, *Vita Mel.*, p. 40.

37. Cf. CR 20:230; 3:1111.

38. CR 2:557. Barnard, p. 264; Raumer, I, 320.

39. Barnard, p. 264. Cf. CR 1:701; 2:952; 10:98.

40. Barnard, p. 264. Raumer I, 320.

41. CR 11:278 ff. Barnard, p. 179.

42. Cf. Camerarius, *Vita Mel.*, p. 71.

43. CR 1:398.

44. CR 10:274.

45. C. L. Robbins, *Teachers in Germany in the Sixteenth Century*, 1912. Used by permission of Teachers College, Columbia University.

46. *Ibid.*, p. 78.

47. George Mertz, *Das Schulwesen der deutschen Reformation* (Heidelberg, 1902), pp. 617, 642.

48. Mertz, *op. cit.*, p. 417.

49. CR 10:918, 920.

50. CR 10:594, tr. Barnard.

51. In 1538 and 1542. Cf. Robbins, *op. cit.*, p. 105.

52. Robbins, *op. cit.*, pp. 106-7.

53. Graves, *op. cit.*, p. 205.

54. Paulsen, *The German Universities*, p. 43.

55. Richard, *op. cit.*, pp. 139-40.

CHAPTER 12

1. CR 1:763-70.

2. CR 1:1040.

3. CR 1:980.

4. DeW 3:328, 351.
5. CR 1:977, 988.
6. Smith, *Correspondence*, II, 465 n.
7. Von Ranke, Bk. V, ii. CR 1:998. Moeller, *Lehrbuch der Kirchengeschichte*, III, ed. Kawerau, 3 aufl. (Tübingen, 1907), s. 98. Cf. *ARG*, I (1903), 172-91.
8. Kidd, *Documents*, No. 103.
9. CR 1:1068-69; 11:1038.
10. CR 1:1083. Melchoir Adam, *Vita Theolog.*, fol. s. 160.
11. Smith, *Correspondence*, II, 470-71. CR 1:1039.
12. Kidd, *Documents*, No. 104.
13. CR 1:1075, 1039. Richard, *op cit.*, p. 176.
14. CR 1:1041, 1046, 1062-63.
15. Cf. Kidd, *Documents*, p. 239 n. Cf. Ney, *Geschichte des Reichstages zu Speier*, pp. 291 ff., 104 ff., 128 ff., 176.
16. Cf. Kidd, *Documents*, No. 105.
17. Kidd, *Documents*, No. 107. Ney, *op. cit.*, p. 243. Smith, *Correspondence* II, 507-8.
18. CR 1:1051.
19. CR 13:823-980, 906; 25:595.
20. CR 1:1059. Smith, *Correspondence*, II, 272-73.
21. CR 1:1048 ff., 1068.
22. Smith, *Correspondence*, II, 490. Enders, VII, 146.
23. CR 1:1093, 1094.
24. Smith, *Correspondence*, II, 471. Cf. *ZKG*, 29 (1908), 341.
25. Schmidt, *op. cit.*, p. 171.
26. Smith, *Correspondence*, II, 473-74.
27. *Ibid.*, pp. 476-77. CR 1:1064.
28. Cf. CR 1:1066. DeW 3:454.
29. CR 1:1071-72, 1078.
30. CR 1:1080-81.
31. CR 1:1070.
32. CR 1:1066. Smith, *Correspondence*, II, 477-78.
33. CR 1:137, 145.
34. CR 1:722, 760-61.
35. CR 1:913; 4:964.
36. CR 1:948-49, tr. Richard, p. 180.
37. Schmidt, *op. cit.*, p. 173. Cf. CR 1:913; 4:964.
38. CR 3:537.
39. CR 1:1048, 974, 1070. Richard, *op. cit.*, pp. 181-82.
40. Th. Kolde, *Der Tag von Schleiz und die Enstehung der Schwabacher Artikel*, Beiträge zur Reformationsgeschichte (Gotha, 1896).
41. WA 30: Part III, pp. 92-93.
42. CR 1:1098, 1099-1106.
43. CR 1:1103. Enders, VII, 168.
44. Koehler, *Religionsgesprach*, pp. 22 ff.
45. Reu, *Augsburg Confession*, Part I, p. 32. Used by permission of The Wartburg Press.
46. *Ibid.*, Part II, pp. 44-47.
47. *Ibid.*, Part II, pp. 46-47.
48. Smith, *Correspondence*, II, 500. CR 1:1098.

CHAPTER 13

1. Von Ranke, *History of the Reformation in Germany,* tr. Sarah Austin, ed. Robert A. Johnson (London, 1905), pp. 592 ff.
2. Reu, *Augsburg Confession,* II, 499-511.
3. Schubert, *Der Reichstag von Augsburg,* pp. 19-20.
4. Von Ranke, Bk. V, ch. ix. End of January, 1530.
5. Richard, *op. cit.,* p. 191. CR 2:20 ff.
6. Reu, *Augs. Conf.,* II, 39, 69-72. Walter, *Der Reichstag zu Augsburg,* 1530.
7. Walter, *Der Reichstag zu Augsburg* (1530), pp. 8-11. Reu, *Augs. Conf.,* I, 43-44. Schubert, *op cit.,* pp. 19-20.
8. CR 2:166-67. Walter, *op. cit.,* pp. 10 ff.
9. CR 2:26, 28, 33. *Lutheran Quarterly,* XXVII (1897), 299.
10. CR 4:999, 972 ff.; 2:47.
11. Jacobs, *Book of Concord,* II, 85-86.
12. CR 2:39 ff.; 4:999.
13. Reu, *Augs. Conf.,* I, 56-57; II, 78.
14. *Ibid.* Cf. Gussmann, *Quellen und Forschungen,* II, 196-97.
15. Reu, *Augs. Conf.,* II, 97 ff. Gussmann, II.
16. *Ibid.*
17. Reu, *Augs. Conf.,* II, 97-98.
18. CR 2:39.
19. CR 9:927.
20. Kolde, *Real Ency.,* II, 244.
21. CR 2:45.
22. CR 2:47.
23. DeW 4:17.
24. CR 2:51.
25. CR 2:60.
26. CR 2:141; DeW 4:44-45.
27. Richard, *op. cit.,* p. 205.
28. CR 8:843.
29. Enders, 8, 20 ff., 190-91, 220 ff., 258-59.
30. *Ibid.*
31. CR 25:207.
32. CR 2:78.
33. CR 2:83.
34. CR 2:88, 90, 112.
35. Reu, *Augs. Conf.,* I, 75. CR 2:59 ff.
36. CR 2:88-89.
37. CR 2:105. *Lutheran Quarterly,* XXVII (1897), 320.

CHAPTER 14

1. Schwiebert, *Luther and his Times,* p. 719. Gussmann, *Quellen,* pp. 249 ff.
2. Schubert, *Der Reichstag von Augsburg,* pp. 21-22. Reu, *Augs. Conf.,* I, 79. CR 2:45.
3. Schubert, *op. cit.,* pp. 25-26. Walter, *op. cit.,* pp. 38-39.
4. CR 2:106. Walter, *op cit.* pp. 38-39.
5. CR 2:115, 106, 114. Walter, *op. cit.,* p. 39.
6. CR 2:106.

7. Reu, *Augs. Conf.*, II, 93.
8. *Ibid.*, I, 93-94.
9. CR 2:111. Reu, *Augs. Conf.*, I, 93-94.
10. CR 2:110.
11. E.g., Kolde, Bezold, Mueller, Ellinger, and Kawerau.
12. Reu, *Augs. Conf.*, I, 95-103. Kolde, *Luther,* II, 592.
13. Th. Brieger, *Zur Geschichte d. Augsburger Reichstages von 1530* (Leipzig, 1903). J. v. Walter, *Die Depeschen des Venezianischen Gesandten Nicolo Tiepolo* (Berlin, 1928).
14. CR 2:59-60, 118-19.
15. CR 2:122.
16. Schirrmacher, *Briefe und Akten* (1876), p. 72.
17. CR 2:122-23. Walter, *op. cit.,* p. 419. Reu, *Augs. Conf.*, I, 100.
18. CR 2:123.
19. CR 2:116 ff. Schirrmacher, *op. cit.,* pp. 58 ff.
20. CR 2:112-13. Reu, *Augs. Conf.,* I, 97.
21. Reu, *Augs. Conf.,* I, 100.
22. CR 2:114-15, 119.
23. Walter, *op. cit.,* pp. 45-46.
24. *Ibid.,* pp. 46 ff.
25. CR 2:122.
26. CR 2:122-23, 112; 26:209-10.
27. CR 2:124.
28. CR 2:127.
29. CR 25:415.
30. CR 2:128.
31. Walter, *op. cit.,* pp. 51-52. CR 2:128 ff.
32. Reu, *Augs. Conf.,* I, 110.
33. CR 2:245-46. Reu, *Augs. Conf.,* I, 112-13.
34. CR 2:145.
35. WA Br., 5:440-41.
36. CR 10:198.
37. CR 2:141, 147, 158. Enders, 8, 33.
38. DeW., 4:82. Enders, 8, 34 ff.
39. Reu, *Augs. Conf.,* II, 315. Enders, 8, 41 ff.
40. Enders, 8, 50 ff.

CHAPTER 15
1. Von Ranke, Bk. V, ch. ix.
2. Reu, *Augs. Conf.,* I, 114-15. Walter, pp. 56 ff.
3. Reu, I, 120-21. Walter, pp. 71-72.
4. CR 2:184-85.
5. WA Br., V, 513-14. Walter, pp. 62-63.
6. Jacobs, *Book of Concord,* II, 207, 209.
7. Jacobs, II, 200.
8. CR 2:187.
9. CR 2:192. Jacobs, II, 188.
10. Jacobs, II, 210 ff.
11. CR 2:221.
12. CR 2:245, 250 ff.; 27:21-23.

13. CR 27:70, 240 ff. Jacobs, II, 239 ff.
14. CR 2:253-54. WA Br., 5:533 ff.
15. CR 2:250; 27:227 ff.
16. Richard, *Confessional History of the Lutheran Church,* p. 132. CR 2:253 ff., 260. Enders, 8, 180.
17. CR 2:245.
18. CR 2:171. Reu, I, 128-29.
19. Von Ranke, Bk. V, ch. ix.
20. CR 2:248.
21. Richard, *Philip Melanchthon,* p. 215.
22. Reu, I, 132.
23. CR 2:300, 281 ff. Von Ranke, Bk. V, ch. ix.
24. CR 2:377-78, 368-71.
25. Enders, 8, 218. WA Br., 5:578.
26. CR 2:299.
27. Reu, II, 386-87.
28. Reu, I, 131 ff.; II, 387-88, 383 ff. Enders, 8, 221 ff.
29. Reu, II, 387 ff. Enders, 8, 234-35.
30. CR 2:312-13.
31. CR 2:336.
32. CR 2:336 ff.
33. CR 2:314.
34. CR 2:362 ff.
35. Reu, II, 391-92.
36. CR 2:289.
37. CR 2:383.
38. Reu, I, 134.
39. Reu, I, 135-36. CR 27:246-378.
40. Reu, I, 136-37.
41. Reu, I, 128-29. WA Br., 5:631-32.
42. Erlangen, 54:194.

CHAPTER 16

1. Mattesius, fol. 143. Cf. CR 2:388.
2. CR 2:438 ff.
3. CR 2:484.
4. CR 2:498.
5. CR 27:227 ff.
6. Von Ranke, Bk. V, ch. ix.
7. Cf. Zöckler, *Die Augsburgische Confession,* p. 95.
8. Jacobs, I, 73-74.
9. Jacobs, I, 300.
10. Plitt, *Apologie der Augustana,* pp. 246 ff.
11. Solid Decl., Rule and Norm of Faith, sec. 11.
12. CR 2:512.
13. Erlangen, 31:268.
14. Richard, *Conf. Hist. Luth. Ch.,* p. 265.
15. Reu, I, 141.
16. Richard, *Conf. Hist. Luth. Ch.,* p. 217.
17. CR 2:430-31.

18. CR 2:740 ff.
19. Vedder, *The Reformation in Germany,* p. 336.
20. Schmidt, *op. cit.,* p. 251.
21. CR 2:397.
22. CR 2:472 ff.
23. CR 2:469.
24. CR 2:592.
25. CR 2:597.
26. CR 2:590, 598.
27. Walch 16:1835-36.
28. CR 11:223, tr. Cox.
29. CR 10:536.

CHAPTER 17

1. Tischreden, fol. 364a.
2. CR 2:611.
3. CR 2:670.
4. CR 2:668 ff.
5. CR 2:726-27.
6. Cf. Schmidt, *op. cit.,* pp. 267-68.
7. CR 2:741 ff.
8. CR 2:740 ff.
9. CR 2:869-70.
10. CR 2:976.
11. CR 2:855.
12. CR 2:873.
13. CR 2:874.
14. CR 2:879.
15. CR 2:1029.
16. Cox, *op. cit.,* p. 337.
17. CR 2:904.
18. CR 2:918.
19. Cox, *op. cit.,* p. 337. CR 2:1010
20. CR 2:907, 910.
21. CR 2:910, 915, 917.
22. CR 2:913.
23. CR 2:520.
24. CR 2:552.
25. CR 2:861.
26. CR 2:947.
27. CR 2:1032.
28. CR 3:26, 25, 37.
29. CR 3:89.
30. CR 3:144.
31. Cox, *op. cit.,* pp. 338-39.
32. CR 2:930.

CHAPTER 18

1. CR 3:537.
2. CR 2:217.

3. CR 2:787.
4. CR 2:470.
5. CR 2:498.
6. Schmidt, p. 315.
7. CR 2:620.
8. CR 2:470.
9. CR 2:675.
10. CR 2:776.
11. Schmidt, pp. 318-19.
12. Richard, *Philip Melanchthon*, p. 251. Schmidt, p. 319.
13. DeW 4:569.
14. CR 2:822.
15. CR 2:807.
16. CR 2:808.
17. CR 2:826.
18. CR 2:824.
19. Schmidt, p. 371.
20. Kostlin's *Martin Luther*, II, 349, tr. Richard.
21. Eells, *Martin Bucer*, p. 201.
22. *ZKG*, Vol. 32 (1911). CR 7:888-89, 877-88.
23. Jacobs, II, 284 ff. CR 3:75 ff.
24. CR 3:81.
25. CR 2:837.
26. Camerarius, *Vita Mel.*, p. 163.
27. CR 3:180.
28. *ZKG*, 32 (1911), 292-93. CR 7:888-89, 877-88.
29. CR 3:514.
30. *Ibid.*
31. *ZKG*, 33 (1912), 286-309.
32. CR 5:112.
33. CR 5:143.
34. CR 5:142.
35. *Ibid.*
36. DeW 5:708.
37. CR 5:461, 464.
38. CR 5:474.
39. Erlangen, 32:39-40.
40. DeW 5:645.
41. DeW 5:697.
42. CR 5:502.
43. CR 5:314.
44. CR 5:746.
45. Faulkner, *Lutheran Quarterly*, April, 1916, p. 68.

CHAPTER 19

1. Jacobs, II, 42.
2. CR 3:258 ff.
3. Jacobs, I.
4. CR 2:108-1022.
5. Jacobs, II, 43.

6. CR 3:271. Jacobs, I, 338-52.
7. Ledderhose, p. 152.
8. Jules Bonnet, *Letters of John Calvin*, I, 122-23.
9. CR 3:647.
10. Ledderhose, p. 160.
11. CR 3:686.
12. Bonnet, I, 93, 122-23, 124, 128, 132, 139, 165.
13. *Ibid.*, p. 124.
14. *Ibid.*, p. 138.
15. *Ibid.*, p. 137.
16. *Ibid.*, p. 130.
17. CR 3:686.
18. Bonnet, I, 130.
19. Ledderhose, 162.
20. CR 3:671.
21. CR 3:676.
22. Bonnet, I, 125-26.
23. CR 3:805.
24. CR 3:801.
25. CR 3:825 ff.

CHAPTER 20

1. Mogen, *Historia captivitatis Philippi magnanimi Hessiae*, 1766. Genealogical table, p. 163.
2. Rady, *Die Reformatoren in ihrer Beziehung zur Doppelehe des Landgrafen Philipp* (Frankfurt, 1890), pp. 43-44. CR 3:851-56, 1073.
3. Cf. CR 3:851-56.
4. J. C. Hare, *Vindication of Luther* (London, 1855), p. 255.
5. Cf. Hare, *op. cit.*, pp. 255-56.
6. Cf. Hare, *op. cit.*, pp. 235-41, with minor changes. Cf. CR 3:856-57.
7. Lenz, *Briefwechsel des Landgraf Philipp mit Bucer* (Berlin, 1880), I, 362. CR 3:849, 1065.
8. Cf. CR 3:xvii.
9. CR 5:709.
10. CR 3:1051.
11. CR 3:581-86.
12. Hare, *op. cit.*, pp. 263-64.
13. CR 3:1077.
14. Vedder, *op. cit.*, p. 354 n.
15. CR 4:761; 5:74.
16. CR 3:1245.
17. *ARG*, III (1905-6), 18-64.
18. *Ibid.*, I (1903-4), 84-97.
19. CR 9:626.
20. CR 4:318. Richard, *Philip Melanchthon*, p. 293.
21. CR 4:346; 9:626.
22. CR 4:413-31.
23. Richard, *Philip Melanchthon*, p. 295.
24. DeW 5:452. Richard, *Philip Melanchthon*, p. 295.
25. Ledderhose, pp. 203-4.

26. *Ibid.,* p. 204.
27. *Ibid.,* p. 209.
28. CR 6:58-59.
29. Funeral Oration, Cf. CR 11:726 ff.; 6:61-62.

CHAPTER 21
1. CR 6:123, 184, 150-51.
2. CR 6:181, 179, 180-81. (June 25, 1546, letter to Amsdorf.)
3. CR 6:183 ff., 150.
4. CR 6:196-97.
5. CR 6:198 ff., 381-88, 390, 409.
6. CR 6:238-39, 230-31.
7. CR 6:520-31.
8. CR 6:532-33.
9. *Ibid.*
10. CR 6:559-60, 599, 532-33.
11. CR 6:563, 578 ff.
12. CR 6:578.
13. CR 6:580.
14. CR 6:605, 610-11.
15. CR 6: Annales Vitae, 1548.
16. CR 6:x-xvi, 26, 640.
17. CR 6:649-51.
18. Cf. Kidd, *Documents,* No. 148.
19. CR 6:839 ff.
20. CR 6:839 ff., 846.
21. CR 6:853-57.
22. CR 6:865-74.
23. CR 6:878-79.
24. CR 6:880-85.
25. CR 6:924 ff.
26. CR 6:888-89, 885.
27. CR 6:892.
28. CR 6:894-95. 904-5.
29. CR 6:924-25.
30. CR 7:12-45.
31. CR 7:92, 97.
32. CR 7:113 ff.
33. CR 7:184 ff.
34. CR 7:215-21.
35. CR 7:246.
36. CR 7:248-49.
37. CR 7:258-59.
38. CR 7:255 ff.
39. CR 7:260 ff.
40. CR 7:275.
41. CR 7:292 ff.
42. CR 7:300-301.
43. CR 7:332.
44. CR 7:364 ff.

45. CR 7:366.
46. CR 7:378 ff.
47. CR 8:171-72; 7:455.
48. *Wider das Interim*, 1549.
49. CR 6:649 ff.
50. *Der Prediger zu Magdebrugk*, 1551.
51. *De Veris et Falsis Adiaphora*, 1549.
52. CR 7:366 ff.
53. CR 7:456-57.
54. CR 7:477-78.
55. CR 7:508, 506.
56. CR 9:1098.
57. Calvin, *Opera*, XIII, 593 ff.
58. CR 9:41-72; 8:840-41.
59. *De peccati originalis*, Flacius.

CHAPTER 22

1. CR 24:43.
2. Galle, *Characteristik Melanchthons*, p. 274.
3. CR 2:546.
4. CR 15:678 ff.
5. CR 23:179.
6. Galle, *op. cit.*, pp. 291-92.
7. CR 21:330.
8. CR 21. *Luth. Ch. Rev.*, XXVIII (1909), 325-26. Used by permission.
9. CR 5:109.
10. CR 22:417; 25:438.
11. *Luth. Quarterly*, XXXV (1905), 303-45. Used by permission.
12. CR 9:766.
13. CR 1:893.
14. CR 2:457.
15. CR 3:380.
16. Cf. J. A. Faulkner, *Luth. Quarterly*, April, 1916, p. 188. Used by permission.
17. DeW 5:70.
18. CR 12:481. Richard, *Luth. Quarterly*, Vol. XXXV, April, 1905.
19. *Ibid.*, pp. 303-4.
20. Strobel, *Apologie Melanchthons*, p. 94.
21. Richard, *Luth. Quarterly*, XXXV (1905), 153 ff.
22. Cf. Faulkner, *op. cit.*, pp. 184 ff. Matthesius, Twelfth Sermon.
23. Richard, *Luth. Quarterly*, XXXVII (1907), 305-27. Used by permission.
24. Reply to Bavarian Articles.
25. CR 16:198; 21:656, 761. Cf. C. F. Fischer, *Melanchthon Lehre von der Bekehrung* (Tübingen, 1905).

CHAPTER 23

1. Smith, *Correspondence*, II, 489. Cf. Kostlin-Kawerau, II, 683.
2. J. E. Volbeding, *Philip Melanchthon, wie er leibte und lebte* (Leipzig, 1860), p. 148.
3. CR 5:322-23.
4. Cf. CR 5:294.

5. CR 5:411-12.
6. CR 5:408.
7. CR 10:406-7.
8. CR 10:475-76.
9. Ledderhose, p. 324.
10. CR 8:65.
11. CR 5:438-39.
12. Cox, *op. cit.*, ch. iv.
13. *Ibid.*
14. CR 1:570, 575, 574, 568. Cf. Keinath, *Concordia Theological Monthly,* Vol. V (1934).
15. CR 1:583.
16. Cf. CR 5:560. Cf. Horawitz-Hartfelder, *Briefwechsel des Beatus Rhenaus,* 1886, s. 304.
17. CR 10:207. Cf. *ARG,* XXI (1924), 78 ff.
18. Ledderhose, p. 333.
19. CR 23:104 ff.
20. CR 3:1073.
21. CR 7:519-20.
22. CR 23:lxxxvii f., 1558.
23. CR 21:866-67. 1543.
24. CR 28:450. 1551.
25. Koethe, *Philipp Melanchthon's Werke* (1829-30), IV, 201.
26. CR 10:628-29. 1555.
27. CR 28:422-23. 1551.
28. CR 21:955-84. Cf. CR 21:604, 561-62.
29. Camerarius, *Vita Mel.,* p. 351.
30. CR 9:914.
31. Cf. Camerarius, *Vita Mel.,* p. 351.
32. Cf. CR 9:789, 792, 845, 1034, 1079, 1094, 1096.
33. CR 9:910.
34. Nikolaus Müller, *Philipp Melanchthons letzte Lebenstage, Heimgang und Bestattung* (Leipzig, 1910). Cf. CR 10:253 ff.

INDEX

[343]

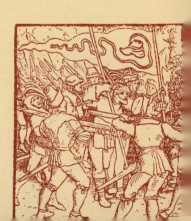